Modern British History

Modern British History:
A guide to study and research

edited by

L. J. BUTLER AND
ANTHONY GORST

I.B.Tauris Publishers
LONDON · NEW YORK

To Professor Derek Oddy and Pat Ryan, former
colleagues at the University of Westminster

Published in 1997 by I.B.Tauris & Co. Ltd, Victoria House,
Bloomsbury Square, London WC1B 4DZ

175 Fifth Avenue, New York NY 10010

In the United States of America and in Canada distributed by
St Martin's Press, 175 Fifth Avenue, New York NY 10010

A full CIP record for this book is available from the British Library

A full CIP record for this book is available from the Library of
Congress

ISBN 1 86064 103 2 hardback
ISBN 1 86064 208 x paperback

Library of Congress catalog card number: available

Set in Monotype Ehrhardt by Ewan Smith, London

Printed and bound in Great Britain by WBC Ltd, Bridgend,
Mid-Glamorgan

Contents

Figures

Contributors

John Armstrong is Professor of History at Thames Valley University

Peter Beck is Professor of International History at Kingston University

Ian F. W. Beckett is Professor of History at the University of Luton

Brian Brivati is Reader in Modern British History at Kingston University

L. J. Butler is Lecturer in Modern History at the University of Luton

John Davis is Lecturer in Modern History at Kingston University

Peter Denley is Lecturer in History at Queen Mary and Westfield College, University of London

Anthony Gorst is Senior Lecturer in History at the University of Westminster

Helen Jones is Lecturer in Social Policy, Goldsmiths' College, University of London

Denis Judd is Professor of History at the University of North London

Ann Lane is Lecturer in Politics at the Queen's University, Belfast

Donald Munro is Assistant Librarian, Institute of Historical Research, University of London

Robert Pearce is Reader in History, University College of St Martin, Lancaster

Elizabeth Shepherd is Tutor and Lecturer in Archive Studies and Records Management, University College London

John Stevenson is Fellow and Tutor in Modern History, Worcester College, University of Oxford

Jim Tomlinson is Reader in Government, Brunel University

Preface

One of the most encouraging trends in higher education in recent years has been that the continuing strength of undergraduate interest in history has been matched by increasing numbers of students seeking to continue their historical studies at postgraduate level, either on taught masters' programmes or through doctoral research. For most new postgraduate students, the transition to higher level work is stimulating and rewarding, yet, at least initially, it can be daunting, and pose a number of new challenges. New skills, such as the reading and assimilation of primary sources in archives, have to be absorbed quickly if the most effective use of precious research time is to be made. Significantly, the need for postgraduate students to be adequately prepared for their work, in order to complete their studies within the mandatory period, has been stressed by the various postgraduate funding bodies such as the British Academy and the Economic and Social Research Council. University departments have responded by providing courses on research methods and skills, often complemented by programmes of research seminars.

There are already several excellent texts on the study of history. Volumes such as G. R. Elton's *The Practice of History* (1969), E. H. Carr's *What is History?* (1961), John Tosh's *The Pursuit of History* (1991), Juliet Gardiner's *What is History Today?* (1988) and Arthur Marwick's *The Nature of History* (1989) have established themselves as indispensable introductions. More recently, they have been joined by thought-provoking studies such as Beverley Southgate's *History What and Why? Ancient, Modern and Post-Modern Perspectives* (1996) and Keith Jenkins's *Rethinking History* (1991). These provide useful guidance, particularly on the more theoretical aspects of historiography, to those embarking on postgraduate study. Experience suggests, however, that for those beginning research, the need to acquire essential new skills rapidly before effective research can begin can be disconcerting. Unfortunately, the kind of practical information required by many novices in research is often widely dispersed and sometimes buried in an over-technical and intimidating format. In this book, therefore, we aim to provide in a single volume practical guidance on research methods together with a survey of the current state of research on modern British history, concentrating on the twentieth century.

In the chapters on methodology, we have attempted to identify the areas of principal interest to those beginning historical research, especially areas involving the identification, location and organisation of primary source materials, and the problems involved in presenting research findings. Accordingly, we have included chapters on the most effective ways to use libraries and archives, on some of the possible research applications of information technology, and on the theoretical, literary and other implications of historical research. In the thematic chapters, the aim is to provide studies of the major specialisms in British history which discuss the current scope and methodological problems of each field – how it has evolved in recent years and how it is likely to develop in the future. Each chapter provides guidance on useful further reading where appropriate. Defining the limits of a book of this type is difficult and inevitably we have had to be selective; therefore, some methodological issues and research themes are not necessarily treated in full. Nevertheless, we hope that the following chapters will not only provide enough guidance and material to equip new researchers to approach their work with confidence, but will also be of continuing use as a resource to which reference can be made when the need arises during the course of research and writing.

We have incurred many debts in preparing this book. We thank our contributors for the interest and enthusiasm they have shown for the project from the outset. We are also grateful to the many other historians we consulted who have expressed their belief that a book such as this would be useful. Our thanks are also due to students on the history programmes at the University of Westminster and the University of Luton. Finally, we would like to thank Dr Lester Crook and his colleagues at I.B.Tauris & Co. Ltd for their enthusiasm for the book and for their help and encouragement in bringing it to fruition.

L. J. Butler and Anthony Gorst
London, 1997

CHAPTER I

Historical writing

Denis Judd

Dr Samuel Johnson once asserted:

> Great abilities are not requisite for an Historian; for in historical composi-
> tion, all the greatest powers of the human mind are quiescent. He has
> the facts ready to hand so there is no exercise of invention. Imagination
> is not required in any high degree; only about as much as is used in the
> lower forms of poetry.[1]

This statement does not make Johnson necessarily an early subscriber
to the Henry Ford 'history is bunk' school of thought, rather it is an
assault on the 'dry-as-dust' presentation of history, a technique which
was common enough in Johnson's day and has, alas, not entirely disappeared in our own.

Apart from recognising Johnson's compulsive, even chronic need to
shock, confront and provoke – after all, the good doctor went out of his
way to insult, apart from anything else, the Scots, patriotism, claret and
the customs and excise – do historians today need to take him seriously?
As a preliminary response, before addressing the main question, a historian might point out that it is virtually impossible, as Johnson claims,
to have 'the facts ready to hand'. Fresh facts about the past can be,
indeed are, discovered almost every day. Sometimes gaps in the retrieved
and retrievable record of human history cannot be closed or made good.
One person's fact, moreover, may be another person's distortion of the
truth. None the less, given a situation where a sufficiency of facts is
available, can their unadorned presentation ever truly enlighten and
engage? If that were so, surely a computer could write history far more
efficiently, quickly and cheaply than a historian. With a reasonable and,
preferably, a readable narrative to string the facts together, however, is
anything else really needed?

Dr Johnson's primary aim, however, may not have been to belittle the historian, although he may, incidentally, have been taking a side-swipe at Boswell – that indefatigable, and Scottish, chronicler of the great man's life. Dr Johnson's main thrust in the above quotation is surely the proposition that the writing of history requires no particular feat of imagination or creativity. This was, and is, palpable nonsense. It is true that history can be a mere accumulation of facts and figures, intertwined with a summary of events; but this would merely provide a meagre and un-nourishing diet even for the most puritanical and self-denying of readers.

To make sense of the past, to discern historical patterns and rhythms, to relate events one to another, the historian arguably needs as much imaginative skill and literary finesse as that employed by the successful novelist. Quite apart from anything else, the need to understand and to bring to life people and cultures often long since vanished demands that the historian has the imaginative qualities to put aside the intellectual and cultural baggage of personal experience, and of his or her own times, and to try to appreciate their equivalents in, say, the Dark Ages or the late-Victorian era.

It is also sometimes necessary to take a leap in the dark, to back a hunch, to follow a line of enquiry which at first sight seems unconventional and potentially unrewarding – maybe even closed according to other authorities – and to see where it will all lead. There can be very few major historians who have not found this approach both rewarding and enlightening.

So, assuming that the historical scholar has gathered the necessary information, perused appropriate primary and secondary sources, marshalled the evidence with competence, considered the argument and structured its presentation, how should the historian best set about his or her task?

First and foremost, it is surely the historian's fundamental duty just to tell a story, and to tell it so well that its readers will be informed, stimulated, intrigued, educated, and transported to different times and different places. It is surely no accident that in the major European languages the word for history is more or less identical with that used for story: French, *histoire*; Italian, *storia*; German, *Geschichte*, and so forth.[2] History even has its own muse, Clio, one of the daughters of Zeus and Mnemosyne, and a sister of other muses who inspire such creative arts as poetry, music and drama. There is no reason to think that Clio enjoys anything but equality and esteem among her more obviously artistic sisters.

The essential point that preoccupies, or at least should preoccupy, each historian is how best to tell the story. There are almost as many forms of historical writing, or ways of telling the story, as there are historians who research and write. In order to achieve its full power, even – occasionally – majesty, a piece of historical writing has to include description, analysis and interpretation as well as a vivid and vigorous narrative.

Let us begin with narrative. Although it might be possible to construct a piece of historical writing in which narrative plays no part, it is difficult to imagine it and even more difficult to imagine relishing the end product. Story-telling is, after all, one of a relatively small number of human activities which provides a chain of experience and enjoyment linking us with the most primitive of our ancestors. By telling a story, presenting a satisfying narrative, it is possible not merely to share certain experiences and even to consolidate group sentiment, but also to impose some sort of acceptable – or at least generally accepted – structure on both the past and the present. In other words, a good historical narrative can be seen as entertainment, education, a form of social cement and an attempt to control both the present and the future. When reading narrative history at its best, not merely are the feelings, scents, sounds and experiences of long-dead people re-created with a freshness and a compelling immediacy, but the modern reader is able to share in an act of re-creation which brings chunks of the past into his, or her, living-room or study. It is surely no accident that some of the most accomplished narrative historians of our own times – C. V. Wedgwood, Arthur Bryant and Winston Churchill – have also been best-sellers;[3] but, then, in the field of contemporary British fiction so have Jeffrey Archer, Jilly Cooper and Jackie Collins.

Few narrative histories could sustain themselves without a hefty garnish of descriptive writing. Indeed narrative plus description are the two most important ingredients in constructing a piece of historical writing that will be eagerly, even greedily, bought and consumed by the reading public. When historians describe past scenes, personalities or events, what they are in effect attempting is to achieve a re-creation of what it was actually like to be there. Such acts of re-creation may be very similar to, and certainly not necessarily inferior to, the descriptive work of the successful novelist, poet or journalist.

There is, naturally enough, an element of fashion in all of this. During the nineteenth century, for example, some of the greatest British novels were written by masters of description like Dickens or Thackeray; similarly two of the greatest nineteenth-century historical writers were Macaulay and Carlyle, both proven masters of historical narrative and description. At its best, descriptive and narrative history can engage, move and divert its readership as readily as any great novel. There is, however, very much more to effective and good historical writing than that. If there were not, the writing of history could indeed be left to novelists or playwrights.

One of the trickiest problems, however, is to decide who can be described as a historian. Clearly there are large numbers of academic historians – mostly at work in the universities, colleges or schools. Much of our history will therefore be written by them. The trouble is that not all of them can write particularly well. It is not merely that a narrowly based highly specialised monograph may arouse little interest outside of a small band of specialists. The truth is that a number of academic historians are unable effectively to bring their subject to life; in their hands, the most tumultuous and potentially exciting of historical descriptions become dross, unremittingly inducing boredom and fatigue in their readers rather than a need to keep turning the pages with zest. It is also the case that lively, accurate and inspiring history can be written by non-historians. Journalists, businessmen, military personnel, ex-civil servants, even – admittedly more rarely – retired statesmen and stateswomen may prove to be writers of fine history.

Whether they are academic historians or simply individuals writing history, however, all who attempt the task of historical writing face certain common difficulties. First, presuming – a big presumption – that the facts have been ascertained and the theories finely tuned, what should then follow? The organisation of the written material is clearly one of the immediate problems that the writer of history faces. It will profit the reader very little if he or she is presented with a jumble of details, descriptions or ideas. It has been powerfully argued that:

> Facts and ideas in disorder cannot be conveyed to another's mind without loss and are hardly likely to carry much meaning even for the possessor. This is because the mind is so constituted that it demands a minimum of regularity and symmetry, even in the arrangement of toilet articles on top of the bureau. ... Organisation distributes emphasis in the right places. The mind cannot give equal attention to every part; it must be guided to those parts – of a sentence or a book – which it should attend to for a correct understanding.[4]

Properly organised, and clearly and effectively presented, historical writing will be much more easy to understand, ideally just as the historian meant it to be. It should be the deep-rooted ambition of every writer of history that his or her reader will take from their experience precisely the meaning that the author intended to put into the piece. Of course, there will always be readers who will wilfully misinterpret for a whole variety of reasons – not all of them admirable – the sense of what they are reading. There will often be the need to project on to the text the personal, cultural or political imperatives of the individual in order to achieve some degree of private satisfaction, justification or objective. The historian had best write off such delinquents as part of the price an individual pays for being allowed, perhaps even paid, for putting his or her ideas before the public.

The historian, in turn, may also be accused of wilfully misinterpreting the material. Information can simply be presented in a biased fashion or, at the very least, in an insufficiently neutral way. The writer of history can select, emphasise, highlight and, either knowingly or unknowingly, distort the significance of this or that event, or the impact and motives of this or that personality. Few historians, I suspect, would be able to claim that they have *never* allowed their own personal predilections and convictions – whether consciously or subconsciously recognised – to shape some part of their writing. The trick is to keep such unprofessional and potentially destructive behaviour within limits. No historian is an inhuman writing machine, but neither, if true to the profession, is he or she a propagandist – even a half-hearted one.

Presuming that the historian can effectively master the primary and secondary material, make judicious and appropriate selections, produce a coherent narrative and lace it with telling and lively descriptions, this still leaves the problem of analysis. To some extent the analysis which the historian brings to bear on his or her material is a deeply personal affair. How could it be otherwise? Every piece of historical analysis presents the writer of history with a number of choices but also an inescapable moment of truth. The historian ultimately has to say what he or she thinks, or at the very least what they believe to be true. For example, in 1882 the British government decided to invade and, in the upshot, occupy Egypt. There are many reasons which can be presented to explain this step. Did the Gladstone administration send in the troops simply in order to keep the Suez Canal open, and safe for international sea traffic? Or did they act in order to protect various European communities in Egypt, some members of which had been killed in the recent Alexandria riots? Or to break the back of a revolutionary military regime which had the Khedive, the hereditary ruler of Egypt, in its thrall? Or perhaps to oust the French from their dual partnership with Britain in the affairs of Egypt? Or was it, conceivably, at some level that was not even clearly recognised and acknowledged, shaped by the fact that the Prime Minister, W. E. Gladstone, had nearly 40 per cent of his private portfolio of investments sunk in Egyptian stock?[5] As in this instance, the historian can synthesise, select and pick and mix from a large number of explanations and causes. In the last resort, however, he or she has to make a decision. There are some historians, however, who believe that it is more important to make up one's mind and to say what one thinks than to weigh the facts and probabilities as precisely as possible. It is sometimes the case that such openly assertive, polemical history, while making the author's meaning plain beyond doubt, leaves the reader with nothing of substance to feed upon, thus denying him or her the satisfaction of an admittedly somewhat passive, but also creative, junior partnership in the process of coming to an historical judgement. Although not exactly a version of 'publish and be damned', the capacity of the historian to say what he or she thinks – short of polemical overkill – is part of an intrinsically dialectical process that should, after various buffetings and toings and froings, lead to some clear-cut and overwhelmingly likely interpretation of events.

At its best an analytical history can be an immensely stimulating and diverting, as well as a satisfying and infuriating, form of enquiry. Essentially historical analysis is a highly refined and almost inevitably skilful form of interpretation. It provides, in greater or lesser degree, a narrative and a chronology of events – although these may be employed only briefly and may sometimes even be taken as read – but overriding these structures is the determination to provide a steady flow of analytical interpretations.

Analysis in history can take different forms and be aimed at different targets. Primarily, perhaps, it attempts to elucidate causes, to explain essentially why events turned out as they did. After all, it would be difficult to provide a satisfactory and conclusive account of, say, the partition of Africa or the General Strike of 1926 simply by producing a narrative of events, no matter how accomplished the narrative might be. Therefore the historian has to create a break or pause in the narrative, and clearly to assess the weight and significance of various factors operating over space and time. The impact of personalities, the allegiances of different groupings and organisations, the interplay of local and national forces, the perceptions – or misperceptions – of the direction of events or of the motives, prejudices and ambitions of individuals, will all play their part in the process of analysis. How do events interconnect? Exactly how does this organisation operate? Who is really – despite appearances – making policy in Westminster or White-hall? The list of questions can be expanded almost at will.

Finally any piece of analysis worth the reading will ask one of the most difficult questions of all: what, in the larger scale of things, does it mean, and should we, as a consequence, alter our view of how things turned out?

Good historical writing should also ask the question 'Why?' as often as the historian thinks appropriate. To a certain extent, the subordinate questions 'When did it happen?' and 'What happened?' are less sig-nificant or, at least, will probably provide less satisfying and less comprehensive forms of explanation. Yet it is not easy to discover 'why' an individual acted as he or she did, or 'why' a war broke out when it did, or 'why' an economy underwent such and such a crisis. Short of psychoanalysing the dead – and there is, incidentally, a flourishing and sometimes very enlightening school of psycho-historians in several Western countries – how exactly can one discover why an individual chose one particular course of action rather than another? How can we ever really tell why a group of people – a trade union, a ship's crew, a college of cardinals, an African tribe – acted as they did? All that can be said is that if the historian fails at least to attempt to answer the question 'why', then the risk is of failing not merely the readers but, more significantly, him- or herself.

One of the greatest of modern British historians, A. J. P. Taylor, took a provocatively quirky line on the question of causality and 'why'. Writing in 1969 he asserted:

> It is the fashion nowadays to seek profound causes for great events. But perhaps the war which broke out in 1914 had no profound causes. ... In July 1914 things went wrong. The only safe explanation is that things happened because they happened.[6]

It takes a certain amount of courage – chutzpah even – to adopt such a position, which is even more spartan than Edward Gibbon's belief that 'History ... is, indeed, little more than the register of the crimes, follies and misfortunes of mankind.'[7] Human beings generally want to know *why* things went wrong; they seek the *causes* of events; they wish to believe that they can truly *understand* the past. Perhaps only by believing that one can understand causality in history do historians, or even their readers, believe that they are, in some measure, in control of the past and hence – far more debatably – in control of the future. Taylor's minimalist view derives either from enormous intellectual and psychological self-confidence or from an almost anarchic attachment to a highly personalised form of chaos theory.

Not that it is, by any means, the duty of the writer of history to make readers feel safe. Vigilance rather than complacency, wariness rather than a weary, depressed acceptance should flow from a study of history. This is not to say that there are a finite and clear number of lessons to be drawn from history. Arguably the only lesson of history is that there are *no* lessons. Nevertheless most readers and students of history hope to gain something from the process, to be able to make sense of the past and perhaps, as a result, to feel more comfortable in making judgements about the present, and maybe even the future. To this end analytical history, supported by the twin pillars of narrative and description, can make the most potent contribution.

Having considered what might make for good historical writing, it is important to note that some historical writing is so cautious that hardly anything is ever evaluated or assessed. Such writing may simply deluge the reader in a sea of grey, factual sludge, in which meaning is drowned and the attempt to interpret never begun. On the other hand, historical writing that contains too many purple passages, florid descriptions and over-heated metaphors can be equally obscure and, ultimately, enervating and dispiriting. An overzealous attachment to metaphor may simply disguise the fact that the writer is taking refuge behind style as opposed to substance. Then there is the overuse of quotations. It can be plausibly argued that 'quotations are illustrations not proofs'.[8]

In the best historical writing, however, quotations certainly can provide crucial assistance in arriving at proof, and thus in consolidating an acceptable interpretation of events. If quotations are employed chiefly to prop up the historian's work, though, scattered like huge stepping stones across the course of a meagre and muddy stream, they will almost certainly be counterproductive rather than helpful and enabling. Similarly generalisations, if soundly based and skilfully deployed, ought to hasten the process of understanding. If, however, they are simply assertions or mere substitutes for more precise forms of exposition and explanation, they can weigh down the historical text, sapping its strength and vitality rather as the Old Man of the Sea threatened to do to Sinbad. Worse perhaps than stodgy generalisations is pedantry. Scholarship is one thing, pedantry quite another. The absurd lengths to which some historians go in order either to verify their sources beyond the hint of criticism, or to prove in an almost paranoid way how thoroughly they have researched their primary and secondary material beggars belief.

Essential though footnotes and bibliographies are, their main function is to provide ballast for the ship of historical writing rather than to drag it down to the bottom of the sea, unremarked and unmourned. There are, of course, some examples of inspired and invaluable historical writing where the author has dispensed with footnotes altogether; in those circumstances the reader is asked simply to take on trust the material presented. It is rare to find many highly regarded examples of this form of historical writing nowadays, and even in the relatively distant past a cavalier disregard for references was open to criticism. It was, after all, the legendary Master of Magdalen College, Oxford, Dr Routh, 1755–1854, who stated: 'You will find it a very good practice always to verify your references, sir!'[9]

Even if the historian has managed to steer clear of the rocks of pedantry and the shoals of an over-abundance of footnotes and references, there are still many more perils to be faced upon the choppy and notoriously treacherous seas of historical writing and interpretation.

An early but fraught defining point is to decide exactly at whom to aim the writing. The respect of one's fellow historians is an admirable thing and much to be desired. On the other hand, there are some historians who seem to be writing only for a few cosseted members of some arcane, minority sect. A subtle allusion here, an obscure reference there, will doubtless set members of the sect glowing with pleasure in the dark corners of library or study, but what will it do for the rest of us, especially for the undergraduate students of history struggling to eke out grants, find part-time employment and merely to keep abreast of their coursework?

Surely one of the prime tasks of any writer of history is to be clear and easy to understand. This is not, it should be quickly said, the same thing as writing headlines and articles for, say, the British gutter press – a form of journalism, as the playwright John Osborne once remarked, generally written by people who cannot write for people who cannot read. Nevertheless, given that the content of the piece of historical writing is soundly based and properly considered, the historian should do his or her utmost to avoid obscurity and to reject jargon. It is worth remembering that the hallowed advice 'never to use a long word if a short one will do' derives not from any desire to patronise the readers but rather from a prudent wish to keep as many as possible with you for as long as possible.

At the same time the historian should never 'talk down' to his or her readership. The reasons for this are self-evident. First, any readers worth their salt will recognise the condescension and resent it. Second, short of indulging in baby-talk, plain language provides a bridge between the highly qualified scholar and researcher and their readership – and one that can be easily and pleasurably crossed. In the process, both parties will keep their integrity and their self-esteem.

Good historical writing should also never play fast and loose with the presentation or interpretation of the facts. This is not to deny that there is considerable profit to be gained from the sensibly constructed 'what if?' questions of history, such as 'What if Oliver Cromwell had not died in 1658?' or 'What if Cecil Rhodes had never gone to South Africa?' The tendency, however, of some writers of the more popular or 'breathless' school of history to impose feelings and reactions on their subjects, despite any concrete evidence that these interpretations are correct, is a sin strictly to be avoided. For example, 'Mary Stuart must have felt as trapped and despairing as a caged bird by these cruel circumstances.' Well, perhaps she did. On the other hand, she might have been thinking about her next meal or dreaming of lost lovers. Who will know? Certainly the cause of historical understanding has not been furthered by such feverish speculation, even though a bodice or two may have been ripped in the imaginative process.

Then there is the delicate matter of assessing the impact of the great man or woman upon events. The historian has to make a crucial decision at the outset. How much weight should be attached to the power of the personality, the intrusion into events of individual men and women? Or is it simply a matter of the virtually preordained interplay of global forces such as the interaction of classes, economic structures or nation states? Naively put: if, say, Joan of Arc or Winston Churchill had never been born, would their work have been done for them by another person, and in roughly the same fashion?

It is fortunately not the brief of this chapter to try to answer that question – although it beggars belief that the individual may not play a vital role, at the very least, in nudging history this way or that. The place of historical biography in the unfolding of history is, however, one that requires some consideration. For too long the purists have tended to dismiss biography as a limited, handicapped contribution to historical understanding. It is certainly the case that some biographers who become besotted with their subject may present a lopsided picture, squeezing the facts to fit the image they have created. This is part of the risk involved in the art of biography; after all, it is a lot easier to fall in love with Sylvia Pankhurst or Joseph Chamberlain than to cherish a passion for the rise and fall of Methodism or the Munich Crisis. Biography may also give short shrift to the historical events which encompass the life under scrutiny. This may arise from the choices made by the biographer; but it may equally derive from the demands of the publisher to play up the 'human interest' or to keep within the word limit.

There are some encouraging signs nowadays that a number of these misgivings may be misplaced. Not only are many historical biographies becoming longer – without, thank goodness, approaching the bloated, multi-volume model so loved by the Victorians – but they also attempt to give as full a picture as possible of the background, in all its complexity. Equally encouraging is the tendency for contemporary biographers to investigate the formation of the personality of their subject in great detail. Rarely nowadays does a historical biography ignore, for example, parenting and childhood experiences in the formation of character and present the reader with an adult protagonist about whose past next to nothing is known.

There are still a daunting number of obstacles to good and effective historical writing beyond those already delineated. Students and readers of history in general should be wary of the traditional vices of the partial historian. These include the proffering of personal prejudice as fact; the playing out of professional jealousies and rivalries in the review columns – all too common, alas; the pushing of political agendas; the snide remarks tucked apparently innocently into articles and books; the presentation of wild speculation as truth; the failure to rein in bias; the taste for polemic rather than rational and generous debate; the floating of the 'bright idea' to the detriment of reasoned analysis; and much more besides.

Finally, any good piece of historical writing should have a memorable opening and an equally memorable ending. This is not the same thing as attempting to be dramatic or trying to attract attention at any cost. Rather it is part and parcel of the creation of an effective and readable work of art – and historical writing, at its best, is precisely that. Obviously there has to be a memorable, or at the very least competent, middle sandwiched between the start and the finish of the piece, otherwise the final product will be valueless. To choose examples of good beginnings and endings is a highly personal exercise, as individualistic as preferring the coastline of County Cork to that of Devon, or Indian food to Italian. Here, for what they are worth, are my choices. They are both taken from books dealing with modern British history.

The opening section is taken from A. J. P. Taylor's masterly, though sometimes heavily criticised, *English History, 1914–45* (1965). It sets the scene in the England of the immediate First World War period:

> Until August 1914 a sensible, law-abiding Englishman could pass through life and hardly notice the existence of the state, beyond the post office and the policeman. He could live where he liked and as he liked. He had no official number or identity card. He could travel abroad or leave his country for ever without a passport or any sort of official permission. He could exchange his money for any other sort of currency without restriction or limit. He could buy goods from any country in the world on the same terms as he bought goods at home. For that matter, a foreigner could spend his life in this country without permit and without informing the police. Unlike the countries of the European continent, the state did not require its citizens to perform military service. An Englishman could enlist, if he chose, in the regular army, the navy, or the territorials. He could also ignore, if he chose, the demands of national defence. Substantial householders were occasionally called on to perform jury service. Otherwise, only those helped the state who wished to do so.[10]

It is possible to quibble over some of the details of this piece. Taylor is actually discussing the United Kingdom, yet rather eccentrically only refers to the English and England – admittedly, perhaps, Ireland was rather a special case in 1914 as it teetered on the brink of both Home Rule and civil war. He only mentions the 'Englishman', ignoring the Englishwoman. He also tends to exaggerate, even romanticise, the freedom of the individual citizen, and so on. Yet the prose is crisp and lucid; the sentences beautifully balanced; the sense of addressing important issues in a direct and illuminating fashion paramount. Above all, the reader wants to know more. What will he say next? How will the story unfold? What paradoxes, what surprises are about to be revealed?

The example of a good way to end a piece of historical writing I have chosen is taken from Robinson and Gallagher's classic analysis of Britain's role in the partition of Africa, *Africa and the Victorians* (1961):

> Because it went far ahead of commercial expansion and imperial ambition, because its aims were essentially defensive and strategic the movement into Africa remained superficial. The partition of Africa might seem impressive on the wall maps of the Foreign Office. Yet it was at the same time an empty and theoretical expansion. That British governments before 1900 did very little to pacify, administer and develop their spheres of influence and protectorates, shows once again the weakness of any commercial and imperial motive for claiming them. The partition did not accompany, it preceded the invasion of tropical Africa by the trader, the planter and the official. It was the prelude to European occupation; it was not that occupation itself. The sequence illuminates the true nature of the British movement into tropical Africa. So far from commercial claims requiring the extension of territorial claims, it was the extension of territorial claims that in time required commercial expansion. The arguments of the so-called new imperialism were *ex post facto* justifications for advances, they were not the original reasons for making them. Ministers had publicly justified their improvisations in tropical Africa with appeals to imperial sentiment and promises of African progress. After 1900, something had to be done to fulfil these aspirations, when the spheres allotted on the map had to be made good on the ground. The same fabulous artificers who had galvanised America, Australia and Asia, had come to the last continent.[11]

There has been no shortage of critics of the overarching thesis contained in *Africa and the Victorians*. Doubtless the extract above will simply confirm them in some of these criticisms. The extract's virtues, however, are manifest. It is a finely balanced summary of the essential points contained in a very tightly argued text of 472 pages; it sticks to what, in the year of its publication, was a revolutionary and enabling reinterpretation; it puts into plain perspective a huge and complex historical process: the movement of European – particularly British – people, capital and commerce into Africa. It ends with a sentence which is so evocative of a worldwide but long dead historical process that it becomes quite moving. Within this sentence the choice of the phrase 'fabulous artificers' is, it seems to me, a stroke of genius.

It is not, alas, given to all of us to be Robinsons and Gallaghers, or an A. J. P. Taylor, Lewis Namier, Linda Colley, Paul Kennedy or

Christopher Hill. We can, however, aspire to the standards which they and a few others set. At the very least we can pay due respect to our muse, Clio, and see to it that she is not disgraced before her sisters.

Further reading

Historians, especially British historians, have generally fought shy of a great deal of theorising over their profession. Latterly this has been less true, and there is now a substantial, and often very rewarding, number of books available – often in paperback. Easily one of the best of recent studies is John Tosh's *The Pursuit of History*, now in a second, revised edition (London: Longman, 1991). This study is exceptionally wide-ranging, articulate, intelligent and equally accessible to students and teachers. Arthur Marwick's earlier, but now updated and expanded, *The Nature of History* (3rd edn, London: Macmillan, 1989) although lengthy, is entertaining and comprehensive.

Among the older classics of the genre are: E. H. Carr's left-leaning *What is History?* (2nd edn, London: Penguin, 1990); G. R. Elton's conservative-inclined *The Practice of History* (London: Fontana, 1969); Marc Bloch, *The Historian's Craft* (Manchester: Manchester University Press, 1954); Pieter Geyl, *Use and Abuse of History* (New Haven: Yale University Press, 1955); J. H. Plumb, *The Death of the Past* (London: Macmillan, 1969); and W. H. Walsh, *An Introduction to the Philosophy of History* (3rd edn, London: Hutchinson, 1967).

More recent publications include: Keith Jenkins, *Re-thinking History* (London: Routledge, 1991) and *On 'What is History?'* (London: Routledge, 1995); Joyce Appelby, Lynn Hunt and Margaret Jacob, *Telling the Truth About History* (New York: W. W. Norton, 1994); A. Callinacos, *Making History* (Ithaca: Cornell University Press, 1988); John Cannon (ed.), *The Historian at Work* (London: Allen & Unwin, 1980); Denys Hays, *Annalists and Historians* (London: Methuen, 1977); Fritz Stern (ed.), *The Varieties of History* (2nd edn, London: Macmillan, 1970); David Lowenthal, *The Past is a Foreign Country* (Cambridge: Cambridge University Press, 1985); John Kenyon, *The History Men* (London: Weidenfeld & Nicolson, 1983); and Howell A. Lloyd, *The Relevance of History* (London: Heinemann, 1972).

CHAPTER 2

History: theory and practice

L. J. Butler

Historians today face a growing challenge to justify their discipline and its methods. Researchers and writers in related or neighbouring disciplines have long criticised historians not only for their apparent failure to think critically about their work and its implications, but also for their reluctance to embrace theory and to bring their work into line with parallel forms of enquiry in the social sciences, where the application of conceptual models is common. Yet, as recent writers have argued, historians cannot avoid being affected by theory in some degree. They do not, for instance, normally approach their work in a completely random manner. On the contrary, their choice of research topic, no less than the methodologies employed to research that topic, will involve active intervention by historians in various stages of selection. Such intervention has important theoretical implications, although these may not always be recognised.

While the scope of historical research has expanded beyond recognition during the twentieth century, a long-standing debate on the nature, methods and even purpose of history has been broadened in recent years by the emergence of 'postmodern' theories which seem to undermine many of the comfortable assumptions historians have traditionally entertained about their work. The resulting literature has, unfortunately, often generated more heat than light, and constructive exchanges between proponents of 'traditional' and 'new' schools of thought have been rare. This chapter does not endorse any particular theoretical perspective: its rationale is simply that at a time when there is a vigorous, sometimes polemical, debate on the very nature of history, students and researchers can no longer afford to ignore what is being said about their subject, and may find a brief résumé of the major themes in this debate useful. It makes no great claims to originality, but draws on some important recent contributions to discussions on the nature and limitations of historical research.

Probably the majority of British historians could be described as being 'traditional' in their outlook. Among this majority, many remain broadly sceptical about the value of theory to historical research. Certainly, many would reject the notion that they themselves employ 'theory' at all: theirs is what is often called the 'common sense' view of history, and traces its roots to the emergence of history as a serious academic discipline under the guidance of the German Leopold von Ranke in the early nineteenth century. The more dogmatic adherents of the Rankean, or 'historicist', approach tend to see this as the only 'real' history, and its hold has been particularly strong among professional, academic historians.[1] In Britain, at least, this may reflect a peculiar, indigenous scholarly attachment to empiricism and a tendency to view with suspicion the claims of theory.

The 'Rankean revolution', notes Peter Burke, was a revolution of both sources and method. Empiricist history is particularly associated with an emphasis on the study and interpretation of documentary evidence. Ranke stressed the importance of studying the official records of the state, in place of former reliance on chronicles of variable provenance and reliability. While this is understandable, given the subjects which Ranke thought appropriate for historical investigation, this meant that other types of evidence could be overlooked, and tended to reinforce the narrow study of national, political history.[2] In this sense nineteenth-century historians, while more rigorous in their handling of evidence, adopted rather narrower horizons than their predecessors during the Enlightenment: whatever could not be dealt with using the new critical tools was liable to be excluded from study.[3]

Traditional history is concerned above all with politics. As the nineteenth-century British historian, Edward Freeman, famously claimed: 'History is past politics, and politics is present history'.[4] This outlook, heavily influenced by the Hegelian attitudes towards the state dominant in Ranke's time, encouraged a preoccupation with the state and its development, and hence led to a stress on national and diplomatic history at the expense of other forms, which were seen as secondary to these more 'important' topics.[5] An unfortunate consequence of this focus on high institutions and 'high policy', with its attendant preference for studies of 'great men' and their actions, was that the mass of the population and their history received relatively little attention.[6] Moreover, the new emphasis on archival research (which in practice often meant research in government archives) discounted the labours of social and cultural historians, as seen in the indifferent professional response which greeted the publication of Jacob Burck-hardt's classic work, *The Civilization of the Renaissance in Italy*, in 1860.[7]

The new historical method, pioneered by Ranke and developed by his disciples, gave rise to confidence that history could aspire to parity with the natural sciences in its capacity to formulate 'the truth'. The critical examination of documents (*Quellenkritik*) was intended to enable the historian to reach into the past, to understand the past *in its own terms* through the perceptions of contemporary witnesses. Cumulatively, these perceptions could provide an understanding of the past unavailable to any single contemporary.[8] An assumption inherent in this approach is that through careful research and the interpretation of documentary evidence, the 'past' is recoverable, that is, that the past consists of a single 'reality' which can be recovered.[9]

The unproblematic approach of the empiricist historian is seen in the claims made for the 'objectivity' of traditional history. In the tradition of Ranke, such historians seek to provide the 'facts', on the assumption that what they provide need not – indeed must not – be biased, but simply 'tells it as it actually was' (*wie es eigentlich gewesen*). This recommendation was intended as a corrective to the kind of visionary history advocated by writers such as Montesquieu during the Enlightenment. History was to be studied, then, not because of its predictive value but simply *for its own sake*.[10] Confidence in the ability of the new 'scientific' history to achieve objectivity was in part a function of the increasing professionalisation of the discipline. Its most extreme expression came, perhaps, with the ambitious attempt by Lord Acton to achieve 'ultimate' history, embodied in the collaborative *Cambridge Modern History*, a project begun in the 1890s. By gathering together a 'complete' collection of the 'facts', each of which had its part to play, a definitive version of the past could be achieved.[11]

This view has been argued forcefully by Geoffrey Elton, one of the leading exponents of the 'common sense' approach, for whom the study of history 'amounts to a search for the truth'.[12] Elton, 'the professional's professional', emphasises a thorough grounding in source criticism and interpretation as the key to uncovering historical truth. The well-trained professional will, according to this view, enjoy an almost 'instinctive' knowledge of the sources, and an equally intuitive knowledge of the questions which need to be asked of those sources.[13] Even though definitive accounts of the past might be elusive – some would say impossible to achieve – empiricist history still strives to re-create the past 'objectively', allowing the facts to 'speak for themselves' without intervention by the historian, whose role is to adjudicate, evaluate the evidence and, in true liberal fashion, attempt to see both sides of a problem.[14] According to this perspective, agonising about the nature of historical knowledge and the wider problems of epistemology simply distracts historians from their proper business: the *practice* of history.[15]

An important corollary of the empiricist standpoint is that the historian should be concerned above all with the people of the past, with their experiences, attitudes and behaviour, avoiding what is sometimes called a 'present-centred' perspective, and attempting to become so immersed in the values of the period being studied that its problems can be understood 'from the inside'.[16] Most importantly, this obliges the historian to put to one side his or her own attitudes and assumptions, not allowing these to intrude into the process of engagement with the past. What this amounts to is a conviction that systematic research can permit the disinterested study of the past, or 'history for its own sake'.[17]

A fundamental assumption of empiricist history, then, is that an objective historical truth exists and, provided that the historian applies rigorously 'scientific' critical methods, this truth can be recovered, showing the past as it was. While no individual piece of research may uncover the entire truth about the past, the cumulative effect of such pieces of research brings the truth closer, incidentally giving historians a collaborative goal and a common ideal.[18]

The desire to be objective also reinforced the prejudice of empiricist historians against social history which, it was thought, unlike political history, could not be studied 'scientifically'. Ironically, however, implicit in the new approach was a growing disdain for sociology, considered to be too scientific in the sense that it seemed to be too abstract and general, and incapable of dealing with the unique character of historical individuals and events. This concern reflected what is still a widely held opinion, that applying theory to specific historical contexts risks oversimplifying the complexities of the historical process and producing 'one-dimensional' history.[19] In the late nineteenth century, the German cultural historian and philosopher, Wilhelm Dilthey, had already highlighted the distinction between the natural sciences, with their concern to explain 'from outside' (*erklären*), and the humanities, such as history, whose goal was understanding 'from within' (*verstehen*), employing the language of 'experience'.[20] In turn, critics of empiricism argue that by attaching such importance to individuals and specific events, traditional historians provide unsatisfactory explanations of the past. For example, nineteenth-century social theorists were unimpressed by historians' claims: while Herbert Spencer dismissed them as providers of raw material for sociologists, Auguste Comte derided the 'insignificant details so childishly collected by the irrational curiosity of the blind compilers of sterile anecdotes'.[21]

The question of which themes were considered appropriate for historical study raises the problem of the preferred medium in which traditionalist historians have attempted to communicate their findings. The particularity of events which the Rankean approach stresses lends itself to a narrative style of writing. This, however, sits uncomfortably with attempts at analysis and generalisation, and is an obstacle to tackling wider questions of social structure and change. At worst, it may encourage an almost antiquarian reverence for discrete 'facts' which hampers the elucidation of patterns of historical change.[22] In turn, traditionalists would argue that theoretical approaches undervalue the 'uniqueness' of particular events and the significance of individuals. This resistance to the 'determinist' implications of theory was expressed forcefully in the writings of A. J. P. Taylor, for whom the accidental (or as recent writers might put it, 'contingent') nature of much human activity was inescapable.[23]

It is empirical historians especially who have drawn the criticism of social scientists, often baffled by the former's apparent myopia, amateurism and poverty of analytical tools. The historian's apprenticeship has, according to this view, usually emphasised the importance of detail and the particular rather than on the detection of general patterns (though this extreme view may reveal more about the preconceptions of social scientists than their understanding of much actual historical research).[24] Equally, by ignoring theory, it is claimed, historians run the risk of disciplinary 'parochialism', becoming prisoners of their own over-specialisation and failing to see parallels between their work and that of other researchers.[25]

Even if its intellectual hold has waned in recent years, Marxism has nevertheless had a profound influence (recognised or otherwise) on historical writing in the twentieth century, such that no historical researcher can afford to be unaware of the elements of Marxist thinking. Almost every branch of historical enquiry has absorbed something from Marxist thought in its widest sense or been prompted into a refutation of its assumptions, in turn opening up new fields of research. Close in spirit to the scientific goal of the nineteenth century, Marxism claims to offer not only an analysis of the past, but also insights into the relationship between the past and the future; like liberalism, Marxism offers a view of history as a process which has both movement and direction, and proposes a history which is both explicitly ideological and is the basis of a political programme for the future.[26]

In place of theoretically deficient 'liberal' or 'bourgeois' history, with its tendency to exaggerate the significance of individual historical actors and the power of ideas while ignoring the importance of economic factors, Marx provided a theoretical model of historical change. For Marx, the key to understanding the past, and to an understanding of how the present is developing, is the study of the evolution of material production. Just as Darwin had sought to explain biological development through his evolutionary laws, so – Marxists believe – Marx recognised the 'laws' of historical evolution, which were fundamentally economic.[27] His approach to history was therefore 'nomothetic', seeking general laws of human behaviour, in contrast to the 'idiographic' approach of Ranke and his followers, whose focus was primarily on the discrete and the particular. The social and political structures existing at any given period were determined, according to Marx, by the economic structures prevailing at that time. Thus the stages of historical development could be traced from early, 'primitive' communities, in which property was held in common; through ancient societies, in which production increased but the growth of private property was associated with increasing social tensions between classes; into feudalism, in which social distinctions were further accentuated by theologically underpinned hierarchies; to the stage of 'capitalism'. Capitalism, associated with increased production through the application of new technology, saw the emergence of new social relations in which capitalists owned the means of production and came to employ the bulk of society as wage-labour, which could be exploited.

According to the Marxist model, society could be said to consist of three levels. The first, the 'forces of production', is fundamental to the other two levels and comprises the technological resources of society, coupled with the human labour which applies those resources. The forces of production in turn shape the 'relations' of production, that is the economic structure of society, including the division of labour and the distribution of economic power. Arising from those forces and relations of production (the 'base') is the 'superstructure' of society – its political and other institutions, together with the dominant set of beliefs (or 'ideology') within that society.[28]

At the heart of the Marxist analysis is the contention that history revolves around the struggle between social classes which have conflicting material interests.[29] Because of its economic power and resulting political influence, the capitalist class could maintain its dominance, but this would ultimately be challenged as the exploited class, the 'proletariat', came to understand its position and common interests – that is, as the proletariat developed 'self-consciousness' of its membership of a single exploited class. This awareness, reinforced by an understanding of the 'laws' of historical development, would in turn make possible the revolutionary replacement of capitalism by socialism. History, for Marx, was essentially the expression of a continuing 'dialectic' between the forces of production and the relations of production: each mode of production (for example, feudalism, capitalism) bore within it the seeds of its successor mode. The contradictions inherent in unequal societies produce class conflict which is the dynamo of history, giving it a progressive momentum. One explanation for the powerful appeal of Marxist thought has been the notion that such conflicts can result in change for the better.[30]

Marx's identification of a close relationship between the economic framework of a given period (its particular 'mode of production'), and the social structure which pertains to that period, has attracted the fundamental criticism that Marxism is inherently deterministic, denying the significance of human agency and choice. Yet Marx's defenders point out that this is to misread Marx's argument: people remain ultimately free agents, but only within economic constraints. For instance, the forces of production include not only human labour and the equipment it operates, but also the intellectual powers and creativity which have enabled humanity to control much of its environment. Equally, the same argument goes, the relationship between base and superstructure is not simply one rigidly 'from the bottom upwards', that is, the superstructure does not simply reflect the material conditions of society, but rather the maintenance of a particular set of economic relations requires a corresponding network of property rights, sanctioned by legal and political systems. In other words, Marx's model allows for reciprocal influences between base and superstructure.[31] Each generation inherits circumstances from its predecessor, and these circumstances include the productive forces acquired by that previous generation.[32]

Marx described his approach as the 'materialist conception of history', and it is Marxism's materialist foundation which has aroused controversy, chiefly on the grounds that it implies too deterministic a course for historical development. This extreme interpretation sees Marxism subjecting history to the rigid control of economic forces, attributing human behaviour to motives of material self-interest and representing history as little more than the story of class conflict. This 'vulgar' Marxism ignores both the complexity of Marx's writings and the considerable developments in Marxist thinking in the last twenty to thirty years.[33] Yet again, Marx pointed out that it is people who make history, not as individuals but as members of social classes, and precisely how and when historical change occurs depends largely on people's understanding of their own condition, and on their capacity to seize the initiative. The paradox at the heart of Marxist analysis is, in John Tosh's words, that 'People are the victims of material forces but in the right conditions they have the opportunity to be agents of historical change.'[34]

The implications of Marxism for historical research have clearly been profound. Marxist theory posed a fundamental challenge to the

Rankean approach (which, for Marxists, was itself a product of the dominant liberal ideology of early nineteenth-century Europe), seen most clearly in the former's insistence that the scope of enquiry must be widened to reflect the contribution to historical change made not only by élites in society, but also by the masses. Marxism, as Southgate comments, therefore changed the criteria by which historians could choose subjects which were historically significant.[35] Moreover, from a Marxist perspective, the conventional historical interest in politics and ideology is seriously flawed unless the economic base from which these arise is also understood. Not surprisingly, the spread of Marxist ideas has done much to encourage research into the deeper economic and social structures hitherto neglected by historians. By analysing these structures, and by discarding the uncritical acceptance of what historical actors have said about their motives, historians can, according to Marxism, strive for a scientifically grounded objectivity.[36]

Although encouraging new perspectives and opening up new themes for research, such as the history of the mass of the population, Marxism has not focused exclusively on 'history from below'. On the contrary, because of their interest in the way state power can be harnessed in the resolution of social conflict, Marxists have been equally interested in the workings of 'high politics' and the mechanisms of the state.[37]

Marxist theory has not, of course, remained static any more than has its application to historical research. The development of the so-called 'new' Marxism in the 1960s and 1970s was taken a step further by the introduction of the work of the Italian Marxist theoretician, Antonio Gramsci, to a wider English-speaking audience in the 1970s and its application to historiography in the 1980s. In contrast to 'vulgar' Marxist identifications of the state with protection of the interests of the dominant class, Gramscian thought encouraged the notion that state power requires not only access to methods and instruments of coercion, but also to techniques of asserting and projecting its own legitimacy in the minds of those who are ruled. In other words, in order to claim legitimacy, and so enjoy unchallenged 'hegemony', the state cannot promote exclusively the interests of the dominant class, but must act more flexibly, making concessions to wider interests: to do otherwise would be to risk fomenting social conflict which might ultimately undermine the security of the existing political and social order. In practice, taking this perspective, the state must exercise a certain degree of autonomy from the class it represents: a process which can give rise to tensions. The implication for historical research is important: Marxist historians cannot simply disregard political history, but rather must pay close attention to the way in which the state has reacted to the demands of conflicting interest groups.[38]

It was in France in the 1920s that one of the most important challenges to traditional history emerged. Under the leadership of Marc Bloch and Lucien Febvre, the *Annales* school (some would prefer the looser term 'movement') attacked the traditional dominance of political history and attempted to replace it with 'a wider and more human history', embracing all human activity.[39] A concern to broaden historical investigation beyond the traditional themes of political and military history actually predated the Rankean revolution. During the Enlightenment, the history of society was seen as an important theme, prompting interest in the development of structures.[40] Even after the development of the new method, the dominance of political history was not total. J. R. Green's immensely popular *Short History of the English People* (1874) offered social history as well as the more conventional political narrative.

What characterised the *Annales* approach was a concern to replace the conventional emphasis on narrative, political history with a problem-solving analysis of structures.[41] Although reacting against the Rankean tradition, the *Annales* group sought to demonstrate that the rigorous methodological standards set by Ranke for the study of political history could also be applied to research on economic, social and cultural themes.[42]

Their interest in addressing the whole range of human history led the *Annalistes* to believe that historians could learn much from scholars in related disciplines, including sociology, geography, linguistics and psychology, Bloch in particular favouring comparative approaches to historical research.[43] In 1929, they founded the journal *Annales d'histoire économique et sociale*, devoted to encouraging interdisciplinary perspectives.

The approach pioneered by Bloch and Febvre was continued by Fernand Braudel, who was equally enthusiastic about the possibilities of interdisciplinary research, seeing a close relationship between history and sociology.[44] The overarching aim of the *Annales* approach was an integrated, or total, history. Braudel sought not to reproduce the minutiae of the past, but to bring together different fields of human behaviour and to emphasise the connections between them.[45]

Many of the group's cardinal principles were encapsulated in Braudel's monumental *The Mediterranean and the Mediterranean World in the Age of Philip II* (1947). Instead of focusing on events, which he regarded as relatively superficial in significance (the 'froth' of history), Braudel sought to examine economic and social changes over the long term, relating these to geographical changes over an even longer term. It was this emphasis on the study of long periods (*la longue durée*) which became a hallmark of the *Annales* group.[46] Significantly, Braudel claimed Marx as an early theorist of *la longue durée*. The abandonment of conventional narratives by the *Annales* school has been seen as central to the group's position. According to Hayden White, the *Annalistes* regarded narrative historiography 'as a non-scientific, even ideological representational strategy, the extirpation of which was necessary for the transformation of historical studies into a genuine science'.[47]

It has to be said that, at least until the 1960s, the *Annales* approach encountered resistance from many British historians, whose empiricism, disciplinary insularity and sacrosanct individualism were formidable barriers to change. Aggravating this was the dearth of adequate translations of the *Annalistes*' work – a problem compounded by the subtlety of some of the school's key concepts. Nevertheless some British writers, notably R. H. Tawney, had recognised the value of the *Annales* approach even before the Second World War. Similarly, in Britain during the 1930s, Lewis Namier had pioneered a structural analysis of political institutions in rejection of traditional narrative approaches. Concerned with the realities of political power, Namier examined the political élite of eighteenth-century Britain by applying a 'collective biographical' approach to the study of eighteenth-century members of parliament.[48] The influence of the *Annales* approach can also be seen in the work of post-war British regional historians, notably in W. G. Hoskins's pioneering *The Making of the English Landscape* (1955). Among British Marxist historians, for example Eric Hobsbawm, the reception given to French historiography has been more generous. As Peter Burke suggests, this may be because Marxists saw in the *Annales* movement a useful collaborator in the continuing struggle against the primacy of political history.[49]

Critics of the *Annales* approach attack what they see as its excessive uniformity, over-reliance on quantitative methods, and determinism. However, as Peter Burke, who describes himself as a 'fellow-traveller' of the *Annalistes*, has argued, this is to ignore the scope for divergences between individual practitioners within the movement.[50] On the charge of determinism, it is worth remembering that Febvre, for example, emphasised not the determining effects of environment, but rather what the environment made it possible for people to do.

Similarly, critics of the *Annales* approach have voiced reservations about the practicability of 'total' history, stressing particularly its failure to engage with political history. As John Tosh has argued, the *Annalistes* have 'conspicuously failed to develop a satisfactory model for integrating political history with the environmental and demographic studies which provide the backbone of their work', Braudel's study of the Mediterranean being a case in point, ultimately failing to integrate a political narrative successfully into the discussion of other themes.[51] In this respect, the same critic argues, the *Annales* method is less convincing than Marxist history, which emphasises the interaction between economy, society and politics.[52] Another basic problem is that the *Annalistes'* preoccupation with analysis can mean the neglect, or obscuring, of the narrative dimension. One solution to this problem is to apply the methods of the *Annalistes* to more manageable subjects, for example the study of localities. This attunes well to the enthusiasm of recent theorists such as Michel Foucault for 'microhistory', and the study of the politics of smaller structures such as institutions and the family.[53] More recently, there has been a noticeable shift back towards political history within the *Annales* school. This reflects not only a reaction against the movement's earlier tendency towards determinism, but also a more fundamental trend among historians to concede the importance of agency, not only structure, in historical explanation.[54]

Arguably an even more fundamental challenge to traditional historiography has been posed by the growth of feminism. For feminists (but for many others also), traditional historical research was inherently flawed in that it neglected the pasts of women. In the past, it seemed, history had been written mostly by men and largely about men, the corollary being that the achievements and experiences of women had been either undervalued or simply ignored.[55] This undeniable imbalance has been tackled in two ways: through the development of a distinctive women's history (or 'herstory'), and through the production of more general narratives which deliberately discriminate in favour of giving women a more prominent position (a form of 'positive discrimination'). While the latter is a consciously biased strategy, it can be defended on the grounds that the bias is explicit.[56] Thus, feminist historians have sought to demonstrate that women 'have played a crucial role, producing, processing, and reproducing the cultural and economic resources of each generation'.[57]

Whether the feminist project to achieve a more balanced history makes possible, as some have claimed, a more 'complete' or more 'true' history has been seen as problematic, in that these kinds of goal are increasingly seen by theorists as unrealisable.[58] Nevertheless, the broad strategy of including in historical research any previously neglected group, let alone an entire gender, can only be beneficial. Like their Marxist precursors, feminist historians have simply refused to be constrained by traditional views about the 'proper' subject matter of history. The fact that women were ignored by historians for so long also, it could be argued, casts doubt on the achievability of 'objective' history, since it was male historians who chose to ignore women as a subject, or failed to recognise what did not suit them. This is reflected in the way in which evidence about women's past has been re-examined, and new kinds of evidence called into play.[59] By restoring many long-forgotten individuals, and by proposing or rediscovering themes which had long been ignored, feminism can be said to have transformed the nature of historical study. Perhaps this is seen most clearly in the challenge feminism has posed to some of the most cherished principles of the 'Rankean' approach, particularly its claim to pursue research free of value judgements. Here, feminist critiques have been intimately associated with fundamental themes at the heart of 'postmodern' perspectives, such as the problematic nature of language. The convergence of philosophy, linguistics and anthropology has done much to undermine the assumption that language simply reflects reality. On the contrary, it is argued, language itself defines reality, not in any fixed way, but in a way that is contingent, or could be different. In practice, contemporary theorists argue, language therefore represents a particular viewpoint, thus excluding other possibilities.[60]

This re-evaluation of language has important implications for feminist theory. History, according to this view, has been written almost exclusively from a perspective which both grew out of, and reinforces, a 'patriarchal' social structure. In traditionally male-dominated Western societies, male values have been cultivated and have permeated everyday language. Inevitably, history has been written not only from a basically patriarchal perspective, but employing a language which is anything but 'neutral' in the way in which it describes gender relations. Historians, even if they are unaware of it, are accordingly subject to an intellectual framework – shaped by the language they use – which undervalues the role of women. The history they write in turn reinforces this essentially patriarchal framework, in that the 'reality' selected for preservation as history is one which underlines men's role in shaping the past. From a feminist perspective, this continuing pattern can only be interrupted by changing the language historians use, allowing it to convey hitherto marginalised female values and attitudes.[61]

Feminism is no more 'monolithic' as an ideology than Marxism. As John Tosh has observed, it consists of two major strands. The first emphasises the importance of patriarchy as the critical factor in determining inequality between the sexes, and sees other forms of social differentiation as subsidiary to this. The second strand (analytically closer to Marxism) promotes a diametrically opposed view, that gender relations reflect the relations of production, specifically being situated between the 'productive forces' in society and the 'superstructure' of society. For some theorists, this relationship can be taken much further, to the extent that gender is itself determined by class.[62]

One very important consequence of the burgeoning of feminist history has been the perceived need to advance from a basically 'celebratory' form to one which is more analytical and explanatory. This in turn has encouraged a view that women's history, and the domination of women by men, can only be understood in relation to the structures and processes involved, which requires the study of both sexes. The consequence of this has been the development of 'gender history', grounded in attempts to examine both sexes and the variety of relations between them. This approach seems likely to have important implications for the writing of all history.[63]

Beyond this, as Beverley Southgate suggests, feminist theory has been important in contributing to the cultural relativism characteristic of much postmodern theory. Its advocates have claimed to demonstrate that any historical account is necessarily partial and contingent, and to have contributed to the 'de-centring' of historical explanation. By widening the focus of historical research in this way, feminism, arguably, opens the way for other basic redefinitions, for example of 'femininity' and even of 'reality'.[64]

As one recent commentator has observed, 'postmodernism' is not an intellectual position but, rather, simply the condition in which we live as the twentieth century draws to a close.[65] This condition is the consequence of the alleged failure of all those post-Enlightenment 'projects' (liberalism, Marxism, humanism and so on) which collectively constituted 'modernism'. As a result, the 'old organising frameworks' or 'metanarratives' have been eroded, and are seen as having never been more than 'temporary fictions' employed to promote particular, not universal interests.[66] Inevitably, the postmodern outlook calls into question those 'certainties' which have conventionally governed the work of historians. Basic Rankean reference points such as 'facts' and 'objectivity' dissolve in the flux of postmodern scepticism. Developing out of earlier challenges to historicism, postmodernism, which embodies recent developments in linguistic and literary theory, social theory and social anthropology, arguably poses the most fundamental challenge to traditional thinking on the nature of history.

A prominent casualty of postmodernism is the traditional empiricist historian's faith in 'objective truth' as an achievable goal. According to the empiricist tradition, it is possible for the historian to be aware of his or her own biases, and to neutralise their effects by attending strictly to what the documents reveal and so achieving 'impartial detachment' – a position described by the historian Raphael Samuel as 'naïve realism'.[67] This optimism is undermined by the observation (crucial to 'postmodern' attitudes, though not in itself postmodern, having been made by the *Annaliste* Marc Bloch)[68] that the sources themselves 'say' nothing: it is 'historians who articulate whatever the "sources say", for do not many historians all going (honestly and scrupulously in their own ways) to the same sources, still come away with different accounts; do not historians all have their own many narratives to tell?'[69] To take this point further, 'the data on which historians work is actually given its meaning by those same historians. It is they who choose it in the first place, who select it from a potentially infinite quarry, and who make some sense of it in relation to a lesson or message that they want to transmit.'[70] The all-pervasive scepticism and relativism of post-modernism are incompatible with the idea that there can be an ultimate, authoritative view of the past. On the contrary, according to this view, no version of history is any more than a 'tentative hypothesis under-pinned by a possibly unstated, but none the less specific, purpose'.[71] In other words, everyone approaches the past from a particular perspective and the 'disinterested' historian proves to be illusory, giving way to the ideal of 'heteroglossia' – the acceptance (even celebration) of a situation in which there can be numerous 'varied and opposing' voices.[72] If it is conceded that all history is written from a particular philosophical or ideological position, then, as Southgate argues, the only questions remaining to be resolved are, first, whether that standpoint should be explicitly acknowledged and, secondly, whether the choices made (in topic, evidence and so on) were consciously made.[73]

The cultural relativism which permeates so much recent historical writing can itself be seen as the outcome of a growing tendency for history to converge with social anthropology, and specifically of the concept that 'reality' is a social or cultural construct.[74] In practical terms, this has not only involved a disintegration of any former con-sensus on what constituted 'good' historical explanation, but also means that historians increasingly find it difficult to communicate with one another.[75]

From the postmodern perspective, even more fundamental doubts emerge in relation to historical evidence. Here, the points raised earlier in relation to feminism and language again have significance. The in-escapable issue is whether the historian's cherished 'facts' are themselves determined by language, that is, whether language does not simply describe a situation but may also help to construct that situation. At its most extreme, it could be argued that this perspective implies that history itself could be 'reduced to a subsystem of linguistic signs constituting its object (the past) according to rules pertaining in the "prisonhouse of language" inhabited by the historian'.[76] Contemporary linguistic theory suggests that language is itself 'produced' by its own context, determining our experience of the world and not vice versa. This prompts the question: does language simply reflect an external reality (that which is 'out there'), or 'is it a "free-standing", autonomous entity that is imposed upon our otherwise random experience – rather like a net being thrown over a swarming group of recalcitrant wild animals?'.[77] If the latter is the case, then this will have important implications for notions of historical 'truth'.

If, as many postmodern writers would hold, we can no longer categorically insist that language is merely representational, then any historical account must be seen as simply a 'verbal construction, lacking any necessary relation to anything outside itself'. Accordingly 'truth' becomes an impossible goal, to be replaced by the only valid criterion of meaning, the 'internal coherence' of the account.[78] One, inevitably controversial, response to this linguistic dilemma has been to emulate the practice of some novelists, by adopting more than one viewpoint or by avoiding a single, 'authoritative' ending, thus allowing readers to reach their own conclusions.[79] Again, to take this process to (one) conclusion, history can be constructed in whatever way we want, since there are no longer any 'absolutes' towards which we can strive.[80]

The employment of theoretical perspectives and the exploration of new themes raise questions about the use of new kinds of evidence and about using traditional kinds of evidence in new ways. For example, oral testimony, long employed by social anthropologists, sociologists and others, is increasingly used where possible by historians, not only to reconstruct the attitudes of key actors in policy formulation and so on, but as a tool in approaching 'history from below' – although it is one which poses special problems of interpretation.[81] Equally problematic is the interpretation of visual sources, now recognised as being rather less 'objective' than was once held. For instance, photographs, no less than written documents, are the result of a process of selection which may be shaped by existing cultural conventions: the resulting image therefore represents, rather than reflects, 'reality'.[82]

The problematic nature of empiricist narrative approaches has also been explored extensively by postmodern writers. The 'stories' which historians have traditionally presented (for example, about diplomacy or the working class) do not collectively constitute 'the past'; on the contrary, to argue that they do is to mistake 'the narrative form in which historians construct and communicate their knowledge of the past as actually being the past's own'.[83] Empiricist narratives, according to this view, are ineluctably compromised because the attempt to relate such 'stories' of the past to the historian's own narrative breaks down since there are no such stories in the past.[84]

Recent historical research has continued the process of opening up the study of long-neglected themes, particularly in the field of social history. From the perspective of 'history from below' has developed an interest in the history of everyday life, a field pioneered in Germany, and arguably a natural outcome of the *Annales* school's early enthusiasm for *la vie quotidienne*. But new perspectives have also been introduced into traditional fields of study such as political history, the difference being that now there is as much interest in the attitudes and responses of 'the led' as in those of their 'leaders'.[85] In part, this embodies a reaction against earlier determinism in favour of empirical descriptions of the relationships, actions and attitudes of ordinary people. Research into 'history from below' and popular culture in turn raises problems of definition, and here, too, the influence of social anthropology has been marked, in the sense that 'culture' comes to be identified with anything which can be 'culturally constituted', including popular attitudes and social institutions.[86] A related theme which has attracted interest is the notion of 'contingency' in history – the idea, again in part a reaction to earlier determinism, that history might have been different. In other words, much of what has happened in the past occurred, and has been interpreted since, in a quite arbitrary fashion. Historians have become increasingly interested in the choices made by individuals, the strategies they have devised to cope with everyday life. This has had consequences for the way in which research findings have been presented, prompting renewed interest in the possibilities of narrative to explore, biographic-ally, the scope individuals enjoy for freedom of action.[87] Recognising that the direction of history can be changed, as Southgate argues, can have an important 'empowering' effect. 'Contingency', then, becomes a liberating factor.[88] Furthermore, the widening of the scope of historical research, together with the use of conceptual tools and methodology borrowed from the social sciences, makes possible not only new per-spectives, but also the opportunity to integrate traditional and new perspectives, exploring, for example, the relationship between 'high politics' and popular political culture.

While the removal of 'objective truth' as the ultimate goal will undoubtedly unsettle traditionally trained historians, there may, as Southgate comments, be compensations. If there is no ultimate truth, there is a need for numerous versions of the past, none of which can claim superior authority, but each of which adds fresh insights from its own perspective. Moreover, acceptance of the limitations confronting the historian's work, and of the equal validity of others' findings, even where these conflict with one's own interpretations, will, it is argued, induce a refreshing and necessary humility. The corollary of this will be a much greater awareness among historians of what their colleagues are doing and where this might lead the discipline. No less significant will be the 'empowering' effects of applying new theoretical perspectives to historiography. As well as revealing the ideological foundations of earlier history, these may suggest 'how our own history may serve as a validat-ing foundation for any future programme'.[89]

Not surprisingly, the erosion of empiricist claims has stung traditionalists into responses, some of which have been characterised by intemperate language. Thus Geoffrey Elton has likened the effects of much recent theorising to those of dangerous intoxicants.[90] Yet it could be argued that recent exchanges between historians on the value of theory have exaggerated the differences between 'traditionalists' and 'new historians'. Much recent writing could be said to be applying a theoretical gloss to the *de facto* pluralism and eclecticism long practised by some of the most respected historians. For instance, the scepticism embodied by postmodern thinking has, in practice, long been part of the historian's armoury. Few practitioners really aspired to an 'ultimate' truth in their work – the mark of a 'good' historian, as of a 'good' scientist, has always been a willingness to accept the limitations of one's own work and the likelihood that one's findings will be tested by others and found wanting.

To conclude with a point raised at the beginning of this discussion, recent contributions to the debate on history suggest that all historians, whether they recognise it or not, employ theoretical assumptions, even at a very simple level. The process of selecting a topic of research, and of selecting evidence through which to approach that topic, will involve the historian in making choices. Controversy among contemporary writers hinges on the implications of this process of intervention by the historian, concerning our ability or otherwise to shed our assumptions, prejudices and personal 'ideological' outlooks, and to engage with the evidence of the past to be able to explain that past in an undistorted way. Proponents of the various positions in this debate continue to present their cases with energy, and there is little prospect of it being resolved in the foreseeable future. Meanwhile, those engaged in historical research need to be aware of the problems raised by any attempt at historical explanation. In order to explain the past, the historian is forced to generalise so as to be able to reach some sort of conclusion. The conclusion which emerges does not need to be, perhaps cannot be, 'definitive'; rather, it takes its place in the continuing, dialectical process of scholarship. The organisation and presentation of ideas in this way prompts fresh research which may confirm or challenge the original claim. Furthermore, even though theoretical differences will continue to divide historians, it would be unfortunate to emphasise the constraints of theory, or to stress only the dangers of determinism: such intellectual rigidities are hardly conducive to vigorous, ground-breaking research. Rather, it may be more helpful to concentrate on the positive, 'heuristic' possibilities of theory – to use theory not in an attempt to find ready-made answers to historical problems, but to suggest new questions, new themes which need to be researched, and new methods of conducting that research.[91] It follows that, faced with the current proliferation of theoretical perspectives, the way forward for the historian may lie in the cultivation of a receptive mind, open to new ideas, but tempered by a healthy and constructive scepticism.

Further reading

As suggested in the opening pages of this chapter, there is now a growing literature on the theoretical problems raised by historical study and research and their implications for historical practice. Among the essential introductory texts are John Tosh's excellent *The Pursuit of History* (2nd edn, London: Longman, 1991) and Arthur Marwick's *The Nature of History* (3rd edn, Basingstoke: Macmillan, 1989), each of which provides a useful bibliography. E. H. Carr's *What is History?* (Harmondsworth: Penguin, 1964) and G. R. Elton's *The Practice of History* (London: Fontana, 1969) have traditionally been seen as good introductions to the debate on the nature of history. For a comprehensive and detailed study of the development of history as a discipline, see Ernst Breisach, *Historiography Ancient, Medieval, and Modern* (2nd edn, Chicago: University of Chicago Press, 1994).

On Ranke and his legacy, Georg G. Iggers and James M. Powell (eds), *Leopold von Ranke and the Shaping of the Historical Discipline* (Syracuse: Syracuse University Press, 1990) is recommended, and contains useful essays by Peter Burke and Wolfgang J. Mommsen. An empiricist discussion of documentary research is provided in G. Kitson Clarke's *The Critical Historian* (London: Heinemann, 1967). A detailed refutation of much recent theorising is provided in G. R. Elton's robust *Return to Essentials. Some Reflections on the Present State of Historical Study* (Cambridge: Cambridge University Press, 1991).

On the *Annales* school, key texts are Marc Bloch, *The Historian's Craft* (Manchester: Manchester University Press, 1992) and Fernand Braudel, *On History* (London: Weidenfeld & Nicolson, 1980). A sympathetic treatment of the movement's contribution is Peter Burke's *The French Historical Revolution. The Annales School 1929–89* (Cambridge: Polity Press, 1990). The Marxist impact on historical research is assessed in S. H. Rigby, *Marxism and History: A Critical Introduction* (Manchester: Manchester University Press, 1987). For an introduction to feminism's implications for history, see Karen Offen, Ruth Roach Pierson and Jane Rendall (eds), *Writing Women's History: International Perspectives* (Basingstoke: Macmillan, 1991) and J. W. Scott, 'Women's History', in Peter Burke (ed.), *New Perspectives in Historical Writing* (Cambridge: Polity Press, 1991).

Important recent contributions include Keith Jenkins's *Re-thinking History* (London: Routledge, 1991) and the same author's *On 'What is*

History?' From Carr and Elton to Rorty and White (London: Routledge, 1995). An extremely lucid introduction to the subtle issues raised by postmodernism is Beverley Southgate's *History: What and Why? Ancient, Modern and Postmodern Perspectives* (London: Routledge, 1996). The impact of recent developments in political and social thought is explored in the important collection of essays edited by Quentin Skinner, *The Return of Grand Theory in the Human Sciences* (Cambridge: Cambridge University Press, 1985). Peter Burke has produced a number of clearly written and valuable studies of theoretical issues in history including, *History and Social Theory* (Cambridge: Polity Press, 1992). Burke has also edited an important collection of essays, *New Perspectives on Historical Writing* (Cambridge: Polity Press, 1991), which includes a number of highly relevant contributions such as Burke's own 'Overture: the new history, its past and its future' and 'History of events and the revival of narrative'.

The American journal *History and Theory* has in recent years published a number of seminal articles on new perspectives in history, and particularly on the relevance of postmodern thinking. Among these are Hayden White, 'The question of narrative in contemporary historical theory', *History and Theory* 23 (1984); F. R. Ankersmit, 'Historiography and postmodernism', *History and Theory* 28 (1989); Perez Zagorin, 'Historiography and postmodernism: reconsiderations', with a reply by F. R. Ankersmit, *History and Theory* 29 (1990); Wulf Kansteiner, 'Hayden White's critique of the writing of history', *History and Theory* 32 (1993); and F. R. Ankersmit, 'Historicism: an attempt at synthesis', *History and Theory* 32 (1995). Something of the polemical flavour of contemporary debates is captured in the exchange between Arthur Marwick and Hayden White, 'Age-old problems', in *The Times Higher Education Supplement*, 25 November 1994. Both these writers have provided more substantial statements of their positions: see Arthur Marwick, 'Two approaches to historical study: the metaphysical (including "Postmodernism") and the historical', *Journal of Contemporary History* 30, 1 (1995) and Hayden White, 'Response to Arthur Marwick', *Journal of Contemporary History* 30, 2 (1995).

CHAPTER 3

Public records

L. J. Butler and Anthony Gorst

Historians of modern Britain are fortunate in having as a major resource one of the richest and best organised archives in the world. The Public Record Office is the national repository of central government records selected for permanent preservation.[1] It supervises the selection and transfer of records from government departments, courts, tribunals and non-departmental public bodies, and makes those records available for consultation by the public. Founded in 1838, in 1992 it became an executive agency and government department, reporting directly to the Lord Chancellor.[2] Although the holdings of the Public Record Office cover the period from 1086 to the present day, this chapter will concentrate on twentieth-century records. The work of the PRO has expanded enormously in the past one hundred years. More people probably now use the Office in a single year than used it during the entire nineteenth century.[3] Its holdings are clearly priceless to the historian of high policy and high-level administrative organisation, central government policy-making and implementation, and so on. But, increasingly, historians with much wider interests, including social and economic historians, are discovering the value of the public records in addressing issues such as demographic change, business practices and medical history, to cite just a few examples.

One point which must be remembered is that the PRO does not exist solely to serve the historian, although this is a useful consequence of its existence. Among the Office's many readers, professional historians constitute only a minority, and many other important 'categories' of readers, such as genealogists, have to be catered for by the Office's staff. It is a testament to the expertise of PRO staff that they have created a system comprehensible to readers with no prior archival experience.

Public records are defined as the records of modern government departments,[4] the armed services, and other organisations associated with government. They consist not only of the records produced by Whitehall, but also include records of the many branches of the Civil Service situated around the country, the records of various government agencies, and those of some, but not all, nationalised industries. Public records, as defined by the Public Records Acts of 1958 and 1967, do not include the records of the departments and courts of Scotland and Northern Ireland, each of which has its own Public Record Office.[5] Nor do they include the records of Parliament or local government. These are housed in various archives, most of which are listed in *Record Repositories of Great Britain*, produced by the Royal Commission on Historical Manuscripts.[6] Conversely, not all public records are housed in the PRO. Around one-fifth of all permanently preserved public records, especially those with a strong local or regional relevance, are located in so-called 'Other Places of Deposit', of which there are over 240 in England and Wales, approximately half of them being local authority record offices.[7]

Government records can cover any aspect of day-to-day government administration and policy-making. The increasingly interventionist nature of government in the later nineteenth and twentieth centuries is reflected in the growing variety and complexity of records produced by government in this period, a trend naturally accelerated by the enormous administrative demands arising from the two world wars.[8] The growing volume of records produced during this century reflects not only the expansion of government business, but also the introduction of new methods of duplicating documents, such as dyeline copying and photocopying. Even after the reductions in the size of the Civil Service during the 1980s, it was estimated that around two million files were being created each year.[9]

Public records include a wide range of physical types of material. While by far the greater proportion of them are written or typewritten records, they can also include maps, sound recordings, photographs, moving images and, increasingly, punched cards and other forms of 'machine-readable' records such as digital computer tapes. The latter, which grew in quantity and significance from the late 1950s onwards, present special problems of conservation and information retrieval. Increasingly, the PRO is receiving documents which were produced using technology which is now obsolete. One solution, actively being explored by the Office, is to transfer these records on to optical disc systems, enabling them to be stored cheaply and retrieved conveniently.[10]

Confronted by the sheer magnitude of the PRO's holdings for the modern period, it is nevertheless worth remembering that what survives represents only a tiny fraction of the original paperwork produced by government. Approximately one per cent of all records are selected for preservation; the remainder, which includes a great deal of material of no administrative significance or historical interest, is destroyed. The practical consequence of this is that the researcher cannot assume that the material he or she needs will have survived. However, the destruction of documents is not necessarily so disastrous for the historian as it might sound; the Foreign and Commonwealth Office, for example, typically aims to preserve around 80 per cent of its main policy papers.[11]

The fundamental principle of modern administration is the concept of precedence, and this plays a large role in determining which records are judged worthy of permanent preservation. Civil servants need to know how problems were dealt with in the past if they are to address them effectively in the present. This concern reflects the traditionally reactive nature of the Civil Service, even of government itself, in which problems are responded to as they arise. Similarly, civil servants need to be able to draw upon the 'collective memory' of their predecessors, to know how and why certain decisions were reached, and what the legal, financial and administrative implications of policies were. This has been reinforced by the growth of research by government departments themselves, designed to evaluate existing or previous policies, or as the basis of policy formation. Fortunately, these are often precisely the kinds of questions which interest historians.

The detailed arrangements for the selection and transfer of documents to the PRO are not derived from public records legislation, but from the recommendations of the Committee on Departmental Records (the Grigg Committee), which gathered evidence between 1952 and 1953, and reported in 1954. Before the Grigg Report, under the 1877 Public Records Act, departments were supposed to apply historical criteria to all their records when selecting them for preservation. In practice, this proved to be problematic: not only was it difficult for selectors to predict the historical value of particular records, but increasingly they were swamped by the sheer bulk of records from the modern period.[12] The Grigg Committee called for improved methods of deciding which records of modern government departments should be preserved. It opted for a two-stage process, known as first and second review. The 'first review' was to be conducted soon after the 'active life' of each record ceased, ideally within five years. The department's own reviewing officer was to determine, by applying administrative criteria, whether the department would require the record for its own use, for example as a precedent or as a guide to possible departmental action in the future.[13] It was anticipated that between 50 per cent and 90 per cent of the records would be destroyed as a result of this first review. The idea that each department, or creating body, should decide which of its records were worthy of preservation reflects a well-established belief among archivists, one argued forcefully by the 'father' of modern British archival practice, Sir Hilary Jenkinson.[14] Jenkinson's point was that the process of evaluation, or 'appraisal', should be impartial, that 'the historical record should reflect the tendencies and spirit of the administration of the day and not those of the academic researchers of the time'.[15]

When records which had survived first review were twenty-five years old, they were to undergo a detailed 'second review' by the department's own records officer assisted by an inspecting officer from the PRO. Because the volume of surviving records would be considerably less than at the first review stage, it would be feasible to apply historical criteria to determine, file by file, which merited permanent preservation. If in doubt, the inspecting officer could consult archivists within the PRO and, if necessary, seek help from the academics and other experts who constitute the Advisory Council on Public Records, chaired by the Master of the Rolls. After this second review, records were either transferred to the PRO to await release to public inspection, or destroyed.

Central to the 'Grigg system' was a recognition that continuity was needed in the handling of records from the time they were in active use to the time they were either destroyed or sent to the PRO. In 1981, the Wilson Committee, itself created partly as a result of fears among researchers about the risk of large-scale destruction of records arising under the Grigg system, restated the fundamental belief that responsibility for the appraisal of records should fall largely on the departments which produced them, with the assistance of the PRO's inspecting officers.[16] Selection procedures can, therefore, be seen as an attempt to strike a balance between the needs of record-creating bodies and the possible needs of future readers.[17]

In the appraisal process, selectors employ three broad, but convenient categories of record. The first consists of policy files: those records which show how a particular policy was evolved, the relevant discussions between ministers and their civil servants, evidence accumulated, and opinions offered by persons outside the machinery of government, experts often drawn from the 'great and the good'. The second category consists of administrative papers, relating to the origins, organisation, functions and personnel of a department, and may include departmental reports, internal departmental manuals and other documents which record procedures. Thirdly, there are so-called 'case papers', often known as 'Particular Instance Papers' or 'PIPs': files relating to the practical operation of a particular policy, including any legal consequences arising from it. The broad subject matter of PIPs will be the same, though each individual paper will relate to a different person, organisation or place. These papers are essential to an administrative system which is grounded in the principle of precedent. Case papers normally survive in huge quantities, giving rise to a conflict between the researcher's desire to see as many as possible of these preserved, and the practical constraints of finding adequate storage for them. Because many case papers concern named individuals, confidentiality requires that they are not open to public inspection for many years, compounding the problem and expense of storage.[18] In practice, the solution is usually to 'sample' such papers in a systematic way, and academic historians are often consulted about appropriate sampling methods.[19]

To the historian, perhaps more interested in the way in which a policy was devised and formulated, it may be puzzling that records relating to the minutiae of that policy being implemented should be valued so highly. However, as the Grigg Committee foresaw, the real value of case papers emerges when they are examined as a representative sample: 'while each individual document may be of little importance by itself, taken together or by way of sample these papers enable certain broad conclusions as to historical, economic or social trends to be drawn'.[20] Ironically, papers which might not meet the first review criteria of departmental need, could nevertheless be historically important because of the data they could provide.

Until the passing of the Public Records Act 1958, there was no statutory right of public access to modern departmental records, although in practice permission was normally granted to readers at the discretion of individual departments.[21] Access to public records is currently governed by the Public Records Act 1958, as amended in 1967. The 1958 Act, embodying the recommendations of the earlier Grigg Report, established a fifty-year release policy, reflecting what had become *de facto* practice among many government departments. Nevertheless, some academics were not satisfied with this, and their misgivings were aired by the Advisory Council on Public Records in 1964 and again in 1965. In March 1966, the then prime minister, Harold Wilson, announced his government's intention to introduce a thirty-year rule.[22] This was achieved through the 1967 Act, under which records normally become available thirty years after they were in active use. Thus, for example, the records produced during 1960 became available for public inspection in January 1991.[23] While advocates of greater freedom of information in government have welcomed this change, and called for further reform, serious doubts were raised prior to the 1967 legislation. Thirty years is, after all, less than an official's working life, and current legislation means that a senior civil servant's earlier career and views may now be open to (potentially embarrassing) public scrutiny. This is a violation of the tradition of anonymity cherished by senior civil servants. Whether records produced from 1967 onwards will reflect officials' sensitivity to exposure, and so be less revealing than earlier records, remains to be seen – when they are opened from January 1998.

In practice, however, there are numerous exceptions to the thirty-year rule. Government departments can, if they choose, release records before they are thirty years old. This provision applies especially to material which is already in the public domain, for example the findings of committees of inquiry. Early in 1972, in a major example of 'accelerated opening', many records from the Second World War period were made publicly available.[24] On the other hand, departments can apply to the Lord Chancellor's Department for permission to defer the opening of records for fifty, seventy-five or 100 years; alternatively, records can even be retained indefinitely by departments.[25] Applications for the closure of records for longer than thirty years have to meet agreed criteria. The subjects considered to be sensitive cover a wide, and sometimes surprising, range. Exceptionally sensitive topics, such as intelligence and security, defence planning and civil defence, and nuclear weapons, have traditionally been subject to so-called 'blanket' retentions on grounds of national security. The types of record closed for extended periods can include papers containing information supplied in confidence by members of the public, papers containing information about individuals which might cause distress or even create risk to them or to their families, and records containing commercial information, again supplied in confidence, which might be of interest to a competitor. Materials gathered for the decennial census are routinely closed for 100 years. Variations from the thirty-year rule require authorisation from the Lord Chancellor, and these instruments can be inspected in the PRO reading rooms.

In 1993, as part of the government's commitment to more 'open' government (the 'Waldegrave initiative'), proposals were set out for reducing the amount of records withheld beyond thirty years, and introducing stricter criteria for the extended closure and retention of records. As a result, over 10,000 documents which had previously been closed became publicly available in the PRO. The majority of these originated in the Foreign and Commonwealth Office and the Ministry of Defence.[26]

Even if a particular document has been closed for an extended period or retained, it is possible to request access to it. In this case it is necessary to apply in writing to the departmental records officer of the relevant government department, whose address the PRO can supply. It is worth remembering that government departments can recall their records at any time, for routine use, for the purpose of compiling official histories, or perhaps for use in exhibitions. In these cases, it may be possible to arrange for these records to be returned to the PRO, although this will take time and require notice.

However, allowing for these potential obstacles, using the PRO is remarkably straightforward, and readers quickly learn the essentials of finding and ordering the documents they need. Indeed, in terms of accessibility, the PRO is frequently compared very favourably to other major national archives, such as those in Washington or Paris. When approaching the public records or any conventionally organised archive for the first time, the most important point to bear in mind is that records are not normally arranged and classified by subject, but according to who created them. At the risk of gross oversimplification, it may help to think of the Public Record Office as a library whose contents are organised entirely according to author, not subject or title. First-time researchers are prone to be frustrated that all the records on the subject which interests them are not conveniently gathered together under the same category or heading. Yet this emphasis on the provenance, or origin, of records is a fundamental principle of archival practice, and a little reflection brings out the force of its logic. Archivists are concerned not only to protect and preserve the records in their care (that is, to maintain physical control over them), but also to keep track of what they are looking after (that is, to maintain intellectual control). Generations of archivists have reached the conclusion that the safest, least subjective way to do this is to preserve the original order of records as it existed when they were in use, and, as far as is possible, never to interfere with this arrangement. Any artificial system of classification, it is felt, risks imposing a false or, at best, temporary value to particular records. Research fashions vary, and what historians consider vital information today, they may, unfortunately, disregard tomorrow. Equally, new developments in historical research can give records a value unforeseen by those who created them.

The records in the PRO are arranged according to the body which created them, which usually means a particular government department or agency, such as the Cabinet Office, the Foreign Office or the Treasury.[27] Each government department or record-creating body has been allocated lettercodes applying to it alone. Many of these will be readily understood, for example 'T' for Treasury papers, 'FO' for Foreign Office documents, and so on. Such relatively self-explanatory lettercodes were convenient for so-called 'dead' archives, to which no further records were likely to be added. However, the PRO eventually exhausted the number of such lettercodes, given the tremendous changes and reorganisations which have taken place in central government in the twentieth century. The PRO therefore employs a system of officially 'meaningless' lettercodes for later creating bodies. Thus, the United Kingdom Atomic Energy Authority was ascribed the arbitrary letter combination 'AB'. Such lettercodes have the advantage that they can readily be applied both to predecessor and successor bodies, and the system can therefore cope with the numerous reorganisations which have occurred in Whitehall in the last fifty or so years, ensuring that successive transfers of records in a continuing series can be placed in the same class regardless of their source.[28]

Within each lettercode, records are arranged in classes, reflecting original series, types or categories of record. Normally, all the records in a class are of the same physical type (for example, files or bound volumes) and the information content (for example, original correspondence, committee minutes or maps). These classes are allocated numbers within the appropriate lettercode. For example the class CAB 65 consists of the minutes of the War Cabinet, 1939–45, while CAB 128 comprises Cabinet minutes produced from 1945 onwards. Each class in turn is composed of pieces, that is individual files or volumes, or 'units of production' supplied to the reader. As far as is practicable, the arrangement of pieces within a class reflects the order of the documents according to their original registration system.[29] A typical document reference, which would be used to order a particular document, and which would be cited in a footnote, might be HO 45/195.[30] The three elements in this reference – the lettercode, the class number and the piece number – are unique to that particular document, making it instantly identifiable and retrievable.

Because so much importance attaches to who created the public records, it follows that it helps to know something about the institutions whose records you intend to read. A great deal of precious time can be saved by thinking in advance about the particular branches of government which might have had responsibility for the subject you are researching. The staff in the PRO's reference room are both knowledgeable and helpful, and will willingly provide advice on locating records, but the demands on their time are great and growing, and it is in the researcher's own interests to reduce the number of unnecessary queries raised with them. A little advance preparation on the researcher's part can achieve much in this respect.

To derive the maximum benefit from the PRO, and to understand the rationale for record preservation, it is helpful to bear in mind the needs of the civil servants who originally created and used these records, and to know something of how central government operates.[31] It is well worth checking whether any histories, official or otherwise, of the department or agency in which you are interested have been written.

The authoritative and semi-official *New Whitehall Series* of departmental histories includes volumes on the Foreign Office, the Home Office, the Ministry of Labour and National Service, and so on.[32] Other useful studies include Peter Hennessy's acclaimed study of the Cabinet and its supporting organisation, and Henry Roseveare's study of the development of the Treasury.[33] The Treasury, as Whitehall's paymaster, itself occasionally needed to produce brief 'blue notes', or administrative histories of government departments, and these can be found in the class T 165.

The PRO produces numerous free information leaflets explaining how to use the archive, along with leaflets devoted either to the records of specific government departments, or to particular topics.[34] A number of extremely useful handbooks have also been produced, for example those on *Making Sense of the Census* (London: HMSO, 1989), *The Cabinet Office to 1945* (London: HMSO, 1975), and *The Second World War: A Guide to Documents in the Public Record Office* (2nd edn, London: HMSO, 1993).[35]

If you are still unsure about the kinds of records you ought to consult, or are unclear how the branches of government relevant to your research operated, your starting point should be the *Current Guide* to the PRO. This is kept in hard-copy form in the PRO reference room, but a microfiche edition is available for purchase or can be consulted in reference libraries.[36] This is updated periodically, and readers can save a great deal of time and effort by familiarising themselves with it. The *Current Guide* is divided into three parts. Part 1 contains brief administrative histories of all government departments and agencies, describing the work done by each department and providing details of the record classes relevant to those responsibilities. Part 2 is a complete alphanumeric list of all the PRO's record classes. It gives the full title of each class, the dates covered by the records in that class, the total number of files, volumes, etc. in the class, together with a description of the class's contents and (often) indications of other, related classes. Part 3 is an index to Parts 1 and 2. It is a massive compilation of index terms, for each of which there will usually be two types of reference: one to Part 1 and one to Part 2. To find out more about the department which created the records which interest you, look up the references to Part 1 of the *Current Guide*. To discover more about the records themselves, look up the references to Part 2.[37]

Having established which record classes are relevant to your needs, you are now ready to consult the detailed class lists, which, in other archives, are often referred to as handlists or simply lists. There are three complete sets of these, housed in the reference room and in the lobby at the PRO. They are arranged alphanumerically, from AB 1 to

ZSPC 11. Class lists are normally produced, under PRO guidance, by the department which transfers the records in question to the PRO. Most class lists begin with an introductory note, providing information about the records in that class and about their administrative context. The class lists themselves typically provide the unique number, date range (vital, as this determines access to the document), and a short description of every individual document or piece. This description is usually either based on, or is a verbatim transcription of, the original file title of the document when it was in active use. It is worth bearing in mind that this description may not be wholly accurate, as items added to a file during its life may have changed the nature or balance of its contents significantly. Also normally provided in the class list is each document's former reference, that is, the filing reference it had when it was in current or active use. This can be extremely useful as a means of tracking down other, related documents. Moreover, this reference will appear on correspondence between the file's creating department and other departments or bodies. If, in a file created by department A, you find a letter from department B, comparison of the file reference on that letter with the file references provided in the class lists relating to department B may enable you to find other relevant material concerning that topic. Class lists also indicate if a particular document has been retained by a department, or is subject to extended closure. The existing class lists are constantly being improved to bring them up to PRO standards, namely a list which follows the numerical order of the original record series. Bear in mind, therefore, that it may be necessary to look through several pages of a class list to find related files. It is also important to be aware that variations exist in the format of class lists. Some are arranged chronologically, topographically or by subject (if so, an index is normally provided at the beginning of the list).

A microfiche version of the PRO's class lists for modern government departments has been produced.[38] Much time can be saved by consulting this to identify useful material before visiting Kew. Similarly, the List and Index Society has produced facsimiles of numerous PRO class lists, including those of the War Cabinet memoranda and most of the classes from CAB 1 to CAB 40. These can be consulted in many reference libraries.[39]

A number of other, more specialised finding aids exist at the PRO. For example, the *Legislation Index* provides a guide to records from various classes relating to the preparation and implementation of Acts of Parliament since 1900. The *Photographs Catalogue*, though not yet a comprehensive guide to the PRO's large photographic holdings, consists of a main catalogue, arranged in PRO reference order, plus separate indexes to places, individuals and subjects.[40] For those interested in the

PRO's huge holdings of maps, three volumes of a printed catalogue have so far been published, and these are supplemented by a card catalogue, arranged topographically.[41] Numerous other nominal and subject card catalogues exist relating to a wide range of classes. These are listed in General Information leaflet 3 *Means of Reference at Kew*.

Some classes of record consist of registers to other classes, especially series of original correspondence. Some of these are on open access in the reference room. Where such registers have survived, they will usually be mentioned in the relevant entry in Part 2 of the *Current Guide*. Thus, for example, CO 554 consists of the original correspondence of the Colonial Office relating to West Africa, while CO 555 comprises registers to this correspondence. By inspecting registers, it is possible to check the contents of a large number of documents very quickly, instead of having to order and inspect each individual document.

Those researching twentieth-century British foreign policy are well served in the range of additional finding aids available to them. In particular, they have access to printed indexes to Foreign Office General Correspondence for the period 1920 to 1951. These indexes provide the original file reference and paper numbers of relevant documents, and the Foreign Office class lists will have to be consulted to convert these former references into current PRO references.[42]

Armed with a list of document references, the reader can then set about ordering pieces. This is an extremely simple process. Ordering is done via computer terminals, following simple on-screen, step-by-step instructions. A maximum of three pieces may be ordered at any one time. Readers are notified of the arrival of their documents by electronic pager, normally after thirty minutes or an hour. Having collected the first document, it is then possible – and, in order to save time, advisable – to order another three documents straight away. Documents can be ordered until 3.30 p.m. each day, and can normally be held over until the following day.

In order to reduce the wear and tear on the most heavily used classes of document, the PRO makes some of these available on open access, without the need to order via the computer system. Thus, for example, electrostatic copies of most Cabinet minutes and papers since 1916 can be consulted in the reading rooms. Similarly, a growing number of classes have been microfilmed, and microfilm readers and self-operated copying machines are available. Make sure that you do not waste time (and create unnecessary work) by ordering documents which are on open access.

Becoming familiar with the format and structure of public records is essential to successful research. Time spent early on learning the way to 'read' modern departmental files will amply repay the effort invested.

Researchers working on twentieth-century history, especially those interested in policy-making and implementation, are likely to find that much of their raw material comes in the form of registered files. These have their origin in the practice by which departments began organising their papers according to subject – keeping together letters received, internal minutes, drafts of replies and so on, in a cover with a unique reference number and, usually, a distinctive title. This more orderly way of arranging business replaced the cumbersome practice of numbering papers individually as they reached a department, or were produced within it, and of keeping registers of these separately numbered items. Some departments were slower to embrace the registered file than others: while the War Office adopted the system in the mid-nineteenth century, the Treasury did not do so until the 1920s.[43] A refinement of the registered file was the 'Home Office' file system, adopted by a number of departments. In this, individual items in a file could be subnumbered consecutively, permitting their temporary removal and replacement.

Record-keeping practices have varied widely between government departments. Some, for example the Foreign Office, long favoured the so-called 'single jacket' file, while others opted for the 'multiple paper' file system. In the single jacket file system, all the papers derived from one communication – related correspondence, drafts, minutes, telegrams and so on – were kept together in a single jacket. A file consisted of a group of related jackets. Though much admired by officials who used this system, it required careful and extensive cross-referencing. With the multiple paper file system, all the papers of a file are kept together, enabling the whole story to be gained from that collection.[44]

Research is a highly personal affair and no two researchers will approach a problem in an identical way; and this chapter does not aim to give detailed advice on research strategies. Nevertheless, a few simple points may be worth considering. When reading a file for the first time, establish straight away how it is organised. Does it, for example, read from front to back (with the most recent item filed at the back) or vice versa? Are minute sheets grouped together on the left-hand side of the file, with letters, drafts and memoranda on the right-hand side? What does the cover of the file tell you? Remember to record the file's original title (bearing in mind that this may be misleading – papers can be added to a file during its working life which give it a scope far beyond that suggested by its original title). Does the file cover bear a printed grid, with each box containing a set of initials and a date? If it does, this will enable you to chart the progress of the file through a department over a given period of time. Take particular care to record document references accurately. These will form the basis of your own footnote references, and care in transcribing them precisely will reduce the need for subsequent laborious amendments and unnecessary repeat visits to the PRO (sadly, all too common during the writing-up stage of research).

When taking notes, try to be selective, and keep the questions you are asking of the records clearly in mind.[45] Do not be overawed by the volume of records, and resist the temptation simply to summarise each file without asking its significance to your research. Marc Bloch's often-quoted observation that documents 'will speak only when they are properly questioned' bears repetition.[46] Of course, this is not to suggest that your research will not evolve, and become more focused, partly in response to exposure to the records and to an empathetic engagement with them.

Generally, when reading a file, try to establish whether it has an outcome, for example a policy statement, a piece of legislation, or instructions to regional officials. Much time may be saved by establishing at an early stage whether it is worth reading the entire file in detail. On the other hand, the very absence of an identifiable outcome to departmental discussions may itself be of historical significance. For researchers into policy-making, it is important to determine where decisions were taken. Were problems resolved within a particular department, or did they require consultation with other departments? Were any Cabinet committees interested in, or responsible for, the topic being researched? Remember that many important questions are dealt with below the level of a full Cabinet meeting. If you are looking at Cabinet or Cabinet committee discussions, try to read the papers presented by officials or ministers in close conjunction with the minutes of their meetings. Fortunately, both minutes and memoranda are normally indexed.

While it is normally quite easy to ascertain the names of ministers responsible for particular topics,[47] a problem which frequently causes initial concern among new researchers is that of identifying the many officials whose names they encounter in letters, minutes, memoranda and so on. The *Dictionary of National Biography*, *Who's Who* and *Who Was Who* are the sources of first resort here.[48] A useful starting point among official publications is the *Imperial Calendar*, subsequently the *Civil Service List*, which indicates the responsibilities of higher-level civil servants, according to department. Some departments produced their own lists of officials, for example the *Foreign Office List* and the *Colonial Office List*. For members of the armed services, the *Army List*, *Navy List* and *Air Force List* should be consulted in the PRO reference room. For officials too junior to be listed in a contemporary guide, it is worth checking guides of a later date. If the individual involved remained in the department, it may be possible to ascertain his or her earlier career. A very useful source of information, which usually gives a much fuller picture of the careers of key officials, is newspaper obituaries, especially those published in *The Times*.[49] It is also worth checking to see whether the department in which you are interested preserved any records from its personnel or establishment branch. Some departments produced occasional circulars for internal use, listing staff moves, promotions, resignations and so on, and these can be very useful in filling in 'gaps' in an official's career.

There is always a danger that the researcher who spends a great deal of time absorbing the ideas of officials will eventually be seduced by the 'official mind': identifying with the problems faced by those officials, losing a proper sense of detachment and, consequently, producing 'semi-official' history. One strategy to combat this danger is to intersperse primary research with secondary reading at regular intervals, exposing oneself to fresh and possibly different perspectives. On the other hand, there may well be a case for a detailed examination of the ideas, assumptions and contributions of senior civil servants. Historians of twentieth-century Britain have increasingly recognised the proactive role played by civil servants in a number of policy areas. Rodney Lowe's study of the Ministry of Labour and its role in the evolution of interwar employment policy is a good example of a work which required a thorough immersion in the day-to-day internal politics of that particular department.[50] Such studies need not result in dry, administrative history, but can enable a real assessment of bureaucrats' role in political life.

Finally, the Public Record Office will supply reprographic copies of documents, subject only to the condition that copying will not damage the originals. A range of reprographic processes is available.[51] For most readers, cost will be an obvious consideration, but for those who cannot visit the PRO easily (for example to check their own notes at a later date), or who are pressed for time, the sheer convenience of having a copy of a key report or set of data may compensate for the financial outlay.

Further reading

A very useful introduction to this subject is N. Cox, 'Public Records' in A. Seldon (ed.), *Contemporary History. Practice and Method* (Oxford: Basil Blackwell, 1988). The archival principles which inform PRO practice are clearly summarised in M. Roper, 'Modern departmental records and the Record Office', *Journal of the Society of Archivists* 4, 5 (April 1972), pp. 400–2. The same author, a former keeper of the public records, has offered some insights into the PRO's wider influence in the archival community in 'The Public Record Office and the profession', *Journal of the Society of Archivists* 10, 4 (October 1989), pp. 162–7. This journal often publishes articles by PRO staff dealing with matters of interest to users of the Office. A wide-ranging selection of essays, produced to mark the 150th anniversary of the PRO, can be found in G. H. Martin and P. Spufford (eds), *The Records of the Nation. The Public Record Office 1838–1988, The British Record Society 1888–1988* (London: The Boydell Press/The British Records Society, 1990). The authoritative history of the PRO has been written by J. D. Cantwell, *The Public Record Office 1838–1958* (London: HMSO, 1991) Some of the problems associated with the destruction of records are discussed in M. Roper, 'Public records and the policy process in the twentieth century', *Public Administration* 55 (1977): 153–68. Thought-provoking comments on the limitations of public records are offered in A. Booth and S. Glynn, 'The public records and recent British economic historiography', *Economic History Review* 2nd series, 32 (1979): 303–15.

CHAPTER 4

Archives

Elizabeth Shepherd

Archives are, by definition, unique. They are created by organisations and individuals in the course of their ordinary business. They reflect the functions and activities of the institution or family. Their original arrangement, form and medium varies, depending on the needs of the creating body. Record creators are not usually conscious of the value of their records to the historian, but are more concerned with the efficient functioning of the organisation, with ensuring that legal and financial requirements are met and with the availability of precedent, procedure, policy and management information to enable effective decision-making to take place. The vast majority of records are of short-term value and are destroyed before they have the chance to fulfil cultural and research objectives as historical archives. The archives that fill the eleven hundred archive repositories in Britain[1] represent only the residue of records which their creators and the archivists, their custodians, deem worthy of permanent preservation for historical research. However, they provide an enormous wealth of primary source material, comprising hundreds of thousands of archive groups[2] and, probably, millions of individual items. Much of this wealth is unknown to the scholastic world and under-exploited by academic researchers. This chapter seeks to provide new researchers with some basic tools to help them to mine this lode of gold.

The term 'archive' is used here to mean a 'body of documents accumulated in the course of business';[3] the institutions in which archives are held are referred to as archive offices, record offices or repositories. The researcher needs to understand how the archival system in Britain works, in order effectively to exploit it and the archives it holds. Too many researchers waste time and become very frustrated because they simply do not understand how the system operates or because their expectations of archival repositories are unrealistic.

In Britain, the archival system has developed over several centuries in an *ad hoc* fashion. Unlike more centralised countries such as France, there is no single national framework which is imposed and funded from the centre; there is no national archives legislation which makes general provision for the preservation and management of archives. There is a mixture of funding sources and of mandatory and permissive legislation for specific types of records. Consequently, there is a variety of approaches to the provision of archive services. For researchers this can cause confusion, since acquisition policies, appraisal and selection of archives, arrangement and description, closure periods for archives, rules on access, record office opening hours and the provision of services such as reprographic copies all vary from repository to repository. More uniformity of approach is being developed through national and international standards: for example on arrangement and description, and the general structure and management of record offices.[4] However, for the present, the researcher should expect variety rather than uniformity.

There are four broad sectors in the provision of archival repositories in Britain. Each of the sectors can be subdivided. The first sector is the national institutions and includes the public record offices (that is the repositories holding administrative and departmental records belonging to the Crown including the courts of law, which are discussed in Chapter 3), the great national libraries which all have manuscript and archive collections, and the national museums and galleries. In addition, there are some special national archives such as the House of Lords Record Office. The characteristic of these institutions is that they have an acquisitions mandate which is nationwide and are funded centrally by a national institution.

The second sector is the local authority record offices. These are run by all the county councils, except Avon, and by some districts in England and Wales and by some regional and district councils in Scotland. Non-metropolitan parts of this sector are, at the time of writing, experiencing wholesale reorganisation and the provision of archive services will change as a result. In Scotland, Wales and in a few parts of England unitary authorities now deliver local services and it is not yet clear how local record offices will be managed. The characteristic of these institutions is that they acquire records from all types of organisations and individuals within a specified geographical area (typically historic county boundaries).

The third and fourth sectors are the domain of specialist repositories. These are the most varied sectors. The third sector is the publicly funded institutions which include university archives and manuscript collections, some research institutes, as well as various specialist record offices such as regional film and sound archives. Some of these institutions have, in effect, a nationwide area of acquisition but others focus on a particular research area (for example trade union archives) or geographical region.

The fourth sector is the independently funded specialist repositories. These range from individual business archive services, through charities and non-profit-making organisations, to historic houses. The characteristic of this sector is that each institution has a specific, specialist acquisition mandate based typically on a single organisation (for example a bank running its own archive service).

There are also three different models of archival acquisition which affect the holdings of a particular archive office in any of the four sectors described above. Some archive services are established by the organisation or family which created the records in the course of its activities. In this case, the whole of the record's life cycle – from creation, through current use, to semi-current storage, to preservation as an archive for research – is managed within the originating institution. For instance, a brewing company manages records to enable it to brew and sell beer now, and also preserves its own archives for internal research (for example, as a source of information about how its products were marketed in the 1950s, for a nostalgia advertising campaign in the 1990s) and for external researchers (for example, an art historian interested in the history of design of promotional materials).

Other archive offices do not acquire the records of the employing body at all, but collect archives or manuscripts on a particular theme from outside the institution, from bodies who created the records but are not able or willing to manage their historical archives. For example, a research institute for military archives attached to a university does not acquire the university's own records, but rather collects private papers of senior members of the armed forces.

A third version of acquisition is the archives office which adopts a 'total archives' model, and acquires both the archives of the employing institution and archives from external organisations and individuals within a defined geographical area or thematic remit. An example is a county archives service which manages the archives of the county council but also acquires archives from local families, churches, businesses, charities, associations and so on operating within the county boundaries. The researcher needs to be aware of the framework and variations in order to learn where to look and what might be found.

British legislation relating to archives is not comprehensive, makes no general provision for the protection of archives and is, in the main, permissive rather than mandatory.[5] In addition, there are few sanctions for non-compliance. Although it has been discussed in the public arena from time to time, there is no freedom of information act. Few organisations are compelled to keep their archives for historical research or to allow researchers any access. In practice, most organisations and many individuals both preserve records and encourage historians to use them. It is worth remembering, however, that researchers seldom have an absolute right to see particular archives and should not assume that access will be provided. This is particularly true for the archives of businesses, which may have commercial sensitivity, and for family papers remaining in private hands.

Public records are normally open to public inspection thirty years after the last date of the record.[6] In special circumstances public records can be kept closed for longer: records containing sensitive personal information, for example, are usually closed for one hundred years. In the absence of similar statutory provision, these provisions are often adopted for non-public records. For local government records, the Local Government Act 1972 s. 228 and the Local Government (Access to Information) Act 1986 make limited statutory provision for access by certain categories of user to certain categories of local authority records.

Three types of archives found in England and Wales have particular protection from legislation: manorial records, tithe records and the records of the Church of England. Manorial documents and tithe records are the responsibility of the Master of the Rolls. He discharges his responsibility through the Royal Commission on Historical Manuscripts (HMC), which maintains a manorial documents register and assists the Master of the Rolls in connection with the Tithe Rules. The records of the established church are regulated by a measure passed by the General Synod in 1978 which has the force of law. Church of England parochial registers and other records over one hundred years old have to be deposited in the diocesan record office, unless the parish can meet quite stringent storage conditions. Records of the Church in Wales are deposited under various agreements with the National Library of Wales or, in the case of ecclesiastical parish records, in the relevant county record office. In Scotland, pre-1855 Church of Scotland parish registers are in the custody of the Registrar General. In Northern Ireland, the Public Record Office of Northern Ireland (PRONI) has oversight of parish records but they frequently remain in parochial custody.

Most archives are unprotected by statute and provision for their care is unregulated, except by adoption of professional standards of management. There are few statutory obligations on businesses or on private individuals to preserve permanently the archives they create,[7] or to make them accessible to scholars. However, in many cases academic and other researchers can obtain access.

The intending researcher needs a 'map' to help him or her to find

a productive route through the plethora of archival institutions described in outline above – to discover what types of archives are likely
to be found where. The four sectors are described in more detail below.
Information about individual archival repositories can be found in a
number of directories and guides.[8]

At the national level, the public record offices and their holdings are
dealt with in Chapter 3. The great national libraries are an important
source of manuscript as well as published materials. The British
Library's manuscript collections date back to the foundation of the
British Museum in 1753 and the special collections now embrace a map
library, music library, manuscripts and philatelic collections, and the
Oriental and India Office Collections. The National Library of Scotland
acquires manuscripts relating to Scotland and the activities of Scots
abroad. The National Library of Wales, Department of Manuscripts
and Records, acquires a wide range of manuscripts relating to Wales,
but also holds archives of more local interest such as diocesan and some
parish records, the archives of Welsh estates and landed families, and
has a Welsh political archive. Each of these institutions focuses on
historical papers of national significance and caters for approved researchers who generally need a letter of introduction to get a reader's
ticket. The published holdings of the national libraries are discussed in
Chapter 5.

Also taking a national view are the national museums and galleries.
Each has a particular subject of interest, whether it be natural history,
warfare, art and design, science and technology, maritime history or one
of many other special areas. Usually these archive services have a dual
mandate: to preserve the archives of the institution itself and to acquire
manuscripts of people and organisations relevant to the museum or
gallery's work. Often the administrative and curatorial records of the
museum are designated as public records and the museum may be
appointed a place of deposit. The deposited collections may be managed
separately or as part of a unified service.

There are some other special, national archive services. The House
of Lords Record Office, in spite of its name, is in fact the archive for
both the House of Commons (although the records only survive in the
main from 1834 since earlier ones were destroyed by fire) and the House
of Lords. It also has some deposited private papers of politicians and
officials, and plans and drawings of the Palace of Westminster.

The General Register Office (GRO), founded in 1837 on the introduction of civil registration of births, marriages and deaths in England
and Wales, maintains the civil registers, some records about British
subjects abroad and some army and air-force records. The GRO forms
part of the Office of Population Censuses and Surveys, but the

decennial national census and other records are held at the PRO. The General Register Office for Scotland was established in 1855 when compulsory registration was introduced. It also holds open census records and Church of Scotland parish registers. The General Register Office, Northern Ireland, has marriage records from 1844 and birth and death records from 1863.

Other publicly funded national bodies which fall outside the public sector, such as quangos, sometimes have their own archive service. In recent years some have transferred their records to the PRO, for example the Medical Research Council.

Over the course of the century or so since county councils were established, local authority archive services have gradually developed. In the English counties, the archive service headquarters is generally in the county town, but increasingly branch offices or service points have been established in other parts of the county. Some cities and districts run their own archives. However, changes to the structures of local government in 1997 in England will alter the provision and funding of archive services. In metropolitan areas, where the county council has been abolished, there is a mixture of county-wide and district services. In London, the Greater London Record Office provides a county-level service for the Greater London area, with the Guildhall Library servicing the City of London. The Corporation of London Records Office manages the official records of the city corporation. Some boroughs run local services. In Wales, single-tier authorities were established in 1996 and existing county-based archive services will be reorganised as a result. In Scotland, regional, district and city councils have been establishing archive services, although there is not yet complete coverage at the local level. Unitary authorities established in 1996 will take on responsibility for providing archival services. In Northern Ireland, PRONI acquires many types of records, such as family and estate papers and business archives, which are found in county record offices in England.

As publicly funded bodies, local record offices are generally open to all, although many will require some proof of identity and will operate a reader's ticket system. Many county record offices are members of the CARN system (County Archive Research Network) and a single reader's ticket gives access to all participating offices. The typical local authority record office holds an enormously wide range of archives of both official and private nature, all of which have a close connection with the relevant geographical area. All local record offices have a dual mandate: they serve as the archive for the employing authority (for example the county council) and, in addition, they acquire records created by other institutions and people. They may also be appointed a place of deposit for public records and may be the diocesan record office. Some key records groups are described below. The description relates mainly to England and Wales and does not cover in detail Scotland and Northern Ireland, where the legislative framework and history is different.

Records reflecting the activities of both the elected council and committees which are responsible for policy and financial decisions and the employed officers who execute the policies are usually opened after thirty years. Council archives cover all aspects of official activity in an area, including education and schools, social services, transport, arts, public health, public buildings, etc. County and district councils have inherited the functions and the archives of predecessor bodies, such as boards of guardians (who oversaw the poor law), highway boards, turnpike trusts, school boards, burial boards and local boards of health. County councils inherited many administrative functions previously undertaken by quarter sessions. The judicial functions of quarter sessions were retained until the establishment of the Crown courts in 1971, but county record offices hold both judicial and administrative records of quarter sessions. In many counties the sessions archives go back four or five hundred years and provide an exceptionally complete and rich source for the locality. Quarter sessions records throw light on many research topics, including crime, jails, policing, trade, nonconformity and recusancy, the treatment of the poor, lunacy, taxation, and local infrastructure such as roads, bridges, canals and navigations, and land use.

Researchers in England are particularly lucky to have access to several fine archives of ancient boroughs. In many cases archives survive from the foundation of the borough in perhaps the twelfth or thirteenth century, comprising borough charters, court rolls and books, mayoral letters and papers, chamberlains' accounts, custumals, freemen's rolls and registers, and so on. These form core archives for city record offices in places such as Chester and Coventry and, of course, the City of London.

Local authority record offices also acquire records from organisations and families, with councils occasionally purchasing these or being given them. Commonly, however, the archives are deposited for safekeeping on long-term loan and the ownership and copyright is retained by the legal owner. Sometimes this means that there are different closure periods or restrictions on duplication or publication imposed by the owner. The range of acquired archives varies from one office to another. English county repositories will generally hold very large quantities of archives of the county's great estates and old landed families.

Local businesses often deposit their archives with a record office either while still in business or on the dissolution of the company. These may encompass family firms, local industries and branches of national companies. Archive offices in industrial areas such as Merseyside, Birmingham or Glasgow have particularly good business acquisitions. Many businesses retain their own archives and these are considered later in the chapter.

Records of nonconformist church congregations may be retained by the individual church or deposited in the local record office. Nonconformist church records often include registers (of members, of births and so on), plans of church buildings, school records, minutes of managing committees, and personal papers of individual preachers and ministers. Many pre-1837 registers were transferred to the Public Record Office.

Since 1979, many county record offices have also been appointed as the local diocesan record office. In this capacity, the offices may manage the archives of the Church of England diocese and its constituent archdeaconries, deaneries and parishes. Diocesan boundaries and record office catchment areas do not always coincide, so it is necessary to check which records are held where.

Local record offices hold a variety of other archives. Local associations, clubs and societies, ranging from a political party to a book club to a Women's Institute, may deposit their records. Local history, archaeological, literary and philosophical societies often have antiquarian collections and other manuscripts which are available through, if not at, the local record office. Personal papers of notable local people such as politicians may also be held. Other local studies material may be held in the record office or local library, including Ordnance Survey and other printed maps; photographs, engravings and postcards; newspapers and cuttings; local ephemera; and copies of original records held elsewhere. These often include microfilm copies of the decennial census return, of manuscripts held in UK and foreign universities and of records still in private hands.

In addition, about 20 per cent of public records for England and Wales are deposited locally in 'places of deposit'. Under this arrangement public records such as those of hospitals, quarter and petty sessions, coroners and shipping registers are available locally,[9] often in the local authority record office.

Publicly funded specialist repositories can be divided into several sectors. Two of the key areas are: first, university archives, manuscript departments and research institutes; and secondly, hospital archive services. University manuscript departments, often located within university libraries, hold significant research collections. The great research libraries, such as the Bodleian and Cambridge University Libraries, have wide-ranging collections of national importance, sometimes accumulated over many centuries. They include the papers of politicians, scientists, statesmen, writers, churchmen and other public figures, as well as archives of national societies, estate and family archives and ecclesiastical records.

Many universities establish research institutes or special collections which focus on a particular research area. Examples include the ESRC Data Archive at Essex University; the Modern Records Centre at the University of Warwick (which holds archives of British political, social and economic history, especially labour history and industrial relations); the Business Records Centre at the University of Glasgow; the Liddell Hart Centre for Military Archives at King's College London; and the Anglo-Jewish archives, and political and diplomatic papers of Wellington, Palmerston and Mountbatten at the University of Southampton. There are many other examples.

Universities and colleges also maintain their own institutional archives, such as statutes, charters and deeds; records of the university council or senate and other legislative and executive bodies; records of university finances, of student registration and examination; and faculty and departmental records. The research and personal papers of important academic figures are also sometimes held.

Archives of hospitals and health authorities are managed in a variety of ways. Some are deposited in the local authority record office, as discussed above. Some health authorities, especially in Scotland, have established archive departments which take in local hospital, asylum and community services records. Major hospitals occasionally have their own archive service to manage the archives of the institution and its predecessor bodies, and sometimes accept other hospital archives from the locality. Some ancient foundations, like the Royal London Hospital, were major landowners and the archives include estate records, ecclesiastical records, archives of associated charities and of eminent physicians and surgeons.

There is also a large number of specialist repositories which are independently funded. Some of the main groups are archive services in businesses, religious bodies, historic houses, national professional bodies and trade unions, voluntary and not-for-profit organisations and other special institutions such as city livery companies, royal societies and the Inns of Court. In this sector, each organisation establishes and funds its own archive office to manage its institutional records. The sector is so diverse that it is difficult to describe it adequately in a brief survey such as this.

One of the largest parts of the sector is in businesses. Some businesses transfer their archives to a local or specialist record office but many larger firms find it worth while to maintain an in-house archive service. Traditionally, some business sectors have been well developed archivally: notably, clearing and merchant banks, pharmaceuticals companies, breweries and nationalised industries. Other sectors, such as professional partnerships (solicitors, accountants), are not so well served. Business archives often include corporate and accounting records, as well as those of marketing, personnel and, where appropriate, manufacturing functions.[10] Pharmaceutical and chemical companies may employ specialist scientific archivists to manage a variety of research media such as tissue samples, slides and so on. Family firms may also hold the personal and legal papers of family members.

Religious archives held in local record offices have already been mentioned, but many denominations have their own national or regional archive office. The Church of England Record Centre holds the archives of the Church Commissioners and its predecessor bodies (including Queen Anne's Bounty and the Church Building Commissioners), the General Synod, the National Society and some papers of leading churchmen. Some cathedrals retain their archives, for example York Minster and Canterbury Cathedral, and there are also some specialist repositories such as Lambeth Palace Library, which holds, among other archives, the records of the archbishops of Canterbury. There are national repositories for the Baptists (at Regent's Park College, Oxford), the Quakers (at the Society of Friends Library, London) and the Methodists (at the Methodist Archives and Research Centre, University of Manchester). Several Roman Catholic dioceses have record offices, such as those in Westminster, Nottingham and Glasgow.

Some historic houses, especially those still occupied by direct descendants of the original family, retain the estate archives and the papers of family members, who often had political and diplomatic connections at local and national level. Personal papers of musical and literary figures may also be found in specialist institutions, such as the Britten–Pears Library in Aldeburgh.

National professional bodies, including various branches of engineering, medicine and finance, and trade unions sometimes establish a repository to care for the institutional records and archives of members who were significant in their fields. Some of the royal colleges which regulate access to professional areas of work under royal charter have significant archives of their own and of their fellows, and acquire manuscripts on related subject areas. Voluntary and charitable organisations also sometimes employ an archivist, as do the various royal societies (which range from geography to history to horticulture and beyond), the Inns of Court and many of the London livery companies.

The researcher is thus faced with a bewildering array of archival repositories.[11] What ought to be clear from this brief description of archives in Britain is that archive services are not, on the whole, arranged by subject or research theme, with everything gathered in one place for the benefit of the historian. The majority of archive services exist to serve a single creating authority or a group of related organisations in one geographical area. Within each record office, the archives are arranged and described according to the principles of provenance and original order – that is, according to their creating institution or family – setting each document in its functional or organisational context rather than categorising by possible research subjects. As Foster and Sheppard note, 'consulting archives is not the same as looking up information in a book ... the reader cannot assume that they are freely available or easily accessible, or even that the originals can be consulted. ... It is easy to fall into the trap of assuming that records will directly answer a specific query.'[12]

A new research student must first ask whether primary sources need to be consulted at this point, since finding them and using them will be time intensive. Once secondary sources have been exhausted, primary published sources are likely to be more easily and quickly accessible than originals. There are several useful bibliographies.[13] Alternatively, copies of archives which are held in geographically remote locations may be available on microfilm, optical disc or as photographic copies. Unless surrogate copies have already been made this may be an expensive route, most useful for further detailed study of key sources after an initial visit to see the original records.

Once the researcher is convinced that it is necessary to invest time and money in using original archives, how can he or she find out where the relevant records are held? For records outside the public record offices, the most useful place to start is the National Register of Archives (NRA) and its counterpart, the NRA (Scotland), run by the Scottish Record Office. The NRA was established in 1945 as part of the Royal Commission on Historical Manuscripts (HMC). The NRA does not hold any original archives, but rather serves as a central point for the collection, storage and retrieval of information about archives and their custodians. The NRA holds copies of over 38,000 lists from all types of record repositories. The hard copy lists are available for consultation by researchers in the central London searchroom and in copyright libraries. In addition, limited specific enquiries can be answered by letter, fax and e-mail. Even more usefully, the NRA indexes are now available remotely. Those of most interest to the researcher are the business, personal and subject indexes.[14] HMC also publishes guides to sources for British history and to new acquisitions to repositories.[15]

There are other advisory bodies specifically concerned with business records, such as the Business Archives Council (BAC) and the BAC (Scotland). The BAC locates and surveys business archives, disseminates information through journals and survey reports, and advises businesses on their archives. The National Cataloguing Unit for the Archives of Contemporary Scientists (NCUACS) locates and catalogues papers of distinguished British scientists and engineers and then ensures their deposit in an appropriate repository. NCUACS is not an archive repository itself.

Another source of information to which the researcher can usefully turn is the published guide or, increasingly, the World Wide Web (WWW) page or other Internet access point for a particular record office. Repository guides, whether published conventionally or electronically, give brief descriptions of each archive group held and general information on the office, such as access restrictions. A growing number of repositories, mainly in the university sector, also make their detailed lists available remotely, electronically. Usually the initial access point is free but to go beyond that, prior application for a password and perhaps payment of a fee is required.

Armed with all this information, the researcher will be able to establish that the archives required are available and accessible.[16] If suitable primary source material does not exist or is unavailable for some reason – either temporarily (for example, awaiting conservation or cataloguing) or permanently (in private ownership, for instance) – the researcher may need to refine or revise the proposed research topic. Such detailed preparation ought also to reveal whether the archives are published or available remotely or in another more accessible format. It not, then the researcher will need to visit in person.

Archive services and archivists have a responsibility in the first instance for the 'physical and moral defence' of the archives in their care. Public service provision is just one aspect of the archivist's work. The resources devoted to public access have to be balanced against other essentials, such as the physical conservation and preservation of the archives, carrying out surveys and acquisition of new archives, and arrangement, description and publication of holdings. These all ensure that archives are accessible to researchers now and that they will be in the future too. For reasons of preservation and security, archives are not loaned to individuals or to other repositories for reference. There is no archive equivalent of interlibrary loans and archives are always 'reference only'. Archives are usually not made available until they are arranged and catalogued. There may also be limits imposed on the number of items a researcher can order at once.

Limited resources mean that record offices often have limited opening hours, and may be closed in the evenings or at weekends. Advance preparation is the best way to maximise the opening hours. Researchers should always contact the record office before a visit to check opening hours and any access restrictions, and to find out whether a reader's ticket, a letter of introduction or other identification is needed. Many repositories encourage readers to book a seat, although some allow researchers to turn up without appointment. If the researcher knows the references of the documents to be consulted, these should be requested before a visit to avoid the frustration of discovering that a key archive is in conservation or in an exhibition and to avoid delays in production to the searchroom. Advance preparation ensures that the researcher will arrive at the records office equipped with the necessary interpretative tools, whether these be medieval Latin palaeography or the information technology skills needed to manipulate electronic records or datasets.

A researcher in an unfamiliar record office will find that time spent at the beginning of the visit becoming familiar with the systems is worth while. Most offices have free information leaflets or an introductory video and all have expert staff on hand to advise. Researchers should find out how to order documents and how long they take to arrive from the strongroom, so that the day's work can be planned. The finding aids are the key to unlock the wealth in the archives and researchers need to understand how they work. Each repository adopts a slightly different approach, but all have a hierarchy of finding aids. The top-level finding aid, giving a macro view of the repository, is the published guide. The next level down is the detailed item list for each archive group. From the list, individual documents can be ordered for consultation. In a few cases, calendars or editions of particular documents have been prepared and published.

Archival finding aids are prepared by archivists to reflect the original order and provenance of the archive group. Researchers, however, often need access points by subject or research topic in order to find the material of most relevance to their enquiry. These are provided by subject, person or place indexes available either as traditional hard copy index cards or, increasingly, by full-text searching or key-word indexing of automated finding aids. Record offices vary in their progress towards automation. Those which have automated finding aids often continue to operate parallel hard copy systems until the backlog catalogue conversion is completed.

An important resource available to the researcher is the expertise of staff in the repository. Whether they be professional archivists or archive assistants, they should all be knowledgeable about the holdings of the office and about the systems. They cannot undertake research on behalf of others but they can advise on possible sources for a research topic. Particularly in specialist and national repositories, the archivists will often be established academics in their own right and can provide specialist subject advice to other researchers.

Archives are easily damaged by poor handling and by copying. Such damage may result either in the archive needing expensive conservation treatment or even in its loss to future researchers. Efforts are made in a number of ways to minimise the damage caused by handling. Book supports are often provided to researchers or weights to hold open rolled maps. Very large documents may have to be consulted on special map tables. Researchers will be asked not to lean on the archives they are consulting and to use pencil not pen for making notes. If a researcher accidentally marks a document with pencil it can be cleaned but pen marks cannot be removed. Some records which are in a very poor physical state or which are very heavily used may only be accessible in surrogate form: usually on microfilm or sometimes optical disc. Microfilm surrogates are less easy to use, while electronic versions are more manipulable, than the original. Use of surrogates is an essential preservation tool since the alternative is that the originals are not accessible at all to researchers.

Researchers often want to take copies of key documents away for further study. These might be individual photocopies or photographs or a longer sequence of documents on microfilm. The cheapest and quickest copying method, photocopying, is the one most likely to cause permanent damage to the original and is therefore often restricted or banned. Usually an alternative, such as photography, is offered. Restrictions on copying are not made to frustrate the researcher, but to ensure that the archives concerned are preserved and continue to be available to future researchers.

Copyright is also a concern for archivists providing copies of original documents. Copyright, that is the exclusive right to exploit an original work, is infringed if the whole or a substantial part of a work, whether published or unpublished, is copied. Copyright in unpublished original literary, dramatic, musical or artistic works lasts for fifty years from the death of the author or from the end of 1989, whichever is the longer. Single copies of documents in copyright may be made by archivists for the researcher's private study only, subject to the copyright owner's permission being given. The researcher will be asked to sign a copyright declaration form about the use of the copies and must not re-copy them for others. If the researcher subsequently wished to include the document, or anything more than a short quotation from it, in a published work, then specific permission of the copyright owner would have to be obtained. The repository can usually advise on the copyright owner for specific archives and how to apply for such permission.[17]

This chapter has considered the immense range of non-governmental organisations and individuals whose records have value as primary sources for historical research. It has described the legislative framework and the structure and management of archival repositories outside the public record offices. It has provided guidance on the types of archives a user might expect to find in the various different kinds of repositories and has considered national resources available to the researcher, such as the NRA. In addition, it has provided some advice to researchers to help them to maximise their time in the record offices they visit. For example, the chapter discussed archival finding aids and reprographic services. The vast wealth of material in national, local and specialist archive offices can only be surveyed briefly in a single chapter. Researchers new to these areas who read this chapter, however, should find themselves better equipped to make good use of the huge range of non-public records held in Britain's record offices.

Further reading

A useful starting point for the new researcher is R. J. Olney's *Manuscript Sources for British History: Their Nature, Location and Use* (London: University of London, Institute of Historical Research, 1995). This brief guide is one in a series published by the Institute of Historical Research, part of the University of London. There are a number of directories which the researcher will find essential. These can usually be found in reference libraries. The most up-to-date and comprehensive is Janet Foster and Julia Sheppard's *British Archives. A Guide to Archive Resources in the United Kingdom* (London: Macmillan, 1995). This directory is arranged by geographical location and is well indexed. The entry for each repository gives brief details including postal address, telephone and fax numbers, opening hours, access provisions, a brief historical background, the acquisitions policy, brief details of the archives and collections held (including non-manuscript material), the facilities available and relevant publications, such as finding aids. A shorter directory is produced by the Royal Commission on Historical Manuscripts, *Record Repositories in Great Britain: A Geographical Directory* 9th edn (London: HMSO, 1992). The National Register of Archives is accessible at Quality House, Quality Court, Chancery Lane, London WC2A 1HP.

CHAPTER 5

Libraries

Donald Munro

Libraries are the gateways to the sources. Their primary functions are the organisation of, and provision of access to knowledge and information. They are the primary locations in which to plan and organise research. Some researchers may be fortunate enough to find all their sources within a single major library. Most, however, will use the library to check out the literature of their subject and establish the locations of likely sources, be they archival, printed or otherwise. Successful research will be greatly facilitated if the researcher makes the effort at the outset to become familiar with the arrangement of libraries and seeks to grasp the differing natures of the several tools and techniques through which the sources may be approached. For the modern or contemporary historian this is especially true as so many of their source materials may be in printed form. Developing a sound knowledge of the bibliographical guides and structures in your subject area is time very well spent.

This chapter will first outline the various types of library, drawing attention to those of particular importance for the historian of twentieth-century Britain. The greater part of the chapter will give some account of the arrangement of libraries, the structure of catalogues and other resources and services offered, together with guidance and advice on how to make best use of these. The emphasis will be on printed materials, although many libraries will hold and house the guides, archival collections and electronic resources described in neighbouring chapters.[1]

A number of prefatory caveats should be noted. First, the range of contemporary information resources is now enormous and seemingly expanding exponentially, but the knowledge required to take full advantage of them has increased as well. The modern historian needs to be familiar not only with the literature of history but also with the literature of other appropriate social sciences. Traditional library resources are being partly transformed and supplemented by new electronic resources, but for all the impressive speed and power, there are major limitations to computer searching. Although the situation is rapidly changing, relatively few libraries are fully retrospectively automated; you cannot assume that the computer shows you everything in a library. Finally, studies of research practices tend to show that even experienced historians and other researchers make limited and inefficient use of the range of resource enquiry available in their subject areas.[2] It is hoped that this chapter may raise awareness and encourage young scholars to develop their critical bibliographical skills. Historical and bibliographical skills, in fact, are complementary.

Libraries in the United Kingdom: an overview

Britain is fortunate in having a well developed and richly varied library system serving national, educational, specialist and public sectors. Libraries as a whole have been faced with a vast expansion in printed publication since the 1960s. There are elements of co-operation and division of responsibility for acquisitions both nationally and in local and regional consortia. Tightening budgets are giving some impetus to these. More recently the information explosion has brought an accelerating proliferation of new sources and alternative means of access in library technology.

An enormous wealth of research material is held in library and information collections in Britain. Some indication of this is the sheer bulk of the *ASLIB directory of information sources in the United Kingdom*, edited by K. W. Reynard and Jeremy M. E. Reynard (8th edn, 1994). At least half of the eight thousand or more entries are potential information sources for the historian of the twentieth century. Postgraduates are likely to use several different sorts of library in the course of their research. They should be aware of the characteristics of the following types, although several major libraries encompass more than one category.

National libraries The British Library (BL) is at the centre of the library network in the United Kingdom. In its various reference divisions it holds the national collection of printed materials.[3] Most importantly from the research viewpoint, under the copyright acts it has the right to legal deposit of British imprints. Broadly speaking, with the exception of more ephemeral and localised Scottish and Welsh materials, the researcher can expect to find any significant publication printed in

Great Britain since c.1852 in the holdings of the British Library.[4] Its main reference branches are the Humanities and Social Sciences (General Collections) in Bloomsbury, London, where the Official Publications and Social Sciences Services, and the Map Library are specialist departments; the British Library Newspaper Library at Colindale, North London; the Oriental and India Office Collections which is the major resource for the history of British imperial rule in India and the Far East; and the Science Reference and Information Service (SRIS) which has three reading rooms in the Holborn area of London.[5]

The BL's other branch of primary importance for the researcher, particularly if based away from the major library centres, is the British Library Document Supply Centre (BLDSC) at Boston Spa which operates a national system of interlibrary lending of books and theses, and the provision of photocopies of journal articles and otherwise unavailable materials in science and technology, the social sciences and the humanities. It holds copies of all significant English-language monographs, most significant serials, exhaustive holdings of conference proceedings, all British official publications since 1962, and extensive stocks of older material.

The National Library of Scotland in Edinburgh and the National Library of Wales in Aberystwyth hold the fullest national collections and exercise their legal deposit copyright more thoroughly for their respective countries. While not strictly national libraries, the Bodleian Library at Oxford and Cambridge University Library share the significant characteristic of enjoying the privilege of copyright deposit.

National libraries are invaluable to the postgraduate researcher. Copyright deposit, even when selectively applied, ensures that their collections of British publications are very full. They have exhaustive holdings of government documentation, and frequently hold popular and ephemeral material not available elsewhere. Apart from their separately stocked lending divisions, national libraries are reference-only libraries. For many researchers the convenience of the wealth of materials in the national collections makes these libraries if not of first, then certainly of second and continuing resort.

A number of other libraries have acknowledged national status without enjoying the privileges of copyright deposit. The British Library of Political and Economic Science (BLPES) at the London School of Economics holds a major national collection covering the social sciences. Since its inception in 1896 it has been building collections in economics, commerce, public and business administration, transport, statistics, political science, and the social, economic and international aspects of history. It is very strong in controversial pamphlet literature, and has unique collections of local authority reports, and reports of banks and railways. Its periodically published subject catalogue, the *London Biblio-graphy of the Social Sciences* (1931–89), has become an extremely useful research tool for the historian seeking an overview of contemporary thinking on social economic and political issues throughout most of the twentieth century.

Other national libraries holding major specialist research collections in their fields are the National Art Library at the Victoria and Albert Museum, the National Maritime Museum at Greenwich, and the Science Museum Library.

University libraries   Most research in the social sciences and human-ities in the United Kingdom is carried out in universities. Their libraries actively seek, within the constraints of declining resources and spiralling costs, to keep up to date with the relevant literature in the specialities of their institutions. In serving their institutional teaching and research, university libraries have frequently been able to build up research collec-tions, many of national importance. This is especially true of the older universities. The newer, post-1960 universities generally have a narrower subject range with less rich holdings of older materials, although some have compensated by acquiring research materials in microform. Few of the institutions recently upgraded to university status have substantial research collections in history. The newer institutions, however, do tend to be more fully computerised and a number of them are at the forefront of developments in information technology generally.

The significant characteristics of university libraries are that they have large general reference collections together with their developed specialisms. They generally have good holdings across the humanities and social sciences. Many materials originally acquired for these dis-ciplines, with the passage of time, have become sources for the modern and contemporary historian. University libraries have been (arguably) relatively well resourced in the past and tend to have more extensive holdings of the larger, and therefore more expensive, bibliographical tools and indexes which smaller specialist institutions can acquire only selectively. Recent cuts in funding have fallen most heavily on periodical subscriptions, with alarming effects even in well-established collections – Leeds University Library, for example, has experienced a reduction of 25 per cent in expenditure on periodicals. Unlike national libraries, substantial parts of university library holdings are available for loan, which can limit the availability of monograph material.

For the modern historian, the most notable university libraries are the Bodleian Library at Oxford and Cambridge University Library, both of which enjoy the advantage of copyright deposit, with a con-sequent richness of British imprints. Similar in size but without the copyright advantages is the John Rylands University Library of Manchester. The university libraries of Leeds, Birmingham and Edinburgh all have libraries of over two million volumes, followed by Glasgow and Liverpool, with Bristol, Nottingham and Sheffield each holding over a million volumes. The University of London Library in Senate House also has holdings of more than a million volumes with very strong collections of bibliographies, and humanities and social sciences periodicals and indexes. University College London and Aberdeen University also have very extensive libraries with substantial holdings of current periodicals. Bristol, Nottingham and Swansea have substantial collections of pamphlets. Besides servicing the student needs of the London School of Economics, the BLPES is a national research collection in the social sciences (as noted in the previous section); it also has the main responsibility for the wider range of twentieth-century primary historical sources within the University of London. Of the newer universities, Warwick is probably the best resourced for the modern economic and social historian.

Special libraries The libraries of research institutes, government departments, business firms and specialist associations complement general academic and national libraries. They will hold fewer of the more general bibliographical tools, but within their individual specialisms they will have more thorough coverage of the literature and guides to the relevant sources. Their librarians are often particularly well informed about the sources and literature of the institutional subject areas, as are the custodians of special collections within university and other libraries. Admission criteria vary. Few are public libraries and scholars are advised to contact a library in advance of a visit. The range of special libraries is enormous but the following may be particularly useful for the modern historian.

The Library of the Institute of Historical Research (IHR), University of London, collects bibliographical and archival guides together with printed editions of the principal primary sources for the history of Britain, Europe and Europe overseas. It holds most of the major journals in history, and a reference collection of University of London history theses. In modern British history there are extensive holdings of primary printed sources for political and parliamentary history (editions of correspondence of major politicians, parliamentary debates, sets of diplomatic papers, etc.), and a greater range of modern and contemporary sources is being built up. Researchers should note, however, that IHR holds few secondary monograph works. These should be available in the University of London Library and the libraries of individual colleges. The strength of the IHR for modern studies is in its specialist bibliographical resources for British national and local history, which are all on open access. Recently its library catalogue has been entirely retrospectively converted and is viewable over the Internet as part of the on-line public access catalogue (OPAC) of the School of Advanced Study, University of London (SASCAT). A wide range of postgraduate seminars in modern political, social and economic history are held in the IHR Library. IHR is also the home of IHR-Info, a multi-functional electronic historical information server (see the subsection on computer facilities and services below).

For the political and social sciences, the major research library is the British Library of Political and Economic Science as already referred to. In addition to BLPES and the University of Warwick Library, several special libraries have strong holdings of research materials for labour and trade union history, for example the Marx Memorial Library in Clerkenwell Green, London; the Trades Union Congress at Congress House; the Bishopsgate Institute, London; and the National Museum of Labour History in Manchester.

The Fawcett Library at London Guildhall University is devoted to the history of women. It has strong holdings of original printed and manuscript sources for the Women's Suffrage movement and women at work. Its valuable annual catalogue and bibliography *Bibliofem* was regularly issued from 1980–86, after which severe financial constraints threatened the viability of the library for a number of years. It is hoped the recent relative improvement in its situation will continue.

The library of the Wellcome Institute for the History of Medicine is well provided with research materials for the history of medicine in its broader social context. Contemporary historians should particularly note the associated Wellcome Centre for Medical Science, which is concerned to provide data for informed policy-making. Many electronic as well as printed resources are available. For the history of technology and science more generally, reference has already been made to the British Library Science Reference and Information Service, and the Science Museum Library.

Recently incorporated into the Cambridge University Library, the library of the Royal Commonwealth Society is invaluable for British imperial historians. It contains many fugitive items relating to the experience and administration of empire. Other major libraries for Commonwealth historians are Rhodes House Library, Oxford and the Institute of Commonwealth Studies, University of London. The British Library Oriental and India Office Collections have already been mentioned as the major resource for the history of British imperial rule in India and the Far East.

For researchers with religious interests, Lambeth Palace Library

(Church of England), Dr Williams's Library (Protestant nonconformity) and the Religious Society of Friends (Quakers) Library, Friends House, all have useful twentieth-century materials. The School of Oriental and African Studies, University of London, has developed strong collections on missionary activities.

Government departmental libraries are less numerous than in 1979. Few are readily accessible, but most will allow access for researchers if prior arrangements are made. The researcher should be aware of the following: Central Statistical Office, Office of Population Censuses and Surveys (easy access), and Treasury and Cabinet Office Library (difficult). The Department of Trade and Industry has several libraries with varying conditions of access, as does the Ministry of Agriculture, Fisheries and Food. The House of Commons and House of Lords libraries will field queries, but are otherwise inaccessible unless you are a researcher working for an MP.

The Ministry of Defence Whitehall Library is valuable for military and defence policy, and several other MoD specialist libraries should not be overlooked by historians researching technical aspects of military, naval and aviation history. The Imperial War Museum is concerned with the military history of the British Empire in the twentieth century and the social experience of war. The National Army Museum concentrates more specifically on the history of the British Army and its regiments.

The burgeoning demand from business and the public for economic and commercial information has led to an increase in the number of libraries attached to individual organisations and companies (for example Bank of England, Midland Bank) and professional associations (for example Chartered Insurance Institute), and to the growth of business information bureaux – both private and attached to public libraries (for example at Leeds, and the City Business Library in London). The British Broadcasting Corporation also has several major departmental libraries and archives.

Although the emphasis in this section has been on libraries in London, many specialist libraries in other localities will be found in the pages of the *ASLIB Directory*.

Public libraries In British industrial and commercial centres, the central public libraries are often regional information centres. The holdings of general reference and special collections in the major civic libraries are not dissimilar to those of university libraries, and like them they may hold some of the major bibliographies and indexes referred to below. In some areas, especially general social and business information (directories, etc.) their current holdings can be richer. They can be substantially superior to nearby new university libraries, particularly in holdings of official publications and local historical and commercial materials. Most local authority libraries have special local history collections in their central library and some have useful collections in branch libraries.

The central public libraries of Birmingham, Glasgow and Manchester, and the city libraries of Edinburgh, Leeds, Liverpool and Sheffield all have significant potential research material, with particularly strong holdings of current periodicals at Manchester, Birmingham and Liverpool. Glasgow and Leeds have strong holdings of official publications. The public library for the City of London, the Guildhall Library, specialises in the history and development of the City, and its economic, social and cultural life. Salford City Libraries, Manchester, has a notable working class movement library.

Public libraries in general have suffered very badly in the years of Conservative government assault on local government expenditure, but although damaged, the major public libraries should be consulted by researchers with interests in the localities served.

Locating libraries

Several lists can help the researcher determine whether they need to consult the materials in a particular library. The most comprehensive is the *ASLIB Directory of Information Sources in the United Kingdom* (1994) which alphabetically lists and describes British special interest and information organisations. It includes a separate section on information sources on the EC Single Market, a useful list of acronyms and abbreviations (forty pages long), and a substantial subject index of 195 pages. *The Libraries Directory 1993–95*, edited by A. Kimura and K. Anderson Howes (1994), gives much useful if extremely compressed information about public and special (including academic) libraries in Great Britain and Ireland. It indicates main subjects and special collections, opening hours and entry requirements for special libraries, special equipment and electronic facilities, classification scheme and the automated library system used. Although not covering the most recent university libraries, Stephen Roberts, A. Cooper and L. Gilder (eds), *Research Libraries and Collections in the United Kingdom: a Selective Inventory and Guide* (1978) is a useful survey of the traditional strengths of the older academic and research sector libraries. The *Guide to Libraries and Information Units in Government Department and Other Organisations*, edited by Peter Dale (32nd edn, 1996), opens with a convenient summary guide to the national libraries (BL, NLS, NLW) followed by special libraries arranged in subject groupings. Valerie McBurney, *Guide to Libraries in*

London (1995) covers all types of library, focusing on non-commercial information services. It includes information about holdings of public libraries, few of which are included in the previously mentioned guides. The Library Association's *Libraries in the United Kingdom and the Republic of Ireland 1996* (1995) is a basic listing of names, addresses, phone and fax numbers, some telex numbers and e-mail addresses, and contact personnel of public academic and selected government national and special libraries. It does not, however, give opening times.

Library arrangement

Library collections consist of a wide range of printed and other materials – reference works, monographs, periodicals, newspapers, government publications, maps, microform publications, CD-ROMs, etc. In most libraries the bulk of the material is arranged in a classified order which collocates like materials according to a well-defined subject classification scheme. In open access libraries this enables efficient browsing in addition to enquiry via the catalogue which is the primary access point. Note, however, that libraries may also hold source materials outside the main classification scheme and which may not be detailed in the main catalogue. There may be collections with separate catalogues, uncatalogued special collections or groups of materials for which published catalogues function as the finding tools. Fortunately most libraries will have guides, resource sheets or 'pathfinders' to assist the first-time user.

Library catalogues The first thing to note about the catalogue is its *scope*. Library catalogues are primarily lists of books and serials. They do not as a rule list contents of books or periodicals,[6] and other materials often may not be listed – for example government documents and the contents of microform sets are seldom fully catalogued. Relatively few automated catalogues include the entire stock of the library; most will hold only acquisitions since a specified date and the earlier holdings of the library will have to be sought in the older card, guard-book, microfiche or other catalogues. When visiting a library for the first time it is important to grasp the relationships and scope of the various catalogues.

Catalogues and indexes are deceptively easy to use. Both students and scholars frequently tend to underestimate the complexity and ingenuity that has gone into their construction. Consequently they often fail to take full advantage of the catalogue's capabilities. Some familiarity with how catalogues are constructed may help towards more effective usage.

CATALOGUE STRUCTURE Regardless of form – card, book or computer-

ised – the principles underlying the construction of library catalogues
remain much the same. Catalogue entries consist of two basic parts: (a)
a bibliographical description of the item, to which are attached (b)
headings for names and subjects, which are used, frequently along with
the title, to construct the indexes to the catalogue.

The description is made up of several basic elements of bibliographic
information copied exactly from the work itself. This identifies the
work precisely and differentiates it from all other items. In card catalogues the main elements are usually grouped into a single paragraph
consisting of title, author statement, edition statement, place, publisher
and date of publication; this may be followed by additional paragraphs
of notes. Many computerised catalogues give a separate captioned line
to each element of bibliographical description. The notes may include
useful information – the relation of the work to other works (for
example translation, or change of serial title). Contents notes may
describe titles in a multi-volume work. The notes are usually followed
by the additional author and subject headings attached to the work.
These can give a good indication of the nature of a work. They are
virtually omnipresent in recent automated catalogues, though they may
not be present in older card catalogues.

Headings are used to construct the indexes to the catalogue. There
are three basic types – author name (authors, editors, corporate bodies),
subject and title, although title indexes are not very common in older
British catalogues. The indexes (usually called catalogues) may be separate files or combined in a single alphabetical sequence.

CATALOGUE INDEXES Most traditional library catalogues use a system
of uniform entry for headings whereby each indexed entity (name, title
or subject) is usually represented in the catalogue by only one index
term, so ensuring that all the works by, say, a single author or relating
to a variously described subject will be gathered under a single form of
heading. Cross-references are provided from alternative forms of a
name. Similarly, alternative spellings and synonyms for a subject will
point to the preferred index term. The list of chosen forms, together
with cross-references from unused forms, is known as a thesaurus or
authority file, which may be available for consultation by catalogue
users, at least for subjects. This is the 'controlled indexing language'
referred to from time to time below.

The practice of cross-referencing is not always found even in the
card catalogue. Unfortunately the provision of cross-references in computerised catalogues is relatively infrequent. Library of Congress (LoC)
subject headings are increasingly used by research libraries in this
country, but institutions may not have implemented full LoC authority

control. The pitfall for readers is that they can readily get the impression that there is no work by a certain author or particular subject in a library because they may have searched under the incorrect form of the name or subject. The user should always be wary and be prepared to try out different forms.

The three types of indexing – title, author and subject – have particular characteristics. Title search is an effective way of locating an item provided you are certain of the first few words of its title. Abbreviated notes and incorrect citations can quickly demonstrate the difficulties of finding a title from inaccurate information. This is less important in some automated catalogues where title search is set up to look for keywords.

Author indexing should bring together all the works by a single author – personal or corporate. In the case of single surnames this usually presents few problems, although in computer catalogues it is advisable to scan the author headings looking for combinations of forenames and initials that may be the same author. Compound names, however, do present problems. In older card catalogues the user should ascertain the library's filing rules and practice for compound name entry. Some may enter under the last element of a British compound name, others under the first. Filing rules may vary also in computer catalogues. Most automated systems in Britain mimic the normal card catalogue practice of filing all occurrences of a single surname with various initials before compound names in which it forms the first element. However, the INNOPAC system recently installed in several British university libraries ignores punctuation and remorselessly indexes ASCII strings so that compound names are interfiled with single names, resulting in for example 'Jones-Baker, Doris' being filed in front of 'Jones, Cecil'. This is all right provided you are aware that it is happening. Corporate bodies – societies, businesses, institutions – are usually entered directly under name, although older card catalogues may gather institutions under place. Government ministries will usually be gathered under a geographic name (Great Britain or England in some older catalogues) although many libraries appear to be adopting direct entry for some government bodies. There is a need for greater standardisation and there may be a trend towards more widespread adoption of Library of Congress headings.

Subject index headings in library catalogues are useful, but they have a number of limitations. Users should be aware that the subject catalogue terms used attempt to describe the subject of the entire book and not the various subjects of its parts. It is unusual for any work to be given more than three subject index headings. Researchers may have to search under terms that are either broader or narrower than that specifically sought. In libraries using Library of Congress subject headings, broader and narrower topics and synonyms can be traced through the tables, enabling the user to search on the likeliest productive terms. Classification schedules in other systems (for example Bliss) can give similar clues. Such schemes, however, are under constant revision to update terminology and the structure of headings. Many libraries have been able to implement these changes on automated files, but not on their unconverted older card files. A further point to remember is that names of persons, institutions and countries may be used as subject headings for works about persons, places and institutions. Where a library has separated its subject and author/title catalogues (card or automated), the user must remember to look in both to find books about a person or institution.

Subject headings can, therefore, be complex and the user needs to be systematic to get the fullest benefit. One helpful feature, however, is that by expanding a search through following the additional subject terms listed at the end of a relevant descriptive catalogue entry the researcher may find other material. This point is alluded to again in the discussion on keyword searching below.

CARD CATALOGUES These were the predominant form of library catalogue until very recently and there are many still about – records of the library's older holdings which have not yet been retrospectively converted. Each card consists of the description of an item with one index term or heading at the top of the card. The cards are filed in alphabetical order under the index terms in one or more sequences.

The precise filing order and presentation of the card catalogue within the alphabetical sequence can be complex and may seem confusing to the unfamiliar user. In having to deal with vast quantities of very different kinds of information in an organised fashion that can assist the user in finding relevant material, a number of helpful devices may be used – uniform title headings for works which appear under several titles, arranged by text, then translations alphabetically by language; under governments and subjects there may be hierarchies of types of material which are not strictly alphabetical (for example in the old British Library general catalogue).

The vital point to remember is that each catalogue has its own filing rules. Some file strictly letter by letter without regard for punctuation; in others there is a hierarchy determined by word and punctuation. These rules can have a very marked effect on where an item may appear in the file. The 'Jones-Baker, Doris' example in the discussion on compound names above would file in most catalogues after 'Jones, Cecil', but in an older card catalogue the lead term could be 'Baker, Doris

Jones-'. 'Smith, Robert J.' can be a long way away from an alternative entry for him under 'Smith, R. J.' Be prepared to browse forward and back to establish the filing order and check that nothing has been missed.

ON-LINE CATALOGUES Most libraries now have some form of on-line public access catalogue (OPAC) where the user enters a search term via a terminal. In some libraries you may be able to download or print the results. The capabilities of the different systems vary considerably.

Virtually all OPACs permit the traditional author, title and classified subject searching. Most OPACs also allow the additional facility of keyword searching, but you should be aware that the extent of keyword indexing varies from library to library. Keywords in the title, notes and contents fields will be indexed in most catalogues; some index all words in classified subject and author headings as well. Keyword searching greatly extends the range of subject searching and allows the user to interrogate the author's vocabulary. Boolean searching – using the logical operators AND, OR and NOT – allows the user to define the structure of a search and combine terms in ways impossible in the controlled indexing vocabulary of the traditional catalogue. Users may also be able to limit searches by date of publication, or to a particular field. Keyword searching can be particularly helpful to the contemporary historian who may be interested in issues and topics which may not yet have got into the controlled indexing language of the cataloguer – for example New Labour, mad cow disease.

While acknowledging its power and flexibility, the user should also be aware that keyword searching has considerable limitations. Titles frequently do not accurately reflect the real subject of a work, and works retrieved on words used by the searcher may have a different shade of meaning or context to that anticipated. Searches by keyword often produce much irrelevant material, especially in catalogues where the entire record is keyword indexed. The user must also try ranges of synonyms to be reasonably sure that a search is comprehensive. Results will be limited to the language of the terms sought. There is a distinct loss of the consistency and breadth of subject searching provided by the controlled indexing vocabulary of the traditional catalogue where all material will be indexed under a single form of each name, title or subject.

The careful researcher can compensate for this loss to some extent by noting the additional subject headings listed at the end of the bibliographical descriptions of relevant materials found under the keyword and searching under those. Allen and Attig point to 'this concept of cycling or using information in the bibliographic records to locate additional materials [as] a key to effective searching in any environment, but nowhere more so than in an on-line catalogue'.[7] Several automated systems now allow the user to do this via a related works or similar entries option which will offer additional searches on the author, and subject headings and classmarks in the work retrieved. It is also possible in some catalogues to convert the supposed 'subject heading' search into a word (that is keyword) search. A further safeguard against variations in cataloguing and spelling is to 'browse' the author and subject indexes in the vicinity of the terms found.

SUMMARY NOTE ON CATALOGUES   In this age of transition the researcher will encounter several types of catalogue, traditional and mechanised. They have many similarities, and both have strengths and weaknesses. The more aware the researcher is of the differences, the better able he or she will be to make efficient use of the catalogues. In visiting an unfamiliar library the researcher should cultivate the habit of checking the scope of the catalogues, the subject classification scheme in use, and the catalogue filing rules. Remember that very different sequences result if filing order is word by word rather than letter by letter. It can be helpful to establish the extent of keyword indexing.

Shelf browsing the library classification   The classified arrangement of libraries was emphasised at the start of this section. It is worth stressing the fact that the classified shelf order of materials in most libraries collocates similar materials. Systematic shelf browsing of relevant classified sections is consequently a valuable supplement to searching the catalogue. This research technique can often be overlooked by scholars beguiled by the immediacy of electronic approaches. The collocation feature of classification schemes enables you to find relevant works you did not know about in advance. Shelf browsing also allows greater depth of access to monographs than the card catalogue does – you are able to scan contents pages and indexes. It can be helpful too if you know the aspect you want of a subject but are uncertain which source will have it. Mann makes the point that it is not simply through luck that you find relevant material on the shelves beside something you have found in the catalogue – it is the classification system working. The reader who is aware of this 'can exploit the system consciously and deliberately rather than haphazardly' – their approach can be one of 'systematic serendipity'. Mann makes the further point that 'the vast bulk of humanity's written memory contained in books is not in the indexes and databases in the first place; and the researchers who neglect systematic browsing of the texts of books are missing a vast store of material that cannot be efficiently retrieved in any other way'.[8]

Cataloguing and classification complement each other. For the advanced researcher an awareness of the outlines, at least, of the library classification scheme will be very useful. Bear in mind that in most classifications the all-pervasive discipline of 'history' is treated both as a subject in itself and as a facet of other subjects – for example works of economic history will normally be treated as a facet of economics rather than being collocated with all 'histories' under the category of history. The user will almost certainly have to look in several parts of the classification. The schedules will normally be readily available for consultation. The system of shelf browsing is obviously most efficient in open access libraries or libraries where permission for access to classified sequences can be obtained.

Library reference tools

Catalogue and shelf browsing reveal only the holdings of that particular library and no library holds everything on a subject. The postgraduate researcher needs to consult other reference resources to reach the wider literature and sources of the subject being studied. The range of these is very extensive – specialist encyclopaedias, directories, dictionaries, periodicals' indexes, catalogues of national imprints, current bibliographies, critical specialised bibliographies, subject guides to sources, national and special library catalogues, union catalogues, abstracting services, citation indexes, biographical sources, book review indexes, among others. It is a constant surprise to reference librarians and information scientists, who are more fully aware of the burgeoning range of reference sources, that so few scholars know of the existence of – let alone use – a number of reference tools which would greatly strengthen their grasp of the potential sources and literature.

It is in this area of reference tools that developments in computerisation and information technology are having greatest impact. Many of the catalogues, indexes and bibliographies about to be referred to may be available in both printed form and in CD-ROM or other computerised form. This section will indicate the more significant individual research tools. The growing number of computer facilities which may offer access to a range of these resources will be dealt with in the subsection on computer facilities and services below. Electronic versions of these tools provide many more access points and faster access to the information than those in other formats. As a general rule the on-line version is the most current, followed by the printed edition, which often includes material ahead of the CD-ROM version. Be aware that CD-ROMs may cover only the more recent years of a reference source. The printed version of earlier volumes may have to be consulted to complete a search. The reader should also remember that the advantages

and disadvantages of keyword searching, outlined in the subection on
on-line catalogues above, apply equally to mechanised versions of bibliographies and indexes.

Among the researcher's main requirements is familiarity with the
literature of the subject. To achieve this they need to know how to find
the established literature, the current output and the sources. Habitually
the researcher's path into his or her sources is strongly influenced by
reading suggested by a tutor or supervisor and continued by following
the footnotes found there. Most scholars will develop the habit of
regularly reading and scanning the literature in a few journals in their
specialist areas. The advanced researcher needs to go well beyond this
if a comprehensive understanding of the research in its period context
is to be grasped.

Several works can help the historian find a way through the modern
bibliographical reference maze. The standard general guide to reference
works in Britain is Day and Harvey (eds), *Walford's Guide to Reference
Material*. Another very useful work is Ronald H. Fritze et al., *Reference
Sources in History: an Introductory Guide* (1990), which gives concise
but informative details of the character and coverage of most of the
major reference works described below and many more.[9]

The reference tools of greatest direct relevance to the modern and
contemporary historian are historical bibliographies, comprehensive
catalogues of printed books and periodicals' indexes, book review indexes and citation indexes, and current research registers. Indexes and
abstracting services are the best way to find journal articles. They allow
the scanning of hundreds of journals at a time and give access to
resources greater than those of any single library. Abstracts contain
brief summaries of articles in addition to bibliographical details. Holdings and locations for works found in bibliographies and indexes can be
located through union catalogues. Most of these research tools will be
available in the major university libraries.

Historical bibliographies The most directly relevant, at least at the
initial stage of research, will be historical bibliographies. These come in
several types: comprehensive (by subject or period), critical (selective/
assessing/instructive), special subject, and current (listing/recording) –
or various admixtures of these. Quality varies enormously. Many,
perhaps most, are little more than listings. Annotation, descriptive or
commentary, is normally a great help in assessing the value of what one
finds. Closely related are subject guides to historical sources, which will
commonly be found on library shelves close to the bibliographies of
printed materials.

The most generally useful for the novice researcher is the critical bibliography which will introduce and guide the user through the significant sources and secondary works of a period or subject. Such bibliographies are invaluable in the twentieth century where the wealth and range of materials can easily overwhelm the inexperienced researcher.

Students and scholars of twentieth-century British history are fortunate in having H. J. Hanham, *Bibliography of British History 1851– 1914* (1976) and Peter Catterall, *British History 1945–1987: an Annotated Bibliography* (1990) – two splendid critical bibliographies comprehensively surveying the historical writing and sources for parts of the period. Both these works are models of their kind, concisely informative about the usefulness, coverage, standpoint and relationships of a work to others in the subject areas covered. They are well indexed (particularly Hanham), helpfully arranged, and constantly engage and stimulate the reader's interest in the literature for their periods. The gap between is partly filled by Alfred F. Havighurst, *Modern England 1901–84* (1987), in which the clear differentiation of types of material (sources, surveys, monographs, etc.) considerably compensates for its sparse annotation. Keith Robbins, *A Bibliography of British History 1914–1989* (1996) appears substantial, but it is not really a critical bibliography and it is very difficult to use efficiently, being poorly edited, unsystematically arranged, and – crucially – lacking a subject index. It does contain more materials for the period 1914–45 than Havighurst, but these are presented only in a series of extensive subject lists which fail to differentiate materials either qualitatively or by form. Besides these bibliographies of mainly printed materials, C. L. Mowat, *Great Britain since 1914* (1970) remains a very useful introduction to the archival and printed sources.

All critical bibliographies are necessarily selective and require supplementing with current bibliographies, which are essentially records of output, and more narrowly focused special subject bibliographies, should they exist. The main current bibliography for British history is the *Annual Bibliography of British and Irish History 1975* which includes a twentieth-century section. It lists books and periodical articles selected from the main journals in British history. This is a less comprehensive and less helpfully arranged and indexed record than its predecessor *Writings on British History 1934 + [to 1974]* but it is respectably current, appearing about ten months after the end of the year covered. It should be further supplemented by *Historical Abstracts* which is the main international guide to current historical periodical literature. Although its coverage of British historical journals is not as extensive as that of the *Annual Bibliography*, and it is about a year less current, it does include a number of additional politics and economics periodicals together with some more general titles. It also includes some books, and you do get an abstract, or synopsis, of the contents of the article which can help the researcher to judge whether the item should be consulted. The printed edition appears in two parts – Part A: *Modern History Abstracts 1492–1914*, and Part B: *Twentieth-century Abstracts 1914–Present* – each issued four times per annum. A consolidated file from 1982 is available in CD-ROM form and some libraries may allow dial-up access to the full computer file back to 1955. A CD-ROM edition of the *Annual Bibliography* is anticipated in the near future.

Subject bibliographies in history can be critical and current. These are much too numerous to list in detail but notable critical ones are G. H. Martin and S. McIntyre, *Bibliography of British and Irish Municipal History, vol. 1, General Works* (1972) and G. Ottley, *A Bibliography of Railway History* (1965), both now obviously older, but invaluable for the coverage of materials up to their dates of publication. Others, such as the highly selective and lightly annotated R. C. Richardson and W. H. Chaloner, *British Economic and Social History: a Bibliographical Guide*, (3rd edn, 1996); the substantial but awkwardly arranged listing by F. Goodall, *Bibliography of British Business Histories* (1987); R. Perks, *Oral History: an Annotated Bibliography* (1990); Philip Rees, *Fascism in Britain* (1979); Harold Smith, *The British Labour Movement to 1970: a Bibliography* (1981) which covers only historical writing from 1945–1970; John Burnett, *Autobiography of the Working Class: an Annotated Bibliography: vols. 2, 1900–45; 3, Suppt 1790–1945* (1987–89); Richard W. Cox, *Sport in Britain: a Bibliography of Historical Publications, 1800–1988* (1991), one of several sterling contributions to sports history bibliography by a systematic compiler; John Kirby, *The Festival of Britain: a List of Information Sources* (1993); and P. H. Jones, *Bibliography of the History of Wales*, (3rd [microfiche] edn, 1989), give some idea of the variety available, and of the need to read the introductions to check the precise approach, coverage and structure of any bibliography. This is an important point. Bibliographies are seldom as comprehensive as their titles might lead one to assume. Frequently they may cover only secondary or separately published materials. Whole categories of material such as periodical articles or printed sources may be omitted.

Numerous specialised historical bibliographies have appeared in journals. Many of these can be found in *Bibliographies in History, vol. 2: An Index to Bibliographies in History Journals and Dissertations Covering all Countries of the World except the US and Canada* (1988). This is based on the files of *Historical Abstracts* and covers journals back to 1954 and dissertations to 1974. Additional current subject materials will be found in annual lists in specialist journals, for example *Business Archives, Urban History, Oral History, Labour History Review* and *Scottish Economic and Social History*. Besides its listings of periodical literature, the *Economic History Review* has carried an annual review of information technology developments since 1991.

Most scholars will find their way to the historical periodicals of greatest relevance through following up bibliographical recommendations and references. The wider range of historical periodicals titles can be found in Eric Boehm and others, *Historical Periodicals Directory, vol. 2, Europe – West, North, Central, and South* (1983).

Comprehensive catalogues of printed books Besides the historical literature, the modern historian needs to be familiar with the relevant contemporary publication of their subject period. The current and historic national imprint contains primary sources for many researchers.

The *British National Bibliography 1950–* (BNB), now produced by the British Library National Bibliographic Service, is a catalogue record of books published in Britain. The entries are classified according to the Dewey decimal classification. Relevant material may be diffused by the classification and there is no critical annotation. The CD-ROM version enables rapid and varied searching. All books in the BNB will be available in the British Library in London. The *Bibliography of Scotland 1976/7–*, published by the National Library of Scotland, records books published in Scotland and works of Scottish relevance published elsewhere that have been acquired by the National Library of Scotland. It is now available on-line.

Before BNB, the *English Catalogue of Books* was the standard list of British books issued by major publishers, but there is no ready way to access the full national imprint. The British Library will have the fullest holdings of works published before 1950. The BL's own printed subject catalogues are helpful if somewhat idiosyncratically classified. The CD-ROM edition of the *British Library General Catalogue of Books to 1975* does allow sophisticated searching by the practised user (refined by date, imprint, etc. as well as keywords). The new BL OPAC97 catalogue is reachable on the web (http://opac97.bl.uk). The *London Bibliography of the Social Sciences 1931–89* (LBSS) is not exhaustive but it does give access to a good range of the literature of contemporary issues through most of the century. It has been succeeded by the *International Bibliography of the Social Sciences* (1952–), an on-line version of which (covering 1981 onwards) is available.

General periodical indexes Finding and locating the periodical literature are skills the serious researcher must develop. There is an enormous number of general and specialised journals and reviews, and even experienced researchers may be unaware of useful titles impinging on their subject area. The standard directory of current periodical publications is *Ulrich's International Periodicals Directory*, (34th edn, 1996). Locating periodical titles will be dealt with in the subsection on union catalogues below.

For current and retrospective coverage of contemporary British periodical literature consult the *British Humanities Index* (BHI) and its predecessor *Subject Catalogue of Periodicals*. Just as the LBSS does for books and pamphlets, browsing the subject-arranged BHI can give the reader some insight into the salient features of political and intellectual debate throughout the twentieth century.

A number of important wider-ranging international periodical indexes include coverage of journals in neighbouring disciplines. The *Humanities Index 1974+* lists articles in many major historical journals and the major historical items in other humanities periodicals. Its sister publication the *Social Sciences Index 1974+* also includes a great deal of historical material which may not reach *Historical Abstracts* or may even be missed by more specialist historical bibliographies. These and other bibliographies from the H. W. Wilson stable (for example *Biography Index*, *Bibliography Index*) are similarly arranged with standardised subject headings and extensive cross-references, derived from Library of Congress subject headings but tending to be more current, direct and precise, and consequently easier to use. These large indexes are available in printed and computerised form. A useful recent addition to the indexes to periodical literature is the *Periodicals Contents Index* (PCI) which includes mainly English-language articles in humanities and social sciences journals from 1770 to 1990/91 – recently produced on CD-ROM by Chadwyck-Healey. This indexes words from the contents pages and includes book reviews. It is laborious to use but it does index a massive number of article titles not previously indexed electronically. PCI is also available on-line via EDINA, a database server at Edinburgh University. The *International Bibliography of the Social Sciences* (1952–) includes extensive coverage of periodical articles. There are numerous other specialised indexes of periodical literature, for example *Journal of Economic Literature*, *Sociological Abstracts*, *ArtIndex* and *MLA International Bibliography*.

Citation indexes   Citation indexes are a specialised form of computer-generated indexes which relatively few British historians appear to use. Produced by the Institute of Scientific Information in Philadelphia, USA, the *Social Science Citation Index* and the *Arts and Humanities Citation Index* (which covers rather more historical literature) can be very useful for the modern historian. These are sophisticated indexes requiring some skill and effort to master; the introductions should be read carefully. Each annual volume consists of a number of indexes, of which the subject (keyword) and citation indexes are generally the most useful. Unlike any other reference tool, citation indexes index footnotes. The researcher can find out who has cited a particular work in a given year so taking him or her forward to the most recent literature on a subject in a way supplementary and complementary to conventional literature searches. This is particularly helpful for scholars working in a very new specialism with one or two seminal works. The keyword index is also very helpful for finding literature on new and contemporary concepts. These citation indexes are available in printed form, directly on-line, or via BIDS (see the subsection on computer files below).

Book review indexes Given the vast scale of historical publication, the scholarly reception of books can be a useful aid to assessing quality and deciding which books to read. Researchers will habitually scan reviews in the journals most relevant to their specialist area, and major review articles in history will be picked up in the *Annual Bibliography* and *Historical Abstracts*. To look further to find fugitive reviews and track the literature of contingent disciplines which may appear in general reviewing journals, quality newspapers and specialist journals in the humanities and social sciences, researchers can use comprehensive book review indexes. Some researchers may find back files of book review indexes helpful in assessing the contemporary impact of works on opinion throughout the twentieth century.

The major comprehensive ones are American, but they tend to include major British reviewing journals. *Book Review Index* (BRI) 1965– (Detroit: Gale Research) is issued six times a year. It gives citations for reviews in 470 indexed journals in the social sciences, humanities and natural sciences. It has a title, but no subject index. The *Master Cumulation 1965–1984* provides access to more than 1.6 million citations. *Book Review Digest* (BRD) (1905–) is more selective, but prints excerpts of reviews and citations of works reviewed at least twice in ninety-five American and UK journals. It has a cumulative *Author/ Title Index 1905–1974* (1976). Both BRI and BRD are available in printed, on-line and CD-ROM editions. A useful CD-ROM updated six times per year is *Books in Print with Book Reviews Plus* which now carries more than a hundred thousand unabridged book reviews from mainly American library and publishers' reviewing journals. This can be a particularly good source for reliable reviews of reference publications (bibliographies, etc.) which often struggle to find reviewing space in British journals.

Union catalogues Union catalogues, printed or computerised, tell you where there are copies. The largest of these are in North America.

OCLC may be accessible in a few British research libraries, and RLIN in fewer still, but COPAC, the on-line public access catalogue of the Consortium of University and Research Libraries (CURL) is being developed into a British national OPAC. It came on stream in 1996 with the computerised book and periodical title holdings of six major university libraries (Cambridge, Edinburgh, Glasgow, Leeds, Oxford and Trinity College Dublin) with another seven expected to be added in 1997. This is an encouraging development, but users should note that 80 per cent of the contents of COPAC have been published since 1960 – holdings before that date are not fully automated. A leaflet guide is available in COPAC libraries. Access is via a text interface Telnet: *copac.ac.uk*, login: *copac*, password: *copac*; or via a WWW interface *http://copac.ac.uk/copac/*.

For locating periodicals the indispensable work is the *British Union Catalogue of Periodicals* (BUCOP) issued in four volumes to 1950, with a supplement to 1960. It is regrettable that despite all the electronic advances of the last two decades no comprehensive update of this invaluable research tool has been forthcoming. SALSER is an electronic union catalogue of the serials holdings of all Scottish universities, the National Library of Scotland and a number of other Scottish libraries, and there are local union lists in major university centres (for example the *University of London Union List of Serials*), but for publications since 1960 the most helpful list is *BSS: Boston Spa Serials* which lists the very extensive holdings of the British Library Document Supply Centre from which volumes can be borrowed or photocopies can be obtained. It also lists the serial holdings of the British Library Humanities and Social Sciences Division, the Science Reference and Information Services Library, the Science Museum Library and Cambridge University Library. Union lists of special materials will be noted in a number of sections below.

Theses and current research   Theses, particularly doctoral theses, are at the cutting edge of research. The research student should check out the thesis literature to see what has been done in the subject area, to perceive new trends, and to avoid duplication of topics. Very few historical bibliographies include theses,[10] mainly because – strictly speaking – they are not publications. There are seldom more than three hardback copies and access to them is either at the institution of origin or by use of a (usually microfilm) copy on interlibrary loan via the BLDSC. The standard British listing of history theses is *Historical Research for Higher Degrees in the United Kingdom* issued annually by the Institute of Historical Research as two separate lists: 'Theses completed' and 'Theses in progress'. There are cumulative retrospective lists,

History theses 1900–1970 by P. M. Jacobs, and *1971–80* and *1981–90* by J. M. Horn. A small number of more specialist compilations exist, for example R. Rodger, *Research in Urban History: a Classified List of Doctoral and Master's Theses* (1994) includes much British material. Lists of work in progress appear in some specialist historical journals, for example *Labour History Review*, *London Journal* and *Scottish Economic and Social History*.

The ASLIB *Index to Theses [with abstracts] Accepted for Higher Degrees by the Universities of Great Britain and Ireland* (1950+) is the standard general listing of British academic theses. The CD-ROM version of volumes 20–43, *Index to Theses: Great Britain and Ireland 1970–93*, is awkward to use and some preference among reference librarians is still held for the greater accuracy of the printed version. *Current Research in Britain: Humanities 1995* and *Current Research in Britain: Social Sciences 1995* (10th editions) attempt to cover post-doctoral research activity. These too are now available in a consolidated CD-ROM format. Information about economic and social research can be found in RAPID, the Research Activity and Publications Database, which will be referred to again in the subsection on computer files.

Other reference tools The preceding subsections have concentrated on general bibliographical tools and those most specific to history. Bibliographic and information sections of libraries will hold many subject bibliographies and guides in related disciplines that will be useful to modern and contemporary historians who should seek them out. Major libraries will also have strong holdings of published guides to archive and manuscript collections. These are dealt with more fully in Chapter 4, but all twentieth-century historians should be aware of the following works: Janet Foster and Julia Sheppard, *British Archives: a Guide to Archive Resources in the United Kingdom* (3rd edn, 1996); Chris Cook, *Sources in British Political History, 1900–1951* (1975–85) in six volumes; and the two volumes of *The Longman Guide to Sources in Contemporary British History* (1994), edited by Chris Cook, Jane Leonard and Peter Leese. Modern historians should also be aware that much useful material can be found in general and special directories,[11] yearbooks, almanacs and handbooks, and specialist encyclopaedias and biographical dictionaries. Many of these may be found in *Walford's Guide to Reference Material* and Fritze, *Reference Sources in History*.

Other materials in libraries

Libraries can hold valuable research materials which may not be readily accessible through the main catalogue. Government and other official documents, microform collections and separately catalogued or un-catalogued special collections can be a virtual treasury for the scholar seeking original source materials – but it is seldom one that is possible to search through the OPAC. These sources have to be more actively sought out in most libraries.

Government publications   National libraries, most university libraries and the major civic libraries have substantial holdings of United Kingdom government publications. These can be conveniently divided into two major categories – HMSO (Her Majesty's Stationery Office) publications and those not published by HMSO. In many libraries HMSO publications are further divided into parliamentary publications and non-parliamentary papers.

All HMSO publications can be traced in the HMSO catalogues issued daily, with indexed monthly and annual cumulations. There is a microfilm version of the *Annual Catalogues of the Controller's Library, HMSO 1922–1972* with printed index. Non-parliamentary papers – reports, surveys, statistical publications – may have entries in the library catalogue, but the lists should be checked for correct title. Parliamentary publications – Command papers, House of Commons papers, House of Commons bills, House of Lords papers and bills, parliamentary debates, statutory instruments, etc. – are seldom separately catalogued but are usually shelved in their numbered or chronological sequences. The HMSO lists should be checked for individual documents. For re-searchers seeking runs of the series, a very useful aid is David Lewis Jones and Chris Pond's *Parliamentary Holdings in Libraries in Britain and Ireland* (PHIL) (Pilot edition 1993), which is a union list of current and historic parliamentary publications in some three hundred public, academic, national and special libraries throughout the British Isles. It provides a useful statement of holdings at a time when numerous collections have been weeded out or disposed of. In some libraries searching for post-1979 parliamentary materials may be supplemented by access to the *JUSTIS Parliament Database* via CD-ROM or on-line.

Non-HMSO publications – research reports and policy documents issued by individual government departments, official bodies, or com-mercially published – can be very difficult to trace. The *Catalogue of British Government Publications not Published by HMSO* (1980–) helps identify more recent publications.

Most large libraries will have an official publications section, with leaflet guides and a specialist librarian on hand who can be consulted. Collections of statistical publications are often shelved near or as part of an official publications department. Contemporary historians should note that a number of the larger libraries are regional European Documentation Centres with holdings of all major documents issued in Brussels, and electronic indexes of documents and briefings on the United Kingdom's implementation of European legislation.

Microforms A great deal of modern and contemporary research material is available in microform – records of political parties, some public records, trade union records, diplomatic documents, materials for women's studies, official publications, etc. Such materials are often difficult to find in libraries. Details of sets are usually in accompanying literature rather than in the catalogue. D. J. Munro, *Microforms for Historians: a Finding List of Research Collections in London Libraries* (1994), lists the material in London libraries. It also includes BLDSC holdings and these are available on interlibrary loan. *Microforms Research Collections in Major Scottish Libraries* (3rd ed., 1994) covers holdings north of the border. The Bodleian Library publishes a list of its microform holdings, and a number of other specialist and individual library lists are available.[12]

Researchers wishing to know what may have been published in microform can consult *Guide to Microforms in Print*, which is published annually in title and subject editions.

Newspapers Newspapers are valuable sources for many aspects of modern historical, social and cultural studies. Because of their extreme bulk and problems in conservation, few libraries hold backfiles of more than one or two major broadsheets. The larger civic libraries are more likely to hold backfiles than most university libraries. Local public reference libraries have resolutely attempted to keep runs of significant local titles, but with uneven results. For the more popular dailies and weeklies the British Library Newspaper Library at Colindale is virtually the only source.

Backfiles of newspapers are often held on microfilm. CD-ROM versions of the major broadsheets have become available since c.1990, but the cultural historian in particular needs to bear in mind that the mechanised editions are text only, usually without illustrations and advertisements, and drastically reduced sports reporting. These are not the editions read daily on the 8.10 from Surbiton.

Few newspapers are indexed retrospectively. Most major university libraries will have *The Times Index (1905–1995)*, the CD-ROM version of which is anticipated. From 1995 there is a CD-ROM *British Newspaper Index* covering the broadsheets.

The *Catalogue of the Newspaper Library at Colindale* (8 vols, 1975) lists the holdings of the most comprehensive collection. For researchers with regional and local studies interests the series of NEWSPLAN volumes, published since 1986 under the auspices of the British Library, are very useful. Designed as surveys of extant holdings of newspapers in libraries and newspaper offices by region with a view to establishing a microfilming preservation programme, the volumes are effectively a series of union catalogues of regionally held local newspapers. Reports have appeared for NEWSPLAN projects in the South West, Northern Region, North Western Region, East Midlands, West Midlands (2 vols), Yorkshire and Humberside, Scotland, Wales, Ireland, and most recently the London and South East Region. Imperial historians can consult Arthur R. Hewitt, *Union Catalogue of Commonwealth Newspapers in London, Oxford, and Cambridge* (1960).

Library facilities and services

A wider range of library services may be available than many researchers will have experienced as undergraduates. Very good services may be provided for an institution's students and staff, but the entire range is unlikely to be available to visitors. The precise range of facilities varies greatly, as does the extent of end-user access, but the following services are likely to be present in some form.

Library information Library guide pamphlets and pathfinder sheets are very useful in orientating the new or visiting reader. A marked increase in the variety and quality of library guidance means that it is now common to find general library guides, floor guides, resource guides to subject areas, guides to general and specific electronic resources, and to other library services available at strategic points in the building. This rapid growth in guidance in part reflects the increasing complexity of the range of resources. Many libraries have developed internal 'information centres' which combine the former general enquiry desk functions with oversight and administration of computerised information services.

Photocopying Self-service photocopying, usually using a prepaid card or ticket system, is available now in most university libraries subject to the restrictions required by the copyright agreements. Few photocopying cards can be used outside the library in which they have been purchased. Researchers using a large number of libraries are well advised to mark their cards with their name (especially in the case of higher value discount cards) and an identifier for the library. This can reduce later frustration and confusion, and help to identify lost cards. Self-service photocopying is not always available in special research libraries. In many libraries the photocopying of older material may not be permitted or may be done only by library staff in a photographic or document delivery department.

Document delivery Document delivery can encompass a variety of activities, and many libraries now have document delivery offices. In addition to the photocopying of restricted materials, elements of the following services are likely to be present.

Interlibrary loan (ILL) is an invaluable facility – particularly for researchers based away from the major research centres. Books and theses may be borrowed and photocopies of articles can be obtained through the national interlending system operated through and primarily based on the stock of the BLDSC. There is usually some cost involved (for example between £8 and £12 for a thesis) but this is negligible when set against costs of accommodation and travel to distant locations. Most academic and public libraries will try to obtain materials for patrons on interlibrary loan. Many reference-only libraries will not lend out material, even on interlibrary loan, but they may be willing to provide photocopies of materials not readily available elsewhere. It is important to have full and accurate bibliographical information when making an ILL application.

Printing the results of computer searches may, depending on local arrangements and network configurations, cover printing records exported from the end-user (that is your own) OPAC, CD-ROM or BIDS searches, files transferred over the network, or the results of searches done for the user by library staff on remote database services. Licensing may restrict researchers' use of some larger computer services to their home library. An expected extension of document delivery will be 'digital books' – on-demand publishing over the wires.

Computer facilities and services New sources and improved means of access are constantly developing in library and information technology. National funding through the Joint Information Systems Committee supports numerous projects under the Electronic Libraries Programme. The implementation of technological advance is very uneven and great variety will be found between the provision in one library and the next. In some universities the library or the information technology department run courses for their staff and students in the use of IT and researchers are strongly advised to take advantage of these where they are available.

OPACS, LOCAL NETWORKS AND THE INTERNET In lending libraries patrons will normally be able to reserve and renew books via the OPAC. They will also be able to view their borrowing record, that is books currently on loan or reserve. Campus networks will enable staff and students to do this from faculty offices. With a modem and tele-communications connections OPACs can be reached from home. Many university libraries allow library OPAC terminal connection to a limited number of neighbouring or relevant library OPACs via JANET (the Joint Academic Network), and any university member with access to the Internet can reach an almost limitless number of OPACs, other bibliographical services and subject information servers worldwide. At the Institute of Historical Research, for example, in addition to the library, members can have access to IHR-Info (telnet: *ihr-uk.sas.ac.uk* or via graphics-based browsers on the World Wide Web at: *http://ihr.sas. ac.uk:8080/*) a multifunctional electronic historical information server providing a Bulletin Board (on seminars, conferences, training courses), electronic publications (bibliographical and other IHR publications), a gateway to electronic sites worldwide (libraries, datasets and other servers), and giving 'easy access to all Internet navigational tools including the latest WWW searchers'. The libraries of most major institutions have Web pages and have developed similar if more general services. In some places you may be able to download records to files which can be used and manipulated by personal bibliographic software packages to produce footnotes and bibliographies. OPACs are usually free. Other services may be chargeable.

COMPUTER FILES Besides CD-ROM versions of bibliographical data-bases and the various types of automated catalogues already referred to, libraries may have database versions of other documentary research resources on CD-ROM (for example *Social Trends*, 1970–95, and *PRO-files*, a series of selected classes from the Public Record Office, published in conjunction with the Institute for Contemporary British History). Many libraries now provide Network links from OPAC or dedicated terminals to machine-readable files elsewhere. Some of these are large commercial or academic databases, which may require user registration and fees for searching (for example DIALOG, BIDS); others may be datasets of statistics generated in the process of some local research project; others still may be useful research tools distributed on floppy disk in a non-commercial basic-cost-recovery publication (for example the machine-readable index to the *Economic History Review*). Like microforms it is sometimes difficult to find out which of these resources a library may have. The *Survey of CD-ROM and On-line Services in University of London Libraries, 1996*, compiled by Charlotte McDonaugh and Carolyn Malsher, gives some indication of facilities in London.[13] It is worth remembering that booking will often be necessary if you want access to some of these computer facilities.

Computerisation has revolutionised literature searching. Electronic tools enable speedy coverage of an increasingly comprehensive range of the relevant literature. An important development is the growth of utilities which are collections of bibliographical databases, so giving users access to a range of research tools on a single host. Researchers should take particular note of BIDS and OCLC *FirstSearch*. BIDS (Bath Information Data Service) offers data from 1980 onwards. It includes on-line access to the ISI *Social Sciences and Arts* and *Humanities Citation Indexes* (see discussion of these under 'citation indexes' above) and the IBSS (International Bibliography of the Social Sciences), one of the largest and most comprehensive social science databases. OCLC *FirstSearch* offers a wide range of American-based bibliographical databases including WorldCat and several of the periodicals' indexes mentioned earlier among many others (for example *ArtIndex*, *BiographInd*, and *SocSciInd*). References can be downloaded to e-mail, disk, attached printer, to a printer in document supply, or not at all, depending on the local configuration of facilities and your status with the home institution. In some libraries the searching services of these and of more complex databases may be offered through library staff.

Another valuable current research tool for the economic and social historian freely available over the Internet is RAPID (the Research Activity and Publications Database, mounted on the EDINA server at Edinburgh University) which contains summary information on ESRC-funded research activity and associated publications since 1985. It can be reached via WWW: *http://edina.ed.ac.uk/rapid/* or Telnet: *ercvax. ed.ac.uk* (129.215.38.1), then username: RAPID, password: RAPID.

Library staff Besides library materials and service facilities, a major resource for researchers is the experience of library staff, particularly those in special libraries or in charge of special collections. There are several good reasons for the researcher to 'cultivate' librarians. Professionally librarians are better placed to keep track of the bibliography of guides and catalogues, and developments in archives. The new researcher and even the experienced historian may miss much of this information. While an individual librarian may know only a limited amount about the substance of an enquiry, they will be knowledgeable about the options for finding information. Librarians of special libraries and collections will have a better overall grasp of the extent of their holdings than the user. They are used to handling the queries of a research clientele and have often built up a reservoir of knowledge and experience that can enable them quickly to answer a query or set the novice researcher off on the right track. Again this is part of their professional function. In many libraries a subject or information librarian may have to do the searching of particularly complex databases having discussed your requirements with you. Librarians are not there to do the research for you, however, and the clearer you are about your requirements, and the more obvious it is that you have done preliminary work but are stuck or uncertain about the next step, the more helpful you are likely to find them. A courteous informed enquiry will be much more productive than a demand. Unfortunately budgetary constraints and automisation of tasks have led to an alarming widespread decline in the numbers of special subject librarians.

Visiting libraries

Preparation in advance can save you much time and enable you to maximise the benefit of visiting an unfamiliar library. The guides to United Kingdom libraries referred to in the section on locating libraries above will help decide which libraries you may need to visit. From these you can find addresses and, from some, opening hours. It is now possible to check current details by on-line access to the Web pages or catalogues of most major libraries. Be sure to note any particular access requirements and go along armed with any necessary letters of introduction and proofs of identity – and, increasingly, the fee for membership or day use. It is often advisable to write in advance; this is both courteous and can save a great deal of waiting about on arrival, as some research materials may be in storage. Writing will frequently be imperative if you intend to use special collections, and a concise explanation of your purpose may have the added advantage of forewarning the custodian, who will have time to think about your visit, and, consequently, be better able to draw your attention to other relevant parts of a collection on your arrival. Unless you are visiting for a very specific purpose, it is advisable for your first visit to read the library's guide on arrival to gain an early grasp of its arrangement and logistical idiosyncrasies – they all have them. Many guides may not be up to date, such is the speed of change, but usually they can save you a great deal of time. Remember that time may be required to register on arrival. Remember also to arrive with adequate writing and note-taking materials; some research libraries have restrictions, for example on the use of pens.

Using libraries – concluding advice

The primary advice to the researcher is to be aware of the breadth of the reference framework which will lead to the relevant source materials: library catalogues, printed reference sources, current and retrospective bibliographical indexes and abstracts, and electronic resources.

Libraries are in a period of very rapid transition. New automated facilities appear almost daily to supplement and sometimes replace traditional hard copy versions of reference resources. Budgetary constraints and automisation of tasks are deeply affecting staff structures in many institutions with a resultant widespread reduction in the number of special subject librarians.

Users should expect differences between libraries. Try to ascertain the organisation and relative relationships of the catalogues in each library. Look out for variations in filing rules. Although they are everywhere, OPACs frequently do not cover all of a library's holdings. Remember the immense utility of library classification schemes but be aware that materials can be scattered within them. Use both approaches – the catalogue and shelf browsing.

In using reference works, researchers should be prepared to take time to understand the structure and master the abbreviations of the source consulted. Creditworthy reference tools will always have introductory sections on how they work. These can sometimes be complex but the greater your grasp of how a particular reference tool works, the better able you will be to use it efficiently and evaluate what you are finding. Good critical historical bibliographies can give you a rapid overview of the literature and sources. Keep up to date by periodically checking relevant current listings and citation indexes.

Beware letting your research be shaped too much by the convenience and facility of a particular tool. No single reference source will give you everything. All have limitations and researchers need to be alert to these. Subject bibliographies date rapidly and updates are less common than might be wished. Often they may be only one person's selection. The standard and thoroughness of indexing varies. Computer-generated indexes are often inadequately edited and the user should habitually scan back and forwards for synonyms and misspellings. Changes in index terms are a hazard of periodical subject indexes over time. Indexes and abstracting services are only as good as their coverage, so check that key publications in your subject area are included. Bibliographical currency is possible only by being selective. Remember to check arrangement: diffusion can occur in bibliographies just as it does in library classification schemes and cross-referencing is seldom as thorough as it should be.

Summarising Mann, researchers need to train themselves in and apply a number of techniques of enquiry: controlled vocabulary subject heading searching, systematic browsing, keyword searches, citation searches, searches using published bibliographies and indexes, computer searches, and talking to knowledgeable people. There are advantages and disadvantages with them all, but each approach can lead to information not reached by the others.[14]

Advanced students should keep their options open and think across the boundaries of their subject. They should become familiar with the specialised reference works in their own and related disciplines. To get the best out of the information sources the researcher needs to develop the 'habits of defining terms, assessing assumptions, and checking details'.

OPACs and CD-ROMs have seen a shift from librarian-assisted computer searching to end-user computer searching. This is much faster than working through card files, but the researcher needs to be aware of the structures. Take advantage of any training courses in the effective use of information technology offered by your library or information technology department. At Glasgow University, for example, the course content aims to give students a grounding in basic search principles, using keywords to define a search, Boolean operators, truncation and adjacency, refining search results, and managing and storing search results.

Remember the limitations of keyword searching, and be aware of the need to try variant synonyms and spellings. If you get a very large number of 'hits' discard the search and try a narrower concept. Browse the indexes in CD-ROM products and OPACs to see the range of terms indexed in the database. Be sure to scan both 'subject headings' and 'keyword' indexes. Boolean defaults 'AND' or 'OR' may vary system to system.

Most systems work by menus. Always read the instructions at the foot of the screen to decide on your next step. Exported output from OPACs and computer services can be in various formats. Choose the format best suited to your needs, that is to your home software. When downloading successive searches be sure to change the filename in your home directory otherwise the system is likely to overwrite your previous search file.

Train yourself in good habits of being consistent in note-taking, especially in your recording and citing of bibliographical references. Abbreviation is fraught with danger, perhaps especially so in this electronic age. Do make good use of skilled library staff; changes are happening very quickly and the professionals are best placed to inform you about new and up-to-date resources.

This chapter has aimed to give some understanding of the methods of librarians and bibliographers. It seeks to encourage research students to learn the new and varied search strategies and techniques required to master the special reference works in their own and in related subject areas. This can require considerable time but it is undoubtedly time well spent, and it will underpin your knowledge and grasp of your field. It is hoped the guidance given here will help researchers to locate their materials more readily in the largely library-resident reference and bibliographic system.

CHAPTER 6

Computing techniques for historical research

Peter Denley

To humanities students, and particularly those who came into the humanities 'to avoid science', the march of information technology can appear relentless.[1] In little over a decade computers have progressed from being a comparatively exotic option for historical research, surrounded by suspicion and scepticism, to a natural and increasingly indispensable part of research culture. That all research is now written up in word-processed form is the first and most obvious cause of this. The fact that in order to access information we now have to use computers (if only to consult library catalogues) is a second. An increasing amount of information distribution and exchange takes place on the Internet and this is in the process of becoming a third cause. At the moment this is still 'optional', but it is less and less possible to ignore information put up on the Internet, and very soon it too will become indispensable.[2]

A fourth factor, the historical database, cannot be far behind. Examples abound already. The current *International Historical Computing Bibliography* has around six thousand entries, the great majority of which relate to database work.[3] These tend to be works written by scholars who have developed a particular interest in the computing aspects of their work; vastly more database projects do not get reported in such literature because their use of the computer is considered to be nothing out of the ordinary.

There are plenty of major examples of the use of databases in modern British historical research. Work on nineteenth-century censuses is perhaps the best known of these, but is by no means the only one.[4] Equally, software is becoming much easier to learn and to use, while good practice for database work in historical research has been developed, taught and documented; the mystique surrounding this activity (some of it, of course, quite superfluous in the first place) is rapidly disappearing. It would not be an exaggeration to say that we are now at a point where, if the proposed research involves significant quantities of structured or structurable information, it would be odd not to look at the possibility of creating a database to hold and manage it.

But the point can in fact be broadened out. All researchers have to organise their material, even if it consists only of notes. The arguments for investigating the most appropriate system for this are strong; there is now a considerable variety of tools which allow access to many types and structures of information. The range of packages now extends from word processors through to conventional database systems (and beyond) through hybrids which treat the data as text but also allow structured manipulation. If one is going to have to go as far as word processing anyway, it is worth considering taking one's computing skills a step further, to allow one not only to store and retrieve one's material but also to analyse it.

This chapter explores the range of possibilities. The first section concentrates on the conventional database system; the second aims to show that this is by no means the only possibility, and presents a loose 'typology' of alternative approaches; and a third section discusses the use of specialised techniques. The chapter emphasises principles rather than specific software, as it is the principles which are crucial and enduring. However, the final section includes suggestions as to how to explore the practical issues and make software decisions.

Databases

The flat-file database Defined most simply, databases are ways of holding information in structured form. The structure is for the designer of the database to determine. There are some basic rules and restrictions, and also some 'good practices', to which the database should conform in order to work effectively. These are not difficult to grasp.

The simplest database consists of a table, in which the rows (known usually as records) each represent an individual case, instance or entry (for example, a person), while the columns (known as fields) represent subsidiary components of information about each case. Such a table is known as 'flat-file' because it is two-dimensional. Figure 6.1 is an example of such a database. It holds biographical information about peers, using data from Cokayne's *Complete Peerage*.[5] Fields have been chosen to hold basic information for each peer, in a way that will allow retrieval and analysis. The data can be viewed in tabular form (Figure 6.1a), or one record at a time, as in a card-index (Figure 6.1b).

Titled Name	Title	Surname	Firstname(s)	DoB	School	University	Career
Buckland	Barony	Berry	Henry Seymour	17/09/1877			
Hanworth	Barony, Visco	Pollock	Ernest Murray	25/11/1861	Charterhouse	Cambridge	Politics
Irwin	Barony	Wood	Edward Frederick	16/04/1881	Eton	Oxford	Politics
Tredegar	Viscountcy	Morgan	Courtenay Charles	10/04/1867	Eton		Military, Politics

Figure 6.1a Tabular view of the database of British peers

Titled Name: Irwin
Title: Barony
Surname: Wood
Firstname(s): Edward Frederick Lindley
DoB: 16/04/1881
School: Eton
University: Oxford
Career: Politics

Figure 6.1b A single record from the database of British peers ('form view')

22 DECEMBER
IRWIN

BARONY.   1. EDWARD FREDERICK LINDLEY WOOD, 4th and yst.
I. 1925.   but 1st surv. s. and h. of Charles Lindley (Wood), 2nd
VISCOUNT HALIFAX (see vol. vi), by Agnes Elizabeth, only
da. of William Reginald (COURTENAY), 21st EARL OF
DEVON, was b. 16, and bap. 28 Apr. 1881, at Powderham; ed. at Eton 1894–
99; matric. at Oxford (Ch. Ch.) 1899; 1st Class Mod. Hist. and B.A. 1903;
Fellow of All Souls Coll., Oxford, 1903; M.A. 1906; Hon. D.C.L. Oxford
1931, and Durham 1933; Hon. LL.D. Leeds 1923, Cambridge, Sheffield
and St. Andrews 1931, Toronto 1932, Liverpool, Dublin and London 1934;
M.P. (Conservative) for Ripon Div. of West Riding of Yorks 1910–25;
served in the Great War, 1915–17, as Major Yorkshire Dragoons Yeomanry
(despatches); Lieut.-Col.; Assistant Secretary, Ministry of National Service,
1917–18; Parl. Under Secretary of State for the Colonies 1921–22; Pres. of
the Board of Education 1922–1924; P.C. 25 Oct. 1922; a British Delegate
to the League of Nations Assembly 1923; Minister of Agriculture and
Fisheries 1924–25. He was cr., 22 Dec. 1925, BARON IRWIN, of Kirby
Underdale, co. York. Viceroy and Governor-General of India 1926–31;
G.C.S.I. and G.C.I.E. 1926; K.G. 1931; again Pres. of the Board of
Education 1932–35; Chancellor of Oxford Univ. 1933. He suc. his father as
3rd VISCOUNT HALIFAX and a Baronet 19 Jan. 1934. Secretary of State for
War and Pres. of the Army Council 1935; Lord Privy Seal 1935–37; Hon.
Col. Yorkshire Dragoons from 1935; he bore St. Edward's Staff at the
Coronation of King George VI in 1937; Lord Pres. of the Council 1937–
38; Secretary of State for Foreign Affairs from 1938; sometime Chairman
of the Medical Research Council; a Knight of Justice of the Order of St.
John of Jerusalem.[1] He m., 21 Sep. 1909, at West Clandon, Surrey, Dorothy
Evelyn Augusta,[2] 2nd da. of William Hillier (ONSLOW), 4th EARL OF
ONSLOW, by Florence Coulston, 1st da. and coh. of Allan Legge
(GARDNER), 3rd BARON GARDNER OF UTTOXETER.

Figure 6.1c An entry from the source for the database of
British peers

A table of this kind looks straightforward, and is very easy to set up
in any database software system. (The examples here were developed
using Microsoft Access.) Before any data can be entered, however, the
fields and their characteristics have to be defined. The decisions involved
at this stage are fundamental and have a profound impact on the way
the research will subsequently go, since it is not very convenient to have
to go back on these decisions and alter the structure of the database.

In this case, the decisions that had to be made were ones involving
selection and structure. The determining factor in these choices must
be the purpose of the exercise. Let us suppose that the object of the

Name	Type	Size
Titled Name	Text	20
Title	Text	20
Surname	Text	25
Firstname(s)	Text	50
DoB	Date/Time	8
School	Text	20
University	Text	20
Career	Text	20

Figure 6.1d Database of British peers: the definition of field types and size

research is to examine the relationship between the education of peers and their subsequent careers. Figure 6.1c is an extract from Cockayne's *Complete Peerage*. It will be apparent that much of the information provided is either too detailed for inclusion or insufficiently relevant to the research. The fields that were created are designed to contain only the information that will be relevant to the research. Having decided on what information is to be included, the researcher has then to divide it up, apportioning the components to fields. The purpose of this is to facilitate retrieval and analysis. The more the information can be broken down at this stage, the easier it will be to manipulate. At the same time, fields should have a clarity of definition which ensures that the information is allocated to a field consistently and unambiguously.

The implementation of the basic structure also requires some decisions to be made in order to allow the software to process it consistently and efficiently. Fields have to be defined as being of a particular data type, and may have specific properties (see Figure 6.1d). The 'default' data type, usually called 'text' (or sometimes 'alphanumeric') allows almost any combination of letters, numbers and punctuation marks to be included. The software will be able to search and retrieve information of this kind, and to sort it in 'ascending' or 'descending' alphabetical order, but will not be able to do more than that. Fields which contain numbers, or dates, or logical switches (for example 'Yes' or 'No') are best defined as being of more specialist data types. If a field is defined as of data type 'Number', it will be possible to perform calculations on it. Calculations can also be performed on fields defined as of data type 'date', as the software 'knows' about the present calendar (though unfortunately commercial packages cannot normally handle other historical calendars).

Fields can also be assigned specific properties. With a text field, for

Enumeration District:	179
Individual ID:	1
Street:	LUDLOW ST
House No:	63
Household No:	1
Family No:	1
Family Name:	SABEY
First Name:	ALONZO
HHold Relationship:	HSLD HEAD M
Race:	WHITE
Sex:	MALE
Age:	38
Marital Status:	MARRIED
Years Married:	11
Num Children Born	0
Num Children Alive	0
Birthplace:	ENGLAND
Father's Birthplace:	ENGLAND
Mother's Birthplace:	ENGLAND
Year of Immigration:	81
Naturalization:	NATURALIZED
Occupation:	LIQUOR BUSINESS
Social Status:	WORKSITE
Function in Economy:	COMMERCE
Months Unemployed:	0
Months Schooling in Year:	0
Can Read?:	YES
Can Write?:	YES
Can Speak English?:	YES
Home Owned or Rented:	
Own Home Mortgaged?:	

Figure 6.2a A single record from the 'Eastside database'
(US Census, 1900)

example, the number of characters it can contain has to be specified. The software will have its own 'default', so this can be ignored, but it is worth making the decisions oneself because one will be able to use the potential of databases more effectively if this is done. There is not much point, for example, in allowing 50 or 255 characters for a field for marital status in which the only values one expects to enter are the letters 'M' (for married), 'S' (single), 'D' (divorced) and 'W' (widowed). It is also possible to specify that only these four entries are acceptable. This is called 'validation', and is a good way to help reduce the input errors which are inevitably going to occur.

These principles hold irrespective of the purpose of the database or the scope of the research. In the example above, information has been abstracted from a compendium. Figure 6.2a illustrates another type of historical database, relating to Jewish immigrants in New York in 1900.[6]

Structured sources such as census returns and other 'tabular' or list-type documents appear to have a natural affinity with databases. Yet even here a number of design decisions have to be made. Some – such as the breakdown of names and addresses into several fields to facilitate retrieval and analysis – are relatively obvious. But there are also some major decisions to be made which could be described as interpretative. If the census entries on occupations are to be of use to the historian, they will need to be grouped or classified. In practice this will entail the addition of a field or fields in which each occupation is assigned to a category according to a scheme devised by the designer of the database. The designers of the New York immigrants database added two fields: one for classification by social status (see Figure 6.2b), the other for function in economy (see Figure 6.2c).

Social Status
NO PAID OCCUPATION
PROFESSIONAL-HWC
PROPRIETOR-LWC
SKILLED
UNCLASSIFIABLE
UNSKILLED, SPECIFIED
UNSKILLED,LABOR/DAY LABOR
WORKS AT-IN
WORKSITE

Figure 6.2b 'Eastside': classification of occupations by social status

Function in Economy
ARTS-MUSIC-ENTERTAINMENT
CLERKS
COMMERCE
CONSTRUCTION
DOMESTICS
EDUCATION
EXTRACTIVE
MFG. FOOD
MFG. HOME FURNISHINGS
MFG. JEWELRY
MFG. OTHER TRADES
MFG. PRINT & ART
MFG.BUILDING MTL
MFG.CLOTHING
MFG.MECHANIC
MFG.METAL
MFG.TRANSPORT TRADES
NO PAID OCCUPATION
NON-PROF SERVICE
PEDDLERS
PROFESSIONS
PUBLIC SERVICE
TRANSPORT
UNCLASSIFIABLE
UNSKILLED-SEMISKILLED

Figure 6.2c 'Eastside': classification of occupations by function
in economy

Note that it is essential that this interpretative task is undertaken in
addition to, rather than instead of, the recording of the information in
the source. A scheme which replaced the source material with the
interpretation of the researcher would lose the original data and make
subsequent reinterpretation impossible. Historians have learnt – from
the experience of the early historical databases of the 1970s and 1980s
– the value of retaining source material and of separating it from
information which is interpretative.

Occupational classification is a much-researched subject. Historians working on such data have constructed a variety of types of schemes, which can be found in the extensive literature presented thus far.[7] Such schemes can be complex, and the very fact that this is a developing area suggests that it is important to allow for the possibility of further modifications – or even of new classification systems. Where such changes are possible, however, the strategy outlined above – of adding a field or fields to the table containing the source data – will soon prove cumbersome. Any further classification exercise, or indeed any modification of an existing scheme, will entail going right through the whole database. A considerable amount of repetition will be involved, not to mention the possibilities of introducing errors.

The need for an efficient system of organising interpretative information is one of the main reasons why historians turn to a more complex, but also more powerful, form of database system.

The relational database The majority of substantial databases consist not of single tables but of a series of tables which interlock in a precisely defined way. This allows for each component of data to be held in a specific place, eliminating data redundancy and streamlining the use of the database.

In the example of the New York immigrants, the argument for splitting the information over two tables is ultimately that the classification system is a system of classifying occupations rather than the individuals who have those occupations. It makes little sense to have to describe each butcher in the database as 'mfg.food' when it is the occupation butcher that we have decided should be described as having that function in the economy. A 'dictionary' or reference table would be a much more efficient way of doing this. It would also allow changes to be made to the classification system without necessitating any change in the transcribed source. The solution is to have two tables, one for the original data and one for the interpretative information, as follows:

Person	Occupation
Enumeration district	Occupation
Individual ID	Social status
Street	Function in economy
House no	
Household no	
Family no	
Family name	
First name	
...	
Occupation	
...	

Individual ID	Family Name	First Name	Occupation
131	ADELMAN	ABRAM	SHOEMAKER
133	ADELMAN	MAX	STUDENT
643	AGGID	SAMUEL	SALOONKEEPER
693	ALKASS	ABRAM	STOREKEEPER
698	ALKASS	DAVID	STUDENT
699	ALKASS	MOSES	STUDENT
700	ALKASS	BENNIE	STUDENT

Occupation	Social Status	Function in Economy
SALOONKEEPER	PROPRIETOR-LWC	COMMERCE
SHOEMAKER	SKILLED	MFG.CLOTHING
STOREKEEPER	PROPRIETOR-LWC	COMMERCE
STUDENT	NO PAID OCCUPATION	NO PAID OCCUPATION

Figure 6.2d A one-to-many relationship illustrated from the 'Eastside' database

The critical part of this design is that there must be an unambiguous way of linking these two tables. In the 'occupations' table, each occupation is listed once and only once, and an interpretative equivalent is then assigned to it. In the 'persons' table, of course, these occupations can and do occur frequently. 'Occupations' is effectively a 'look-up table' or dictionary which can be referred to from the main table. Because each entry in the 'occupation' column of the 'person' table has a corresponding value in one, and only one, row in the 'occupations' table, it is possible to retrieve the occupational code assigned for each person in the database (see Figure 6.2d).

What has just been described is the fundamental principle of relational databasing. Relational databases consist of a series of flat-file tables, linked together by a series of relationships of the kind just illustrated. The type of link described is known as a 'one-to-many relationship'. In the example above, the 'occupations' table is at the 'one' end of the relationship and the 'persons' table at the 'many' end, because one entry in 'occupations' can have many corresponding entries in 'persons'. The relationship is often illustrated graphically, as below:

The <> symbols are the conventional notation for one-to-many relationships.

The mechanism which links the two tables is clearly defined. There has to be a field which appears in both tables.[8] However, this field has a different function in the two tables. In 'occupations' – the 'one' or 'parent' table – the occupation field is defined as a primary key. For each record in 'occupations' there must be an entry in this field, and it must be unique – that is, different from all the other entries. In 'persons' – the 'many' or 'subordinate' table – the occupation field is defined as a *foreign key*. This is because it is, effectively, 'borrowed' from another table where it is the primary key. The values that appear in occupation in the 'occupation' table can all occur in occupation in the 'person' table, but for the relationship to be truly one-to-many, no other values may occur (otherwise it would no longer be possible to link all the records in the two tables). These are the basic rules, or conditions, which have to be met in order for such a link to be made properly.

Relational database design: a worked example The need for 'look-up tables' or reference tables in which interpretative information is held separately from the source is one possible reason for going beyond the single flat-file database and down the more complex route of multiple tables linked relationally. The source data may point to this route. A register of marriages would at first sight seem a straightforward candidate for a flat-file solution. Each entry gives details of the bride, the groom, and the place and date of marriage. A list of fields could be drawn up as follows:

> Husband's first name(s)
> Husband's surname
> Husband's date of birth
> Husband's place of birth
> Husband's occupation
> Wife's first name(s)
> Wife's maiden name
> Wife's date of birth
> Wife's place of birth
> Date of marriage
> Place of marriage

A researcher wishing to investigate nuptiality over a short period will be content with this. However, over time, the single file will lead to shortcomings. People can remarry, either after the death of a partner or – recently a much more frequent cause – after divorce. In a flat-file system there will be no easy way of identifying those who remarry. It would therefore make more sense to break the data into two tables, one for men and one for women, and then to attempt to make the appropriate connections. The two tables would then look like the ones set out below.

Husband	Wife
Reference number (H_UID)	Reference number (W_UID)
First name(s)	First name(s)
Surname	Maiden name
Date of birth	Date of birth
Place of birth	Place of birth
Date of marriage	Date of marriage
Place of marriage	Place of marriage
Wife (W_UID)	Husband (H_UID)

Note that we have introduced a system of cross-referencing. Each person has a reference number, called a 'UID' (for Unique IDentifier). This makes it possible for a 'husband' record to refer to a specific 'wife' record without repeating all the information it contains.

This has still not solved the problem of what to do about second or further marriages. We cannot put more than one entry in a field, and if we create a separate field for, say, 'Wife 2' we will quickly run into serious problems in managing the data, while the problem of further marriages would necessitate yet further, for the most part empty, fields. Expressed visually, the problem is as follows. A single marriage is a one-to-one relationship – husband to wife.

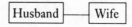

However, a database recording the marriages of men and women over time has to take account of the fact that both men and women can have many spouses during the course of their lives as expressed graphically below.

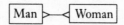

This is not a relationship which a database system can handle using the rules described above, as there is no way in which the system can know which man to connect to which woman. It is therefore necessary to break this 'many-to-many' relationship down into a series of one-to-many relationships, by finding a connector. The solution is to have a third table containing the information about the marriage itself, as shown below.

In this model, each person can have several marriages, but each marriage links information from the two tables while also including the information that makes it unique. The tables now appear as in the set of tables below

Man

Reference number (H_UID)

First name(s)
Surname
Date of birth
Place of birth

Woman

Reference number (W_UID)

First name(s)
Maiden name
Date of birth
Place of birth

Marriage

Date of marriage
Place of marriage
Wife's reference number (W_UID)
Husband's reference number (H_UID)

Note that the distribution of the information is now also more efficient and less repetitive (the two 'date of marriage' fields have been replaced by a single one). The links between the tables are made by the mechanism of primary and foreign keys, as introduced above. In the example above the underlined fields are defined as primary, while those in italics are foreign.

One final point. It may be objected that this looks like involving a lot of inconvenient data entry. The information in each record in the original source will have to be divided across three tables. While this may not look like an obvious way to proceed, it should be stressed that there are ways of designing data entry forms which largely obviate this problem. Good database packages now available include formidable tools for making data entry and retrieval much more user-friendly than the data model suggests.

The above example is a simple, and simplified, instance of a source which is most appropriately represented by a group of interconnected tables. Many real instances can entail more complex structures. For example, marriage registers often contain information about the occupation of the husband (at least). Representing this for analytical purposes might mean combining the linking of different tables of source information, as above, with interpretative information as in the previous example. Complex databases can consist of a whole web of tables linked through one-to-many relationships.

Methods of relational database design   The design of such databases is a complex task, and just looking at data without a methodical approach can lead to bewilderment and confusion. There are two main systematic approaches in the database world, both of which have much to offer the historian. The first of these, Entity Relationship Modelling (ERM), is a formal version of the procedure that was adopted in the worked example above: taking an overview of all the information to be included in the database, grouping it provisionally in clusters which could become separate tables ('entities' is a technical name for tables), identifying the relationships between these tables, breaking down any 'many-to-many' relationships into a sequence of 'one-to-many' relationships, and then filling in the detail of fields. The most common alternative procedure, Relational Data Analysis (RDA), takes a 'bottom-up' approach, starting with the identification of all possible fields, and then distributing them across a set of interrelated tables according to a series of rules designed to eliminate repetition and inappropriate dependencies. Both of these methods have evolved for professional databasing. Neither is trivial, and many historians find them daunting. Happily some very accessible historical literature now exists which takes the reader through both processes using historical examples.[9] For researchers proposing to use anything beyond the simplest of flat-file databases, investigation of these techniques is recommended. But some qualifications also need to be made. The question remains of how much historians should listen to computing experts, and how suitable sophisticated databasing techniques are for historical information.

Relational database management systems (RDBMS) evolved as methods for administrative and commercial purposes. Many of their features are geared to multiple use and to constant change; efficient RDBMS allow many people to access their different components in different ways, and make regular and instant updating possible. Much of the complexity of these systems ensues from this flexibility. For historians, most of these features are an irrelevance and a distraction. On the other hand, historical data has many features which RDBMS are not designed for or particularly well equipped to deal with. Many historical sources have complex structures, entailing irregular string lengths and large amounts of text which cannot be easily compressed to suit tabular representation. Historical data is often incomplete. This can lead to substantial wastelands of largely empty fields, but it can also mean tantalising inconsistencies which weaken the potential for analysis (for example, an entry in a 'date' field in an RDBMS has to have a complete date – '1956' is not acceptable). Historical data can contain a great variety of measurement schemes, and differing concepts of measurement and accuracy; even the incorporation of the good old pounds, shillings and pence involves quite a bit of adaptation of current commercial database systems. Finally, much historical data is what data specialists call 'fuzzy', and this places special demands on computer systems.[10]

These points are not meant as an argument against using RDBMS: they are still, by far and away, the most effective way of processing structurable information. It is, however, wise to inject a note of caution about how slavishly historians need to follow the intricacies of database theory in order to achieve the results they want. Compromise is usually a necessary part of the outcome, and common sense as important an ingredient as all the theory. Perhaps the most important elements of database theory that the historian can profitably absorb are some general points offered below.

FITNESS FOR PURPOSE There is no 'right' design for every database project. The more specific the questions at issue for the researcher, the clearer it will be which components of the original data will be worth including and the uses to which they are likely to have to be put. Conversely, research which begins as a comparatively open-ended exploration of sources (albeit with hypotheses in mind) will benefit from close adherence to those sources. What has been excluded or glossed over at the beginning is rarely returned to.

One should also bear in mind the appropriateness of one's data model to the size of the database and the uses to which it will be put. A lot of historical data can be most fully represented by a model of some complexity. But that may be more trouble than it is worth; particularly with a small sample, it can take longer to perfect and work with a complex model than would be the case with a simpler design in which – dare one say it – some corners have been cut.

A common experience among historians designing databases is that it is a three-stage process. First, a relatively simple design is established. As it is tested out with the entering of small amounts of actual data, the model is amended and goes from simplicity to considerable complexity. At some point it is realised that some of these elaborations have brought their own complications and are more trouble than they are worth, and further rationalisation and simplification take place. The cycle can be frustrating, but it is actually a natural one which is necessary in most cases; if problems have been confronted and overcome, the end product will be an improvement.

CLARITY AND UNAMBIGUITY OF STRUCTURE Whatever design is evolved, it is important to ensure that the design of the database is such that it is absolutely clear which components of information are to be recorded in which field and how. This is harder than it sounds, but inconsistency in data entry can lead to serious problems of retrieval and analysis.

NO REDUNDANCY OF INFORMATION Perhaps the main reason why the relational database should be explored even by those who are suspicious of it is that it is the only way to avoid data redundancy. The duplication of information leads very quickly to serious difficulties.

BUILT-IN VALIDATION Researchers who enter their own data may find it difficult to imagine just how easy it is to make errors during the process. An element of information typed in the wrong column, or an inaccurate date or numerical value, can easily be overlooked. Giving the software criteria for the acceptance or rejection of what is being input is one way of reducing the danger; another is to perform checks such as listing the contents of fields in alphabetical order to help to identify typographical errors.

GOOD DOCUMENTATION A much neglected aspect is the importance of recording the details of how the database has been designed and why. It is surprising how quickly one can forget the details of decisions one has made and the criteria on which those decisions were based. Good documentation is also an essential part of the presentation of the work, and is indispensable if the database is subsequently to be deposited in a data archive for use by other scholars (which many grant-awarding bodies make a condition of funding).[11]

This last point introduces an area in which historians can undoubtedly learn from the experience of other computer users – project management. The use of computers in historical research introduces a new dimension to the work, work which already requires training, the acquisition of knowledge and skills, planning, design, execution, reporting and writing up. The database work thus becomes a subset, and usually an important subset, of the research project as a whole. However, its interrelationship with the more conventional part of the work (reading, writing and so on) is not obvious. Without a firm timetable, the database side of the research can easily spin out of control – yet historians coming fresh to databasing will be poorly equipped to make realistic assessments of the time this aspect of the project will take. If any advice can be given (other than the depressing observation that no first database project has ever over-estimated the time involved), it must be that one should do one's best to evaluate the number of stages involved in the research, and make systematic estimates of the time required for each. For data entry, such estimates should be based on a period of sample work rather than arbitrary guesses.[12]

Beyond the relational database

So far we have concentrated on databasing, the most frequent computing technique used by historians. It is far from the only one, however. A number of other possibilities are worth exploring.

Spreadsheets and statistical packages This book has not emphasised quantitative approaches to historical research, and consequently neither has this chapter. For historians whose main concerns are essentially quantitative, and whose data is highly structured in a simple way, spreadsheets – such as Microsoft Excel – may offer a more powerful solution than databases. The two types of software actually have much in common, and each now includes at least some of the features of the other. Complex statistical operations are undoubtedly easier to carry out in spreadsheets (which are also good at graphing data), while complex retrieval and complex data structures are more appropriately handled in databases.

Like database systems, spreadsheets are also designed with commerce and administration in mind, and are geared to the possibilities of instant and frequent updating. Quantitative historians eventually often reach the point where statistical packages are necessary. Some of these are written specifically with the needs of the social sciences in mind (like SPSS, Statistical Package for the Social Sciences). There is no shortage of specialist literature in this area.[13]

Flexible data files: the textbase Whether or not the researcher has a need for the analysis and retrieval of structured data of the kind that has been described above, he or she will almost certainly have substantial quantities of material – both primary and secondary – which require at the very least filing and most probably also effective mechanisms for retrieval. Typing such notes up in word processed form is one obvious solution, which an increasing number of scholars are adopting. (The growing number of laptop computers used in libraries and archives is just one indicator of this.) Software exists, however, to help take care of this in a more systematic and powerful manner. Packages such as Ask-Sam and Idealist cater much more flexibly for those who have substantial amounts of textual material which they wish to hold, retrieve and, to an

10.
WID345   345/28   Minutes of Court
27th Mar 1821
Drink   Customer Relations   Seamen   Discipline
pp.56-7   The mate of the ship Aime reported leaving the docks drunk.
To be reported to the ship's owners.

2.
WIDCHAR298   W.I.D.C.O. Annual Accounts for Parliament, 1799-1831
1st Feb 1806
Charity Gratuities
Donations and Gratuities for year ending above DATE:

£	s	d	
5	5		Poplar Charity School
5	5		Lime Street School
36	19		Aldgate Ward
20			London Hospital
21			Widow of Lieut. Lock
15	15		Messengers & Watermen

Figure 6.3 Two records from the Port of London database
(using Idealist)

extent, organise and cross-refer. I describe these as 'textbases' because their emphasis is on the holding of information essentially in textual form.

Figure 6.3 shows examples of records from a textbase held in Idealist.[14] This package allows records with different structures to be held together in the same file. Transcriptions of sources, notes from secondary literature, and bibliographical references can all be held together (as they might be in conventional paper filing systems). The advantage of this is that retrieval of information can be performed on individual fields common to different records, or across all fields. As the whole text is indexed as it is entered, retrieval is very fast. Dictionaries of synonyms can also be built up, allowing conceptual indexing, or even the construction of multilingual dictionaries. Above all, the system is easy to grasp and get to work with.

There are limitations on what can be done with the data beyond retrieval; Idealist is not intended as an analytical package. However, some major research projects have found it to be a very flexible tool, and it is worth investigating as a natural step beyond word processing.

Textual analysis An area of computing that is comparatively under-explored by historians is the electronic analysis of text. The development of these techniques (for literary and linguistic research) predates the growth of historical computing and databasing in particular, and has much to offer the historian. Texts held in electronic form can be studied for their vocabulary, their linguistic and stylistic characteristics, and indirectly for content[15] in quantitative ways. Historians have found such techniques useful for two kinds of analysis. Authorship attribution, or determining through stylometric analysis whether someone known to have written a work or group of works can be deemed to have written another work, has had its enthusiasts among historians; content analysis, which studies the vocabulary and rhetoric of discourse with its interconnections and associations, has been useful in exploring concepts in French revolutionary literature, for example, as well as the tactics of Austrian neo-Nazi propaganda.[16]

Neither of these techniques is easy to learn or to implement. Substantial amounts of text are needed for such work, together with equally substantial amounts of control sample (to ensure that the findings of the analysis are actually significant). The software used is by and large either not commercial or outdated.[17] The area is none the less worth investigating, and, with the increasing availability of key literary and historical texts in electronic form and the development of more powerful access systems, the potential for the future is considerable.

Images, 'multimedia' and presentation It was said above that databases hold information in structured form. It was not, however, stated that that information had to be textual or numerical. If it can be either of these, it could equally be visual or audio, taking the form of images, sound recordings or video. Relational database management systems are including ways in which databases can incorporate links to data of these kinds, and the industry is moving in the direction of 'object-oriented' databasing.

For the historian, the implications of this are far-reaching. The structured retrieval and analysis we have been talking about can embrace all forms of historical evidence. Links between the various items of data can be made systematically (through searches and database-type queries) or directly and 'hypertextually'. The most common way in which historians are using these possibilities is in creating presentational, teaching and 'edutainment' material. Less visible but as important is the impact that the world of multimedia is having on the creation of archives of historical material.[18] Though neither of these is obviously relevant to research at the doctoral level and scale, researchers with substantial amounts of visual material could do worse than investigate the state of the technology and the possibilities for historians.[19]

Mapping A special case of the above is the need to link data held in a database with cartographical representations. We regularly see this on television screens (and overdose on them on election nights), but historical mapping is much more complex: first because many aspects of maps change over time, and secondly because the investment required to get as far as an initial base map is considerable. The relationship of historical geography to the world of Geographical Information Systems (GIS) is complex. Various projects are under way, foremost among them the Great Britain Historical GIS Programme,[20] with its map of Registrar General's Registration Districts which can be used in conjunction with Census Reports, and which is being enlarged to include parish boundaries.[21] Unfortunately, as yet, these techniques have not been made easy for historians to learn and implement. For the researcher who would like to include just the occasional map, it is disappointing to have to advise that – for the time being – this may be more trouble than it is worth. However, if there is a more substantial geographical side to the proposed research, it is worth seriously exploring these techniques with historical geographers.[22]

Integrated software and source-oriented data processing One other approach should be mentioned both for the sake of completeness and for the light it sheds on current thinking about historical data and computers. Since 1978 Manfred Thaller has been developing discipline-specific software. The premise was and is that historical sources present specific problems for which historians have a right to expect solutions in an integrated form. The result was κλειω (or kleio), a multi-purpose system which has gone through various forms from a mainframe version (1984) through to PC DOS (1988; first English-language version 1993), Unix, and now Windows 95.

Κλειω works on a data model which is fundamentally different from that of relational databasing. The relationships between different data elements are much more flexible, and are essentially defined by the user in accordance with a minimum of rules. The object is to allow the data to be held in a form which mirrors the implicit or explicit structures of the source as far as possible, and then gets the program to do the work, as it were, of interpretation and analysis. Respect for the historical peculiarities of the data and of its structures are accompanied by a clear separation of source data from interpretative data. Alongside the source is an 'environment' through which the data can be interpreted. The basis of this is provided by the system (which, for example, recognises seven different historical systems of chronology) and can be built on by the user, who adds the appropriate information (for example, about currency, geography, orthography). Features in κλειω include a large proportion of those likely to be required by historians: catalogues and classification systems, tools for textual analysis, mapping, record linkage algorithms, and output for statistical analysis or publication. The feature that is currently attracting most interest is the recent extension of these principles into the world of image processing. Κλειω provides a high-quality tool not only for the storing and retrieving of images but also for their manipulation and enhancement, and for the structured processing of images as integrated parts of a database. Images – which can of course be manuscripts – can be bound, section by section, with a textual counterpart in the database, and can thus be searched for content.

The influence of κλειω has been considerably wider than the extent of its actual use; many of the underlying principles, particularly regarding source-oriented data processing, have been adopted by the historical computing community. The software is another matter. For all its features and potential, κλειω has not proved easy to learn, and many have preferred to stick to conventional solutions. Since it is most effective at the representation of source material, it is perhaps not surprising that it has attracted pre-modern historians more than twentieth-century specialists. However, a number of modern projects have also been undertaken, and the image processing version of the software has been adopted by a number of major projects for the creation of electronic archives. The largest of these is the computerisation of the records of the extermination and concentration camps at Auschwitz, being undertaken by the Auschwitz Museum in conjunction with the Max-Planck-Institut für Geschichte at Göttingen.[23] Indeed, κλειω's principal function in the future may well be as software for electronic editions and archives, including multimedia ones.[24]

Specialised techniques

The previous sections have attempted to give an indication of the range of types of computing solutions which historians have found useful. In the course of their work with these, historians have had to confront problems and use specialised techniques which have either developed within the profession, or been borrowed from the other disciplines or from the pool of techniques common to several of the social sciences. Some of these are highly sophisticated. The techniques of historical demography, family reconstitution, and, more recently, event history analysis are areas in which rich traditions and extensive literature exist.[25] The same is true for the use of computers in historical psephology,[26] prosopography[27] and oral history.[28] They are beyond the scope of this chapter, not least because budding specialists will already know how to find their way in these areas. Two aspects of historical computing, however, are found across a range of research areas and merit brief treatment.

The classification, and thus the 'coding', of historical information is an indispensable part of the process of analysis, as illustrated above. The coding and classification of occupations has had a particularly prominent place in the work of historians. Computerisation has elevated this to prominence. Much has been written on systems of occupational coding in modern British history, and this is now being complemented by useful comparative work.[29] Part of a current project is the development of a systematic occupational coding scheme for nineteenth-century census enumerators' books.[30] An awareness of the variety of existing schemes and the problems associated with their creation and use is, at the very least, useful for all potential projects in social and economic history.

Another widespread problem for which computers are increasingly being used is the linkage of records concerning individual people. The moment research extends over more than one source, the identification of individuals in one source with those in another is often a critical part of the exercise. Is the John Smith who appears as a 'rope maker' in a census list the same as the J. Smith who appears as 'textile worker', living at the same address, in a document from a decade later? Or at least what is the probability that they are identical? The criteria by which such matches could be made are complex. Schemes for considering each possible factor and allocating a weighting of probability have been evolved, and these lend themselves readily to systematic treatment and thus computerisation. One feature of such work that has proved useful is an algorithm for the identification of variants in spelling. Soundex, a system created in the 1920s for US social security administration, converts names into numerical codes according to a set of mainly phonetic criteria.

Nominal record linkage is a complex technique. To date, British research has concentrated on 'list unique' linkage, that is the establishment of links between lists in which individuals can only appear once. They have proved particularly important for social and political history. Multiple linkage, and linkage between different but related people, are yet more ambitious, but are also capable of computerised, or at least computer-assisted, solutions.[31]

Points of departure

Where to start? This chapter has mentioned some specific software, but has deliberately avoided detailed discussion of the relative merits of different systems and different specifications of computer. This is in part because the technology is constantly and rapidly changing, and any specific advice could well be out of date by the time it went to press.

There is, however, a stronger reason. The best single piece of advice has to be that researchers should seek the advice of their local institutions before all else. All universities have computing services which are geared to support. The likelihood is that they will hold suitable software solutions to the majority of computing problems at the early stages; they will probably also run introductory courses in the software and have the expertise to help with it. Following this route opens the door to help and exchange of experiences with colleagues, not to mention frequent and often substantial educational discounts in the purchase of software.

Where local expertise and infrastructures cannot help, the historical profession has its own institutions. The Association for History and Computing has a lively membership, annual conferences, workshops and training sessions, and a journal. Although it does not act as an answering service, it provides a forum for the interchange of ideas and information. The Computers in Teaching Initiative Centre for History, Archaeology and Art History (CTICH) has a responsibility for training in the use of computers in the teaching of history. Although this brief does not correspond particularly closely to the interests of researchers, there is considerable overlap, as is demonstrated by CTICH's publications which include a software guide and a newsletter, *Craft*.[32] The recently created Arts and Humanities Data Service (AHDS) co-ordinates information and publishes guidance about a large variety of humanities computing matters. The History Data Archive at the University of Essex, formerly part of the ESRC data archive, is now part of the AHDS, and has special responsibility for holding historical data sets deposited with it.[33] Finally, the Institute of Historical Research includes historical computing training courses in its portfolio of short courses and workshops.[34]

Further reading

The literature on historical computing is now immense, and is directed at both beginners and more specialist levels. Pointers to specific topics have been given in the notes to this chapter. The most comprehensive general introductions are Charles Harvey and Jon Press, *Databases in Historical Research* (London: Macmillan, 1996), and Daniel I. Greenstein, *A Historian's Guide to Computing* (Oxford: Oxford University Press, 1994). Evan Mawdsley and Thomas Munck, *Computing for Historians. An Introductory Guide* (Manchester: Manchester University Press, 1993) is a slightly older guide. A good practical coursebook is M. J. Lewis and Roger Lloyd-Jones, *Using Computers in History. A Practical Guide* (London: Routledge, 1996).

For an admirable review of the current state of historical computing, see Andrew Prescott, 'History and computing', in Mullings et al., (1996 [see note 18]), pp. 231–62. See also R. J. Morris, 'History and computing', in *Encyclopaedia of Computer Science and Technology*, vol. 31, supplement 16, pp. 293–308, and 'Computers and the subversion of British history', *Journal of British Studies* 34 (1995): 503–28.

History and Computing, the journal of the Association for History and Computing, is taken by many university libraries and provides an up-to-date picture of the main issues and techniques in which computing historians are engaged.[35]

Bibliography on historical computing currently takes a number of forms. The excellent thematic bibliographies in Harvey and Press and in Greenstein (see above) are good starting points. A full retrospective bibliography containing around six thousand entries is the *International Historical Computing Bibliography*, edited by Peter Denley with Debra Birch and Raivo Ruusalepp (and published by the Centre for Historical Computing at Queen Mary and Westfield College for the Association for History and Computing). This is published on disk, using the software package Idealist (described above), and therefore searchable by title contents. An older version is searchable on the Internet, http:// grid.let.rug.nl/ahc/biblio2.html. An annual descriptive bibliography is also published for the Association for History and Computing by the Laboratoire d'Etudes et de Recherches sur l'Information et la Documentation, Université de Liège: *History and Computing 1993* and *History and Computing 1994*, Halbgraue Reihe zur historischen Fachinformatik, A24; St Katharinen: Scripta Mercaturae Verlag, 1994 and 1995 respectively.

CHAPTER 7

Managing and funding research

Peter Beck and John Davis

'There are 100 vice chancellors out there playing fantasy football', even outstripping football managers in 'going around with bulging cheque books and attractive sweeteners attempting to spot and buy "talent"'.[1] These observations, reflecting the contemporary vogue for viewing research in higher education by reference to footballing analogies, were prompted by frenzied competition between colleges for the 'academic stars' deemed likely to score well, and hence ensure a good result, in the forthcoming 'big match' – that is, the 1996 Research Assessment Exercise (RAE). Universities, seeking variously to achieve higher ratings for specific research assessment units (RAEUs), like history, or to retain top ratings secured in the 1992 RAE, recruited researchers with strong lists of recent publications to posts often carrying minimal, if any, teaching responsibilities.

RAEs have been presented by the Higher Education Funding Councils (HEFCs) as the most rational way to allocate research funding, especially as the mechanism, like the ongoing Teaching Quality Assessment (TQA) exercise and Higher Education Quality Council (HEQC) Audits, satisfies governmental pressures for public accountability and transparency. Thus, quality ratings on a seven-point scale (i.e. 1, 2, 3b, 3a, 4, 5, 5*), in conjunction with numbers of active researchers by RAEU, determine the amounts distributed to colleges during the next funding cycle. Research, albeit needing still to be balanced against teaching, has received greater priority within colleges, even if the results of the TQA – history was included in an early round held during 1993–4 – suggest a significant correlation between the quality of research and teaching.[2] Inevitably, RAEs, reinforced by their significant funding, staffing, postgraduate recruitment, public relations, teaching quality and other implications, have given research a stronger profile at both college and national levels.[3]

For history, the 1992 and 1996 RAEs, like their predecessors in the 1980s, primarily involved academic staff, whose quality of research, in conjunction with history's research income and environment, represented a prime determinant in the rating awarded to any college's RAEU. The research of each historian as embodied in up to four outcomes published between January 1990 and March 1996, was assessed against perceived standards of national and international excellence. However, history postgraduates are not unaffected by RAEs, TQAs and institutional audits. Numbers of higher degree students, supervisions and doctoral completions – alongside evaluations of monitoring and support structures for postgraduate students – were also taken into account.[4] Inevitably, prospective postgraduate applicants are encouraged by recruitment literature and advertising to interpret RAE and TQA ratings and HEQC institutional audit reports as a reflection of the quality of individual history departments/sections, while extra funding consequent upon an improved RAE performance may yield job opportunities for promising history postgraduates who have just completed or are near completion of higher degrees.

Within all colleges, RAEs have fostered increased attention on research management and monitoring as a means of raising both the level and quality of research, and the number of active researchers in history and other RAEUs; thus, the aim is to ensure not only a strong showing by leading researchers but also improved performances by less experienced staff. The 1992 RAE, demonstrating that 'ratings were in part a function of the quality of the college's paperwork', placed a premium on good documentation: 'Colleges claiming to perform quality research should ensure that research is managed and monitored in an appropriate manner capable of ensuring the production of a comprehensive and accurate return.'[5] It is of little use aspiring or claiming to conduct research worthy of a high rating, while operating a second-rate managerial and support structure. Returns to the history panel for the 1992 RAE indicated that most colleges were at an early stage of the management process; indeed, several seemed to have given little or no thought to the topic.[6] Certainly, the 1996 RAE, trebling the number of pages allowed to cover such matters, placed greater emphasis upon this element. Even so, research should not be over-managed. This is vital in history, where research often assumes a more individual character, otherwise scarce resources, including time and energy, will be diverted towards administration rather than the advancement of historical knowledge.

Obviously the situation varies between colleges, given the manner in which any history RAEU operates within the broader institutional framework and the fact that HEFC revenues deriving from RAE ratings accrue to universities and colleges of higher education in general rather than directly to specific RAEUs within them. As a rule, management and monitoring procedures have been refined on a continual basis, frequently in line with plans outlined for the RAEs. This has been demonstrated by efforts to build upon current achievements and strengths, foster new research directions on a selective basis, maximise staff research aspirations within the agreed framework, and enhance the history RAEU's visibility at the college, national and international levels. Inevitably, forthcoming RAEs have figured prominently in research planning; thus, the prime objective has been to ensure that history RAEUs are well managed with a view to the optimisation of their respective performances in the next RAE. In addition, any management strategy must be flexible in terms of possessing a capacity to respond to alternative reporting arrangements and requirements resulting from, say, changes in RAE publication categories or modes of interpreting rating criteria, even if there are signs that the HEFCs are seeking to provide greater continuity between RAEs (for example, through stability in panel membership).

Unsurprisingly, research strategies based on clear and coherent plans have been implemented in various ways. These include the identification of the history RAEU's priorities, given the need for a targeted strategy (for example funding, timetable relief, study leave) to enhance the quality of staff outcomes (for example monographs rather than articles, publication of articles in more prestigious refereed journals), encourage long-term projects, and support new research directions; the placement of greater emphasis upon research records and/or potential in the appointment of new staff; the encouragement of staff to seek external funding and the supporting of them during the process; the overview of support structures and facilities for both experienced and inex-perienced researchers and postgraduate students; the linkage of research in a meaningful, informed manner to postgraduate education as well as to staff appraisal and staff development procedures; and the use of databases and annual critical review mechanisms to monitor progress.

Inevitably, individual universities, motivated by specific agendas, have sought to use the RAE for their own purposes, such as to exploit the public relations value of high ratings, secure 'new' money, or interpret RAEs as a way of forcing uncompleted or delayed staff projects to a published outcome. One group of old universities, dependent on research's contribution to some 30 to 50 per cent of total funding, has pressed for resources to be concentrated on a few highly rated 'research' universities, leaving less favoured colleges to perform a predominantly 'teaching' role. By contrast, 'new' universities, welcoming the 1992 RAE for bringing in 'new' money alongside a recognition of a hitherto under-estimated activity, favour an alternative strategy using developmental funding to improve research's contribution to their budgets (at present, it is frequently as low as around 1 to 7 per cent), even if – to employ another sporting analogy – they realize the impossibility of achieving a level playing field for research purposes during the foreseeable future.[7]

Although they have merits, RAEs have frequently occasioned more negative reactions, which have raised question marks about their future. Two leading historians, Rees Davies, president of the Royal Historical Society, and Sir Keith Thomas, president of the British Academy, have highlighted unwelcome 'unforeseen' side effects, like the football-type transfer market and the fact that researchers' former institutions, having provided the supportive environment responsible in part for their highly esteemed status, receive nothing by way of compensation for the loss of a major, perhaps irreplaceable, part of their team. Both Davies and Thomas complained also about the apparent stress on publication as an end in itself, and the resulting reluctance of historians to undertake praiseworthy scholarly work not taken into account by the RAE.[8]

Maurice Kogan, resenting external intervention in academia, has criticised the RAE's efforts to assess the unassessable, but perhaps for historians, like other academics, the fundamental question is – to quote Rees Davies – 'how do we measure quality?'[9] Will history panel members know quality when they see it, especially as the seminal quality of work often takes time to become apparent? Other problem areas include:

- Do RAEs encourage short-term research horizons at the expense of larger historical projects produced over the longer term?[10]
- 'What is the evidence that, consequently, more worthwhile research is being done?'[11] This question, articulated by one historian, Michael Bush, reflected fears that the resulting quest for published outcomes prompted 'more and more on less and less' and merely created – to quote Warwick University's Lincoln Allison – 'a mountain of wasted words'.[12]
- Is history ill served by being judged as part of an exercise imbued with the paradigms and assumptions of the natural sciences?[13] Is it possible to apply RAE criteria, particularly those relating to standards of national and international excellence, in a fair and consistent manner across the range of RAEUs? For example, the history panel for the 1992 RAE was not only criticised for being harsher than its counterparts but also experienced difficulty in defining international excellence.[14]

- Can any one history panel, even one drawing on *ad hoc* expert external advice, assess adequately the wide range of research outcomes placed before it?
- Does the exercise encourage the concentration of resources on established names at the expense of younger researchers?
- Has the pressure to publish resulted in the isolation of historical researchers at certain colleges, unfortunate divisions between teachers and researchers, and the neglect of undergraduate and even postgraduate teaching?[15]
- Has the RAE caused excessive attention and resources to be devoted to managing, rather than conducting, research? Or does the resulting management structure merely provide a useful role for – to quote Michael Bush again – 'clapped out scholars'?[16]

Frequently, complaints about the system's iniquities – in one case (not history) it even led to legal action – were prompted by lower than expected ratings awarded by the 1992 RAE to specific college RAEUs, as evidenced by the controversy surrounding Oxford University's 4 rating for history.[17] No doubt the 1996 RAE's results will evoke similar resentment. There are, of course, other areas of debate, which have led some to wonder whether the 1996 RAE will ever be repeated. After all, RAEs are basically funding not research exercises, and much depends on whether the HEFCs, pressurised by the British Academy and other bodies, discover a more effective and acceptable mode of allocating research funding.

British research councils, like the Engineering and Physical Sciences Research Council, Natural Environment Research Council, and the Economic and Social Research Council (ESRC), represent the prime alternative source of research funding to HEFCs. Recently, the British government's 1993 White Paper entitled *Realising our Potential: a Strategy for Science, Engineering and Technology* led the research councils to attach greater recognition to 'the importance of research undertaken to meet the needs of users and to support wealth creation'.[18] The current mission of the ESRC, a research council of particular relevance to staff and postgraduates working on economic and social history as well as the history of education and technology, is:

a) to promote and support, by any means, high-quality basic, strategic and applied research and related post-graduate training in the Social Sciences;

b) to advance knowledge and provide trained social scientists which meet the needs of users and beneficiaries, thereby contributing to the economic competitiveness of the United Kingdom, the effectiveness of public services and policy, and the quality of life;

c) to provide advice on, and disseminate knowledge and promote public understanding of, the Social Sciences.[19]

Perhaps business historians writing a company history would have no problem with these criteria, but most historical researchers fit uneasily in the utilitarian framework fostered by the *Realising our Potential* initiative. Historians, though confident about articulating the merits of their research outcomes and history's contribution to the quality of British life, prove uneasy about tailoring their work to specific demands emanating from users in commerce, industry and government.

In practice, most historical research, particularly by postgraduates, is funded according to alternative criteria defined by the Humanities Research Board of the British Academy (HRB). During the reappraisal of research councils of the early 1990s, the British government resisted strong pressures for the creation of a Humanities Research Council. This is not the place to go into the details of that debate, except to say that during 1993–4 the negative outcome led the British Academy – which had hitherto held responsibility for research, scholarship and postgraduate awards in the humanities – to devolve its funding role to the HRB, a new body funded by a grant-in-aid from the Department of Education and Science.

At first sight, the humanities appeared to have secured by the back door the much favoured research council. However, the HRB, though echoing ESRC claims to support high-quality research, publications and related postgraduate training, proves very different in terms of mission, role, type of research support, and the amount of funding for distribution (Table 7.1).

The ESRC's emphasis on relevance – and particularly its distinction between basic, strategic and applied research – is alien to the funda-

Table 7.1 ESRC and HRB funding

	Total funding (£millon)	Postgraduate studentships (£millon)
ESRC		
1994/5	58.9	16.96
1995/6	61.48	18.38
1996/7	63.08	18.25
HRB		
1994/5	15.78	13.72
1995/6	16.89	14.13
1996/7	17.39	14.13

mental nature of humanities research, and particularly the HRB's concern with the advancement and dissemination of knowledge and understanding for its own sake and its acknowledgement of the humanities' indefinite links with user communities. With the exception of teaching, there are few such linkages, even if employers, though disinterested in the topic of a history thesis, may interpret a doctoral qualification as evidence of a trained mind equipped to deal with problems in an analytical, balanced, critical and flexible manner. Nevertheless, the utilitarian pressures of the time proved inescapable, as evidenced by the HRB's receipt of a mission statement and assignment of a functional role to encourage a broader understanding of the nature and value of humanities research, expressed in terms such as promoting knowledge, enhancing British cultural life, and fostering skills suitable for employment.

The HRB, acting through its Postgraduate and Research Committees composed largely of conveners of subject-specific panels (for example history), represents the principal source of research funding for the humanities, including history. The Research Committee, assuming responsibility for conference, publication and research grants, academy research projects and research leave awards, is concerned primarily with postdoctoral research, but its budget (1995/6: £2.26 million) compares extremely unfavourably with the amounts available for such research through the ESRC (c. £40 million) and other research councils. The bulk of HRB funding is devoted to the studentships awards scheme administered by the Postgraduate Committee and intended 'to provide resources for research and scholarship within the United Kingdom in the humanities; to provide training for students who wish to prepare for academic careers in the humanities; and to provide training in high-grade scholarly and analytical skills for students who will use them in a wide variety of other careers'.[20] The studentships budget does not fall far short of that for the ESRC's comparable scheme (see Table 7.1), but both the humanities and social sciences fare badly by comparison with the large sums expended on studentships in the natural sciences and engineering.

The wide-ranging nature of historical research means that the work of postgraduates often extends into other subject areas within the humanities (literature, history of ideas and so on) and beyond the field as well, most notably the social sciences. In this vein, the ESRC and HRB, acknowledging both the 'fine' line dividing the humanities and social sciences and the growth of interdisciplinary projects, have defined their respective spheres of responsibility in a flexible manner. The HRB, stressing complementarity, provides postgraduates with clear guidance about the most appropriate funding body:

The borderline between the HRB's and the ESRC's subject remit is defined by content and methodology, not by the period to be studied. The HRB is primarily responsible for biography, administrative, legal, military, political and religious history, the history of science and of ideas and historiography. The ESRC is primarily responsible for social and economic history, including the history of education. In social history, if the emphasis is qualitative (e.g. a study of status and deference in 17th century England) you should approach the HRB. If the emphasis is quantitative or demographic, using social science methodology, approach the ESRC.[21]

In 1996 the HRB, advised by a working party report on the 'Subject domain of the humanities', compiled a register of courses falling within its remit, and hence eligible to receive studentship awards.

The above-mentioned guidelines raise interesting questions for the future, given the HRB's definition of its sphere of responsibility largely by reference to individual RAEUs, including history, and the 1996 RAE's placement of economic and social history – this had a separate panel in 1992 – as a subgroup of the history panel. In the meantime, it remains possible to submit economic and social history to another RAE panel, such as economics, if deemed more appropriate for any particular college.

The HRB administers two schemes for postgraduates: Competition A for one- or two-year studentships, primarily for Master's degrees or research training, and Competition B for completion of a doctoral research programme undertaken over periods of either three years full-time or five years part-time study. Applicants, eschewing the 2+2 year alternative, increasingly assume a 1+3 year structure for awards. All history-related applications go to members of the history panel, which comprises four experienced researchers appointed for three-year periods and reports through its convener to the Postgraduate Committee. Continuity of expertise is ensured through the staggered service periods of panellists, while the Postgraduate Committee seeks to ensure comparability and consistency between the various subject panels.

Competitions A and B operate separately. In general, for Competition B, more is expected (particularly on qualitative aspects) and hence the same application will not be suitable for both schemes. Successful completion of a Competition A award helps, but does not guarantee success in Competition B. Nor does failure to secure an award for Competition A rule out subsequent success in Competition B; indeed, a growing number of applicants for Competition B have not received a prior HRB award. Meanwhile, the extremely competitive nature of Competition A means that perhaps the majority of history postgraduates now resort to self-funding for a Master's course, which then provides the basis for a Competition B application.

Assessment of individual applications is based on two components: a selectors' mark and a qualification mark. Selectors' assessments are guided by clearly defined criteria, monitored at a preliminary meeting to ensure comparability of gradings, and finalised by consensus at the history panel's final meeting. Their mark, constituting a crucial determinant of any application's outcome, represents the selectors' consensus view about the merits of supporting a particular student for a particular programme of historical study at a particular institution. Selectors, interpreting all available information in the light of specific HRB guidelines and their extensive expertise, base their judgements on a range of considerations. These include:

- The perceived capacity of the candidate, including academic performance at undergraduate and, if applicable, postgraduate level.
- The feasibility and coherence of the proposed programme of study as a historical research project. For Competition A, the focus is placed upon its suitability as a course and/or scheme of research training in its own right or as a foundation for further study; whereas for Competition B, the emphasis is upon the proposal's suitability as a worthwhile doctoral project.
- An assessment of the applicant's sense of commitment to the project, its relationship to his or her previous undergraduate/postgraduate studies, the candidate's preparedness for postgraduate study, and statement about the reasons and purposes for undertaking the programme, including future plans.
- The quality of departmental support and supervision (for example relevant staff research expertise, appropriate research methods training, research seminars, supervisory provisions, library resources, archival accessibility, computing facilities) offered to history postgraduates in general and the applicant in particular. Statements about support and facilities will be evaluated in the context of the department's record in supporting previous award-holders. For Competition B, completion rates (that is, proportion of recent successful, on-time doctoral completions) are increasingly relevant, given the HRB's efforts to raise what are generally viewed as unacceptably low overall figures. Rightly or wrongly, British governments view completion rates as a major performance indicator.

For both competitions, selectors' marks are combined with the history panel's assessment of candidates' qualifications marks to determine final rankings. Inevitably, postgraduate performance proves vital for Competition B.

Potential applicants must scrutinise closely the fine print of the HRB scheme concerning, say, residential requirements, acceptable academic

Figure 7.2 HRB postgraduate studentships in history

Date	Awards	Applicants	Success rate (%)
Competition A			
1994	82	430	19
1995	92	450	20
Competition B			
1994	85	319	27
1995	91	367	25

qualifications, deadlines, and the treatment of each annual competition as a separate entity; thus, awards cannot normally be carried over to the following year. Contrary to occasional complaints about ageism, 'there is no age limit for applicants, and applications from candidates of whatever age will be considered on their merits', and by reference to the objectives of the studentships scheme (that is as preparation for academic and other careers).[22]

Obviously, it is difficult to come to any hard-and-fast conclusions about the HRB awards scheme. What one can point to is the extremely fierce nature of both competitions. In recent years, applications have ranged between 2,500–2,650 and 1,700–1,900 for Competitions A and B respectively. During the 1990s the continued rapid rise of around 80 per cent in applications across the range of humanities subjects, in conjunction with funding constraints, has meant that the number of highly-graded applicants far exceeds the number of available awards (1995: 536 and 500 awards for Competitions A and B respectively). Roughly speaking, history applicants have between a one in four and one in five chance of success (see Table 7.2).

For Competition A as a whole, in 1995 93 per cent of HRB awards went to candidates with a first. At one time, a first-class degree almost ensured success. Today, a first, though almost essential, is no longer a guarantee of a positive outcome; indeed, the success rate for such students hovers around – even below – 50 per cent. As a result, greater importance attaches to the quality of the actual grade, since the qualifications mark acknowledges three categories of first (that is exceptional, solid, low/borderline). For applicants, the aim must be to secure as good a first as possible. For academic staff marking undergraduate degrees, there should be a clear differentiation between the quality of students falling within the first-class band. Moving on to Competition B, in 1995, 96 per cent of awards went to those with postgraduate experience, thereby demonstrating another recent development: the need for a strong postgraduate mark, supported by a good first degree result. But academic qualifications represent merely one factor. A more decisive influence on ranking is the selectors' mark. Selectors, guided by the above-mentioned criteria, have to weigh up in a pragmatic and balanced manner a wide range of considerations on the basis of what is provided in varying degrees of comprehensiveness and clarity on application forms. Inevitably, much depends on the quality of the paperwork, as submitted by the applicant, referees and the receiving institution. Selectors can only assess information placed before them; thus, an application may be put at risk by shortcomings in any part of the application forms. Fortunately, referees and institutions are beginning to realise this point, even if certain references and supporting statements regarding the institutional framework suggest that some staff/colleges have yet to get the message, such as by failing to provide what is specified on the forms. In the meantime, the onus remains on applicants to ensure that the forms do themselves justice, such as by doing their homework about what is required and seeking informed assistance on the topic and programme of study, the choice of referees, and the most appropriate university for the project.

Moreover, things change. For example, the 1996 competition brought redesigned and reworded application forms, the restriction of applications to only one institution, and two additional schemes for Competition B. For the first time, awards became available for five years' part-time doctoral study, while the HRB introduced an experimental partnership scheme, reviewable for 1997, for awards made and funded in co-operation with institutions. Neither scheme is intended to offer a soft route to an HRB award. Part-time applicants will be judged in competition with full-time candidates, while the partnership scheme is intended to allow an institution-driven alternative to the existing student-centred approach. Thus, students, though able to link up with ongoing historical research programmes, are expected to undertake a worthwhile self-standing project.

Like the HRB, the ESRC, whose previously quoted mission statement reflects its increasingly utilitarian focus, provides two types of studentship. Research studentships are tenable only at higher education institutions (HEIs) formally 'recognised' by the ESRC for the quality and relevance of their research training and standards of supervision; thus, applicants must check the latest *List of Recognised Outlets*. The ESRC's explanatory guidance about borderline historical topics resembles that provided by the HRB: 'if the emphasis is on Social or Economic History, or the History of Education or of Technology, the ESRC should be approached'.[23] Historical projects employing social science methodology in such fields as cultural and media studies, politics and international relations, and women's studies might also fall within the ESRC's sphere of responsibility.

Advanced Course Studentships are available on both a quota (courses at certain HEIs hold a specified number of studentships) and competitive basis for students taking full-time Master's courses, which are normally of one year's duration. In fact, only 10 per cent of studentships are awarded through the competition. Most awards are offered on the basis of quotas allocated to courses on the basis of their track record. Quotas will be reviewed in the major recognition exercise in 1996. Studentships are distributed over fifteen subject areas, including economic and social history, according to an allocation determined by previous student demand and the requirements of the academic labour force, among other factors. In the competition, applications are assigned to relevant subject areas, and assessed alongside other applicants within that area.[24]

Standard Research Studentships, awarded for postgraduate degrees by research, are normally tenable for three years' full-time or five years' part-time study. Continuity of funding for the second and subsequent years is conditional on the demonstration of satisfactory progress. The ESRC, pointing to the resulting academic and employment merits, requires award holders to acquire the broadly based skills of practising social scientists.[25] As a result, students may only apply to what are described as Mode B 'recognised' departments when they can demonstrate that they have already undertaken formal research training as part of a Master's degree. Other applicants must apply to Mode A departments, which offer training programmes in line with the ESRC's *Postgraduate Training Guidelines* (1996). Typically, about 60 per cent of a student's first year will be taken up with research training involving, say, bibliographic and computing skills, research design and strategy, theories and philosophies of social sciences, ethical and legal issues, written and oral communication to different audiences, teaching skills, and quantitative and qualitative social scientific methodologies.[26] For economic and social history students, the ESRC requires additional specialised training 'to promote the ability to undertake historical research in a social science perspective', such as through courses in historiography and historical explanation, economic and social theory and analysis, quantitative methods and computer applications.[27]

Recently, the ESRC, pointing to the needs of users, has concentrated resources on selected themes; thus, at least 60 per cent of research studentships *across all subject areas* (that is not within economic and social history alone) will be made to applications relating to nine specific themes, which currently include 'environment and sustainability' or

Table 7.3 ESRC postgraduate studentships in economic and social history, 1995

	Awards	Applications	Success rate (%)
Advanced courses			
Quota awards	20		
Competition awards	4	11	36
Research	19	73	26

'governance and regulation'. Of course, it remains possible to submit a 'non-theme' application, but clearly there is ever-increasing pressure to choose a theme-related topic. Also relevant here is the ESRC's sanctions policy, which renders certain HEIs ineligible to receive ESRC studentships for a two-year period. Thus the ESRC, having deliberately pushed up its overall submission rate (for theses completed within four years) from around 30 per cent in the early 1980s to over 70 per cent, requires institutions to achieve a four-year rate of at least 50 per cent over a three-year period. This figure will be increased to 60 per cent in 1998.

In the 1995 studentship allocations (excluding housing management awards) 682 advanced course and 505 research studentships were awarded. Table 7.3 shows the position for economic and social history. Six part-time research studentships were awarded, but no applications were received for economic and social history. The excess of applications over available studentships means that both schemes are extremely competitive. Strong applications, supported by very good degree results, prove essential. ESRC guidance notes for applicants helpfully outline the Board of Examiners' marking procedures, and potential applicants must read relevant sections, given the specific targeting of marks. Arrangements are both similar to, and different from, those of the HRB. For Advanced Course Studentships allocated through the competition, 65 marks are available to indicate the Board's assessment of the student's basic suitability for postgraduate study in general and the proposed course in particular on the basis of his or her record, references and statement of reasons for the application. Up to 35 marks reflect the undergraduate grade (that is 35: first; 30: top third of upper second grade; and so on).[28] The scheme for Research Studentships is more complex, but, roughly speaking, the Board of Examiners may use a maximum of 50 marks to evaluate the coherence, justification and feasibility of the project as well as the candidate's perceived ability successfully to undertake doctoral research.[29] A further 15 marks (7.5 maximum for each) will be awarded on the basis of two references, while up to 35 marks are used to reflect the match between supervisor and applicant as well as the perceived training requirements.

Supervision aspects, which must be clarified prior to application, prove 'critical' and exert a 'large impact on the success of your application'.[30] For this reason, doctoral applicants are advised to undertake considerable 'research' prior to application on 'recognised' Mode A/B colleges and suitable supervisors, especially as – to quote the ESRC – 'the system used for judging applications is designed to ensure that candidates' research interests are well matched with those of the departments in which they choose to study'.[31] Early contact with the supervisor is vital since, in the words of an ESRC spokesperson, 'what the supervisor says about the topic has an impact on the peer review process that decides your fate'.[32] The ESRC also advises students 'to ensure that you are undertaking a Ph.D. topic which is realistically achievable within a three year period'.[33]

The late 1980s and early 1990s saw frequent complaints articulated by postgraduates about the quality of their educational experience. Repeated surveys, reinforced by the work of the National Postgraduate Committee, highlighted serious shortcomings concerning, for example, semi-detached or unhelpful supervisors, the lack of appropriate research training, and inadequate library, IT and other facilities.[34] Although the situation for current postgraduates may still not be perfect, the 1990s have witnessed significant improvements. For history postgraduates, the recently created HRB, though the actual source of funding for only the fortunate minority, proves prominent as the main potential source of funding. Although its thematic and utilitarian focus raises question marks about its continuing relevance for history postgraduates, the ESRC remains important for those studying economic and social history. Indeed, the ESRC does not consider that the position of economic and social history, with respect to postgraduate studentships, has been weakened by recent developments.

Despite seeking to avoid becoming too prescriptive, the HRB – reinforced in its quest for quality by the RAE, TQA and other developments – has proved a formative influence upon humanities postgraduate education. Its impact is evidenced by the increased focus of one-year Masters courses on research methodology, the manner in which the 1+3 year model has made prior postgraduate experience almost the norm for doctoral awards, the emphasis upon more effective departmental/institutional support structures for postgraduates, and pressure on colleges to improve completion rates. The ESRC has been equally active in its sphere of responsibility; indeed, its stress on research training, quality of supervision and submission rates has been even more strict than that of the HRB.

Frequently, changes have been introduced by history departments/
sections in pursuit of a coherent research management strategy based
on clearly defined plans and priorities, and particularly the perceived
needs of the ESRC, HRB, RAE, TQA and so on. Improvements, though
patchy in impact across the higher education sector, have included
induction programmes for new postgraduate students; research methods
training; more formal postgraduate seminar arrangements; improved
office space and IT provision for postgraduates; draft guidelines/codes
of practice for supervisors and students; annual monitoring procedures;
formal mechanisms for student feedback, complaints and appeals (such
as questionnaires and postgraduate committees); and enhanced teaching
opportunities for postgraduates. In addition, the need to raise completion rates prompted reviews of the criteria expected of doctoral
candidates. Thus many universities, following ESRC and HRB practice,
now assume that a doctoral thesis should be a piece of work which can
be produced by a capable, well-qualified and diligent student, properly
supervised and supported, within three years.

In general, most innovations have been welcomed as exerting
beneficial consequences for postgraduates, but there are alternative perspectives; for example, traditionalists often deny the case for training
supervisors, while others fear that three-year limits for doctoral theses
may compromise standards. Obviously such debates will continue, even
if there is general recognition about the crucial importance of the
quality of supervision, as acknowledged by Brian Brivati (a colleague at
Kingston) in an illuminating article about the ups and downs of
historical research for a doctorate: 'good supervision can make the
difference between passing and failing'.[35]

Recently, the Dearing Committee commenced its investigation of
higher education as a whole, and undoubtedly the resulting report will
prove relevant to postgraduate education and funding. For the time
being, the major debates on these aspects will focus on HEFCE's *Review
of Postgraduate Education*, a report produced by a committee chaired by
Martin Harris (Manchester University) and published in May 1996.
The report touched on a wide range of questions, including the purposes of postgraduate education, the increased emphasis on lifelong
learning, the view that demand from individuals and employers 'will
continue to grow' but will have to be accommodated without further
funding, and the increased reliance on personal contributions to funding.[36] An emphasis upon excellence in research education led to a
demand for institutional codes of practice for postgraduate education
based on quality provision with respect to areas such as supervisory
arrangements, research infrastructure and environment, and monitoring
procedures.[37] In turn the report, arguing that research funding should

be concentrated on departments possessing at least a 3 RAE rating, gave a new edge to the ongoing debate about the pros and cons of an élite group of research universities, while reinforcing linkages between the RAE and postgraduate education.[38] Against this background of continuity and change, key questions need to be asked by prospective history postgraduates (see Appendix 1).

However, the perennial problem for historical postgraduates remains one of money (Appendix 2).[39] Rejection letters are received by the large majority of ESRC and HRB studentship applicants, who are forced to consider self-financing, alternative funding sources (Appendix 2) and modes of study (for instance part-time), or giving up their research aspirations.

Meanwhile, colleges are becoming more aware of the continuing need to improve the quality of the postgraduate experience, while recent meetings of the HUDG (History at the Universities Defence Group) Steering Committee suggest that the late 1990s will witness debates about postgraduate recruitment as well as about the standards and format of higher degrees in history.

Further reading

Prospective history postgraduates, informed by this short study, should employ the following titles as a basis for further research. Careers offices, libraries, research offices, etc. at most universities/colleges of higher education should provide readily available, up-to-date information on key funding sources, addresses and so on. HRB and ESRC guides, as cited in the notes, are essential starting points, especially as the ESRC's *A Guide for Postgraduate Award Holders* (pp. 81–8) includes an invaluable information section. Also relevant are L. Williams (ed.), *The Grants Register 1995–1997* (London: Macmillan, 1994); Association of Commonwealth Universities, *Awards for Postgraduate Study at Commonwealth Universities 1995–1997* (Bexhill: Chandlers, 1995); and C. Stratton (ed.), *Postgraduate Study 96* (East Grinstead: Reed Information Services, 1995); and, for the USA, *Directory of Grants in the Humanities 1995–96* (Phoenix, Ariz.: Oryx Press, 1995). *Higher Education in the UK: Research Opportunities 1996–97* (London: Higher Education Business Services, 1995) and *Higher Education in the UK: Guide to Graduate Courses 1996–97* (London: Higher Education Business Services, 1995) offer invaluable summaries of history courses/studentships by college. The broader history scene today is covered by Alan Booth and Paul Hyland (eds), *History in Higher Education* (Oxford: Blackwell, 1996).

Doctoral applicants should consult Estelle M. Phillips and D. S. Pugh's *How to Get a Ph.D.: a Handbook for Students and Their Super-*

visors, 2nd edn (Buckingham: Open University, 1994) and J. Woodley's *Key Issues in Supervision Practice in the Social Sciences* (Swindon: ESRC, 1994). Student perspectives are offered in P. Salmon's *Achieving a Ph.D. – Ten Students' Experience* (Stoke on Trent: Trentham Books, 1992). History doctoral students should read Brian Brivati's 'Stormy sixties love affair', *Times Higher Education Supplement*, 6 December 1991, while consulting Joyce M. Horn's annual guide *Historical Research for Higher Degrees in the United Kingdom. Part 1 Theses Completed* and *Part II Theses in Progress* (London: Institute of Historical Research). In 1996 the Institute of Historical Research's annual publication *Teachers of History in the Universities of the United Kingdom: Special Research Edition* detailed staff research interests, which will be updated on an occasional basis.

The weekly educational press, most notably *The Times Higher Education Supplement* and *Education Guardian* (part of Tuesday's *Guardian*), publish up-to-date details on course/studentships offered by individual colleges. Source materials are becoming available on the Internet (for example, *Prospects Postgrad 1996* at http://www.prospects.csu.man.ac. uk; *Teachers of History* at http://ihr.sas.ac.uk:8080/).

HRB and ESRC help in providing information is gratefully acknowledged.

Appendix 1

Questions for the prospective history postgraduate student

General

Why do you want to undertake postgraduate study in general and in history in particular?

Are you prepared to spend the requisite period (likely to be between one and three years depending on the course, but even longer for part-time) on postgraduate study?

How do you propose to meet course fees and related costs, since it is easier to secure a place than a grant?

• What are your prospects of getting an award from the Humanities Research Board (HRB) or, for economic and social history, the Economic and Social Research Council (ESRC), given the extremely competitive nature of both schemes and the consequent need for a good first degree?

• Have you identified and contacted colleges offering bursaries/awards for history postgraduate students?

• Alternatively, are you (or your family) able to provide funding from your own resources or borrowing?

- Are you prepared to consider part-time study as either an alternative to full-time study or as a preferred choice, especially as both the ESRC and HRB fund part-time doctoral research?

Choice of college

Having surveyed college/departmental prospectuses and general post-graduate course guides, which college(s) appears to be the most suitable place for your proposed course, and particularly for your likely area of specialisation? For the ESRC, have you checked the list of recognised Mode A or B colleges? For the HRB, is the Master's course eligible for studentships?

What can you discover about your preferred history department/section, as indicated by, say, numbers of academic staff and history post-graduates or areas of staff specialism?

What does publicly available information (i.e. RAE and TQA ratings, the HEQC Audit, ESRC recognition) tell you about the quality of the history department/section's postgraduate work? For economic and social history, has the department secured Mode A/B recognition from the ESRC?

What types of course are offered, most notably, regarding research methodology? Are courses full- and/or part-time?

What facilities are available for postgraduate students respecting desk/office space, photocopying, computing, regular research seminars, residential accommodation, sports facilities, creche arrangements and so on? Are these facilities also available in vacations/evenings?

What library, archival and other resources are available? Do post-graduates have to pay for interlibrary loans? Are there reciprocal arrangements with other college libraries?

Are your main archival and other sources geographically proximate to the college?

Is financial help provided for conference attendance?

Are there teaching opportunities? What are the payment rates?

What are the procedures regarding, say, admission, registration, monitoring progress, assessment and examination?

How are the views and interests of postgraduate students represented at departmental/institutional level? Is there an active postgraduate community?

Have you asked existing postgraduates there for their views?

Additional points for doctoral research

Who will be your supervisor? What are his or her recent publications?

How close are his or her research interests to your proposed project? How much experience has he or she of research supervision to completion? Do you think that you will get on with each other for the next three or four years? Are any other staff/postgraduate students there working in a similar area of expertise?

What arrangements will exist between your supervisor and you regarding, say, his or her role, frequency and duration of contact, and reading and commenting on your written drafts? Is your supervisor planning to take any extended sabbatical leave during your projected period of study?

What is the college's doctoral completion rate for history? Is the history department subject to HRB/ESRC sanctions for low completion rates?

What are the key procedures regarding aspects like admission, registration, monitoring progress, transfer from M.Phil. to Ph.D., and vivas?

Does the supervisor feel that your proposed programme of doctoral research is realistic, coherent, clearly focused and capable of completion within 3 years full-time or 5–6 years part-time?

Will relevant research methods training and other courses (for example foreign languages) be available, if required?

Appendix 2

Main student schemes for history

	Master's degree research training	Doctoral study	Comments
Humanities Research Board of the British Academy (HRB)[1]	Competition A	Competition B	Extremely competitive For most types of history
Economic and Social Research Council (ESRC)[2]	Advanced course studentships (competitive and quota basis)	Research studentships	Extremely competitive For economic and social history, history of education/ technology

[1] Students in Scotland, Channel Islands and Isle of Man should apply to their own education authorities.   [2] Students in Northern Ireland, Channel Islands and Isle of Man should apply direct to their own education authorities.

Other possibilities

It is impossible to summarise adequately the wide variety of award schemes offering support for either higher degrees or *ad hoc* projects, like archival/library visits in Britain or overseas or completion of existing research. You should consult the further reading list, since only a rough guide follows.

a) Other British schemes

    i) Many universities/colleges operate grant/studentship schemes (require direct application).

    ii) General schemes include Sir Richard Stapley Educational Trust, Wellcome Trust.

b) Schemes for overseas study

    i) General schemes include Leverhulme Trust's 'Study Abroad Studentships' (c. 20 awards *per annum* for 12–24 months' duration anywhere except UK and USA).

    ii) Various academic bodies offer awards for the history of specific areas/themes. Examples include the German Historical Institute, German Academic Exchange Service, Society for the Promotion of Roman Studies, British Institute in Eastern Africa, British School of Archaeology in Jerusalem, Japan Foundation, Pacific Cultural Foundation, Polish Cultural Institute, Sir Robert Menzies Centre for Australian Studies (for example, Northcote Scholarships), Society for the Study of French History, etc.

    iii) Many overseas universities offer studentships.

    iv) Archival/library visit grants, for example most American presidential libraries.

c) Self-funding

    This option proves expensive for full-time study, even if self-funding a one-year Master's course offers the foundation for, say, HRB Competition B applications for doctoral research. Self-funding part-time study is much cheaper, and worthy of consideration.

d) Part-time study

    The HRB and ESRC offer awards for part-time doctoral programmes. For those failing to get a studentship, this is a cheaper alternative mode of study, but is demanding in terms of time and effort.

CHAPTER 8

The Internet for historians

Anthony Gorst and
Brian Brivati

Traditionally historians have acquired their data by visiting libraries and archive collections; this mode of working has arguably, despite prolonged debates on the nature and philosophy of history, changed little during the twentieth century. Even the information technology revolution of the last twenty years has had comparatively little impact on the methodology of the majority of historians. Personal computers, the most obvious tool of this revolution in information technology, have mainly been used simply as replacements for pen and paper, as little more than glorified typewriters or calculators to manipulate and represent data collected in the archive. In the last five years, new developments in information technology have meant that a growing amount of primary source material has become available to historians' desktop computers via the Internet. This development has significant implications for the researcher in modern British history, as it potentially changes the way historical research will be undertaken in the future. However, as important as understanding the potential of this technology is an understanding of its problems and limitations.

The technology that has the potential to bring the archive to the historian is generally known as the Internet. At a technical level, the Internet is simply a worldwide system of computer networks linked electronically. Although the Internet is now almost synonymous with commercial Internet Service Providers (ISPs), especially since the arrival of giants such as Compuserve, Microsoft and America On Line, it had its origins in the late 1960s and early 1970s in an experiment by the United States defence establishment, which created a small network of computers for 'command, control and communications'. This initiative, which led to the rapid growth of electronic mail as means of exchanging information between scientists, was extended by the United States National Science Foundation to the American academic environment during the 1980s using a number of super computer centres as nodes. From this relatively narrow base of users the Internet has grown rapidly, as more computers and networks have been grafted on to this spine, particularly with the involvement of commercial ISPS. It has now reached the point where it is an established technology, though not without its problems, which, precisely because of its phenomenal growth and accessibility, has to be taken seriously as a research tool by academic users.

The terms 'Internet' and 'World Wide Web' (WWW) are sometimes used interchangeably; however, the WWW is in effect only a subset of the whole Internet. The Internet covers the whole 'matrix' of technologies and systems with a variety of interfaces, including 'gopher', whereas the WWW is a mature hypertext system – developed originally by the *Conseil Européen de Recherches Nucléaires* (CERN), now the European Laboratory for Particle Physics – which has enabled organisations and individuals to publish material on web sites which are browsable and searchable using hypertext links from anywhere in the world with a computer and Internet connection. The explosion in the usage of the Internet over the past few years can, in large part, be directly attributed to the take-up of the WWW by both web authors and users. The latest generation of Hyper Text Markup Language (HTML) editors means that little or no technical or programming knowledge is needed to generate individual web pages and web sites beyond that required to use a word-processing package. Moreover, these web pages are easily accessible using WWW browser software such as Netscape Navigator or Mosaic which, using an intuitive 'point and click' interface, are simple to master. A not inconsiderable advantage of the latest WWW browsers is their ability seamlessly to integrate other Internet standards, such as gopher and telnet, thus removing from the historian the onerous task of mastering often impenetrable command line interfaces.

The speed with which it is changing makes the measuring of the growth of the World Wide Web close to impossible. According to one source, in December 1994, there were a mere 11,576 web sites in existence of which only 18.3 per cent were commercial sites, the overwhelming majority being educational and governmental. Latest figures suggest that there were over 1.6 million web sites in January 1997, with the proportions reversed. Usage of the Internet is also difficult to measure but the same source suggests that there are now approximately 102 million people with access to the Internet and current industry projections suggest a doubling year on year to over a billion users by the turn of the century, as more and more home computer users become connected to the web through ISPs.[1]

Great claims have been made for the Internet: in Britain political parties are united in recognising the educational potential of the 'information superhighway', indicated by their aspirations to connect all libraries and schools. Equally, however, there is widespread scepticism about both its utility and durability, with some dismissing the Internet as a temporary phenomenon. This chapter presents an attempt to assess the potential of the Internet as a tool for the researcher in modern British history. It assumes some knowledge, given that most history students at undergraduate and postgraduate level will now have free and unlimited access to the Internet – through workstations in laboratories or in the library or resource centre, following heavy investment by universities in computing facilities – and many students will have a formal information technology component built into their degree programmes. It is very easy to be seduced by the undoubted advantages of the Internet, a tool which in theory provides access to a storehouse of information without leaving the desktop in the office or library. However, in addition to technical considerations and issues, the Internet raises questions about the nature of historical sources and methodology which cannot simply be dismissed as mere 'luddism' on the part of a technologically resistant profession.[2]

The Internet is commonly assumed to be analogous to an enormous and ever-growing library, with the information held digitally and accessible from the desktop at home (via a modem connected through a telephone line to an ISP) or at work (via a networked computer). It is, however, a library with a difference in that it is not controlled by any one agency or institution. Anyone connected to the Internet with their own home page or web site can put any information on their 'shelves' at any time, and indeed can then remove it at any time; they can 'shelve' this information in any category that they choose and 'reshelve' it in another location, in another category, at a later date should they so wish. Worse still, from the point of view of historians accustomed to permanence in their sources, both the structure and content of web pages can change radically in a short space of time while still keeping the same title and address. The indexing system of the Internet is therefore inherently problematical as the cataloguing is in effect done by individuals; similarly the retrieval and delivery system is idiosyncratic, at times moving very slowly and prone to breaking down at regular intervals for no apparent reason. The user of the Internet for academic purposes cannot, therefore, simply expect to approach the Internet and locate the information they need in the same way as they would in a conventional copyright library or archive. Because of its size, the speed of its growth, and the fact that anyone can put up a home page and become an 'information provider', the Internet is fundamentally an anarchic organism. It is, therefore, imperative that anyone seeking to use the Internet in the course of their research takes a systematic approach and is prepared to think flexibly in order to locate relevant information.

This also raises significant issues about the nature and integrity of material on the Internet at a number of different levels. First, information on the Internet is in no sense pure or untainted: individuals consciously choose to put the information on-line and, in some cases, their motivation is political rather than scholarly.[3] What at first sight appears to be a historical site devoted to the Holocaust can turn out to be a 'revisionist' propaganda site aimed at denying its existence. Second, there is no quality or editorial control for much of the material on the Internet: the WWW is a leveller in which undergraduate essays and projects, scholarly articles and primary source materials have much the same status as far as search engines are concerned. Third, it is possible to stumble across links to sites that are offensive, perhaps containing material of a pornographic nature, when undertaking innocuous searches: it is not just that pornography is available on the Internet but rather that it is difficult to avoid it. In March 1997 for example, the British press reported a story in which schoolchildren, attempting to find information on the Internet for a school assignment on Louisa May Alcott's *Little Women*, entered the term 'little women' in a commercial search engine and produced a number of hits – the first being a link to a pornographic site.[4] The user of the Internet for academic research must therefore exercise great care and judgement if a good deal of time and effort is not to be wasted.

Before moving on to investigate the substantive content of the World Wide Web from the perspective of the researcher in modern British history, it is worth while pausing to examine some of the features and facilities of the Internet which, while not dependent on the World Wide Web, are easily accessible through the Web. Electronic or e-mail is a useful tool for researchers as it enables free (or cheap) and, if all goes well, practically instantaneous communication between individuals. The ability to send computer files of all types – whether text, spreadsheets or graphics and images – electronically across the Web via e-mail has the potential to revolutionise collaborative projects (indeed, much of the final revision of this chapter was carried out via e-mail). Moreover, e-mail allows access to the world of news groups (USENET) and discussion lists, which at their best represent themed electronic seminars where ideas, sources and methodologies can be discussed via e-mail and information exchanged. The best of these (such as H-DIPLO, which is devoted to the study of diplomatic history) are now widening their coverage from purely e-mail based discussions to include extended essays and book reviews for debate by subscribers. Much of the H-NET discussion lists are American-centred in both their content and their subscribers, a fact which led to a lively debate within H-DIPLO in 1997; by contrast, the British equivalent of H-NET, Mailbase, remains comparatively underused by British academics.[5] News groups within USENET tend to be much more informal than academic discussion lists and, from a narrowly academic point of view, the debate is often less useful – not least because there are often somewhat sterile counterfactual debates hi-jacked by individuals with political and religious agendas, often expressed in somewhat robust language. That said, some of the USENET groups are very good, especially, for example, those with a technical bent such as the aviation groups (for example <rec.aviation.military.naval> or <soc.history.war>) where 'amateur' historians can provide useful information and leads when dealing with specific technical and objective questions. The academic user will, however, need to exercise discretion and judgement in selecting which groups to access if they are to avoid wasting time reading puerile ahistorical arguments interspersed with adverts from people offering the chance to get rich quick.[6]

Academic library catalogues are increasingly available on-line over the Internet, usually through a link from the WWW pages of their home universities, so that it is possible to conduct complex searches using the LIBERTAS system via a telnet connection from the desktop. Index pages exist for all academic libraries in the United Kingdom at NISS (National Information Services and Systems). Moreover it is possible to search groups of library catalogues through, for example, the M 25 consortium (which includes all higher education libraries within the London orbital motorway). Usually these access the OPAC (On-line Public Access Catalogues) via a hypertext link that opens a telnet connection. However, a recent development is COPACS, going on-line with a simple WWW forms based search engine which accesses a database of selected university libraries in the United Kingdom. Although its coverage at the time of writing is confined to six major collections, its ease of use makes this an invaluable aid that will improve further as more libraries are added to its database.[7] Given the increasing number of history titles being published year on year, this facility is an invaluable aid both to the construction of preliminary bibliographies and the checking of references in footnotes when writing up research. Further bibliographic help can be had if your institution is registered to use the Bath Information and Data Services (BIDS): this is particularly strong in on-line searches for journal articles, which are notoriously difficult to keep up to date with. Again, searches in BIDS can be entered via a simple forms based interface.[8] The Institute of Historical Research is gradually putting all its useful reference material on-line, including *Teachers of History in the Universities of the UK* and *Historical Theses Completed and in Progress*, dating back to 1992: at present these are held only as text files and cannot be queried and sorted as a true database but they remain very useful tools for finding other historians working in the field.[9]

After some years of discussion, electronic journals are now beginning to develop in a systematic way and again are available on-line through the World Wide Web. The Institute of Historical Research has been at the forefront of these developments in Britain and edits and publishes *Reviews in History* which aims to provide reviews of scholarly works (including 'new thoughts' on classic texts) soon after publication. This journal will doubtless build over the years to a fine scholarly resource for the researcher in modern British history. From an author's point of view the advantage of such journals is speed from submission of an article or review to publication. Moreover, there is a strong case for research assessment panels in history to recognise electronic outputs as comparable in status to traditional paper formats; for this to happen the editorial and refereeing process of the traditional journal must be fully implemented electronically. How far true electronic journals are able to overcome scepticism and establish themselves depends on attracting established scholars as contributors and, crucially, on them establishing and maintaining editorial standards: in order to supplement traditional 'hard copy' journals which will undoubtedly remain one of the mainstays of the historical profession, on-line journals must have editorial boards to validate their contents. The *Canadian Journal of History* represents an interesting and well-thought-out hybrid format for electronic publication which combines the advantages of hard copy with the speed and accessibility of the World Wide Web. From 1996 the journal's contents have been available on-line, and articles can be viewed and downloaded; the only difference between the hard copy and electronic versions is that the footnotes to articles are not available on-line.[10]

Increasingly, history departments in universities in the United Kingdom and abroad are establishing their own Internet sites. These are, however, at the time of writing, usually concerned merely with advertising the department and its courses, and often contain little more than information relating to staff and their research interests. The Internet also has obvious applications for distance learning – supplying teaching materials to students electronically – something in which the Open University, for example, is actively engaged. The crossover point in this technology will come when it is used not merely to teach subjects related to itself (as currently, for example, it is predominantly in the teaching of computer science and programming), but becomes a medium for communicating knowledge of any kind, including historical knowledge. Its advantages over more established media such as CD-ROM include the ease of updating and simplicity of access from a larger number of access points. The use of the World Wide Web in this way is still very much in its infancy in the United Kingdom and the material available is of variable interest and quality, but the implications for both teaching and research are profound if it is taken to its logical conclusion, with lectures and seminar materials being distributed through the Internet to multimedia workstations.

Ultimately, using the Internet as a teaching delivery system to provide primary source material for traditional 'special subject' case studies will depend more on the resolution of copyright questions and copyright costs than on technical questions, which have now more or less been resolved. A good example of the kind of themed site that is developing around primary source materials is that of the *World War One Document Archive* maintained by subscribers to the World War One Military History list and hosted at Brigham Young University.[11]

An interesting development from the point of view of the researcher beginning a project in modern British history has been the establishment of WWW sites by museums and archives in the United Kingdom. At present many of these are still in their initial stages and tend to replicate existing printed guides and catalogues, although doubtless these will be further developed in the near future. The Public Record Office, for example, has a four-year plan, *Archive Direct 2001*, to make many of its finding aids available on-line in a searchable form. One institution which has clearly identified the Internet as a means of improving accessibility of its services is the Royal Commission on Historical Manuscripts, whose Internet site includes a link to ARCHON: an on-line database of all the main archives in the United Kingdom. Remote access is easy, though the interface is rather user-unfriendly, and, although it is not possible to undertake a subject search, searches by name are relatively simple. The papers of Montgomery of Alamein, for example, can be located – including the main collection at the Imperial War Museum and subsidiary collections and correspondence located in deposits in other repositories.[12] The site also has a list of other archive web sites for the UK and abroad. Although many of these merely give location, opening hours and contact number, there are exceptions: the Liddell-Hart Centre for Military Archives at King's College, London has a very well-developed site which includes the facility to search their catalogue in order to identify relevant files.[13] It is therefore comparatively easy, particularly when searching for an individual, to locate primary source materials.

Much of the laborious preliminary preparation of a literature search can thus now be undertaken through the medium of the Internet. Secondary sources can be identified and a working bibliography created. A list of the location of relevant primary sources can be generated. Research topics may be discussed and refined, and possible contacts identified with other historians on-line who are working in the field. The use of the Internet as a research tool does not absolve the researcher and the author from the obligation of making due acknowledgement for help received and providing full and proper footnotes and references. There is considerable debate about the conventions for citing materials that have been accessed via the Internet or other electronic mechanisms. Reproduced in the Appendix to this chapter are guidelines proposed by Melvin E. Page, of the history department at East Tennessee State University. These guidelines are not altogether uncontested and there is an emerging literature in the United States on the merits of different models and their relation to conventions for the citation of non-electronic sources. We have favoured the Page system for its comparative simplicity but the debate is ongoing and conventions may well change.[14]

Whichever citation system you decide to use, the most critical element of the citation is the date of access. One of the core problems with electronic sources available on-line, as against CD-ROM or other digital formats, is their impermanence. As a general rule and for the foreseeable future, the safest option is to check electronically accessed material against the hard copy source where available and then reference the hard copy source, even if the material initially has been located on the Internet. This has a number of important advantages for the research student. First, it is verifiable by examiners and supervisors, who may retain a certain – and legitimate – concern over the integrity and accuracy of on-line electronic sources, particularly where they have been re-keyed. Secondly, by identifying a hard copy source, the author can be sure that the material will be available for future reference. In cases where the means of access is solely on-line or the record is a uniquely electronic one, then the conventions proposed by Melvin E. Page should be followed, trusting that the material will be archived and thus made available permanently.

Arguably the real potential of the Internet lies in its ability to deliver primary source material to the desktop, thereby avoiding travel and accommodation costs for the impecunious researcher. However, there are a number of difficulties with using the Internet as a core tool for researching primary source materials for a dissertation in modern British history, all of which relate to the fact that there is no systematic initiative to place historical source material on the Internet. At present primary source material is being put on the Net almost at random, with an inherent loss of the essential contextualisation of documents.

Moreover, much of the information on the Internet is at present fundamentally irrelevant to the historian – particularly so since the growth of 'personal home pages' created by individuals, largely though not exclusively, on commercial Internet sites such as AOL and Compuserve. There are exceptions, such as the interesting pages devoted to the attack on the USS *Liberty* by Israeli aircraft in 1967 created by a surviving crew member, which contain a range of contemporary media coverage together with oral testimony, but these stand out against the mass of pages devoted to the leisure interests of their authors (including pictures of family and pets). These may, or more likely may not, be of historical interest but the historian is in danger of drowning in a sea of contemporary ephemera. (Eventually of course this may become of interest to the cultural historian of the 1990s, provided it is archived and available.) This problem can only worsen as disk space for the creation of multiple home pages for individuals is provided by ISPs to all subscribers: the solution will probably lie in the continuing refinement of search engines to make them more discriminating.[15]

Much of the information on the Internet created by institutions (whether government or business) is contemporary and current information, typically dating back only as far as the early 1990s. However, some executive agencies of the United States government appear to be developing their web sites as a public relations medium of communication with the on-line public. The United States *Naval Aviation News* is an example where a hard copy magazine is beginning to be published electronically and back issues made available on-line. Undoubtedly over time this will build into a valuable historical record (always provided, of course, that the back catalogue remains available on-line), but for the present it is of more use to the student of contemporary strategic issues than to the historian. However, some of the historical sections of the executive agencies of the United States government are providing chronologies, commentaries and analyses of historical questions in which their departments are interested in the form of on-line books: the United States Naval Historical Center is particularly strong in this regard. In this area, as in so many others in Internet usage, the United States is ahead of other countries in recognising the potential of electronic publication and communications. However, even in the United States the amount of material put on-line in any field is uneven and the process of creating a historical electronic record will obviously be an incremental one.[16]

The vast majority of the small amount of genuinely historical data on the Internet reflects the fact that the US is the most 'advanced' in terms of both the coverage and usage of the Internet (related no doubt both to the lower cost of computer equipment and lower on-line costs for the private citizen), and therefore the historical material on the World Wide Web tends to be American in origin, American in content and reflects the interests of the American public. There are numerous sites devoted to Native American history, the American Civil War, the Vietnam War, etc. Again, some of these are very good indeed: as an example of what can be done the researcher should examine a site devoted to the career of Senator Joseph McCarthy. This site, with its combination of transcripts of speeches, academic essays, annotated bibliographies and downloadable multimedia sound and video files is a model for British historians to emulate.[17] A further example is the '50 Years From Trinity' site created and maintained by the *Seattle Times* to commemorate the fiftieth anniversary of the invention and use of the atomic bomb in 1945. While perhaps containing less substantive material, this site is well designed and – in common with many well maintained sites – contains links to other sites of relevance to those interested in atomic weapons history, including material on the original Manhattan Project and a Brookings Institution Nuclear Weapons Cost study site.[18]

How then can primary source material related to a modern British history research topic be located on the Internet amid the morass of contemporary American ephemera? There are already a number of good index sites which provide links to British history material. Undoubtedly the best is that located in the subject index of BUBL Information Service at Bath which has a comprehensive listing of history resources on the WWW, including British history, and is annotated with generally sound judgements on the nature and the content of the sites that are listed.[19] Also useful are the home pages of institutions that are overtly dedicated to the study of history. By far the best, in terms of content, are the pages of the Institute of Historical Research: these pages provide gateways to other history sites and are probably the best starting point for a preliminary search of the WWW for the first-time user.[20] A further way into historical resources on the Web is through commercial search engines such as Yahoo.[21] Queries and searches on these, however, demand careful thought and construction in order to sift carelessly worded titles to ensure that the search results reflect your interests and the purpose of your research. Researchers must be precise in their search queries and should spend some time thinking about their search terms before sitting down in front of the screen and typing; this will save some time and frustration when waiting for the search engine to deliver a list of sites – only to find that much of the list is irrelevant.[22]

It is therefore possible to use the Internet to conduct research in modern British history, notwithstanding the fact that this can be a frustrating experience involving the researcher in struggles with incomprehensible error messages while attempting to follow dead and out-of-date hypertext links. Ideas for research topics can be refined in ongoing discussions conducted via e-mail and through discussion lists, while secondary material and bibliographies can be generated with an ease which is remarkable when compared to such activities in the 1980s – less than a decade ago. Moreover, it is even possible to find some relevant primary source material on the Internet.

Notwithstanding all the essentially technical difficulties identified above, there are a number of more fundamental methodological issues raised by the use of the Internet as a source for historical research which go to the heart of the practice of history as a serious academic discipline in Britain. First, history will be written from the sources available and, at the time of writing, those on the Web are overwhelmingly American. When this is allied to the incremental and ongoing process that is inevitably part of the creation of a web site, a rather strange impression – to say the least – can be given of modern British history, with whole areas and sub-specialisms simply unrepresented on the World Wide Web. Secondly, history stands or falls by its accuracy. Leaving aside the question of wilful and malicious tampering with sources, can a historian rely on material that is selected for unknown reasons and has to be re-keyed in order to be put on the WWW, thus raising inevitable questions of accuracy? The replication of images on the web is relatively easy: they can be scanned at high resolution and held as a file that can be downloaded and printed with a high degree of reliability. The problem area is with files that are made up predominantly of text. Here there are two alternatives: the first is that taken by Project Gutenberg, which for entirely understandable reasons of accessibility and the size of a downloadable file, puts its electronic texts in what it calls 'plain vanilla ASCII' files, reasoning that 99.9 per cent accuracy is good enough and that the original look of a book is not absolutely necessary for its readership.[23] For the historian, for whom the appearance of a document can be essential in understanding its status, this may not be good enough. The second approach is to scan the text document and hold its pages as images – almost as a digitised photocopy. The problem for the historian here is that multiple page documents have to be held in multiple files which are often quite large; moreover, because these are image files, they cannot be as easily manipulated as pure text files. A solution may be found through a development of the Adobe Acrobat format which preserves the appearance of a document but enables several pages to be linked in one file. Finally, historical research and writing is based on a fundamental principle that the evidence on which arguments are based has to be verifiable by other scholars. Thus sources have to be transparent, checkable and reproducible; with a medium as ephemeral and volatile as the Internet this is not the case. Yet the Internet, whether we like it or not, is here to stay and it is for historians to shape how history is created and perceived by the growing number of people who use the Internet to explore and learn about the world.

Having gathered material, what matters is what you do with it: the Internet is only one tool of many to be used by the historian. No marks are gained for the use of technology to collect data: this is the least of the historian's skills and the WWW a mere novelty in this respect. It is the assimilation and analysis of data that are the skills of the historian. Whether disseminated electronically or in hard copy between the covers of a book, journal or thesis, the final piece will stand or fall by the traditional virtues of scholarship.

Further reading

In addition to those locations and sites mentioned in this chapter, the prospective first-time Web user may wish to start at the *Index of Resources for Historians* maintained by the department of history at the University of Kansas and Regensburg University at URL <http:// kuhttp.cc.ukans.edu/history.htm/index.html> and the *Directory of Historical Resources* at URL <http://www.directnet.com/history/hddirect. htm>. Both these files are very large and can take a long time to access. Yahoo maintains a running index of history sites at URL <http:// www.yahoo.co.uk/Arts/Humanities/History/>: this can at times be rather an eclectic mix. Users should follow up on-line links as far as they can: one link will often lead to another. They should also visit relevant sites as often as possible as most Web sites are always being added to.

Appendix 1

The Melvin Page citation system
(http://h-net2.msu.edu/~africa/citation.html>, April 1997

Bibliographic citations

Basic citation components and punctuation

Author's Last Name, First Name <author's internet address, if appropriate>. "Title of Work" or "title line of message." In "Title of Complete Work" or title of list/site as appropriate. <internet address>. [menu path, if appropriate]. Date, if available. Archived at: if appropriate.

The samples below indicate how citations of particular electronic sources might be made.

Listserv Messages

Curtin, Phillip <curtinpd@jhunix.hcf.jhu.edu>. "Goree and the Atlantic Slave Trade." In H-AFRICA. <h-africa@msu.edu>. 31 July 1995. Archived at: <gopher.h-net.msu.edu> [path: H-NET E-Mail Discussion Groups/H-AFRICA/Discussion Threads/Goree and the Atlantic Slave Trade—item number 465].

Lobban, Richard <RLobban@grog.ric.edu>. "REPLY: African Muslim Slaves in America." In H-AFRICA. <h-africa@msu.edu">. 4 August 1995. Archived at: <"http://h-net.msu.edu/~africa/archives/august 95>.

Walsh, Gretchen. "REPLY: Using African newspapers in teaching." In H-AFRICA. <h-africa@msu.edu>. 18 October 1995.

World Wide Web

Limb, Peter. "Alliance Strengthened or Diminished?: Relationships between Labour & African Nationalist/Liberation Movements in Southern Africa." <http://neal.ctstateu.edu/history/world_history/archives/limb-l.html>. May 1992.

FTP Site

Heinrich, Gregor . "Where There Is Beauty, There is Hope: Sau Tome e Principe." <ftp.cs.ubc.ca> [path: pub/local/FAQ/african/gen/saoep.txt]. July 1994.

Gopher Site

"Democratic Party Platform, 1860." <wiretap.spies.com> [Path: Wiretap Online Library/Civic & Historical/Political Platforms of the U.S.]. 18 June 1860.

Graeber, David <gr2a@midway.uchicago.edu>. "Epilogue to *The Disastrous Ordeal of 1987*". &ltgopher://h-net.msu.edu:70/oo/lists/H-AFRICA/doc/graeber>. No date.

Usenet Group Messages

Dell, Thomas <dell@wiretap.spies.com>. "[EDTECH] EMG: Sacred Texts (Networked Electronic Versions)." In <alt.etext>. 4 February 1993.

Legg, Sonya <legg@harquebus.cgd.ucar.edu>. "African history book list." In <soc.culture.african>. 5 September 1994. Archived at: <http://www.lib.ox.ac.uk/internet/news/faq/archive/african-faq.">http://www.lib.ox.ac.uk/internet/news/faq/archive/african-faq.general.html>.

E-mail Messages

Page, Mel <pagem@etsuarts.east-tenn-st.edu>."African dance...and Malawi." Private e-mail message to Masankho Banda. 28 November 1994.

Footnote and endnote citations

Basic citation components and punctuation

note number. Author's First name and Last name, &ltauthor's internet address, if available>, "Title of Work" or "title line of message," in "Title of Complete Work" or title of list/site as appropriate, <internet address>, [menu path, if appropriate], date if available, archived at if appropriate.

The examples below indicate how citations of particular electronic sources might be made.

Listserv Messages

Phillip Curtin, <curtinpd@jhunix.hcf.jhu.edu>, "Goree and the Slave Trade," in H-AFRICA, <h-africa@msu.edu>, 31 July 1995, archived at <gopher.h-net.msu.edu>, [path: H-NET E-Mail Discussion Groups/H-AFRICA/ Discussion Threads/Goree and the Atlantic Slave Trade —item number 465].

Richard Lobban, <RLobban@grog.ric.edu>, "REPLY: African Muslim Slaves in America," in H-AFRICA, <h-africa@msu.edu>, 4 August 1995, archived at <http://h-net.msu.edu/~africa/archives/august95>.

Gretchen Walsh, "REPLY: Using African newspapers in teaching," in H-AFRICA, <h-africa@msu.edu>, 18 October 1995.

World Wide Web

Peter Limb, "Relationships between Labour & African Nationalist/ Liberation Movements in Southern Africa," <http://neal.ctstateu.edu/ history/world_history/archives/limb-l.html>, May 1992.

FTP Site

Gregor Heinrich, <100303.100@compuserve.com">, "Where There Is Beauty, There is Hope: Sao Tome e Principe," <ftp.us.ubc.ca>, [path: pub/local/FAQ/african/gen/saoep.txt], July 1994.

Gopher Site

"Democratic Party Platform, 1860," <wiretap.spies.com>, [path: Wiretap Online Library/Civic & Historical/Political Platforms of the U.S.], 18 June 1860.

David Graeber, <gr2a@midway.uchicago.edu>, "Epilogue to *The Disastrous Ordeal of 1987*," <gopher://h-net.msu.edu:70/00/lists/ H-AFRICA/doc/graeber>.

Usenet Group Messages

Thomas Dell, <dell@wiretap.spies.com>, "[EDTECH] EMG: Sacred Texts (Networked Electronic Versions)," in <alt.etext>, 4 February 1993.

Sonya Legg, <legg@harquebus.cgd.ucar.edu>, "African history book list," in <soc.culture.african>, 5 September 1995, archived at <http:/ /www.lib.ox.ac.uk/internet/news/faq/archive/african-faq.general. html>.

E-Mail Messages

Mel Page, <pagem@etsuarts.east-tenn-st.edu>, "African dance...and Malawi," private e-mail message to Masankho Banda, 28 November 1994.

CHAPTER 9

Political history

Robert Pearce

'History', said Sir John Seeley, quoting Edward Freeman, 'is past politics, and politics present history.' It was a neat formulation but also a very complacent and inadequate one. History is, of course, far more than merely past politics. Over the last thirty years there has, for instance, been a remarkable efflorescence of interest in social history, on history 'from below' rather than 'from above'. Many have cast scorn on what Marx once dismissed as 'high-sounding dramas of princes and states' and have attempted to investigate the lives of the exploited many rather than the actions of the politically powerful few. They have, quite rightly, refused to take past political figures at their own generally egotistical and excessive valuation. No one nowadays takes for granted the centrality of political history, and many of those who study what could be called political history prefer to call themselves simply historians rather than political historians. Nevertheless political history remains an important genre, popular alike with students and the general public. It provides an interesting and significant perspective on the human past, and has done so since the time of Herodotus and Thucydides. It also has many valuable features which other subdivisions of history sometimes lack and is certainly unlikely to lose its attractions in the new millennium.

Defining political history is far from straightforward. Literally, it means history deriving from the polis, or city-state in ancient Greece, the members of whom were citizens with a sense of corporate identity. Thus it is about a relatively advanced stage in the evolution of mankind, when individuals felt the need to organise themselves into groups larger than the family or extended family. In 1970 Geoffrey Elton called political history 'the history of ... the activities of men in society'.[1] Not everyone would accept such a wide-ranging definition, but it is important to remember that political history is far wider than mere 'high politics' or party politics. Politics is neither pure nor simple, and therefore neither can political history be. Its theme is power and influence in society and its subject matter is the organisation and deployment – and often abuse – of that power and influence. It encompasses not only government, administration and legislation at local, national and international levels, but also, at one extreme, the theories and philosophies that inform politics and, at another, the multifarious activities with which governments are associated: including war, economic and social organisation, conflict and co-operation, and so on. The concerns of British government have expanded during the twentieth century, and during the two world wars they were virtually all-encompassing; the interests of political historians have increased accordingly. There are also political aspects to groups which, ostensibly at least, disavow any political function, such as some churches, professional associations and trade unions. There are 'low' or 'popular' politics, as well as high. Nor should it be thought that the élite practitioners of high politics were necessarily divorced, either in their aims or their unspoken assumptions, from larger groups – certainly not in this relatively democratic twentieth century. In fact, there are political aspects to all human relationships and will be until the dawn of the classless society and the withering away of the state – in other words, until the end of history.

Above all, political history is about people – individuals, as well as groups, classes and nations. It is about events in all their similarity and uniqueness; and about the passage of time. These are three aspects of human reality which will surely register as important for any historian. Yet its boundaries are fuzzy rather than distinct, a welcome recognition of the totality of the human past and of the arbitrary, man-made nature of all divisions. Ronald Hutton has rightly called political history the most protean variety of history. In Elton's more homely metaphor, political history is to some extent 'a portmanteau affair, a vacuum cleaner sucking in the products of other forms of historical study'.[2]

Political history can be written as if politics were part of a closed world, in which only important individuals matter. Maurice Cowling is one very successful exponent of this historical school.[3] There is some justification for examining high politics in this way: if a task is worth doing it is worth doing in as much depth as time, the sources and printer's paper and ink will allow. But this cannot be the end of the enterprise; it is then up to others to place politics in the context of society as a whole.

Yet how much more intellectually rewarding it is for political historians themselves to see politics as an integral part of a larger whole. Such efforts at contextualisation are now increasingly common. Take, for instance, British political history from 1945 to 1951: the period of the Attlee administrations. Any thorough study – and there have been several[4] – will examine the central institutions of government, including the Cabinet and its committees, the different ministries, Parliament itself and also the Civil Service. A good deal of attention will be devoted to a relatively small number of important individuals, including politicians and bureaucrats, many of whom will have left behind private papers and diaries which political historians will subject to minute scrutiny. But a good proportion of most historians' work will also be devoted to grass-roots political activity in local party organisations. (How else can we understand the dissatisfaction of Labour supporters with the government by 1950 and the Party's reaction to Bevan's resignation – or, for that matter, the resurgence of the Conservatives?) The economy will also loom large, as historians investigate the economic effects of the war and also the post-war efforts to overcome the balance of trade deficit. This will involve study not only of the Treasury and macroeconomic planning, but also of economic performance in particular regions and of relations with the trade union movement. Similarly, the study of government-inspired austerity is likely to bring in aspects of social history, including, for instance, women's fashions and the 'New Look' (which the Chancellor of the Exchequer, Stafford Cripps, deplored for its profligate wastage of valuable cloth), and the all-time high popularity of the cinema and British sport. Not just the political inauguration but also the impact of the National Health Service, and of other reforms, must also find their place. There will be due recognition of foreign policy and of Britain's role in world affairs. This will not be any 'optional extra', since the cold war – and Marshall Aid, increased defence spending, the Korean conflict, and cutbacks in social spending – left an impress on so many government policies. Decolonisation must also be included, and so must many other aspects of these crowded years, including the changing intellectual climate of opinion. The list, of course, could go on and on. In short, very few political historians will be content merely to chart 'political' events in their imagined purity. We must work alongside social, economic, diplomatic and industrial historians in a collaborative venture, seeing our own research in the context provided by that of others. Even the study of the 1945 election is not pure politics. How could it be when we have to try to assess popular attitudes? We must give due recognition to the speeches, the broadcasts, the manifestos and all the other para-phernalia of electioneering. But we also have to take into account the social context. Unless we are aware of the high degree of political apathy and ignorance that existed, for instance, we may entirely misread the significance of Labour's victory, which was once said to show the public's readiness to accept revolutionary changes.[5]

In some ways, then, there is now a new look to political history. Yet in other ways it is still concerned with traditionally important historical tasks. What matter if, to some, these may even seem old-fashioned? Political historians should not feel obliged, for instance, to apologise for their concern with narrative; after all, analysis and interpretation depend upon establishing exactly what happened, when and how. (This is no easy task, as bewildering discrepancies in works relating to even the well-documented modern historical period will testify.) Anyone doubting the validity and utility of formulating as accurate a chronology as possible should read George Orwell's *Nineteen Eighty-Four* (1949), where the inhabitants of Oceania's Airstrip One have no reliable information about the past: they cannot even date remembered events to within a year or two. As a consequence, they are reduced to a state of credulous imbecility. Big Brother – and his real-life equivalents – allow no study of political history; otherwise they would lose control of the past, and without this they could not control the present and the future. Unless we study political history seriously, in order to get as close to the truth as possible, the past will be prescribed for us in accordance with some party line. This is Orwell's essential message; it is a stark warning, and an important one. (That Orwell, in his non-fiction writings, sometimes played fast and loose with factual accuracy is another matter.)[6]

It is true that, over past generations, political history has been knocked off its pedestal. Surely no one subdivision of history can now claim to be the most important. There is no 'infrastructure' to historical studies, influencing if not determining the lesser historical offshoots in the superstructure. If we accept any such crude model, we are prejudicing what should be an open-minded enquiry into historical change and causation. Yet if political history has been demoted in historiographical importance, that is to be welcomed, for it has emerged from the debate with its critics much strengthened and reinvigorated, surer about its relevance and with a wider approach to its subject matter. We have been reminded – or perhaps jolted into recognition – that 'political history' should be interpreted widely, not narrowly. We all now see the political nexus in a wider perspective, and so are less likely to try to write 'pure' – that is limited, incomplete and uncontextualised – political history. The history of past politics must, to be fully intelligible, embrace at least aspects of social and economic history. It was once almost fashionable for hard-headed Eltonian political historians to mock the pretensions of cultural, economic and social historians; now we are more likely to accept their findings, to view them from a political perspective and to build on them. A political history which embraces other subdivisions is better political history. The result is that present-day political history is professional and intellectually demanding, while at the same time being – at its best – stimulating, well written and refreshingly free of specialist jargon. It is history at its most accessible and often at its most engaging. Indeed it is generally the public face of the discipline – for the simple reason that it is far more readable than other forms of history. Political historians tend to believe that their study of human experience should be presented in a form intelligible to a wide range of human beings with a variety of interests, and not just to those specialising in the same area. They have not forgotten that though historical research is an arduous activity, which requires methodical and rigorous study, writing and communicating history is equally important. It is also equally arduous. It is an art demanding clarity of thought, an aesthetic sense and even empathy with one's likely readers. The best political historians have always looked upon history as part of the national culture. Other historians – especially those whose arcane offerings sometimes seem on a par with the more obscure passages in metaphysical philosophy or nuclear physics – have much to learn from political historians.

In short, political historians tend to be practical: more concerned with writing about the past than with writing about writing about the past. If, on the whole, they lack a grasp of conceptual theory, they make up for this with empirical rigour. As a result, there are very few important 'schools of thought' among them. They tend to get on with their work in their own way. They are less specialised and less theoretical, but more prolific and more popular than other historians. They are concerned with what happened, when, how and why. Hence they get to grips with individual people and are adept at telling a good story well. These are skills not to be scorned; and this approach to history is not to be undervalued.

'History gets thicker as it approaches recent times.' How right A. J. P. Taylor was, and the thickness of historical texts has increased markedly since he wrote this in 1965.[7] Therefore it is true of the twentieth century, as Lytton Stratchey wrote of the Victorian Age, that its history will never be written, for 'we know too much about it'. The first requisite for the historian, wrote the paradoxical Strachey, is ignorance: ignorance 'which simplifies and clarifies, which selects and omits'.[8] The overwhelming mass of surviving evidence provides at once the greatest opportunity but also the gravest challenge for the historian. Clearly, therefore, researchers into political history must be specialists, learning more and more about less and less. But, even so, specialisation provides no short-cut to historical understanding. There is only an unending war to be waged against ignorance and misunderstanding, involving the hard, sheer intellectual slog of reading and assessing vast amounts of source material. But even this is not the end of the process; in addition, we have the Herculean task of working through the secondary literature, in order to place our findings into a larger context and thus assess their significance. All this requires not only the obvious intellectual qualities but also – and perhaps of equal importance – moral qualities of patience, determination and staying power: in short, strength of will.

Scott Fitzgerald once said that the test of a first-rate intelligence is the ability to hold two opposing ideas in the mind at the same time and still retain the ability to function. This is of clear relevance to the historian. We have to realise the impossibility of ever getting at the truth about the past while continuing to seek, with all our powers, to do just that. Every research student must try to write something definitive. That means choosing an area to investigate which is small enough to be practicable. The good news is there are many such areas, especially since history is expanding as the present becomes the past. The bad news is that nothing definitive is ever written. But that should not blunt our enthusiasm. There is much significant work waiting to be done, including work that will seem definitive for a time.

Scott Fitzgerald also said that 'the cleverly expressed opposite of any generally accepted idea' is worth a fortune to somebody. Political history is full of such reversions of accepted interpretations and denigrations of previously unassailable reputations (though not many fortunes have been made as a result). But a word of caution is needed here. The deliberate attempt to sensationalise political history by emphasising one-sided viewpoints is easy enough: we simply have to select evidence to support our contention, and the more doggedly we do this the more publicity will be attracted to our findings. But this is bad history, and we must always be on our guard against it. If research is to be academically respectable, it can be exciting and offer new insights – but it must be sober and judicious. It must bear hostile scrutiny. Surely the human past is interesting and exciting enough, without our having to resort to fiction?

The whole of twentieth-century British political history has seen remarkable historiographical changes over the last generation. Nevertheless we should not cast aside the historical scholarship of, say, the years before 1967, when the thirty-year rule came into operation. There is an understandable tendency to do this: after all, we would be out of a job if, at least to some extent, history did not have to be written afresh each generation, as new documentary resources become available and new perspectives present themselves. But the fact is that good scholarship does stand the test of time. I am thinking particularly of *Britain Between the Wars 1918–1940* by C. L. Mowat, first published in July 1955. This is one of the seminal works of twentieth-century political history – or, one should say, of largely political history for, like all good works in the genre, it has interesting things to say about economic and social developments as well. Over forty years after its first appearance, it is still an indispensable book for students of the interwar period. Despite being unable to use government papers, Mowat was an erudite historian with a mastery of the published sources; he also had the political historian's eye for a telling quotation and a plain, unambiguous writing style which communicated clearly on a first reading – the sort of style which seems remarkably easy, until one tries to emulate it. He achieved an aura of solid dependability: partly by his use of voluminous evidence, partly by his avoidance of flashy but superficial half-truths. Much more could be said about the strengths of the book, but a brief consideration of what, from the perspective of 1996, seem to be its weaknesses will reveal a good deal about the progress of scholarship in the last generation and thus about the present state of twentieth-century British political history.

First of all, his book began in November 1918 and did no more than glance backwards at the war and pre-war years. There is in fact a long-standing tendency, going back before the extreme version of the theory put forward so memorably by Sellar and Yeatman (in *1066 and All That*, to regard the First World War as a major turning point, with the implication that it caused a cleavage between the pre- and post-war years. Today periodisation tends to be less sharply defined. Admittedly scholars of the nineteenth century have tried to claim 1900–14 as part of the 'long nineteenth century', but no self-respecting historian of twentieth-century British political history would gloss over these years – years which saw such vital legislation as the 1909 People's Budget and, in 1911, the National Health Insurance Act, the Parliament Act and the payment of MPs. The end of the war does indeed present a seductively opportune time to begin a volume on modern political history, especially since the new Representation of the People Act trebled the electorate and gave a new look to elections and to Parliament itself. From 1918 we can realistically speak of something approaching real democracy in Britain. But this was political evolution not revolution.

Twentieth-century historians now treat the years before 1918 as a vital part of their field. The two broad interpretations of Edwardian England which once held the field – the mythical 'golden age' when it was summer all year round, and the contrasting vision of a country racing headlong towards its own violent destruction – have now been replaced by a much more realistic assessment of a society of contrasts and variety. Similarly, the war no longer seems quite the clear-cut turning point of yesteryear.[9] Admittedly, there are contrasts between the pre- and post-war periods; but those who seek for continuities will find these as well – even demographic ones. Indeed many of the changes wrought by the war would probably have come about anyway, sooner or later. The perennially debated issue is the future of the Liberal Party. It is impossible to write off the influence of the war, but nor should the fundamental problems of the Liberal Party – in terms of ideology, identity and constituency activity – be ignored. Similarly the new position of women in the wartime workforce, which looked at the time like a significant shift, turned out to be only a temporary phenomenon. Nevertheless, to trace the ramifications of the war into the interwar period is an enormous undertaking, and one very much awaiting its historian.

On the politics of the interwar period, Mowat, like most good political historians, eschewed blanket generalisations. Interested in the particular, he generally avoided lumping the politicians together. But he did, after analysing the fall of Lloyd George in 1922, refer to 'the rule of the pygmies' which lasted until 1940, when Churchill became prime minister.[10] It is a revealing phrase – and, quite possibly, a valid interpretation. Later historians, like Robert Skidelsky, have drawn attention to the mood of national self-doubt and pessimism which characterised the period: the failure to tackle unemployment was intimately linked with the failure to stand up to Hitler.[11] Indeed many have seen the interwar years in general, and the Thirties in particular, as the waste land – a blighted period, symbolised by the dole queue and by Chamberlain's fatuous 'piece of paper'. In fact, there is in Mowat a recognition of the variety of the interwar years; but, even so, negative features predominate over positive ones in his account. His politicians were well-meaning but lacking in dynamism and in genuine constructive abilities.

It is not surprising that Mowat held these views. First, he did not have the advantage of access to government papers and so could not see the period from the vantage point of the policy-makers themselves. In addition, being born in 1913, he was writing about politicians whose lives overlapped with his own. Most of us find it hard to credit contemporaries with the stature of the great figures of the past; distance does sometimes lend enchantment to the political view. These are not handicaps from which today's historians of the 1918–40 period suffer. Indeed so voluminous are the official papers that there is a danger of what has been called 'archivitis': we come to appreciate the official point of view so well that it becomes our own, and our acceptance of official explanations misleads us into imagining that no other, more beneficial responses to problems were possible.

Yet there is an even more important reason for Mowat's slant on his period. He was writing at a time of overwhelming historiographical consensus – a rare condition, it is true, but a dangerous one because it stops us thinking. Historians believed that the interwar politicians had made two overwhelming errors: they had tolerated mass unemployment, which never dipped below a million after the immediate post-war boom and which had reached three million at the start of the 1930s; and, even more catastrophically, they had allowed Hitler to rearm to a position where he brought about the Second World War. Furthermore, it was accepted, in the 1950s and 1960s, that these errors had been eminently preventable. When Mowat was writing there was full employment: it seemed that, by keeping demand high and by other Keynesian techniques, governments could prevent unemployment. But had not Keynes advised governments in the interwar period to pursue similar policies, and especially to abandon both the gold standard and the fetish of a balanced budget? Obviously, then, the interwar politicians had not had the nous to take good advice. Had they done so, the mass unemployment, hardship and discontent would not have occurred. Similarly, if only the politicians had taken their lead from Churchill and rearmed rapidly, and stood up to Hitler instead of pandering to him, the Second World War would not have occurred. The most destructive war in history was, therefore, as Churchill put it, the 'unnecessary war', caused at least in part by the short-sightedness and craven fear of British politicians. Chamberlain and the rest were 'guilty men'.

It all looks very different from today's perspective. No longer do we feel obliged to pay homage to Keynes. Today's mass unemployment seems an intractable problem, and so – once again – does that of the 1930s. Perhaps indeed Keynesian policies might have made matters worse; certainly they would have created a crisis of confidence among businessmen. Nor do historians accept the stereotyped image of the 'hungry Thirties'. There were far more positive aspects to the decade, and indeed to the whole interwar economy, than was once admitted. Mowat's perspective reflected the nostrums of his time (just as, more recently, the perspectives on the 1930s of 'Thatcherite' historians have done). In addition, recent research has convincingly shown that Chamberlain and the other appeasers were doing their best to wrestle with almost impossible foreign policy problems. It can still be argued that he was misguided, but it is no longer possible to see Chamberlain as a craven figure of fun. There has in fact been a remarkably stimulating historiographical debate on appeasement, overturning the simplistic notions of a previous generation.[12]

There are other differences too between Mowat's approach and that likely to be taken by historians now. Today there is a much greater recognition of the important dimension conferred by local history. We are far more likely to see national political parties in the light of the work of constituency associations; Stuart Ball, for instance, has pioneered this approach for the Conservative Party.[13] Similarly we are likely to be more aware of the local aspects of general elections and of national events, like the general strike.[14] But in fact there is far more research to be done on local issues if historians of the twentieth century are to produce anything like as complete a picture as that provided by historians of the nineteenth century.

There are many other aspects of interwar politics which have now been taken much further than in Mowat's time. We know, for instance, much more about the 1931 political crisis, an issue which modern scholars have subjected to detailed study.[15] We are also much more aware of the importance of the Civil Service, which can no longer be seen as merely an impersonal machine efficiently putting political orders into operation. Figures like Maurice Hankey and Thomas Jones are now viewed as important figures in their own right.[16] Another important issue is the study of British fascism. Mowat gave only two pages out of almost seven hundred to the British Union of Fascists, which emerges from his pages as an unimportant body doomed from the start to abject failure. Today, however, we have a much fuller picture.[17] The historical study of British fascism has come of age as an important subdivision of modern political history, and moreover a field in which political historians have collaborated constructively with other historians. Fascism has much more to tell us about British traditions and interwar society as a whole than Mowat realised.

Fascism is also one of the very few fields in which there is a significant European dimension to our historiography, the other being the allied field of appeasement.[18] But in fact the European perspective on interwar history should be taken much further. We need direct comparisons between British and continental politics, for instance in the fields of industrial relations and social policy. European perspectives can provide stimulating new angles of vision on topics with which we may seem over-familiar. Certainly a study of interwar Europe throws the survival of democracy into greater relief. The British tended to take this for granted, as have too many subsequent historians, but it was perhaps the great achievement of the interwar years.

When we come to the Second World War, Mowat is no longer relevant. Nor, perhaps, is there any historian who has written a synthesis of comparable stature. Instead there are more specialised volumes, and no shortage of them. Most studies of wartime politics have centred on the role of Churchill – too much so, given the vital importance of other figures – and so this is perhaps a convenient time to say something about the role of biography in modern political historiography. Much nonsense has been written on this issue. For instance, very many commentators have insisted that biography – which often degenerates into hagiography or 'hatchetography' – is bad history.[19] Admittedly there is something to be said for this contention. Many biographers do have a habit of becoming like their biographees, vicariously sharing their triumphs and disasters, resuscitating old quarrels and settling old political scores in print. Where, for instance, is the biography that can realistically portray Attlee without diminishing Morrison, or do equal justice to both Attlee and Bevan? But this is only to say that biography demands all the skill a political historian can muster and that, like other historical works, biographies can be written well or badly. But this approach to political history is a viable one. No one chastises historians for investigating an event or issue in as much detail as possible, so why should not historians re-create the life of a politically powerful individual in as much depth as the sources will allow? If an individual is lifted out of the context of his or her times, so that the figure seems unnaturally dominant, this is the fault of the individual writer, not a necessary fault in the biographical genre. Which political historian of the interwar years has not benefited from reading John Grigg on Lloyd George, David Marquand on Ramsay MacDonald, Middlemas and Barnes on Baldwin, or David Dilks on Chamberlain? Similarly, which student of the war years has not profited from Alan Bullock's coverage of Ernie Bevin, Ben Pimlott's life of Dalton, or Martin Gilbert's monumental study of Churchill?[20]

Churchill's roles, both as an anti-appeaser in the 1930s and as wartime premier, have led to wide-ranging historiographical debates. Our distance from the war has enabled a new generation of historians to attempt to cut away the wartime myths and present a merely life-size, unglamorised Churchill, warts and all – or, sometimes, warts alone.[21] As a result, fascinating debates have occurred on Churchill's role and historical importance. Similarly there has been a fruitful debate on the thorny issue of whether there was a wartime consensus between the parties in his coalition government. At present the differences between the parties are being emphasised, but we may be sure that the debate is not ended and that studies of particular ministries or political aspects will add to our understanding.[22]

A similarly rich and controversial period is 1945–51, which is producing a veritable spate of general studies, monographs and biographies.[23] Many of these reflect current beliefs about how best to manage the economy, and it is often easy to spot the politics of the various authors. Perhaps the best of them come clean and admit allegiances. Even so, there has also been much scholarship of a very high order, as can be seen in several of the editions of historical sources that have been published. Who could possibly improve on these wise words of caution, with which Ben Pimlott prefaced one of his volumes of Hugh Dalton's diaries?

A diary is often supposed to show 'the truth' about its author. Yet the truth of a diary is always partial, and in spite of the diarist. Whether or not a diary is intended for public scrutiny, its author selects and fashions with great care. A diary may be a depository for disagreeable attributes – a confessional, as in the case of Beatrice Webb, or a kind of emotional latrine, as with the startling, explosive diary of Lord Reith. On the other hand, it may be an expression of conceit, or a vehicle for self-justification. A diary may be only written up at moments of unhappiness, or only at times of light-hearted relaxation. A cheerful person can write a gloomy diary, or an arrogant person a humble one. Dalton's diary certainly does not give us a proper picture of Dalton.[24]

Here is a recognition that, while passionately involved with the characters or issues he is writing about, the political historian must also strive and strive again for scholarly detachment. There are also pleasing signs that the post-1951 period is resulting in rich, detailed investigations. These should multiply as time allows material released under the thirty-year rule to be digested.

But do we really need to allow thirty years to elapse before serious historical study is undertaken? There is a vogue at the moment for studies which go very close to the present day. Recent titles include T. O. Lloyd's *Empire, Welfare State, Europe: English History 1906–1992* (1993); Bernard Porter's *Britannia's Burden: The Political Evolution of Modern Britain 1851–1990* (1994); Glyn Williams and John Ramsden's *Ruling Britannia: A Political History of Britain 1688–1988* (1990); *British Political History 1867–1995* by Malcolm Pearce and Geoffrey Stewart (1996); and Stephen J. Lee's *Aspects of British Political History 1914– 1995* (1996). Also noteworthy is the number of political diaries and memoirs (of Crossman, Benn, Castle, Callaghan, Thatcher, Clark, Jenkins, Owen and others) covering the last generation. In addition, there has been a crop of biographies of recent political figures: Cosgrave on Powell, Pimlott on Wilson, Zeigler on Wilson, Campbell on Heath and Young on Thatcher, to mention only a few. To these should be added newspaper sources and the 'oral testimony' of recent political players. Furthermore, there has been a host of recent historical TV documentaries, with interviews and film extracts – on the Thatcher years and on the European movement, for instance, and on individuals like Powell, Hailsham and Jenkins. Historians' shelves these days bulge with almost as many videos as books. One is forced to ask whether there will be much to add in future years to this 'instant history'.

The answer, of course, is that there will be much to add, and many new and varied interpretations to make. Historians often justify the study of history by pointing out that the present cannot be fully understood unless its roots are traced back into the past: and there is thus an obvious justification for very recent history. But we cannot achieve much perspective on the present until it has become the past. Those who assign significance to today's events do so at their peril: future developments may make their interpretations look remarkably silly. If history teaches anything, it is that contemporaries often get it wrong. The history of the last twenty or so years is, therefore, at best only provisional history.

Future historians, looking back on the last quarter of the twentieth century, will certainly have their work cut out, and it will be different work from that of today's political historians in many ways. There will be a much greater emphasis on Britain as part of a larger unit, in terms not only of Europe but of the world. (Perhaps they will also focus much more on the history of Britain's relative decline, though of course this does not mean that there will be a decline in national history.)[25] Also they will have to use television archives as one of their main sources, not only because of some admirable investigative work by journalists but also because television has become the prime forum for political debate, and political image-making and manipulation. Historians will be indebted to the techniques forged by students of media studies. But the work of future historians will also, in some ways, be similar work: certainly there will be too much to do, so that they will have to stand on the backs of colleagues known and unknown. It will still be exhausting and unending, and humbling – in that the more we know and understand the more we will realise just how little we really know and understand. Yet it will also be endlessly fascinating and challenging. Why else would we do it?

Further reading

There is an embarrassment of riches in modern political history. But it is worth becoming familiar with solid reference books. Three of these are in the Longman series of Handbooks and Companions: *The Longman Handbook of Modern British History 1714–1987*, Chris Cook and John Stevenson (eds) (2nd edn, 1988); *The Longman Companion to Britain in the Era of the Two World Wars*, Andrew Thorpe (ed.) (1994); and *The Longman Companion to Britain since 1945*, Chris Cook and John Stevenson (eds) (1996). Also absolutely indispensable is David Butler and Anne Sloman, *British Political Facts, 1900–1979*, 5th edn (London: Macmillan, 1980). Cameron Hazlehurst and Christine Woodland (comps), *A Guide to the Papers of British Cabinet Ministers 1900–1951* (London: Royal Historical Society, 1974) is also an excellent source. The Royal Commission on Historical Manuscripts (Quality Court, Chancery Lane) is always most helpful in answering queries about the whereabouts of particular collections of papers. Finally, C. L. Mowat's *Great Britain Since 1914: The Sources of History* (London: Hodder & Stoughton, 1970) is heartily recommended.

There is no single journal pre-eminent in the field of twentieth-century political history. In order to keep up with the output of scholarly historians, students should consult the range of journals available in university libraries. However, four journals can be particularly recommended: the *Historical Journal*, *Twentieth Century British History*, *Contemporary Record*, and, especially, for its reviews, *History*.

CHAPTER 10

Diplomatic history

Ann Lane

The ending of the Cold War in 1989 brought a new climax to the process of reflection on the state of diplomatic history[1] which has concerned the profession for the greater part of the twentieth century. Diplomatic history, as a sub-field of historical scholarship, reached the zenith of its élite status in the 1920s and early 1930s during the initial enthusiasm, both scholastic and popular, for seeking an explanation for the outbreak of the Great War of 1914–18 in the nature of the international system in general and the conduct of great power diplomacy in particular. Since then, the assumptions of Rankean method, with its hermeneutic approach and conception of the international order as determined by the foreign policies of states, have been under persistent and sustained attack. In the first instance, it was the economic determinists, both from Marxist and English radical traditions, who mounted the challenge by arguing that markets and raw materials, not foreign policy, are the driving forces in history, and that *ergo* the reading of diplomatic correspondence was of questionable value. Since then the relevance of the field has been variously dismissed by social historians, who criticise its élitist approach and so establish by default an élitism of their own; by economic historians, who until very recently appear to have ignored diplomacy altogether; and by adherents of the new and allegedly separate discipline of international relations. The latter take especial pains to distance themselves from historians of international relations, a strategy made necessary by their objective of developing a 'science' of international relations as a distinct and supposedly superior field of scholarship.

From time to time, senior scholars in the field of diplomatic history have taken issue with these critics: for example, in 1955 W. Norton Medlicott, in his inaugural lecture as Stevenson Professor of International History at the London School of Economics, addressed in characteristically diplomatic language the challenges then being posed to the historians of international relations.[2] Writing at the height of the Cold War, Medlicott concluded that it was not the historian's task 'to direct policy or point a moral, but to supply data on which others may act'. For a more fulsome response, however, it is necessary to turn to Medlicott's successor but one, Donald Cameron Watt, who over the years has been ready to articulate the most eloquent and reasoned ripostes to the points raised by the discipline's critics. One of the most accessible examples of this defence is to be found in the introduction to his volume dealing with the Anglo-American relationship, *Succeeding John Bull: America in Britain's Place, 1900–1975* (1984), in which he not only provides the reader with an 'exposition' of the concept of diplomatic history as the history of international relations, but points out the interrelationship between this and the theoretical concepts associated with 'social science'. Indeed it was Watt, who identifies himself as 'a historian and a student of international relations', who as early as 1965 published a volume the stated purpose of which was 'to bridge the gap' between his discipline and that of the political scientist. Watt's *Personalities and Policies* is a self-conscious attempt to demonstrate the existence of an interface 'by borrowing concepts from political science which might assist the elucidation of the historical problems which bedevil [the historians'] field'.[3] As such, this exploration of British foreign policy as the product of an 'oligocratic society' and Watt's own definition of the power-holding élite in Britain, a theme to which he subsequently returned in numerous later publications, serves as a model of history which is both archivally derived and conceptually formulated.

The study of diplomatic history emerged as a response to the need for an explanation for the catastrophe of the First World War which marked the collapse of the congress system by which the international balance of power had been maintained since the Treaty of Vienna in 1815. The perception commonly held after 1914 among informed public opinion in Britain was that the secret diplomacy of the pre-war years had been partly, if not largely, responsible for the cataclysm that ensued; Woodrow Wilson gave this notion powerful endorsement in calling for 'open covenants openly arrived at'. At the same time the movement towards greater public scrutiny of diplomacy, spearheaded in Britain by the Union of Democratic Control, combined with the growing desire of the governments of the principal protagonists in the Great War to make public some of the official record in order to influence opinion on the question of war guilt. This led to the rapid acceptance of the principle that contemporary international relations were an acceptable and appropriate subject for historians to study, even though historical study of the modern period was concerned in the 1920s with nothing more recent than the Napoleonic Wars.

Diplomatic history was then, and has remained, closely associated with the study of the origins of wars with particular concentration on the major wars – two hot and one cold – which have shaped international affairs during the twentieth century. This fact has contributed greatly to bestowing on diplomatic history the reputation of being traditionalist to the extent that the study of diplomacy at moments of international tension has inclined historians to focus on the actions of a relatively small group in society, that is those with the power and authority to recommend policies or take decisions at the highest level.[4] The logic of such an approach inevitably gives the individual some paramountcy in the policy-making process.

The historians' enquiry into the British role in the onset of each of the major twentieth-century crises, while serving as a study in itself, is almost always underpinned by a sub-discourse relating to the state of British power and British decline which has been an underlying concern of British historians engaged in studies dating from the Victorian era to the present day. The most recent survey of British decline as an international player is that by David Reynolds, *Britannia Overruled: British policy and world power in the 20th century* (1991), which argues the case for power as a reflection of the strengths and weaknesses of competitors, and British power therefore as relative to the changing balance of forces within Europe during the twentieth century. It is worth contrasting this with the argument in Paul Kennedy's *The Realities Behind Diplomacy: Background Influences on Britain's External Policy, 1865–1980* (1981). Whereas Reynolds emphasises the importance of political decisions and the element of choice, Kennedy argues the case for the relative decline of Britain as an economic power as 'the most critical conditioning element in the formulation of the country's external policy over the last hundred years'.[5]

British scholarship in the field of diplomatic history has drawn heavily on the traditions of German scholarship. The hermeneutic approach, the notion that diplomatic documents would somehow 'lead to the centre of historical reality', was derived from the methodology of Leopold von Ranke who devoted much of his later career to perusing the sixteenth-century Venetian *Relazione* as the source material for his writings.[6] So it was that in the early 1960s, the British school received fresh stimulus in the debate about the origins of the First World War as a consequence of the publication in 1961 of Fritz Fischer's *Griff nach der Weltmacht*, subsequently published in English in 1967.[7] This study of Wilhelmine Germany's foreign policy not only stoked the fires of renewed debate about who was to blame for the First World War, but also pointed the way towards a new school of thought about the sources of foreign policy itself. Fischer observed that the explanations of pre-1914 German foreign policy could be found in domestic and social pressures. Although this was almost incidental, its importance for countering still-accepted Rankean assumptions about the nature of foreign policy proved enormous in the intellectual climate of the 1960s, when growing disillusionment with American policy in the Cold War combined with the philosophical tenets of radical thinkers on both sides of the Atlantic. This led to the development of a new framework for understanding the driving forces of foreign policy and the economic dimension provided much scope for experimentation.[8]

However, the more immediate by-product of Fischer's work was to disturb the intellectual consensus in Britain about the origins of the First World War, the very debate out of which the discipline of diplomatic history developed. The debate, which started almost immediately after the war's outbreak in 1914, had concluded essentially that no individual power could be blamed; but Fischer – by placing emphasis on the expansionist tendencies of Germany under the Kaiser, and attributing these to technological and industrial developments as well as the existence of Chancellor Bethman Hollweg's detailed annexationist policies – effectively revived the idea of German responsibility for the war. This approach has been found less valuable for the understanding of British foreign policy in this period. Zara Steiner, for instance, argues in *Britain and the Origins of the First World War* (1977) that the social structure of Edwardian England, with its firmly defined élites and chains of command, inclines her to the more traditionalist approach: 'British action', she concludes, 'was the response to cultural events and that these were made by a few men ... the decision to go to war was the result of deliberations of a handful of men'. Underlying her thesis is the equally Rankean assumption that foreign policy deals with problems at the international level which are 'qualitatively different from the issues of domestic politics'.[9]

One historiographical consequence of the uncertainty about the justification of the war guilt clause enshrined in the Paris Peace Settlement was that the debate about the causes of the First World War became inextricably linked with that about the origins of the Second World War. The early acceptance by historians of the notion that the immediate responsibility for the Second World War lay with Hitler and Nazi-Socialist Germany was, of course, a direct outgrowth of the official position adopted in mobilising the population to meet the circumstances of 1939. However, the thesis of this as the 'unnecessary war' – which facilitated the attack on the politicians who sought to appease Hitler's pre-war demands – became an established part of historiography partly

as a result of the publication of memoirs, written by leading personalities in the debate that went on in Britain in the 1930s, which sought
to absolve their writers of any association with the policy of appeasement. The most important and intriguing of these for this purpose are
those of Anthony Eden, which are an excellent demonstration both of
the value of such sources as historical record and also of the penchant
for selective memory which generally bedevils politicians when they sit
down to recount for the public their role in the great events of history.
While the judgement of A. J. P. Taylor that memoirs are 'a form of oral
history set down to mislead historians' is taking the argument of
instrumentality on the part of the writers to an extreme, Eden and
Winston Churchill were unashamed nevertheless in their efforts to
establish an 'authorised' view of their policies through the device of
publishing selections of their official correspondence cemented together
with judicious narrative.[10] The impact of these on historiography can be
seen by reference to John Wheeler Bennett, *Munich: Prologue to Tragedy*
(1948), and Martin Gilbert and Richard Gott, *The Appeasers* (1963).

During the 1950s the official version of the origins of the Second
World War was already being subjected to scrutiny by some whose work
began to point the way towards a revisionist interpretation. Both
Medlicott and Watt had voiced dissent from the 'unnecessary war' thesis
by the time that Alan Taylor's most controversial and provocative piece
of historical writing appeared in print.[11] *The Origins of the Second World
War* (1961) was successful in challenging, in somewhat immodest terms,
every important assumption made by the historical profession about the
personalities and policies of the 1930s. While purporting to be a work
of traditional scholarship, derived from readings of diplomatic correspondence, its style and accessibility, combined with Taylor's vaunted
reputation as provocateur, gave it unusual power in historiographical
terms – a fact which was speedily recognised by the diplomatic history
fraternity. If Taylor had been seeking to galvanise diplomatic historians
to revise and defend their theses and even their methods in seeking and
understanding the diplomatic origins of the Second World War, he was
amply rewarded. The greatest minds in the profession mobilised to take
issue with Taylor's thesis and an impression of the quality and intensity
of the debate can be garnered from Esmonde Robertson's edited
volume, *The Origins of the Second World War: Historical Interpretations*
(1971).[12] A succession of monographs and articles, many of which follow
the traditionalist methodology, soon followed. However, for a different
perspective it is necessary to turn to Tim Mason who, in a thesis
reminiscent of Fischer's interpretation of the foreign policy of Wilhelmine Germany, took issue with Taylor's approach through diplomatic
documents, arguing that important social, cultural and economic

developments within Germany had to be taken into consideration if the war's origins were to be understood.[13] The thesis of British failure to intervene in the 1930s, as a consequence of internal developments both political and economic, is cogently elaborated in F. S. Northedge, *The Troubled Giant. Great Britain among the Powers 1916–39* (1966).

It was at much the same time that the Cambridge historian, F. H. Hinsley, wrote his detached and classic study of the history of international relations, *Power and the Pursuit of Peace* (1963). Rather than tackle the subject through the origins of wars, Hinsley analyses the disorders of the first half of the twentieth century from the perspective of the failure of the international system to provide for perpetual peace – an aim, he says, which 'cannot be much less old than the practice of war'. Hinsley attempts to explain the crisis in terms of imbalances in the European power structure, caused initially by the removal of Russia and the weakening of France and dismemberment of Austria-Hungary, which left Germany unchallenged as potential hegemon on the Continent. After levelling some criticism at diplomatic history for its narrative approach, Hinsley sets forth his objective of moving towards the direction of a theory of international relations through an amalgamation of 'some of the findings of all the relevant disciplines', including legal history and the history of ideas 'around the evolution of the modern system of relations between states'.[14]

Following the controversy of the early 1960s, debate about the origins of the Second World War tended to fragment and it was only with the fiftieth anniversaries associated with that war that works of genuine synthesis began to appear, often as part of established series, such as the Longman series on the *Origins of Wars* and Macmillan's *The Making of the Twentieth Century*.[15] As part of this process of reconsidering the diplomatic origins of twentieth-century wars, attention has focused increasingly on the changing role of foreign ministries themselves. There is an excellent monograph on the making of British foreign policy before the First World War by Zara Steiner, *The Foreign Office and Foreign Policy, 1898–1914* (1969).[16] However, by the 1930s the importance of the Foreign Office in shaping foreign policy had been diminished considerably, a result in part of the deep distrust of professional diplomats that had been engendered by the commonly held opinion that their activities had led Britain into the 1914–18 conflict.[17] The significance of this change is evident in the growing importance of the Treasury and Bank of England in the policy-making process which was evident in the 1930s and has become more so since, a development which is reflected in the trend over recent years for diplomatic historians to devote much of their research time to trawling through the archives of these two institutions. One further (and comparatively recently developed) line of enquiry by British historians has been that of approaching diplomatic history through the history of diplomacy, a recent example of such scholarship being provided by Keith Hamilton and Richard Langhorne in *The Practice of Diplomacy: Its Evolution, Theory and Administration* (1995).

Diplomatic history has enjoyed – or endured – an almost symbiotic relationship with 'official' history and the publication of diplomatic documents. Indeed, the origins of the two world wars are some of the best documented events in modern times, and this is due primarily to the publication of documents for purposes of persuasion which facilitated and encouraged the development of a school of diplomatic history in the first instance. Certainly, this process has not been limited to publication, but historians have been used by foreign ministries across Europe and North America for the purposes of editing selections of material from the archives for publication, and preparing 'official' histories of the events themselves. In Britain a mixture of these practices has been adopted. This process began in the 1920s when historians and governments were goaded by the German project to gainsay the war guilt clause of the Paris Settlement through the vehicle of its documentary series *Die Grosse Politik* (1922–27). The British Foreign Office, concerned at the impact of this series on public opinion, especially in the United States, after some delay, authorised its own series *British Documents on the Origins of the War, 1898–1914* (1926–1938) which was edited by G. P. Gooch and H. V. Temperley.[18] The impact of *Die Grosse Politik* on historiography and, furthermore, on contemporary public perception was profound, and shortly after the outbreak of the Second World War, Llewellyn Woodward reflected that the Wilhelmstrasse had scored something of a diplomatic triumph in presenting its case so quickly and cogently; the impact it had had on American opinion was not without significance for Britain's position in the renewed conflict. To prevent this happening again, the British and American governments sought in 1945 to get their interpretation across first by arranging – immediately on the war's end – the editing and publication of the captured German foreign ministry archives.[19] Woodward himself was one of the founding editors of the parallel British series which covered the interwar years, *Documents on British Foreign Policy* (1949–1983) and also jointly authored the five-volume official history of Britain's wartime foreign policy.[20]

The diplomacy of the war itself was slower to attract attention from historians. This had much to do with the fact that the official records remained closed. One of the effects of the publication progammes and public debate of the interwar years was to make officials and governments more wary, and the device of the fifty-year closed period for all documents provided a useful cloak to protect ministers and their mandarins from premature trial by a jury made up of members of the historical profession. However, the decision taken by the Wilson government in 1967 to reduce the closed period to thirty years, and their subsequent decision to release the records pertaining to the Second World War en bloc in 1972, provided historians with an earlier than expected opportunity to overturn official orthodoxy. Much of the resulting work was traditionalist in style and some of the best, such as Elisabeth Barker's *Churchill and Eden at War* (1981), gives effective treatment of the political issues through the diplomacy of pre-eminent personalities. The most recent, and one of the most accessible accounts of high-level diplomacy is Robin Edmonds, *The Big Three: Churchill, Roosevelt and Stalin in Peace and War* (1991), but for students of British involvement in the war in the Far East, Christopher Thorne's monograph, *Allies of a Kind: the United States, Britain and the War against Japan 1941–45* (1978), remains a classic which explores not only the policies of the protagonists but also offers an interpretation of the Anglo-American relationship.

Students of the Cold War are much less well served by Britain's official historians; the American series, *Foreign Relations of the United States*, is better resourced and in consequence is well ahead of its British counterpart, *Documents on British Policy Overseas*, which only began to appear in 1984 and so far runs to just eleven volumes on selected themes for the period 1945–52.[21] Researchers seeking an introduction to the British documentary material on the post-war period will find it useful to combine their perusal of these volumes with *Documents on International Affairs*, the companion edition to *Survey of International Affairs*, which was published by the Royal Institute of International Affairs between 1925 and 1963.

The British school on the origins of the Cold War has emerged since the late 1970s as documents have become available for public inspection. The existing scholarship which was largely of American origin and equally America-centric – classified as 'Orthodoxy' (the Russians were to blame) and 'Revisionism' (American capitalism was the root cause) – shared the common theme of depicting the Cold War as essentially bipolar in nature, defined by a stand-off between America and the Soviet Union dating from 1945, or 1917, and perhaps even earlier, in a conflict which was seen as beginning in Europe and spreading to the Middle East, Asia and Africa. While it cannot be gainsaid that the European dominance of the international system disintegrated during the first half of the twentieth century and was replaced by one in which the United States and the Soviet Union predominated, a bipolar approach to the diplomacy of the period treats the countries of Europe as though they were mere spectators at the game of superpower politics. Despite the crippling effects of the war, European powers in reality played an important part in the re-ordering of the international system during the 1940s, and the history of the Cold War is incomplete without a proper assessment and acknowledgement of their role.[22]

A significant body of literature based on the British documents has emerged, often in the form of monographs examining bilateral issues, which at one and the same time justifies this perception while also inclining towards an Anglo-centrism – just as the American scholars working from the archives in Washington produced an interpretation which was America-centric.[23] An example of this is Anne Deighton's *The Impossible Peace* (1991) which contends that Britain took the lead in promoting the division of Germany, thereby contradicting the conventional wisdom that for two years after the war ended, Britain sought to achieve agreement to control Germany within the framework of the Potsdam Protocol of 1945, and that it was only at the end of 1947 that Bevin and his senior officials reluctantly concluded that Soviet intransigence made 'four power' control impossible. Geoffrey Warner is a persistent and vocal critic of this interpretation and his exposition of the counter-argument on this critical issue can be found in *The End of the Cold War* (1990), edited by David Armstrong and Eric Goldstein.[24] John Kent is another who has developed a challenging thesis with wide-reaching implications which has been published as *British Imperial Strategy and the Origins of the Cold War* (1993). Kent argues to the effect that British foreign policy was not dominated by Cold War considerations at all, but rather that Bevin sought to build up Britain as an independent 'third force' based upon its leadership of a bloc of colonial powers. He is a supporter of the Britain first thesis to the extent that he argues that 'Bevin's imperialism does suggest that his policies could only lead to Cold War confrontation and were therefore more a cause of Allied disagreements than a response to them'.[25]

There is little consensus in the British school about where the Cold War began – or even when. Soundings can be taken of the state of progress with new research at various junctures through the range of edited volumes produced as a result of national and international conferences, which (despite their inevitably uneven quality) offer both valuable insights on specific topics and introductory chapters which usually give a fairly clear indication of current concerns. Among the most helpful for the early Cold War period is Ritchie Ovendale, *The Foreign Policy of the British Labour Governments 1945–51* (1984), which examines the major issues of the late 1940s thematically and includes a contribution by one former diplomat, Frank Roberts, whose various postings as First Secretary at the British Embassy in Moscow (1945–47) and Private Secretary to Ernest Bevin (1947–49) more than justify his frequent appearance among such collections as a contemporary witness. Anne Deighton's *Britain and the First Cold War* (1990), the product of a similar conference held at King's College London in 1989, is both more wide-ranging and more specialised in content but is a sustained example of the Anglocentricity of the British school. The literature on this period is enormous but if there are such things as indispensable volumes on the early Cold War then I would recommend two which examine diplomacy through the eyes of those at the summit. The first is Alan Bullock's third volume in his biography of Ernest Bevin, *Ernest Bevin, Foreign Secretary 1944–1951* (1983), which is much more than biography, providing an immensely detailed narrative of diplomacy at the highest level. The second, Hugh Thomas's *Armed Truce* (1986), is far more wide-ranging in that it discusses the world as seen through the eyes of the leaders in each of the principal countries involved in the post-war settlement, but deals only with the years 1944–46; however, it is valuable not least for the lively pen-portraits of the participants.

Nevertheless, it is clear that Britain, as the erstwhile guardian of the European balance of power, was highly significant in the early Cold War and this has much to do with its relationship with the United States. On both sides of the Atlantic scholars of diplomatic history had accepted by the early 1980s that an understanding of America's relationship with Britain in the mid-1940s is vital to achieving an understanding of the American road from the Second World War to the Cold War. Immediately, we are plunged back into the task of separating myth from informed historical opinion in tackling the historiography of this relationship during the war and its aftermath. David Reynolds, whose monograph *The Creation of the Anglo-American Alliance 1937–41: a Study in Competitive Co-operation* (1981) is a valuable starting point, reminds us elsewhere that the wartime alliance 'was Winston Churchill's creation', that it was Churchill who popularised the epithet 'Special Relationship' in his Fulton speech of 5 March 1946, and used his memoirs (published between 1948 and 1954) in part to perpetuate this same theme.[26] C. J. Bartlett has explored Anglo-American relations since 1945 as political history in *The Special Relationship* (1991), while Alan Dobson, whose approach is part theoretical and part historical, provides a useful perspective on the economic aspect in *The Politics of the Anglo-American Economic Special Relationship* (1988).[27] The published version of Watt's 1981 Wiles lectures has been mentioned elsewhere but it is important in this context, not least for its use of the metaphor of Pax Britannica replaced by Pax Americana as a device for comparative purposes.[28]

The British school has shown a preoccupation with several key

themes in addition to the nature of the Anglo-American special
relationship: arguably the most significant and topical is the question of
Britain's relationship with Europe. The early post-war years have already
been the subject of much attention, with scholars having found evidence
of not inconsiderable pro-European enthusiasm on the part, first of
Churchill, whose views are none-the-less inconsistent, and the Labour
Party during its first two administrations. Reflecting the precipitous
decline of Britain from great power status which followed the war,
scholars have sought explanations of Britain's failure to lead Europe
both in the lack of the material resources necessary to maintain a strong
alliance against the Soviet Union and in the institutional differences
between Britain and its would-be European partners – a case which is
argued by Avi Shlaim in *Britain and the Origins of European Unity*
(1977).[29] But it is to the economic rather than the diplomatic historians
that one has to turn for an examination of the economic questions
which have made British membership so difficult; the standard work is
that by Alan Milward, *The Reconstruction of Western Europe, 1945–51*
(1984). Although it will become increasingly difficult for diplomatic
historians of the post-1960 period to tackle this subject as traditional
diplomatic history, British relations with the European Union (or
European Economic Community, as it used to be known) must surely
dominate the history of Britain's diplomacy from the early 1960s onwards. Separate introductions to the general development of Britain's
policy towards the European Community since 1945 have been provided
by John Young and also by Stephen George, whose *An Awkward
Partner: Britain in the European Community* (1990) is perhaps the most
well-established work, particularly for the period after Britain's entry
into Europe in 1973.[30] Central to each is the question of how far
membership effected 'a profound revolution in British foreign policy',
as historians such as David Reynolds suggest, or whether, as George
argues, there has in fact been 'no conversion to the idea of Europe'.[31]

The precipitousness of Britain's decline since 1945 has inevitably
provided a background theme for studies dealing with the post-war
period. The Suez crisis of 1956 was, according to traditional historiographical wisdom, a key moment in this process: it gave immediate rise
to an 'after the fall' approach to the study of British foreign policy,
exemplified in the work of F. S. Northedge, *Descent from Power: British
Foreign Policy 1945–1973* (1974). This thesis owes much to defections
of public servants at the time, as well as the division within the country,
and the opportunity it provided Harold Macmillan to redefine British
overseas commitments. The whole episode, and particularly the collusion aspect, was so disturbing because it revealed the realist basis for
British foreign policy, belying the supposed moral leadership Britain

enjoyed in world affairs – a reputation built up on the popular perception of the 'great power' politics of two world wars, and one on which Britain had traded heavily in the ideologically charged climate of the Cold War. It is little wonder that Anthony Eden and those loyal to him went to such enormous, if inevitably futile lengths to deny and cover up the fact of collusion with Israel. All this was exposed at the time, and it is interesting to contrast the Eden episode with Bevin's non-interventionism in the Middle East which formed the theme of Roger Louis's masterly study, *The British Empire in the Middle East 1945–1951* (1984). Since the opening of the records in 1987, these debates have been largely superseded and attention has turned instead to discussing why Britain embarked on this operation and then, having been drawn so deeply in, abandoned it short of achieving its objectives.[32] The standard account based on multi-archival sources is Keith Kyle, *Suez* (1991) which is a model of painstakingly researched narrative history; it should be read in conjunction with W. Scott Lucas's monograph, *Divided We Stand: Britain, the US and the Suez Crisis* (1991, reprinted and revised 1996), which is more provocative and also points to the preoccupation of so many scholars coming fresh to diplomatic history during the 1980s when the principal concern, if not actual obsession, was the hunt for the missing dimension of foreign policy – the input of the intelligence services. Lucas develops an interesting argument with respect to the role of the intelligence services, and specifically the relationship between overt and covert diplomatic methods. For an entirely different perspective on Suez, it is worth turning to another American scholar, Diane Kunz, who has approached the question from the point of view of economic diplomacy which, she argues, determined the course of the crisis 'from beginning to end'; her *Economic Diplomacy of the Suez Crisis* (1991) examines the proposition that Britain's relative decline enforced dependence on the US and that this meant the loss of policy autonomy for Britain.

The current historiographical orthodoxy on British foreign policy since 1945 has two themes: the first is concerned with the concept of avoidable decline and manifests itself at times in the more extreme iconographical works, such as John Charmley, *Churchill: the End of Glory* (1993) and the more academically sound but no less provocative works of Correlli Barnett. The second theme is the argument that the attempt to cling to British great power status has led to the squandering of resources, and so hastened and magnified this decline.[33] The latter thesis is exemplified in Michael Blackwell's *Clinging to Grandeur: British Attitudes and Foreign Policy in the Aftermath of the Second World War* (1993). At the same time the study of diplomacy itself, in terms of its mechanics, has become an increasingly fashionable subject – reflected in the establishment of postgraduate courses around the United Kingdom in centres such as Keele and Leicester, not traditionally noted for the study of diplomatic history, and the continued popularity of established courses at the London School of Economics (International History), Birmingham (Diplomacy), and Aberystwyth (International Politics). Among the best introductory textbooks to the study of diplomacy in a theoretical sense is *Diplomacy: the Dialogue Between States* (1982) by Adam Watson, himself a former member of the British Diplomatic Service, who addresses the fundamental questions of the nature and potential of diplomacy. More recently, Geoff Berridge has produced a useful text, *Diplomacy: Theory and Practice* (1995), which is a by-product of his Master's course at Leicester University and places emphasis on the different modes of diplomacy. Each is obliged to draw heavily on diplomatic history. The essential companion for those seeking some knowledge of the mechanics of diplomacy is R. G. Feltham's *Diplomatic Handbook* (1993), now in its sixth edition, while the historical origins have been explored by M. S. Anderson, *The Rise of Modern Diplomacy 1450–1919* (1993).

The discipline itself has its own journals: the well-established *Diplomatic History* which is produced by the Society of Historians of American Foreign Relations (SHAFR), and the more recently conceived British counterpart *Diplomacy and Statecraft*, which has been edited at the University of Birmingham since 1989; but see also the Canadian journal *International History Review*. The hunt for documentary material on British diplomacy can take the researcher far and wide. As with other branches of historical studies, relevant collections of private papers have been deposited in university libraries up and down the UK and a trawl through the standard guides to UK manuscript sources can yield some unexpected finds. However, it is the official records which must supply the bulk of the source material. It is no longer sufficient to write the history of British diplomacy solely from British sources: the multi-archival approach is now almost de rigueur. This now includes investigation of material in Russian-language sources which brings us to the major omission in British scholarship at the present time – an examination of the Soviet perspective. Jonathan Haslam has produced two volumes on Soviet foreign policy in the interwar years, but there is nothing comparable to this for the Second World War or Cold War period from British scholars. This is partly a reflection of resistance among British students to the tackling of the Russian language at university level, but is also an indication of the degree to which the scope of Cold War research projects have been determined by the availability first of documents in English-language sources, and secondly of funding for travel to more remote locations. The problems of handling the archives in Moscow have been well-aired; nevertheless, scholars in the United States and elsewhere are demonstrating that it is possible and valuable to take on this challenge. An introduction to the state of scholarship on this aspect can be found in the works of Vojtech Mastny and David Holloway's fascinating monograph, *Stalin and the Bomb* (1994).

A cautionary note should be sounded to all who venture into the diplomatic archives: diplomatic correspondence is seductive; it 'combines skilful exposition with rhetorical force ... it abounds with formulations that remain in the memory' and, by implication, can transfer themselves on to the written page of the unwary researcher.[34] The doyen of diplomatic history written as a narrative of diplomatic correspondence, Ranke, was firmly of the belief that the rigorous use of primary sources would entail objectivity; but such an approach without some contextualisation of the material would be open to criticism even from those scholars who have not rushed to embrace postmodernist, poststructuralist thinking in their research methodology. The use of oral eyewitness accounts is often helpful in giving depth to a piece of written research, but the problems of squaring the accounts of survivors, who may or may not have axes to grind or whose perspective was limited (the Civil Service in Britain is so compartmentalised that, with the exception of the most senior officials, this is almost invariably the case), with the official record which if thoroughly worked over provides a much broader but by definition 'uncritical' perspective, is a well-known problem in all fields of contemporary history where actors in the events studied are still living.

Some recent historiographical anthologies have also reflected the influence of the new cultural history which, in placing emphasis on the social construction of memory, postulates that historical memories are socially acquired and collective and are also constantly refashioned to suit present purposes.[35] Applied to history this means a 'denial of the fixity of the past, of the reality of the past apart from what the historian chooses to make of it, and thus of any objective truth about the past'.[36] Michael Hogan's edited collection, *Hiroshima in History and Memory* (1996) demonstrates how this thesis can be used to stimulate a fresh examination of old debates in diplomatic history. Hogan juxtaposes essays by American and Japanese scholars on the construction of official memory and the challenge posed to this version by alternative memories, while giving the debate some cohesion by inclusion of an historiographical overview and 'traditionalist' analysis of the decision-making process which led to the dropping of the bomb on Hiroshima.

The alleged predictive value of theorising received something of a setback with the ending of the Cold War which proved as unexpected to social scientists as it was rapid. One consequence has been the partial demolition of a range of academic theories which have found their way into diplomatic history, among them totalitarianism; moreover, the collapse of communism has left economic determinists with the burden of proving the validity of their interpretations.[37] The sharp controversy about poverty of theory in diplomatic history can be traced most readily through back issues of *Diplomatic History*. In practice, however, there remains a large area of crossover between political science and diplomatic history: philosophical problems are bound to impinge on the writing of diplomatic history of any worth, while the abstractions of the theorist are of little moment without drawing on the detailed empirically based analysis of the historian. As one distinguished historian of British diplomacy once observed: 'History is not narrative of the past as it was, nor is it a quest after the facts – it is a discipline dedicated to the eternal recurrence of revision ... endless arguments, debates and controversies about what exactly did happen, why it happened and what would be an adequate account of its significance.'[38]

CHAPTER 11

Military history

Ian F. W. Beckett

In the last thirty years, historians have increasingly come to recognise the often pivotal role played by war and conflict in historical development. In the process, the interpretation and understanding of the impact of war upon states, societies and individuals has been transformed, with a transition from what might be described as traditional 'drum and fife' or 'drum and trumpet' military history and its concerns with battles, campaigns and generalship to the study of 'war and society'. The latter, indeed, is often characterised as 'new military history' which, in turn, has applied the new methodologies to the historiographical backwater of operational art so that the scope of research has continued to expand to the benefit of wider historical understanding.

Something of the transformation that was taking place thirty years ago can be gauged from a comparison of Michael Howard's classic military history, *The Franco-Prussian War*, published in 1961, with his *War in European History* which appeared fifteen years later. However, while conforming to certain traditional parameters and describing military actions in what John Keegan characterised a little unfairly as 'neo-classical' style, the former was already breaking from those conventions in examining the war against the political, social and economic background of France and Prussia. Indeed, Howard delivered a lecture to the Royal United Services Institution in that same year of 1961 arguing that military history required study in far wider terms than either the traditional campaign narrative or what Tim Travers has called the analytic–utilitarian approach of trying to discern 'lessons, principles, and rules of war'. Indeed, Howard insisted that military history must be 'directed by human curiosity about wider issues and by a sense of its relevance to the nature and development of society as a whole'.[1]

As Travers has reminded us, both the narrative and the analytic–

utilitarian styles were long established among British writers, the first real campaign narratives emerging from the Marlburian wars and the first real campaign analysis from Henry Lloyd's work on the Seven Years War. Epic works such as Sir William Napier's *The History of the War in the Peninsula* (1828–40), A. W. Kinglake's *The Invasion of the Crimea* (1863–88) and Sir John Fortescue's *History of the British Army* (1899–1930) continued in the narrative vein while G. F. R. Henderson's celebrated *Stonewall Jackson and the American Civil War* (1898) and the military authors of later Victorian texts such as the 'Wolseley', 'Special Campaign' and 'Pall Mall' series maintained the analytic approach. Indeed, the search for the 'principles of war' remains at the core of the contemporary revival of the study of operational military history at both the Royal Military Academy, Sandhurst, and the Staff College, Camberley.[2]

In looking beyond these persistent traditions, however, those – like Howard – who were striving to establish military studies as a respectable academic pursuit faced the additional difficulty of the increasing number of accounts of the two world wars being published to feed a burgeoning popular history market in the late 1950s and 1960s. Partly no doubt due to what John Keegan has called the 'historiographical heritage of the Second World War', and reflected in the success of television series such as the BBC's *The Great War* in 1964,[3] there was also a sense in which this increasing popularity of military books served the spirit of that particular period in the characterisation of war as futile. Indeed, they frequently said more about the culture of the 1960s than about the military past.

This was especially true of the treatment of the First World War, with the 'butchers and bunglers' approach to British generalship evinced in such books as Leon Wolff's *In Flanders Fields* (1958) and Alan Clark's *The Donkeys* (1961), and in the Theatre Workshop production, *Oh! What a Lovely War* (1963), directed by Joan Littlewood. In fact, this trend still survives in such recent works as John Laffin's *British Butchers and Bunglers of World War One* (1988) and Denis Winter's *Haig's Command* (1991). However, as Brian Bond has commented, 'despite the saturation coverage ... little was produced of lasting scholarly value because there was so little attempt to place the war in historical perspective'. Indeed, while purporting to be revelatory, many of these books merely rekindled the historiographical battles of the 1920s and 1930s as established in participants' memoirs. Thus, influential memoirs such as Churchill's *The World Crisis* (1923–29) and Lloyd George's *War Memoirs* (1933–36) continued to dominate popular historians' bibliographies, even as the introduction of the fifty-year rule by the Public Records Act of 1958 and of the thirty-year rule by that of 1967 were making Cabinet papers and memoranda available to the historian for the first time.[4]

The continuing appearance of what can only be described as 'military pornography' or 'tabloid military history' has been particularly unhelpful given the suspicion that can still be attached to the academic study of war. Nevertheless, Howard's pioneering efforts were vital in establishing the importance of what he was to refer to in *War in European History* (1976) as the 'environmental framework' of war and conflict. Another in the forefront of change was Arthur Marwick, whose study of British society in the First World War, *The Deluge* (1965), was followed by *Britain in the Century of Total War* (1968) and *War and Social Change in the Twentieth Century* (1974). Just as Howard's influence was felt in the syllabus of his War Studies Department at King's College, London in the 1960s, so Marwick's work became familiar to a wide readership through the 'War and Society' course taught by him and his colleagues at the Open University in the 1970s.

In contrast to to older scholars – such as the American, J. U. Nef, whose *War and Human Progress* (1950) represented war as having a purely negative impact on historical development – Marwick built on the correlations between wartime participation and the subsequent levelling of social inequalities made by other more perceptive authors in the 1950s, such as Richard Titmuss, Stanislas Andrzejewski and G. N. Clark, to establish war as a catalyst and determinant of far-reaching social change. In particular, Marwick established an analytical framework for the study of 'total war', four 'modes' in *Britain in the Century of Total War* becoming a 'four tier model' in *War and Social Change in the Twentieth Century*. In this framework, total war would be characterised by destruction and disruption on an unprecedented scale; the challenging of existing political and social structures; the increased participation through total mobilisation of previously disadvantaged social groups; and the psychological impact of the war experience – the whole culminating in real and enduring social change. Some other historians at the time, such as Angus Calder and Henry Pelling, were more cautious in their assessment of the impact of total war as evinced in *The People's War* (1969) and *Britain in the Second World War* (1988) respectively. Marwick, too, has since modified his interpretation, as evidenced in his introduction to *Total War and Social Change* (1988) and the second edition of *The Deluge* (1991). Nevertheless, Marwick has had a profound impact on the historiography of war.[5]

The emergence of the new approaches of Howard and Marwick bore fruit in new academic series in the 1970s and 1980s such as *War and Society* from Fontana; *War, Armed Forces and Society* from Manchester University Press; *Studies in Military and Strategic History* from

Macmillan; and *Origins of Modern Wars* from Longman. To these have been added in the 1990s, *Modern Wars in Perspective*, also from Longman; *Modern Wars* from Edward Arnold; and, most recently, *Warfare and History* from UCL Press. Academic journals have also appeared, notably the *Journal of Strategic Studies*, the American *Journal of Military History* (formerly *Military Affairs*), the Australian *War and Society*, and, most recently, *War in History*. Other academic journals of course carry material of relevance, and the size of the useful annual summary of this literature, *War and Society Newsletter*, published as a supplement of the German journal, *Militärgeschichtliche Mitteilungen*, has increased dramatically since its first appearance in 1973. Increasingly, too, courses and chairs in war studies have become available at universities beyond King's College, London and the University of Oxford. Individual courses and special subjects appeared in many history departments in the late 1960s and 1970s while the MA in War Studies at King's College has been supplemented by an MA in Military History at the University of Leeds, and King's College itself has now introduced an undergraduate degree in War Studies. Postgraduate work had also become sufficiently frequent for military studies to receive a separate heading in the *Index to Theses* from 1977 onwards.[6]

As a result, the comprehension of the significance of war and conflict in British history and among British historians has increased substantially, and this has by no means been confined to the 'total' wars of the twentieth century. As early as 1969, for example, Geoffrey Holmes recognised that few facets of British life between 1689 and 1714 remained untouched by the fact of war and that it had had a major impact upon the progress of the British economy throughout the eighteenth century. The argument has been carried much further more recently by John Brewer in *The Sinews of Power* (1990). Indeed, however appalling, war can no longer be considered purely in terms of disaster and destruction: on occasion, positive benefit may be derived in social, economic or even demographic terms, as is made clear by the work by Jay Winter in such texts as *War and Economic Development* (1975) and *The Great War and the British People* (1986). Ten years after Holmes, Clive Emsley argued that the impact of the French revolutionary and Napoleonic wars between 1793 and 1815, and not industrialisation, was the prime factor in determining the course of British social history. Yet, these conflicts were essentially 'limited' compared to those of the twentieth century although, as John Childs has pointed out, the concept of limitation is somewhat relative. Indeed, the manpower problems Britain experienced during the Crimean War were not dissimilar to those encountered in the First World War; and the losses sustained between 1793 and 1815 were almost certainly proportionately higher in terms of men under arms, and the level of military participation probably greater in proportion to male population between 1793 and 1815 than between 1914 and 1918. In fact, seen in these terms, the resulting social, economic and political upheaval in the immediate post-war period from 1815 onwards was of more significance for the future pattern of British society and democracy than developments in the aftermath of either world war.[7]

In many respects, therefore, the military historian has been required to master the methodologies of social, economic, political, cultural and local historians. This is most apparent in syntheses such as Howard's *War in European History* (1976) or John Gooch's *Armies in Europe* (1980), which derived from the undergraduate course in war and society he had introduced at the University of Lancaster in 1970; John Child's *Armies and Warfare in Europe, 1648–1789* (1982); John Hale's elegant contribution to the Fontana series, *War and Society in Renaissance Europe, 1450–1620* (1985) or the *Manchester History of the British Army*, a nine-volume sub-series of that mentioned earlier from Manchester University Press, which seeks to integrate the new social, political and economic scholarship with more traditional campaign studies. A typical volume in the latter series, such as Edward Spiers's *The Late Victorian Army, 1868–1902* (1991), thus addresses such subjects as military organisation, training, recruitment of officers and men, conditions of service, and the wider relationship of army with state and society before concluding with a survey of colonial campaigning and a case study of the South African war.

From such studies emerge not only the complexity of the relationship between armies, states and societies but also the myriad ways in which war and conflict might impact upon them. Even in the case of a largely anti-militarist state such as Britain, in which an army usually recruited by voluntary enlistment was largely unrepresentative of its parent society prior to the introduction of conscription in the twentieth century, there was still an interdependence existing side by side with popular indifference to military matters. Thus, the presence of even small numbers of regular soldiers inevitably meant trade for local businesses, but the army also provided spectacle and often considerable inspiration for the purveyors of popular culture. Indeed, one theme explored by Edward Spiers in his volume on the late-Victorian army is why it was that a military career was held in such low esteem when the army's overseas achievements were acclaimed in popular art, literature and theatre. Equally, one recent examination by John Fuller of the way in which the morale of the British army on the Western Front was so robust between 1914 and 1918 while that of other armies largely collapsed postulates a solution in the effective exportation to the army's rear areas in France and Flanders of mass popular culture.[8]

Consideration of morale and discipline in itself can also conveniently illustrate the variety of sources which can be interpreted by the military historian. Fuller's primary source, for example, was a sample of surviving trench journals produced by soldiers themselves for an audience of soldiers. Another approach has been to examine reports by the military censors and yet another to pursue those statistical indices utilised by the army's own general headquarters, namely incidences of trench feet, shell shock and military crime. In both these latter approaches, surviving official records in the Public Record Office provided the sources and, as further official records are released relating to wartime courts martial – personnel files are usually closed for a minimum of seventy-five years – so more statistical data will become available. In addition, however, historians are able to draw upon the private papers of soldiers of all ranks retained in such repositories as the Imperial War Museum, National Army Museum, the Liddell Hart Centre for Military Archives at King's College, London and the Liddle Collection at the Brotherton Library of the University of Leeds. Indeed, Gary Sheffield's doctoral research on the significance of officer–man relations for morale and discipline was largely based upon such collections.[9]

As in other modes of historical investigation, there is little substitute for solid research in the written archives. However, while those repositories named above and other national collections – such as those of the British Library, Churchill College, Cambridge and the India Office Library – will inevitably consume much of the military historian's research time, the rich diversity of the country's County Record Offices and other local archive libraries and offices should never be underestimated. For the study of what might be termed the 'amateur military tradition' of home defence forces such as the Militia, Volunteers, Yeomanry, Territorials and Home Guard, for example, recourse to locally held collections is essential. Some guides are now available to such records[10] but these can be supplemented by the indices maintained by the National Register of Archives, and the latter is also a ready source of information on other privately held collections. For the papers of prominent soldiers, a new and welcome development is the Survey of Military and Naval Records of Senior Defence Personnel project jointly administered from the Liddell Hart Centre for Military Archives and the University of Southampton Library. This aims to bring together, on linked on-line computer databases, information on the whereabouts and content of the surviving papers of all defence personnel who achieved the ranks above and including Major-General, Air Vice Marshal and Rear Admiral between 1800 and 1975.

Such official, demi-official and private papers will be subject, of course, to the same strengths and weaknesses as similar source material in any other branch of history. Moreover, as in other areas, historians of twentieth-century military affairs have embraced new sources such as film and other visual media and oral testimony. In many respects, the exploitation of oral testimony in military history was part of the movement in the late 1960s and 1970s towards the exploration of the 'personal experience' of war – or, as Peter Simkins has expressed it, 'everyman's experience' of war. Initially, this was an increasing feature of popular rather than academic military history, one New Zealand exponent of oral testimony likening the rush among authors to interview surviving Anzacs of the Great War as a 'smash and grab raid on history'. In Britain, popular authors such as Martin Middlebrook and Lyn Macdonald combed the dwindling ranks of Great War veterans and, in turn, stimulated still more publications in the same vein. An interesting by-product was a distinct shift in emphasis from an earlier obsession with Passchendaele towards the first day of the Battle of the Somme and the fortunes of the Pals Battalions in particular, as the typical Great War experience.[11]

More conscious of the limitations of oral history, professional military historians have used it as 'just one skein in the tapestry' to supplement other sources but, as in the case of Alistair Thomson, have also approached it in far more sophisticated ways. Moreover, *inter alia*, they have concluded that, since no one unit was like any other, the individual experience cannot be generalised in the way often attempted by the popular historians. Similarly, historians connected with the Imperial War Museum have greatly extended the utility of visual evidence to the military historian, exploring the wealth of film and photographic archives to good effect.[12]

So far, the impression has been created that popular military history has little to offer, but it must be acknowledged that it has been beneficial in encouraging further interest in the subject. Thus, to add to the older Society for Army Historical Research established in 1923, new specialist societies emerged such as the Victorian Military Society (1974) and the Western Front Association (1980) – their respective journals, *Soldiers of the Queen* and *Stand To*, as well as their study group and branch structures, providing a generally effective forum for dialogue between the professional and amateur military historian. Ian Knight's meticulous examination of the circumstances surrounding the British defeat at Isandlwana, in *Zulu: Isandlwana and Rorke's Drift, 22–23 January 1879* (1992), is an excellent example of the kind of quality work emanating from members of such societies. Moreover, amateur enthusiasts have also contributed valuable local studies such as Frank Hussey's *Suffolk Invasion: The Dutch Attack on Landguard Fort, 1667* (1983) or A. Rootes's *Front Line County* (1980) on Second World War Kent. Genealogists and family historians are similarly contributing to the WO 97 project administered by the Friends of the Public Record Office, by which an especially large collection of soldiers' documents from the eighteenth and nineteenth centuries will be rendered more easily accessible to all. Local record societies have also performed the same function with respect to militia muster rolls, lieutenancy correspondence and so on for many years.[13]

There was also a further service rendered by the essentially popular interest in the war experience of ordinary soldiers since, in concentrating upon the social organisation of armed forces, many professional military historians had arguably lost sight of the fact that these forces were ultimately intended to fight. Indeed, in a debate on the nature of military history published in *History Today* in 1984, John Childs had pointed out that the 'new military history' was not actually military history at all in the sense that the latter should be concerned primarily with battle. In the following year, a pioneering social study of the British army in the Great War, *A Nation in Arms*, was assailed by one traditional military historian, John Terraine, as 'a work of sociology, not military history'. However, a military sociologist, Gwynn Harries-Jenkins, noted that while studies of 'the complex relationships between armed forces and society are usually works of sociology. This is not; it is military history.'[14]

Nevertheless, Terraine had a point in commenting that 'something essential is escaping – the War itself, in fact' and Peter Simkins, whose own *Kitchener's Army: The Raising of the New Armies, 1914–16* (1988) had been a formidable contribution to the study of the army as a social organisation, also pointed out as recently as 1991 that 'all too few military historians in this country possess *intimate* knowledge of the tactical and sociological factors affecting the conduct of units in battle'. Consequently, his call was for 'more operational histories and studies of battlefield performance' in order to dispel remaining myths and half-truths about the First World War.[15]

In a sense, the return of the professional military historian to the physical and psychological reality of the battlefield environment was marked as long ago as 1976 when John Keegan's *The Face of Battle* brilliantly exposed the deficiencies of traditional military history in explaining precisely what had happened on past battlefields, using Agincourt, Waterloo and the Somme as case studies. Hew Strachan also focused on operational rather than institutional developments in *European Armies and the Conduct of War* (1983), and supplemented his institutional and social study, *Wellington's Legacy: The Reform of the British Army, 1830–54* (1984), with *From Waterloo to Balaclava: Tactics, Technology and the British Army, 1815–54* (1985).

Keegan used overwhelmingly secondary sources but subjected them to more careful scrutiny than had been common among previous military historians, who had tended to favour a rather broader and stereotyped brush for battle descriptions. He was also not afraid to apply the findings of American social scientists and psychologists, who had analysed behavioural patterns among Second World War servicemen in immediate post-operational investigations. A similar method to that of Keegan was used by Paddy Griffith, whose detailed 'tactical snippeting' applied to soldiers' accounts of battle might mean, for example, not overlooking a passing reference to the discarding of packs as a key to a serious intention to aim for total victory on an American Civil War battlefield. Griffith's work was manifested first on a broad scale in *Forward into Battle* (1981), covering the whole of the development of warfare from the Peninsular War to Vietnam; then on the smaller canvas of the American Civil War in *Rally Once Again* (1987); and, most recently, in *British Battle Tactics on the Western Front* (1994). The Keegan methodology also had a wider currency in the re-evaluation both of classical warfare in *The Western Way of War* (1990) by the American scholar, Victor Davis Hanson, and of the English Civil Wars by the American-based historian, Charles Carlton, in *Going to the Wars* (1992).

The challenge posed by Peter Simkins has also been taken up by other historians and it is noticeable that there is increasing emphasis on operational studies relating to the British army in the Great War. Tim Travers, for example, has sought an explanation to the British army's slow learning curve between 1914 and 1918 in largely managerial terms, set in the context of the hierarchical nature of the army's officer corps; whereas Trevor Wilson and Robin Prior have explored a technical solution in detailed analysis of such issues as the understanding of evolving artillery techniques. A significant development has been to push the search for a key to operational evolution down the chain of command from army level to corps and divisional level. In this respect, two potentially exciting projects, which further apply new methodologies to military history, are the British Divisional Commanders during the Great War project directed by John Bourne at the University of Birmingham and the SHLM project at the Imperial War Museum, so named after Peter Simkins, Bryan Hammond, John Lee and Chris McCarthy. The former is intended to establish a 'multi-biographical' database of the 222 individuals who exercised divisional command on a permanent basis on the Western Front, while the latter seeks to establish a similar database to assess and compare individual divisional combat performance according to set criteria such as strength of enemy defences, degree of supporting fire, terrain, and climatic conditions.[16]

The growth in academic study of operations has thus far tended to reinforce the pattern of contemporary professional military concerns in concentrating upon what French soldiers knew as *la grande guerre* or large-scale warfare. In reality, the actual practical soldiering experience of western soldiers in the nineteenth and twentieth centuries has more generally been in some form of low-intensity conflict; Davis Hanson would date the preconceived notion of the nature of 'real' war, in the sense of meaning conventional large-scale battle, to classical Greece. Its attraction has been a matter both of institutional conservatism and of the lack of decisive results to be obtained in such distinctly unglamorous warfare. Equally, those who were formerly largely concerned with (nuclear) strategic studies – usually social or political scientists rather than military historians – have generally refashioned themselves as regional security specialists in a post-Cold War era and they, too, remain as oblivious to the significance of low-intensity conflict as previously. Yet, military historians have increasingly acknowledged that the total wars of the twentieth century are wholly abnormal in the context of the overall pattern of military activity over the past two centuries, and are now devoting greater attention to counter-insurgency campaigns and doctrine.[17]

One particularly valuable development has been the way in which the New Zealander, James Belich, in *New Zealand Wars and the Victorian Interpretation of Racial Conflict* (1986) and the South African historian, John Laband, in *Kingdom in Crisis: The Zulu Response to the British Invasion of 1879* (1992) have substituted indigenous for imperial perspectives of the historiography of such colonial campaigns. In so doing they have added yet another layer of understanding to that supplied by historians like Keegan and Griffith to the received versions of traditional military history. In terms of more modern counter-insurgency campaigns, North American historians like David Charters and Tom Mockaitis have been in the forefront but, as the thirty-year rule advances, more material will become steadily available for the study of Britain's post-1945 campaigns – indeed, younger British postgraduate researchers are already beginning to work in these areas.[18]

Despite the enormous range of research on British military history over the last twenty years, it can also be said that much remains to be done. As might be expected, the thirty-year rule tends to have an undue influence on postgraduate work. The most recent edition (1995) of the Institute of Historical Research's *Historical Research for High Degrees in the United Kingdom: Theses in Progress*, for example, lists just three topics related to the British army for the seventeenth century; four for the eighteenth century; and nine for the nineteenth century; but twenty-three for the twentieth century. Similarly, the companion edition listing theses completed in 1994 shows two for the eighteenth century, one for the nineteenth century, and eight for the twentieth century.[19]

Generally, there is still too little interest in the seventeenth and eighteenth centuries. Beyond the preponderance of publications on the impact of the English Civil Wars, there is still comparatively little, although John Childs has completed a notable trilogy on the period between 1660 and 1702. For the eighteenth century, valuable work has been done by historians such as Alan Guy, Tony Hayter and the Canadian, John Houlding, but much remains to be scrutinised and, for all the past popularity of the Peninsular War, an overall reassessment of the whole period between 1783 and 1815 remains lacking and, significantly, the relevant volume of the Manchester series has yet to be contracted. The period after 1815 is much better covered but a recent revival of interest in the Victorian army has demonstrated that there is still much here worthy of examination.[20] Indeed, the Army Records Society, founded in 1984 to publish an annual volume of historical documents, has published two successive Victorian volumes dealing with Lord Roberts (1993) and Lord Chelmsford (1994), and could still arguably turn with profit to the papers of such luminaries as Viscount Gough, Sir Charles Napier, the Duke of Cambridge or even Edward Cardwell. A yawning gap still remaining in the study of auxiliary forces is in that of the Yeomanry.[21]

In such a brief survey, it is impossible to do more than convey an overall sense of the work that has been and is being accomplished in the field of military history: there are many contributions which, perforce, it has been necessary to omit. Nevertheless, it should be apparent that the range and reach of the subject has been continuously expanding over the last thirty years. Indeed, it might be argued that no other branch of history has had quite so great an impact on other practitioners of the historian's craft as has the 'new military history'.

Further reading

It is immensely difficult to select a handful of titles to represent the work of the last thirty years but the following can be recommended as conveying the sheer variety of military history that has become available. Note, the choice has not been restricted to British military history or to British military historians. Among those already mentioned in the chapter, Sir John Hale, *War and Society in Renaissance Europe, 1450–1620* (London: Fontana, 1982), Sir Michael Howard, *The Franco-Prussian War* (London: Hart-Davis, 1961) and John Keegan, *The Face of Battle* (London: Cape, 1976) demand inclusion for the sheer elegance of their exposition. Similarly, Peter Simkins, *Kitchener's Army* (Manchester:

Manchester University Press, 1988) and Edward Spiers, *The Late Victorian Army, 1868–1902* (Manchester: Manchester University Press, 1991) are fine examples of the most modern analysis of the relationship between war, army and society. To these might be added Geoffrey Parker, *The Army of Flanders and the Spanish Road, 1567–1659* (Cambridge: Cambridge University Press, 1972) and John Lynn, *The Bayonets of the Republic* (Champaign: University of Illinois Press, 1984), while a neglected masterpiece is Marcus Cunliffe, *Soldiers and Civilians: The Martial Spirit in America 1775–1865* (London: Eyre & Spottiswoode, 1969). Remaining with American themes, two greatly contrasting volumes are the scholarly Eric Bergerud, *The Dynamics of Defeat: The Vietnam War in Hau Nghia Province* (Boulder: Westview Press, 1991) and, a fascinating example of 'amateur' military history, Peter Svenson, *Battlefield: Farming a Civil War Battleground* (London: Faber & Faber, 1992), mixing history with the experience of farming on the former 1862 battlefield of Cross Keys.

CHAPTER 12

Imperial and Commonwealth history

Robert Pearce

Over the last century a twofold imperial revolution has occurred: not only has the British Empire been decolonised, but so has imperial historiography. A century ago historians who were themselves committed imperialists held the field. In 1884 Sir John Seeley was able to paint a glowing picture of the acquisition of the Empire and to point confidently to a future of ever greater expansion. He believed that history should 'not merely gratify the reader's curiosity about the past, but modify his view of the present and his forecast of the future'.[1] In fact, he believed, like the Duchess in *Alice in Wonderland*, that everything has a moral if only you can find it, and the moral of British history was to his mind quite simple: imperial expansion, which was central to the British past, would continue also to dominate its future. It was, therefore, easily the most important theme or subdivision of historical studies. Such was the overweening confidence of imperial historians a century ago that it led many an academic to switch from historian to prophet in propounding a new Whig historiography.

Nostalgia for an imagined past of imperial glamour and greatness may not have entirely disappeared today. But, on the whole, the grand imperial schemata of past generations have themselves become the subject of historical scrutiny. Seeley's place in imperial history is assured – not as an historian but as a propagandist of imperial greatness. While reinforcing imperial values, he was also reflecting the imperial mind-set of his generation, and thus he is a figure well worthy of study. Since then, however, there has been a transvaluation of imperial values. The imperial world-view has been turned upside down, and imperialist imperial historians have been largely replaced, in an age of decolonisation, by anti-imperialist ones – the debunkers of imperial myths, the celebrants of new larger-than-life nationalist heroes, the confident but indignant exposers of neo-colonial machinations. But, of course, they too had a political agenda. Theirs has been an engaged reading – and writing – of history: knowing what they were looking for, and being determined to find it, they were easily able to confirm their theories. Hence they tended to emphasise only one strand from imperial history and, by implication, to deny either the existence or importance of other strands, in order to extract a simple moral. Perhaps the most obvious example of this is Peter Fryer's *Black People in the British Empire* (1988). But such analyses have seemed to many to bear an uncanny resemblance to systematic denigration.

Imperialism has always been a political minefield – an uncomfortable, but not altogether uncomforting, thought for the hard-working scholar immersed in painstaking research among voluminous documentation. At least it gives the consolation of importance to his or her work. Far more disconcerting has been the line taken by another group of historians, who have decided that imperialism is no longer of relevance. Not Disraeli at the Crystal Palace in 1872, but Gladstone at Midlothian in 1879 had been correct: the essential strength of Britain lay not overseas but in these isles. The Empire had been an essentially false trail: it had led nowhere, except perhaps to the unreality of Commonwealth rhetoric, and so could now be conveniently forgotten. What was the point of charting a meaningless evolutionary dead-end? Was not imperialism a virus to which, despite the virulent contagion of the few, the bulk of the population had been immune? The majority of the British people – and also of politicians – had, after all, been steeped in abysmal imperial ignorance. When surveys of the public's knowledge were held after the Second World War, it was found that few could name either a single colony – the United States or Rutland being among the hazarded answers – or item of colonial produce, let alone define the difference between a colony and dominion. The only issue on which the majority was correct was in its assumption that most people in the colonies were non-white. These results added to anecdotal evidence that responsible ministers were little better informed than the population at large. It was said that J. H. Thomas, Secretary of State for the Colonies in 1924, thought Uganda a term of abuse rather than an East African protectorate. Nor was this a particularly new phenomenon. At the end of the nineteenth century, Mary Kingsley had complained that British people could not tell 'a paw paw from a palm oil puncheon'.[2]

The moral from such reasoning was that Britain's destiny certainly did not lie in the Commonwealth; if overseas, it was merely across the English Channel. Furthermore, although no one could deny that the

Empire had existed at one time, there seemed no reason to study 'imperial history' as such. It could be swallowed up quite satisfactorily by other historical subdivisions, and especially 'area studies'. Africanists and other geographical specialists were needed; and by seeing imperial rule as a brief episode in a much longer story, they would reduce the significance of Britain's imperial impact, which the ethnocentric Victorians had so arrogantly inflated. Hence former colonies had not only won their independence, they had also won back their own histories. The imperial factor was thus relegated to the margins of 'Third World' history by grass-roots historians of the 'subaltern studies' school. If any morsels remained from imperial history, they could be devoured by mainstream political, international, economic, social and intellectual historians, as well as by old-fashioned biographers and new-fashioned exponents of development studies and race relations. Imperial historiography looked likely to be decolonised out of existence. Perhaps imperial history would follow another once-vaunted field of study, constitutional history, and lose its relatively free-standing significance. Might it even, despite the existence of well-endowed chairs in imperial history, go the way of that once fashionable prop of imperial rule, craniology? Was the imperial sun finally setting on studies of empire?

We cannot balk the question of whether there is any need for a specifically imperial history. Take away its component parts – divide them up among other forms of history – and what is left? According to David Fieldhouse, writing in the 1980s, there is a common denominator: in the interaction between the history of Britain and the histories of those peoples brought together by British expansion. Hence there is a place for the Janus-like imperial historian, facing both colony and metropolis, placing 'himself' in the 'interstices of his subject'. Imperial history thus provides a context – one among many – whose significance is worth investigating.[3]

But does imperial history need such a defensive apology? After all, Fieldhouse was basically saying little more than that the Empire had metropolis and periphery, which should both be studied. This is true enough, but hardly profound. Should it not 'go without saying'? Were imperial historians, for so long conscious of the superiority of their themes, now succumbing to an inferiority complex?

Simple explanations are often the best. We study the British Empire in the twentieth century because it existed. Is that not sufficient justification? The Empire, and its Commonwealth counterpart, did exist: therefore we do not have to invent them, but we do, as historians, have to reconstruct them. Even if imperial history could be dissolved entirely into its component parts, that would not eliminate this basic reason. Indeed it is precisely because imperial history is so multifarious – and, as a consequence, so challenging and stimulating – that it is such a rewarding field of study. Where else would we find so fascinating a combination? We must be jacks of all trades in order even to begin to master the history of the British Empire and Commonwealth.

Reports of the death of imperial history have been wildly exaggerated. Today the subject is alive and flourishing, not only at the level of doctoral research but in schools. British imperial and commercial expansion appears in key stage three of the National Curriculum and, at key stage four, elements of imperial and Commonwealth history feature in the British core unit for the twentieth century. A sign of the times is the recent appearance of Frank McDonough's *The British Empire 1815–1914* (1995) in Hodder and Stoughton's popular *Access to History* series. The forthcoming *Oxford History of the British Empire*, guided by Roger Louis, is an even more welcome development. Indeed there seems a possibility, greater than at any time hitherto, of disinterested study free of any political agenda. After all the business of the historian, *pace* Seeley and also the anti-imperialists, is merely to gratify our curiosity about the past, without consciously seeking to modify our view of the present or forecast of the future. Nor, in an effort at intellectual empire-building, need we argue that our area of study is the most important one possible. Imperial history will not provide any key to modern Britain, as was once naively supposed; alas, no such key exists. But it does provide a revealing perspective from which to view aspects not only of twentieth-century Britain but of much of the wider world.

No doubt later historians will spot characteristic biases of imperial researchers at the end of the twentieth century. This is inevitable with any form of history. But it does seem at least possible that there may now be a less prejudiced historiography, free of either imperialist hagiography or anti-imperialist venom. Such neutrality, consequent upon the passage of time, is to be welcomed; good historical writing requires broad imaginative sympathy not particular political passion. Peter Marshall has recently voiced hopes for a new, more openly enquiring historiography. It would, he writes, 'be a sign of maturity of British society if young people could learn to look at the imperial past as an historical problem to be judged like other problems, rather than one which evokes automatic and unthinking affirmations of loyalty or rejection'.[4] There are pleasing signs that this is happening. As imperial passions subside, the history of the British Empire is coming of age, as a dispassionate study – neither celebratory nor apologetic – which accepts a plurality of viewpoints.

The British Empire never made much sense to the tidy-minded strategist. It was, as Liddell Hart put it, the greatest example of over-extension in history. And he was writing only of the 'formal' Empire;

there was also the 'informal' one. Similarly imperial history has always taken an unwieldy shape. It has all the trackless inconvenience of a jungle. And when there is a path, seemingly broad and straight, it often turns out to be one of the perverse variety which Mary Kingsley tangled with during her travels in West Africa – occasionally the type that would make a deliberate bolt for the interior of Africa before metamorphosing into a stream, so that she suspected it might be the incarnation of a local devil. It is the same with the Empire. The subject matter seems almost limitless and is definitely unpredictable; certainly it resists precise definition, but it is only the myopic or the intellectually weary who assert that it is nothing but a dead-end. If imperial history has sometimes the inconvenience of the trackless African bush, it also occasionally has the resonant beauty of the African rainforest. This, while denigrated by many, including Joseph Conrad and Albert Schweitzer, appeared to Mary Kingsley to be composed of 'ever varying scenes of loveliness whose component parts are ever the same, yet the effect ever different. Doubtless it is wrong to call it a symphony, yet I know of no other word to describe the scenery. ... It is as full of life and beauty and passion as any symphony Beethoven ever wrote.'[5] The history of the British Empire and Commonwealth is similarly full of life and interest to those who approach it in the right spirit. No one should ever be shamefaced about studying imperial history.

Imperial studies have widened significantly over the last dozen years. There is now a much greater recognition of the centrality of the Empire to the British experience – and not simply to those relatively small numbers of individuals, in the exiguous white line, who worked in India or the colonies, or to those connected in other direct ways with overseas territories. J. A. Mangan has pioneered the study of imperialism and private education, so that the Empire may be seen as the public school writ large. In similar vein, Donald Leinster-Mackay has seen the nineteenth-century preparatory school as 'cradle and creche' of Empire. Nor was the state system immune, as will be readily apparent from reading works like Robert Roberts's memoir *The Classic Slum*,[6] though this is an area where far more systematic and detailed research is needed. The impact of imperialism on British education – and vice versa – is only one element in the patterns of socialisation to which the Empire contributed, and which ensured that individuals, in Britain and overseas, were imbued with appropriate attitudes and values. Whether imperialism actually amounted to a 'dominant ideology' – or 'emergent', 'alternative' or, in some ways, even 'oppositional' – can be left for sociologists to argue about. What is certain is that much more work remains to be done in this fascinating field, which embraces areas of popular culture formerly thought to be outside the purview of imperial history.

The British public may, on the whole, have been profoundly ignorant of the details of colonial life, but that their attitudes – their values and the things they took for granted – were affected by imperialism cannot now be doubted. (Surely we half-realised this before, but perhaps it was too obvious: like the taste of water in the mouth, it is always there and so we seldom notice it.) The existence of the British Empire affected not only education but literature, the cinema and even 'ephemera' (the cumulative effects of which were often long-lasting): all these, and more, served as 'vehicles of imperial propaganda'. John MacKenzie's seminal publication from 1984, *Propaganda and Empire: the Manipulation of British Public Opinion, 1880–1960* must be seen as a landmark in the new self-confident expansion of imperial history. This opening volume in his *Studies in Imperialism* series for Manchester University Press – now the premier series for imperial history – helped to establish the viability of studying imperialism as a wide-ranging cultural phenomenon. Despite focusing particularly on the late nineteenth and early twentieth centuries, he has argued that Britons' complacent habits of superiority only really ended as late as the 1960s. This is a provocative judgement which challenges imperial historians to subject the period from 1914 to a more rigorous study than has yet been provided. How important was the First World War in stimulating new attitudes? How far did Hitler's racism not only boost nationalism in the colonies but cause a fundamental change in British imperial thinking? Admittedly, much work has been done on the 'official mind'; but how did popular assumptions change? Also, how significant was the outburst of imperial feelings during the Falklands War? It may, in future years, be decided that MacKenzie has overstated his case. Dickens's prescription, in *A Tale of Two Cities*, of 'the best of times' as also 'the worst of times' may well be applicable to this case, as to so many others: an age of imperialism generally turns out also to be an age of anti-imperialism and, furthermore, an age indifferent in parts even to seemingly all-pervasive imperial values. Nevertheless, we all have cause to thank MacKenzie for expanding our imperial horizons.

Historians have long been familiar with the intellectual exercise – stimulating but necessarily never-ending – of trying to construct some sort of 'balance sheet' for the effects of imperial rule in the colonies. Now we must try to evaluate the effects of imperialism on Britain itself. What might seem an obvious pursuit for the adventurous has in fact been surprisingly neglected. Shula Marks has appealed for such a British-directed study of empire, so that we may see what the Empire has meant to 'us'.[7] But who are 'we'? Imperial history can surely go some way to providing the answers.

Mangan, MacKenzie and others have established that imperial consciousness was one facet in British national identity early this century. But the Empire has produced a far more profound change in the composition and identity of the British nation, with the large-scale immigration into Britain from the 'New Commonwealth' after the Second World War. On 22 June 1948 – a symbolically important date with which future schoolchildren may became very familiar – the *Empire Windrush* docked at Tilbury, with 492 Jamaicans on board. The changing racial and cultural composition of its population is obviously an important element in the history of any country. It is certainly not the exclusive preserve of the imperial historian; but, on the other hand, it cannot be understood without copious references to imperial history. It was the imperial connection – especially in the forms of imperial propaganda in the colonies and of colonial economic development or underdevelopment – which helps to explain the motives behind much post-war immigration, both 'pull' and 'push' factors. Similarly, imperial assumptions underlay the reiteration of Britain's traditional 'open door' policy in the 1948 British Nationality Act. (And it was only a reiteration, despite the fact that some non-imperial historians believe that the 1948 legislation created a new dispensation for colonial migrants.) Furthermore, it is impossible to comprehend the immigrants' reception without some understanding of the ideas and images of black people nourished during the heyday of imperialism. Colonial rule over the 'subject races' would probably have been impossible without consistently-held assumptions of their cultural and racial inferiority. After 1945, of course, such beliefs were decidedly embarrassing to successive governments, which wished to dismantle the Empire rapidly and inaugurate the multiracial Commonwealth. But popular attitudes could not be so speedily transformed. Indeed it has often been said that the treatment of 'black Britons' mirrored that of the 'subject races' in the Empire, so that Britain was the last colony of the British Empire. But those who have indulged in such paradigm production have generally had little specialist knowledge either of imperial history or of black experiences in Britain. A little knowledge can be a dangerous thing, and we need a substantial input from imperial historians in order to avoid accepting half-baked clichés and stereotypes of what were in reality extremely complex and diverse phenomena. The views of contemporary journalists and political scientists must be supplemented by the empirical work of historians. Certainly there are rich seams of hitherto unmined primary resources awaiting future researchers, as Paul Rich has emphasised in *Race and Empire in British Politics* (1985).

More specifically, further research is needed on the Immigration Acts of 1962, 1968 and 1971, which first restricted and then virtually ended primary immigration from the New Commonwealth. These

measures not only affected Britain; they were also crises in Commonwealth relations. Indeed they must be seen as acts of decolonisation,
ending Britain's role as the so-called 'mother country'. Given their
implications for the Commonwealth, and the reactions they prompted
not only in Britain but in Asia, the West Indies and Africa, they call
above all for the attentions of imperial historians (who must be not so
much Janus-faced as hydra-headed to trace all their many aspects).
Doctoral research is under way on the origins of the 1962 Act, but
there is room for many more researchers in this fascinating field.[8] The
racial politics of the 1960s and 1970s must also be considered a suitable
field for imperial historians. The defeat of Patrick Gordon Walker at
Smethwick in 1964 is as much part of imperial as of domestic political
history.[9] Similarly, Enoch Powell's (in)famous speeches from 1968 – at
Walsall, Birmingham and Eastbourne – cannot be fully understood
without due recognition of the imperial dimension. Right-wing organisations like the League of Empire Loyalists and the National Front,
and left-wing mirror-images like the Movement for Colonial Freedom,
which can be so difficult for the uninitiated to understand, will be
readily understood by historians familiar with the climate of imperial
thinking in Britain at the start of the twentieth century. The study of
twentieth-century extremes (like Freud's analysis of neurotic personalities) can, by contrast and comparison, tell us much about more
mainstream behaviour.

It has long been recognised that the 1956 Suez crisis must be seen
in the context of imperial history. Historians are also investigating the
imperial component in an allied field: British decline, interpreted both
narrowly, in economic terms, and more generally as a national phenomenon. It is essential that specifically imperial historians should join the
debate and not leave the field solely to colleagues who may be too
inclined to generalise on, without precise knowledge of, imperial
matters. Similarly there is an imperial component behind Britain's move
towards the European Union. Many argued in the early 1960s that
Europe was a surrogate for empire, fuelled by those who had never
come to terms with multiracialism. (Is there, perhaps, an imperial dimension to almost every topic in twentieth-century British history?)

Nevertheless, it should not be thought that the more traditional
overseas concerns of the imperial historian are not also flourishing. There
is a steady flow of books on the old, white Commonwealth. In addition,
the late nineteenth century has long been of major concern to imperial
historians and continues to be so. The debates of the 1960s and 1970s
on the origins of the 'scramble for Africa' and the South African – or
Boer – War continue to excite historical passions. Perhaps the most
accessible and succinct summary of the state of play on pre-First World

War historiography is to be found in P. J. Cain and A. G. Hopkins, *British Imperialism: Innovation and Expansion 1688–1914* (1993), which establishes the concept of 'gentlemanly capitalism'. Similarly their companion volume, *British Imperialism: Crisis and Deconstruction 1914–1990* (1993), provides a stimulating discussion and sketches in a wide-ranging context; but on this period there is far more original research waiting to be done. Decolonisation is surely the major theme for imperial historians over the next decades. Official papers at the Public Record Office for 1966 – for that crowded period of African decolonisation – are now available. (Documents in colonial archives have generally not been subject to the same restrictions, but – at least if my own experiences in the Nigerian and Sri Lankan archives are anything to go by – availability is subject to a host of other problematic factors, not least the ravages of local fauna.)

Pioneering studies – both on particular territories and as general overviews – have been written on decolonisation already, but we may be sure that the study of this vital area is still in its infancy. One particularly gratifying sign is that source material has been, and is being, published. No survey of modern imperial history can avoid paying tribute to *Constitutional Relations between Britain and India: the Transfer of Power* (edited by Nicholas Mansergh, 12 volumes, 1970–83) and to *Constitutional Relations between Britain and Burma: the Struggle for Independence* (edited by Hugh Tinker, 2 volumes, 1983–84). In addition, the early volumes from another massive project, *British Documents on the End of Empire* (under the general editorship of D. J. Murray and S. R. Ashton), have also appeared, with the promise of more in the future. The only problem with such endeavours, valuable though they are, is the illusion that their formidably weighty tomes contain all the material which historians need to see. The diligent researcher, however, knows that this is far from the case. The same delusion does not attach to the briefer selection of documents contained in *British Imperial Policy and Decolonization 1938–1964* (edited by A. N. Porter and A. J. Stockwell, 2 volumes, 1987 and 1989), another welcome sign of the proliferation of interest in imperial studies.

Yet written documents ought ideally to be supplemented with other, especially visual, sources. Perhaps such a venture might one day be available on CD-ROM, or some even newer form of computer software. Film is certainly an important, though generally neglected, medium. Brian Lapping's Granada television series *End of Empire*, with its accompanying book (1985), is an excellent example of how archival film may be interspersed to good effect with other material. But so far little real historical analysis of the film sources themselves has been made. Lapping also used extracts from interviews to good effect, and in this field historians have been much more busy. The journal *Contemporary Record* features transcripts of interviews and colloquia on imperial themes. Also very valuable are the transcripts – and other voluminous documentation – collected by the Oxford Development Records Project, most of which are available at Rhodes House.

Yet documents, of whatever type, cannot disguise the fact that, sometimes, the turning point in colonial policy can precede by several years or even decades the actual transfer of power. Nor can we be confident that colonial policy as such gives us an explanation for the end of the British Empire. Who was the puppet, who the puppeteer? Who was pulling the strings of the governors, secretaries of state and civil servants? How important were local nationalists – and who was pulling their strings? How vital were the colonial, the national and the international contexts? And what of the intellectual climate? In particular, how important were economic changes? What is the reality of neo-colonial explanations? Have the predictions of Gallagher and Robinson, in their formative article from 1953 on the imperialism of free trade, been vindicated, so that the end of empire may be seen as merely a reversion – attempted or real – to Britain's always preferred choice of 'informal empire'?[10] There is no shortage of theories – far too many exist to summarise them here – but as yet there is no sign that any answers are likely to hold the field for long, especially since individual case studies often conflict with the theories of the system-makers.

The real problem is that those who seek an explanation for decolonisation at any particular level of causation – colonial, metropolitan, international, economic, etc. – are all too likely to find one. But how are we to choose between interpretations which have so few, if any, points of contact and thus of comparison? Francis Bacon judged that if we begin with certainties we will end in doubts, but that if we begin with doubts we will end in certainties. It is a good maxim for the researcher, though experienced historians are often certain only of the perennial nature of doubt.

The comparative study of decolonisation is also in its infancy. Many historians have written that the Second World War killed the Empire, and certainly most observers – including Clement Attlee – believed that the days of the Raj were numbered. But the speed of African decolonisation surprised many who were involved in the dismantling process. How important was the Indian example? D. A. Low has judged that 'many of the most critical battles for colonial Africa were fought, not on the banks of the Volta, the Niger, or the Zambezi, but on the Ganges'.[11] Yet such a view remains speculative rather than conclusive. Also, how important was the Pan African Congress, run by Nkrumah and Kenyatta, in Manchester in 1945? We are on firmer ground in insisting that Ghanaian independence stimulated other nationalists to spurt to the tape, but the whole issue of international nationalist, or South–South relations is another field of study likely to testify to the continuing vitality of imperial history.

Given the scope of British imperial history in the twentieth century, this section on methodologies could be the longest part of the chapter. But instead it will be the shortest. There is, in fact, no special methodology which separates imperial from other forms of history. It requires all the historical skills featured in this book. But because this form of history involves more than just Britain, it is perhaps necessary to stress two points in particular: the importance of bridging what may be called the 'imaginative gap' between Britain and the overseas territories, and the necessity of seeing one's research in context.

The former colonies and dominions are separated from Britain not just by time but by space – and also by differences in culture and tradition. Hence the possibilities of incomprehension and misunderstanding are daunting. But how can the imaginative gap be bridged, if indeed it can be? One answer, perhaps, is by travel, which may go some way to breeding greater understanding and sympathy/empathy. Much has changed in the old colonies, of course, but at least the climate – and something of the general atmosphere – remains the same. Film resources can also be useful. But perhaps the easiest resource is imaginative literature. Novels – for instance those in the readily available Heinemann *African, Caribbean and Asian Writers* series – can help us enter imaginatively into other worlds. Certainly if we are studying the colonial era, using predominantly official sources, the study of colonial novels can help us to become aware of ethnocentric bias. Surely no one who has read Chinua Achebe's *Things Fall Apart* (1958), which portrays Iboland from the inside and thus sympathetically, could ever study Lugard's despatches from northern Nigeria – let alone *The Pacification of the Primitive Tribes of the Lower Niger* – without, almost automatically, reading between the lines. Similarly, Achebe's *No Longer At Ease* (1960) must be a prime source for understanding the dilemmas of young western-educated Africans and the spiralling corruption of the 1950s and after.

It should be added that imaginative literature can be our source material as well as our tool. The perspective of the imperial historian provides a novel and important angle from which to view writers like Joseph Conrad, E. M. Forster, George Orwell, Graham Greene and others from the imperial era. After all, is not literary criticism too serious a business to be left to literary critics?

Another methodological problem is that it is easy for researchers, especially when fresh from undergraduate studies, to become so obsessed with their particular topic of study that they fail to put it into context, and thus fail to see it in proper perspective. In this way inflated – and sometimes even grotesque – significance can be assigned to particular events, issues or people, and we may mistake the exceptional for the typical. One answer to this is the conscious attempt to see one's project in relation to the broadest context possible, perhaps the comparative study of different empires. Knowledge of other empires is obviously valuable in itself; and, in addition, an effort to see one's own 'patch' in such a broad context does help us to assess and reassess its true significance. It will also produce recognition of how much we owe to other historians, from this country and overseas. British imperial history can then take its place as an important form of international history with the object, like that of the Commonwealth itself, of enhancing international collaboration and understanding.

Further reading

Apart from the books and articles referred to in the body of this chapter and in the notes, students are advised to consult the premier journal in this field, the *Journal of Imperial and Commonwealth History*. This regularly features details of recent theses, as well as publishing articles and reviews of merit. *African Affairs* is also very valuable, especially for its regular bibliographies and select lists of articles on Africa in nonspecialist periodicals. Among good general works on imperial and Commonwealth history, the following are just a few of those which can be confidently recommended: John Darwin, *Britain and Decolonisation* (London: Macmillan, 1988); John D. Hargreaves, *Decolonization in Africa* (2nd edn, London: Longman, 1996); David Birmingham, *The Decolonization of Africa* (London: UCL Press, 1995); Judith Brown, *Modern India* (2nd edn, Oxford: Oxford University Press, 1994); William Beinart, *Twentieth-Century South Africa* (Oxford: Oxford University Press, 1994); and Bernard Porter, *The Lion's Share* (3rd edn, London: Longman, 1996).

CHAPTER 13

Social history

John Stevenson

Social history has become such an all-embracing category in recent years that it has, at times, threatened to swallow its parent subject whole. Not very long ago it represented a somewhat ill-defined area, a residual category concerned with the manners, habits, artefacts and environment of the past: a background 'set' against which the more important aspects of history were acted out. In Britain, at least, there was an implicit hierarchy of status in historical studies: political, diplomatic and constitutional history occupied the central positions of the historical canon at school and university. Usually social history was lumped in with economic history, but whereas the latter had a coherent theoretical base in economics and an increasing tendency to develop its own methodology based on statistics, social history often appeared a poor relation. Social history was seen as essentially a literary-based form, drawing much of its source material from literature and visible remains. When social history did begin to develop signs of a theoretical structure, it tended to be derived from sources which were themselves eventually seen to be problematic. 'Classical' sociology and anthropology, the former often with a distinct Marxist or functionalist tinge, and the heavily deterministic *Annales* school of writing, were soon to find their critics in turn. New areas of social history such as women's history and gender relations, crime and deviancy, and the 'new' cultural history have found their own methodologies outside the paradigms offered by the giants of twentieth-century social science or the *Annales* school.

G. M. Trevelyan's pioneering *English Social History*, first published in 1944, stood for many years as a prime example of the genre. His famous definition of social history as 'history with the politics left out' was both frequently cited and as often interpreted as an acknowledged abdication of the 'high ground' of historical studies – politics and diplomacy – by social historians. Read with more care, Trevelyan in fact argued the case for the importance of social and economic history in shaping political events. But despite its great depth and insight, Trevelyan's use of chapter titles based on leading literary figures of the day made it all too easy to dismiss social history as impressionistic and caricature it as a 'crinolines and candlesticks' approach.[1] As a result, in the huge expansion of higher education which took place in the 1960s, and which saw the creation of new chairs, departments and sub-specialisms in history, it was economic history which provided the more obvious focus for organisation. It appeared to have a theoretical basis and methodology, a recognised cluster of problems and issues, and its own professional association and journals – notably the *Economic History Review*. Social history tended to get drawn along in its wake as another 'non-political' category of history, but one far less coherent than its stable-mate. This yoking together of economic and social history, apparently so obvious, did not bear much relation to the way the two areas were to develop during the 1970s and 1980s. Initially, social history was the distinctly poorer relation, the tail wagged by the dog of economic history. Not only did the established position of economic history as a more clearly defined discipline tend to overshadow social history, but new departments of economic and social history were often placed in faculties of social science, while history remained firmly anchored within the harbour of traditional arts and humanities. Administrative separation between history and economic and social history may have been both symptom and cause, but it threatened to impose some intellectual barriers between a 'social science history' and what was happening in history departments. Economic history, as it became more influenced by economic theory and growing statistical sophistication, was beginning to suffer its own crisis of conscience. Not surprisingly, there was some pressure from those who wished to preserve the integrity of economic history to move more determinedly into closer association with economics and to reinforce its statistical basis, especially with the development of cliometrics and more powerful means of computation. The economic rigours of the 1970s and 1980s brought some of these tensions to crisis point. It is no disrespect to the many able and dedicated practitioners of both economic and social history to argue that where separate departments were established they often tended to suffer from falling into the interstices between conventional departmental and faculty boundaries in British universities. By the mid-1980s many such departments were in a parlous state, usually small and often uncomfortably positioned in relation to larger 'arts' history departments. Many struggled to obtain institutional backing, and single honours degrees in economic and social history experienced difficulty in attracting student applications.

In that environment it was sometimes difficult for social history as a distinct discipline to flourish and take off: none-the-less important and valuable work continued to be done. One area which did flourish was that devoted to the social consequences of industrialisation. The agenda provided by the pioneer historians of the industrial and agricultural revolutions concerning the impact of economic change upon population, the standard of living, urban growth and the development of social and labour movements were of significance for a wide range of historians. Some of the major debates, such as that over the standard of living, became part of the mainstream of historical debate. One area which developed a momentum of its own was the history of the labour and trade union movements, one of the natural outgrowths of interest in the response to industrialisation and the rise of industrial society.

'Labour history', as it began to be called, was sometimes regarded with suspicion as an area dominated by historians of the Left, pursuing an agenda and priorities of their own. There was much solid and useful work, however, with important contributions on the social history of industrialisation, an important effect of which was to broaden history 'from below'. The formation of the Society for the Study of Labour History, formed in 1960, which also published a regular *Bulletin*,[2] and that of History Workshop in 1967, resulted in two groups which were, in their different ways, both committed to the history of organisations and individuals which conventional history courses left out. History Workshop, the first of which was held at Ruskin College, Oxford – a trade union college for adult men and women – had already existed for some years prior to 1967 as a loose coalition of amateur worker-historians and full-time teachers and researchers. Its expressed aim was to foster a 'people's history' which 'will bring the boundaries of history closer to those of people's lives'.[3] The contribution of labour history to a broadening of historical enquiry is easy to underestimate. It is almost certainly the case that no labouring population anywhere in the world has been so intensively studied as that of Britain in the two centuries or more since the beginning of industrialisation. While traditional labour history has excavated to quite unprecedented depths the personnel and character of labour organisations and trade unions, there has also been an impressive range of case studies of particular groups, industries and localities. Interest has been stimulated in the proto-industrial and early modern period, as well as in rural labour, and the position of less well-organised groups such as women and immigrants. Labour history, as reflected in the annual bibliographies and listings of work in progress published by the *Bulletin*, has proved one of the major contributory streams to British social history.

As significant, if not more so, in the evolution of British social history was local and regional history. It is a moot point whether W. G. Hoskins's *The Making of the English Landscape* (1955) did more than E. P. Thompson's *The Making of the English Working Class* (1959) to stimulate a broader view of history among British historians. But complementing the work of labour historians, works like that of Hoskins and Asa Briggs's *Victorian Cities* (1963) did much to enlarge the vistas of historians to the world beyond Westminster and Whitehall. The opening of county record offices and other local archives helped to generate a fresh wave of interest in county and urban history. The 'county community' as a vehicle for the study of the political and religious conflicts of the seventeenth and other centuries, and the burgeoning of what became known as 'urban history' owed an enormous debt to the silent revolution which had been gathering pace in the preservation of parish registers, estate records and data on urban development – a silent revolution which, in turn, provided the raw material upon which a growing body of postgraduate researchers and established historians could work. New technologies assisted; the computer enormously assisted work in demography – one of the most impressive areas of development – and with this work came a reconstruction of the population history of Great Britain, pioneering analyses of family and household structure, and major advances in our understanding of the interrelation of the demographic record with economic and social change. The portable tape-recorder became the mainstay of the new field of oral history, particularly significant for work on aspects of the recent past which had hitherto received little systematic attention.[4]

But the movement was far more widespread than one inspired solely by new sources and new technologies. Running through the burgeoning of activity was concern with a broader history. In part it drew inspiration from the *Annales* school, with its aspirations to a total history encompassing all aspects of human activity, stretching from the geographical determinants of climate and physical structure, through those shaped by medium-term changes in social and economic environment, down to more localised features of social life. The concept of *mentalité*, focusing upon culture, belief and custom, proved one of the most fruitful influences upon social history, stimulating interest in areas such as witchcraft, carnival and popular protest, as 'windows' into the world of otherwise inarticulate sections of society. The contribution of the social sciences was also important, seen in the interest shown by historians in the work of social anthropologists, sociologists and criminologists. An increasing cross-fertilisation of ideas around such key social concepts as 'class', 'culture', 'community' and 'deviance' produced a fresh generation of work much, of which found expression through the pages of journals such as *Past and Present*. Social history also became one of the key areas for interest in the history of medicine, a history which was moving beyond a mere chronology of heroic breakthroughs in medical technology to a wider appreciation of such matters as the development of new structures of thought and belief about illness and its treatment. Similarly, it was hardly surprising that the rise of the feminist and gay movements would have important consequences for an area of history which now seemed to embrace almost all aspects of human activity. Women's and gender studies, histories of sexuality, became one of the growth areas of social history in the 1970s and 1980s. Just as a decade or two earlier it had been the history of the labouring classes – usually thought of as male and activist – that had spurred an interest into new areas, it was now the female half or more of the population that had so far remained largely 'hidden' which drew increasing attention in the shape of research, courses and publications.

Social history now represents a large, somewhat inchoate grouping of subjects and subdisciplines; it defies close categorisation and many have felt that even as a loose umbrella category, it lacks coherence. On the one hand social history could be said to encompass almost everything apart from the most determinedly 'high political' and abstrusely technical cliometric analyses. Its rationale lies in the proposition that it is concerned primarily with all aspects of history which deal with societies in the aggregate or with those which pertain to them as aggregates. The latter is an important qualification for it has allowed social historians to make very detailed investigations of individuals, environments and events, such as Carlo Ginzburg's *The Cheese and the Worms* (1982) or Emmanuel Le Roy Ladurie's *Montaillou* (1978) or *Carnival à Romans* (1980), with a view to elucidating broader structures of belief and activity. On the other hand it can be argued that, properly speaking, social history should be the application to the past of social science theory – a form of historical sociology. Few, however, would now accept so narrow a definition, for two main reasons. First, it has been found that attempts to apply theoretical models from the social sciences have often proved extremely arid and, perhaps more importantly, invert the normal processes of historical enquiry. Historians have not, on the whole, been happy with attempts to fit data into *a priori* models. Second, the positivist social science which gave itself to this approach has come under attack from within its own disciplines, and now seems outmoded. Indeed there has been an increasing willingness on the part of social scientists to learn from historians about how theoretically informed empirical enquiry must be carried out.

Vagueness of definition and boundaries has not prevented a continuing output of fresh research, a torrent of specialised monograph and article literature, and a proliferation of journals concerned solely with aspects of social history. But synthesis in so wide and varied a field presents some special difficulties. Analysis always carries with it the danger of fragmenting the world of experience of real, living people into a series of abstract categories; detailed recapture of such experience may defeat the object of general statements, descending into a new kind of antiquarianism. The problem has been tackled in various ways, ranging from studies which concentrate on particular themes to intensive focus upon particular episodes or periods. Others have employed something akin to a *pointilliste* technique to build up a broader picture from a myriad of small details and characterisations. Moreover, in spite of some significant studies dealing with lengthy periods, one of the most challenging difficulties faced by social history is that of representing change. The *Annales* school, in particular, has been criticised for its tendency to deal with structures at the expense of change and development. Many of the great classics of the *Annales*, such as Braudel's study of the Mediterranean and Le Roy Ladurie's *Montaillou*, dealt with pre-modern societies, either relatively stable in themselves or confined within some clearly defined geographical or social setting. Both in terms of the balance between analysis and the reality of social experience and of the relationship between structure and change, the social history of any lengthy period, particularly one of rapid change, presents daunting problems.

Indeed it has recently been argued that the *Annales* school has suffered its own crisis of conscience. Having stimulated interest in a vast range of activities which might be seen to embrace 'total' or 'global' history – the long-term effects of climate and geography, of the patterns of work and leisure, of the attitudes to the human body and sexuality, of social ritual and popular culture, and of states of mind, *mentalités* – some of its practitioners have orientated themselves more towards narrative, the area of historical studies that they once almost despised. Much the least important branch of historical studies for the practitioners of the *Annales* school was the history of day-to-day events – what was dubbed *histoire évènementielle*. Braudel, in particular, was fascinated by structure at the expense of the transitory, ephemeral short-term events which had dominated so much history writing in the past. In his most famous work, *The Mediterranean and the Mediterranean World in the Age of Philip II* (1947), he described the structures which dominated life in the Mediterranean: the mountains, plains, sea routes and seasons which imposed patterns upon all human activity.[5] Faced with the massive effects of these long-term trends and continuities (*la longue durée*), *histoire évènementielle*, the turn of events, the personalities of rulers, and the outcome of battles, made up only minor concerns of history. What was so striking about this version of history was that it hugely played down what so many historians had attached importance to in the past, notably the importance of the great ideological cleavage between Christian and Muslim in the seventeenth-century Mediterranean and, in turn, the significance of what had in the past been described as one of history's 'decisive battles': the defeat of the Ottomans at Lepanto in 1571. For Braudel, both Christian Spain and Ottoman Turkey had to contend in like manner with the ultimately decisive effects of climate and geography, which implicitly mattered far more than any ideological differences between them. Similarly, Braudel relegated what had once been regarded as one of the crucial turning points of early modern history – the defeat of Ottoman naval power in the Mediterranean – to the last, lesser section of his work. Nowhere was the effective contempt for the history of events made more evident, characterised as the trivial, superficial 'crest of the foam', carried by the tides of history.[6]

Nor was this attitude confined to the older generation of *Annalists*. It was reinforced in the work of Le Roy Ladurie, whose interest in collective *mentalités*, seen most extensively in his *Montaillou*, found brilliant and systematic exposition in the almost static, recurring structures in the lives of a section of the French medieval peasantry. Similarly, Ginzburg's *The Cheese and the Worms*, the study of the mental universe of an Italian miller tried before the Inquisition in the early seventeenth century, was used as a window into a wider and enduring world of what Ginzburg called the 'little tradition' of pre-Christian belief and superstition shared by the lower orders of medieval and early modern Europe. Similarly, Jacques Le Goff, a prominent contributor to *Annales* and a professor at the École des Hautes Etudes en Sciences Sociales, published in 1978 an edited collection, *Nouvelle Histoire*, which confidently set out an agenda for future work in the manner of the forebears of the *Annales* school. But, as Malcolm Vale has recently reminded us, such confidence was somewhat short-lived. Within ten years a second edition was casting doubt on the earlier certainties. Confronted by what he called the unexpected 'return of the event', the renewed indeed reinvigorated tradition of writing narrative history, political history and biography, Le Goff conceded that these forms might provide the means of producing both analysis and a sense of dynamic events.[7]

What Le Goff was expressing, perhaps somewhat belatedly, was the so-called 'revival of narrative' heralded by Lawrence Stone in his essay of 1979, 'The revival of narrative: reflections on a new old history'.[8] Stone, along with others, expressed the growing belief in the inadequacies of model-building and of the kind of structural history which the *Annales* had brought about. Structural history was just that, static, and much of it was exceedingly dull when not in the hands of its most skilled practitioners. However, as Clayton Roberts has argued, much of this apparent stasis was illusory. Braudel declared the fascination of the *moyenne durée* where shorter-term cycles of change interposed themselves between the *longue durée* and day-to-day events. The historian, too, had a duty, according to Braudel, to be 'aware of the three *durées*' and 'to discern and set forth the dialectic that takes place amongst them'.[9] In any event, historians voted with their pens. Le Goff followed his partial recantation with a massive biography of Louis IX (1214–70) of France, weaving into a conventional biography lengthy discussions of historical context.[10] This form of 'thick narrative' has become one of the favourite genres of recent historical writing, seeking to convey much of the structure and context of day-to-day events alongside the narrative of day-to-day events.

But even as these autonomous changes were taking place within the mode of historical writing which had proved increasingly pervasive over the past generation, other tendencies and influences were making themselves felt which would have an important impact upon social history. One of the new issues to affect the historical scene in the 1970s was feminism. In part it was an outgrowth of the radical and popular History Workshop movement which developed into a Women's History group in the early 1970s. If people were reclaiming history, then women had voices to be heard. It also clearly reflected a wider burgeoning of interest in feminism and gender studies which sought new agendas and approaches to history. The prioritisation of gender issues and its potentially revolutionary project were well summed up by Hélène Cixous:

> Then all the stories would have to be told differently, the future would be incalculable, the historical forces would, will, change hands, bodies; another thinking as yet not thinkable will transform the functioning of all society.[11]

With this kind of agenda, feminist historians were somewhat impatient with the conventional structures of historical writing which, almost by definition, tended to accentuate the doings of men rather than of women. The explicit aim of many early feminist writers was to give proper weight to women's experience. Inevitably, there was an attempt to emphasise those areas that had dominated women's lives, for better or worse, in the past; areas such as the family, child care, domestic economy and management, sexuality and gender relations, were treated as particularly significant. At its most radical it sought to retell history in such a way that a more rounded and 'complete' history of 'humankind' would be possible rather than the male-orientated focus of the social history of the past. This had particularly telling results in areas such as labour history, long one of the seed-beds of social history but with an agenda which tended to be attuned to the story of the male workforce with its full-time, hierarchical structures, rather than the more fluid, part-time, patchwork of economic activities which reflected many women's experience of the world of work. This was but one example of a larger historiographical issue, one central to feminist critiques of past history, including social history, in which the whole language and practice of the existing discipline posited upon an essentially 'patriarchal' structure. Because men and male attitudes have been dominant for so long in western society, it was argued, attitudes and priorities perceived as being 'male' have been deliberately fostered. As a result, our whole past and our account of that past is written in a language which writes women out of history. The feminist project then could be seen as not merely to expand the sphere of social history by extending it to give greater emphasis to issues such as housework and reproduction, but, like Marxism or some other radical ideology, to reorientate entirely the whole direction of historical study away from its patriarchal bias.

In practice, the impact of interest in feminism upon social history was rarely as dramatic as that, many opting for a pluralistic dimension of 'women's history' or 'gender studies' which could be accommodated by an expansion of the curriculum and a greater acceptance of the centrality of women's experience to the study of the past. One, at least, of the services of women's historians was to retrieve women, both ordinary and prominent, from the margins of history. Paradoxically, almost in contradiction to the claims that women were deliberately written out of history, closer attention to the past showed them as more prominent in many more spheres than had often been allowed.

But one of the other results of the feminist challenge to the agenda of social history was the attention it focused on language. The 'linguistic turn' in recent historical studies has argued that much of what we experience as 'fact' has been fashioned or conditioned by language. For Marxist or feminist historians the 'deconstruction' and subversion of existing dominant structures of language was a vital part of expanding and realigning the horizon of historical knowledge. Words, it is alleged, have no fixed and authoritative applications or referents to which they correspond. Language rather than reflecting reality actually defines it. This linguistic turn has had an immense influence in what is now sometimes cited as the 'crisis of postmodernity' – a crisis which affects social history in common with other aspects of history. For historians who had hitherto set out to describe some external 'reality', whether of events or phenomena, it was suggested that this was a futile exercise. Instead history consisted of a range of 'discourses' and 'narratives' based upon a multiplicity of readings of 'texts' and 'symbols', depending upon the perspective and language of the observer. This suggested again a radical fragmentation of social history rather than a single 'narrative' based upon an established reality. The effect upon conventional approaches to history was well summed up by two historians for their own area of interest – nineteenth-century Scottish history – as follows:

> The story of our nation has now become history, herstory, theirstory, ourstory – regions, industries, interest groups, ethnic groups, religious groups, technologies, professions and sexual orientations are all developing their own stories.[12]

Accordingly, much social history is now written with a vocabulary which embraces the 'new historicism'. It has had a particularly dramatic effect upon cultural history, where the 'reading' of cultural artefacts, icons and ritual has offered a fertile field for new research and insight. Few areas of history have remained unaffected, however, in a postmodern critique which questions any aspirations towards objectivity and absolute reality. Thus it has been argued that social history has moved, as has history as a whole, from a once fashionable search for scientific objectivity – particularly strong in the early years of social history – towards what has sometimes been dubbed a more 'poetic' approach to the construction of historical writing. Historians have been urged to adopt the techniques of the novelist rather than the scientist, adopting more than one viewpoint, and leaving open and alternative endings to the narrative. Beverley Southgate concludes a recent survey of new directions with the comment:

> Paradoxically, then, historical study seems now to be becoming less autonomous, or less than ever constrained within the imposed (and, again, contingent) boundaries of a single disciplinary structure: and the old Aristotelian distinctions between history and poetry, reason and imagination, are becoming increasingly eroded.[13]

Such a fluid and indeterminate situation might provoke concern that social history, indeed history itself, is in crisis. Judged by the scale and range of output, nothing could be further from the truth. What is clear is the acceptance of a pluralism across a range of writing which now embraces both the legacy of earlier inputs and the new tendencies in historical writing as they affect social history. Labour history, in spite of the collapse of Communism, appears to live on, continuing in British circles to be represented in the annual bibliographies of the recently renamed *Labour History Review*. Anyone today reading *Annales* or *Past and Present* would find the traditions of the earlier wave of interest in the social sciences, geography, and demography still being reflected in a continuing output. More radical cultural and feminist perspectives have also come to find their niche within an increasingly 'broad church' of history. In this context the distinction between 'social history' and other kinds of history has come close to being abolished. Who, it might be said, is not dealing with some kind of social history unless they are investigating the more arcane areas of high diplomacy, high politics or economic statistics. Moreover, a sign of intellectual maturity within the discipline is the ability to produce integrative texts and signposts, for example in F. M. L. Thompson's *The Cambridge Social History of Britain, 1750–1950*, published in three volumes in 1990, where a balance was found between narrative and analysis through thematic chapters, and scope for a local and regional element by a selection of regional chapters contained within a single volume. Similarly, the Penguin *Social History of Britain* sought to break British history down into broad chronological divisions with thematic chapters within. Other approaches have been to devote whole volumes to broad text-like treatments of particular themes as in the Longman *Themes in British Social History* series, with volumes dealing individually with areas such as education, crime, health, poverty and sexuality. At the other extreme we still have the highly detailed study working out from the analysis of a small event or series of events to a wider set of contexts and meanings. Work such as that of Barry Reay on the uprising in Kent in the 1830s or Ruth Harris's work on the Lourdes apparitions suggests that the more sophisticated treatment within the social history canon can still proceed with modest enthusiasm and coherent rationale.[14] So far, at least, the so-called 'crisis of postmodernism' has not paralysed the pens of the social historians.

CHAPTER 14

Gender history

Helen Jones

This chapter shows how gender historians approach their research and writing by offering an introductory survey through specific examples from writings on late nineteenth-century and twentieth-century Britain. It discusses the methods of research and the areas of greatest interest among gender historians; it briefly points to the distinctions and overlaps between gender, feminist and women's history, and the impact gender history has had on mainstream history.[1]

In the 1970s a community of scholars engaged in feminist, gender and women's history gradually emerged. The publishing boom dates back to the publication in 1973 of Sheila Rowbotham's *Hidden from History: 300 Years of Women's Oppression and the Fight Against It*. Rowbotham stated that she wanted to explore the conditions in which women produced and reproduced their lives, both through their labour and through procreation; and how the free expression of this activity has been distorted and blocked by circumstances of society. She wanted to explore what has been specific to women as a sex and the manner in which class has cut across their oppression. Although emphasising women's constraints and oppression in her introduction, her chapters on the twentieth century actually concentrated on women's political strategies for overcoming them: she wrote about suffrage; women, trade unions and the unemployed; the family and sexual radicalism; birth control, abortion and sexual self-determination; and feminism and socialism.[2] She did not carry her story beyond the 1930s and indeed it is still the case that few feminist, gender or women's historians venture further. Although this was by no means the first book in the field, previous historical studies of women had been written in isolation. Soon there was to be a network of historians in the area. In the 1980s gender history courses in higher education began to appear; in 1982

History Workshop Journal became a journal of socialist *and feminist* historians (in 1995 it dropped both adjectives); in 1986 the Women's History seminar at the Institute of Historical Research, London began to meet; and three new journals *Gender and History* (1989), *Journal of Women's History* (1989) and *Women's History Review* (1992) were launched. What significance do we give to these terms 'feminist', 'women's' and 'gender' history?

All three approaches typically (and they are not alone in this) have exploited oral sources, autobiography and collective biography. There is an awareness of the construction of the sources, which 'reflect' as much as 'provide' evidence, so that they are seen as a matter of investigation in their own right. Further, the researcher acknowledges her or his own personal project and subjectivity, so linking the private world of the historian and the public world of the sources. The interaction between the private and public worlds of their subjects is also emphasised. There are important differences, nevertheless, in all three approaches, although these differences are more clearly drawn, and strongly contested, in the USA than in Britain.

In a nutshell, feminist historians utilise feminist theories, such as radical, Black or liberal ones, in order to analyse the past. Women's history takes women as the subject of study; it may or may not be feminist or gender history. Gender history is both a sphere of interest and a methodology, and as such it has implications for the way we study history as well as what we study. It is as much about methodology as it is about subject matter. Gender history is about relationships between women and men; the social construction of differences between women and men, and the social processes by which definitions of femininity and masculinity are constructed. It maintains that 'woman' is not a single category and that women's experiences will differ according to their age, class, ethnic origin, and whether they are married or single, mothers or childless. For its deconstruction of the term 'woman', gender history has been criticised by those who argue that women's, not gender, history should be prioritised. Briefly, the argument in favour of women's history is that it keeps women at the centre of research and writing so that women are not again marginalised as happened in traditional history; gender history, by focusing on constructions of masculinity and male sensitivities, diverts attention from male privilege and power, and for this reason gender history is 'safe' and acceptable in the US academic world. By emphasising differences between women it denies that women are a political category and subordinate class.[3] The divisions between women's history and gender are, however, more sharply drawn in the USA than in Britain. Much of the work now undertaken in women's history contains the key elements of gender history, and much of it is also feminist history. The self-conscious and public use of women's history as part of the contemporary feminist project is much less prominent now than twenty-five years ago, however, when historians, such as Anna Davin and Sally Alexander, were teasing a feminist analysis out of a culture of socialist history.

In the late 1960s and early 1970s the women's movement, rather more than the history profession, stimulated a renewed interest in women's and gender history; this partly explains why they are more interdisciplinary than many other historical approaches. At the same time as gender history was developing, so too was a gendered approach within a whole range of disciplines, in particular anthropology, psychology and sociology, and many made a conscious effort to learn from cross-fertilisation. Twentieth-century British gender history has also been influenced by historians from other periods and countries;[4] it is slightly artificial, therefore, to peel it off for independent dissection.

At the same time as gender history is part of a very large intellectual project it is often scrutinised from a self-consciously personal perspective. For this reason some gender historians explicitly state their personal involvement as they engage with the material and subject of their study. A number of historians have provided accounts of their personal experiences in the opening up of gender history. Sally Alexander, for instance, writes of her, and others', burgeoning personal feminism, which she sees as having psycho-sexual origins and manifesting itself in the politics of the body. Her early feminist work was a challenge to the Marxist/materialist interpretations which, along with all other approaches of historians, had marginalised women.[5] Her linking individual psychological influences with wider political developments is typical of much of Alexander's work, although for feminist historians of twentieth-century Britain it is not so typical. Psycho-history remains on the margins of gender history. Catherine Hall identifies a year, 1968, as the moment of revelation and, like Alexander, links it to her own personal circumstances.[6] Carolyn Steedman's *Landscape for a Good Woman* interweaves autobiography with the construction of her mother's biography, and in so doing she shows how she sees the process through which her own thinking changed.[7] As well as linking their personal development with their public work as historians, many gender historians also link the personal and public worlds of their subjects.

Twentieth-century gender historians have examined the 'private' world of women and the family, asserting the importance of understanding gender relations in the home and the validity of analysing people's day-to-day lives, often through oral history. Andrew Davies, for instance, in a study based on a wealth of interviews, vividly shows the pre-war gendered experience of poverty in Manchester and Salford.[8]

Joan Sangster has recently discussed the reasons why oral evidence has been attractive to the historical study of women: while traditional sources have often ignored women, oral evidence is a way of blending women into historical scholarship, and of challenging established definitions of social, economic and political history. Oral evidence can put women at the centre of history, and highlight gender as a category of analysis. It is also a means by which the 'subjects' of history can influence the historiography by pointing to what is important to them. It is another tool for exploring diverse perspectives. Sangster goes on to argue that it is a means of seeing how and why women explain, rationalise and make sense of their past, so that we can better understand the social and material framework within which they operated and perceived choices; the cultural patterns they faced; and the complex relationship between individual consciousness and culture.[9]

The importance of making public what goes on in private is partly a reflection of the influence of those feminists who believe that the prime site of women's oppression is in the home. While such radical feminists are challenged, in particular by Black feminists, the family remains an important area of gender history and one which is likely to grow. Gender and women's history have used oral history methods to delve into the private worlds of women earlier this century and have undertaken local studies in order to build up detailed pictures of women's day-to-day lives which are less refracted through the eyes and artefacts of official records.

Elizabeth Roberts's *Women and Families: An Oral History, 1940–1970* (1995) is illustrative of research into private daily lives; it builds on her earlier study which covers the period 1890–1940. Roberts's study is untypical of current research in that it focuses on the post-war years, a period which certainly deserves greater attention from gender historians. She displays no interest in theoretical questions, however, which makes the study readable but does mean that there is little attempt to scrutinise her own oral history methods. She does not attempt to make comparisons with other investigations or to explain any differences with other work in the field. There is no discussion of the problems of people's memories or of interviewing techniques. So, for instance, she tells us that some husbands and wives sat in on each other's interview whereas others did not, but this does not seem to be problematic for her as she claims it did not influence respondents' evidence 'as far as we could tell'. Further, given the centrality of women's oppression for many feminists, exposing the less appealing side of many marriages has been important to a number of writers; however, her study makes no attempt to follow this line of enquiry.[10]

In her earlier study Roberts claimed that working-class women's control over the household budget gave them power within the family (a view which has not gone unchallenged). What is interesting in her latest study is the impact consumerism appears to have had on power relations in the home. Roberts argues that women's traditional skills of managing to make ends meet, and of careful budgeting, became less valued after rationing ended and more consumer goods became available and affordable. Women had more money to spend but the percentage of the household income under women's control shrank. Some couples chose to share responsibility for household budgeting and in some marriages husbands wanted more control over their wages than their fathers had enjoyed. Wages increasingly came to be seen as the property of those who earned them. While historians have written of women in the post-war years remembering their mothers' lack of control over their lives and being determined to escape the constraints on their mothers' lives by, for instance, having fewer children, it is interesting to read that men too looked back in horror on their fathers' lives and wished to escape their limitations. It is also an illustration of the importance of examining the experiences of men and women in relation to each other (see below).

Judy Giles also ventures into post-war Britain. She organises her argument – based on oral testimonies, letters, fiction and the written pronouncements of professional observers – around the themes of growing up, housing, relations between servants and mistresses, and notions of respectability, and argues that it was in their private life that most women tried to define and understand themselves. The importance of subjectivity and women's consciousness is, as in so much gender history, prioritised. Giles underlines that the home could be both constricting and fulfilling for women. Influenced by post-structuralist thinking, Giles wants to draw attention to the way in which both written and spoken sources represent rather than simply reflect their subjects' worlds.[11] The nature of sources and the way in which they are used is important for gender historians. Liz Stanley argues that research material – written, oral, visual – which feminists use should be treated as topics of investigation in their own right, rather than as resources of something beyond themselves.[12]

By exploring the private worlds of women, and in trying to reconstruct a picture of how they perceived their situation and coped with it, gender historians have come to realise how effectively women managed. This emphasis is in contrast to some earlier writers who found a victim in every (dead) woman's life history. Two historians, Ellen Ross and Elizabeth Roberts, illustrate this newer approach well.

Most historians looking at private charitable help have concentrated on the work of middle-class lady philanthropists; in contrast, Ellen

Ross has drawn attention to the informal welfare operated by working-class women in London: how they would help out in times of serious illness or eviction, and how working-class women fought back when attacked by men because they had not, unlike middle-class women, internalised deference towards men. Women would organise themselves into childcare groups with neighbours, and in extreme circumstances they would informally adopt children. A picture emerges of multiple strategies and networks for coping, and of strong women able to pack a punch when necessary.[13] Ross has gone on to show that in the late nineteenth and early twentieth centuries poor London mothers' skills were deployed in managing the family income, earning money, and looking after and controlling children. (This struggle for survival meant that the emotional and intellectual nurture of their children inevitably had a low priority.)[14] Elizabeth Roberts, through her interviews, opened up a world of women in the North West who also developed successful strategies for their daily lives in order that they might not just exist, but live with a degree of dignity.[15]

As well as no longer looking for victims, the search for heroines has also been called off as historians are exploring the complexities and contradictions of women's lives to a much greater extent than in the past. Partly this shift reflects a loosening of the ties between the women's movement of twenty years ago and women historians, while post-structuralism has mounted a challenge to the artificial construction of binary opposites so beloved of Enlightenment Europe.

Another way, other than through oral history, of retrieving a version of women's lives is through the use of autobiographies and biographies. Auto/biography and collective biography have been enthusiastically, although not uncritically, taken up. Two of the most interesting developments in this field have been collective biographies and the re-reading of biographies written by women, notably in the work of Carolyn Steedman in her biography of Margaret McMillan, a pioneer of nursery schools. Steedman explores the way in which Margaret used the biography she wrote of her sister Rachel to tell the story of her own life; indeed Steedman argues that at times Margaret and Rachel are interchangeable in the biography. It is Steedman's method of writing her biography of McMillan, as well as what she tells us about McMillan's life, which is especially interesting.[16] Seth Koven adopted the same approach in an essay on Henrietta Barnett. He explores the way in which Henrietta Barnett depicted her own life in her biography of her husband, Samuel. The ways she chose to depict spinsterhood and marriage in the biography, and the place she gave herself in the biography, went to make it as a much an autobiography as a biography of Samuel.[17]

Barbara Cain has penned a case for collective biography. She argues that by looking at a group of women there is greater scope for exploring the interaction between particular women, the range of choices and experiences open to women, and the extent to which the structures of society, whether legal, social or familial, can be adapted either by individuals or through networks of relationships. Cain argues that locating women's lives within networks of relations, friends, lovers or associates is the characteristic which distinguishes feminist from traditional biography. By adopting a group biography approach the 'exceptional' framework is removed from the study of women's lives. Further, it acts as a warning against crude labelling of people as feminist or anti-feminist. Cain gives the example of Jane Lewis's *Women in Social Action in Victorian and Edwardian England* (1991) which shows, among other things, how difficult it is to distinguish between the ideas of those women active in public life who supported, or opposed, suffrage.[18] It is, too, another example (along with victims versus heroines) of the attempt to demolish false binary opposites and of the influence of post-structuralist thinking on gender history.

Olive Banks has attempted to construct a collective biography of 116 active feminists (overwhelmingly, but not exclusively, female) divided into four cohorts, the last cohort being born between 1872 and 1891. By exploring the life histories of groups of feminists Banks studied the extent to which feminist beliefs reflected childhood experiences, especially with parents, and the experience of marriage in shaping feminist attitudes: again she was exploring the relationship between the public and private.[19] Johanna Alberti also adopted a collective biographical approach towards fourteen women who had been active suffragists before the First World War and whose political activities continued after the war. Alberti explores the links between their personal lives and relationships and their public activities.[20]

A distinct methodology for feminist biography has been argued for by Liz Stanley. Stanley traced the connections between Olive Schreiner, Eleanor Marx, Emma Cons, Edith Lees, Constance Lytton, Dora Montifiore and Virginia Woolf in her work on Olive Schreiner. In tracing these webs of friendship she found their personal involvements often repaired organisational divisions. Stanley identifies what she sees as important elements of a 'feminist biographical method': biography should be seen as composed by textually located ideological practices and analysed as such; there should be a textual recognition of the labour process of the biographer as researcher in reaching interpretations and conclusions; a 'spotlight' approach on a single individual should be avoided; and the fact that informal networks among feminists through friendship can be as important as the formal organisation of feminism to an understanding of these women's lives needs to be recognised.[21]

The popularity of a collective approach to women's history is reflected in the large number of studies which focus on women's organisations. The suffrage campaign, for instance, has still lost none of its interest for historians. Explaining the apparent decline of organised feminism has also been a preoccupation of historians. Earlier, it was assumed that after 1918 organised feminism went into decline; later, historians found various strands of feminist organisation in the 1920s and the feminist desert then shifted to the 1930s. More recently historians have looked beyond the most obvious constituents of the women's movement to make a claim for a feminism inherent in organisations such as the Women's Institute, and I argue that there is a false dichotomy in claiming that feminism was overtaken by more important events in the 1930s – unemployment at home and fascism abroad – when a number of campaigners focused on the gendered impact of both unemployment and fascism, even though feminist organisations were not flourishing. Earlier studies of feminist organisations were undertaken largely in an attempt to find heroines who could be assembled as a canon of worthies parallel with, and indeed, to rival the canon of great men. A few feminist heroines were sought out among a mass of female victims.

Among twentieth-century historians the move away from seeing women simply as victims to seeing them as also perpetrators of oppression was led most controversially by Claudia Koonz in her study of women in Nazi Germany;[22] less noisily, historians of twentieth-century Britain have also brought out the complexities of women's motives. In my study of Violet Markham a seemingly contradictory woman emerges who, before the First World War, campaigned against women having the parliamentary vote but offered help to working-class girls in her Settlement; she argued that women's interests should lie in local, not national or imperial concerns, and yet she was actively interested in imperial affairs and loved mixing with politicians such as the imperialist Lord Milner. Between the wars she advocated new job opportunities for middle-class women but only a traditional job (domestic service) for working-class women; she continued to believe that biological differences between men and women meant that women and men were ideally suited to separate roles in life, yet recognised the impracticality of this and encouraged the employment of women in paid work, and certainly never shirked high-profile work in a man's world herself.[23] Dea Birkett and Julie Wheelwright, in their studies of unconventional women, have not glossed over their unappealing aspects. Julie Wheelwright examines the life of Flora Sandes who was the only woman to fight with the

Serbian army in the First World War. Her lust for the military life, and her lack of interest in turning her experience to the advantage of other women are all discussed. Wheelwright tries to explain why Sandes never showed any interest in changing the gender order.[24] Yet, should we be surprised? Women who flout gender stereotypes at one moment or in a compartment of their lives do not necessarily deploy their experiences in other areas or for other women. Women pursuing their own interests are not necessarily feminists. By the same token, some historians now classify certain men as feminists. Olive Banks, for instance, includes men in her study *Becoming a Feminist*. Indeed, an interest in gender history from the point of view of men and the construction of masculinity has been an important development in gender history in recent years.

'Femininity' has to be analysed in relationship to 'masculinity', for both have always been defined in relationship to each other. One cannot understand women's (changing) position in the family or labour market without knowing how men's role has been constructed and defined. From the mid-1970s various historians such as Natalie Zemon Davis, Jane Lewis, Anna Davin and Alun Howkins have all called for men's position in society to be analysed in conjunction with women's position. In 1985 Davin and Howkins argued that men should not be reduced to crude stereotypes as this plays into the hands of anti-feminists who see both women and men with set characteristics. Rather, one should look at men, as well as women, as a social group and a gender category.[25] In 1991 Michael Roper and John Tosh made clear that 'masculinity' is no less problematic than 'femininity' and that it is an evolving social construction. They argued that traditional historians, preoccupied with the location and exercise of power, need to acknowledge that men's power has resided in their masculinity as well as in their material privilege and manipulation of law and custom.[26] The study of the construction of masculinity has, however, remained fairly marginal to gender, as well as mainstream, history. Joanna Bourke has recently tried to bridge the gap. She argues that during and after the First World War the mutilated bodies of servicemen shifted people's perceptions of masculinity.[27] Indeed, the history of the two world wars is one area where gender history has made a genuine impact.

The gender history which has had greatest impact is that which manages to combine both gender history with traditional mainstream history. The two world wars have proved fruitful areas for this project, and have been relatively well researched by both traditional and gender historians. There is a well-developed debate over the extent to which the wars challenged or reinforced gender relations and the extent, therefore, to which they changed women's lives. In studies of the First

World War, for example, the contribution of women to the war effort has long been worked on; the regulation of women's sexuality has also provided a meeting point for different approaches. During the First World War, venereal disease came to be regarded not only as a civilian problem affecting the quality of the race, the future of the nation and the protection of the innocent, but also as a military problem undermining the fighting strength of the forces. As a result, unsuccessful attempts were made to regulate women by prohibiting any woman previously convicted of soliciting from residing in, or frequenting, the vicinity of stationed servicemen.

No good social and political history of the Second World War can afford to ignore John Macnicol's argument that family allowances were finally introduced in 1945 not because of a concern with the family, but rather with the labour market in mind, as family allowances were seen as a means of avoiding a minimum wage and encouraging mobility of labour.[28] Penny Tinkler looks at the gender dimension of the ballooning youth service scheme. The emphasis differed between boys' and girls' leisure; the involvement of girls was to minimise the military connotations of boys' activities; girls were organised in civilian not military linked organisations; unlike boys, they were often trained in flexible and transferable skills rather than job-specific ones; and there was no effort to train girls for future roles associated with marriage and motherhood.[29] This contrasts with the work of Denise Riley who has examined government policy towards nursery schools, putting it in the context of state welfare and family policies, and who argues that during and just after the war these policies were surrounded by the language of pronatalism.[30] The contradictions in wartime government policies were explored by Penny Summerfield, who highlighted the conflicts between the demands of the traditional family and the labour market.[31] Historians researching the history of the family and the welfare state explore the meanings behind these and related terms, such as 'mother', and emphasise that they are not objective terms set in stone but shift in meaning according to time and place. The ideology of motherhood, the role of women in the family, and the development of state welfare have been explored by various writers.[32] Ideological assumptions behind terms such as 'family' and 'mother' have also informed the debate about women's health and women's contribution to health promotion – both informally and as paid health workers. The reasons for 'official' interest in women's health from time to time and the social construction of meanings of 'health' have all been analysed, and the impact of these constructions on women's day-to-day lives considered.[33]

Gender history has also interacted with social and economic history as attempts have been made to explain the sexual division of labour. In an effort to explain the long-standing sexual division of labour and the subordinate position of women in the labour force, a substantial body of literature now offers explanations ranging from women's psychology, socialisation, domestic ideology and male work culture. Most of the research on which these arguments are based relates to working-class, manual occupations, or women's contemporary position in the labour market. Where women's professional experience is investigated, writers tend to focus on a single occupational group, such as teachers, nurses or civil servants. During the interwar years women both challenged and reinforced the sexual division of labour and domestic ideology, and as a group displayed a contradictory and ambivalent attitude towards women's professional employment. On the one hand, many young women were especially attracted to those occupations requiring 'feminine' qualities and some women campaigned against the employment of married women. On the other hand, women attempted to open girls' eyes to a range of career openings, and campaigned for equal opportunities within the professions. There is, of course, nothing remarkable about women holding different views on their personal career plans or on the appropriate place for women in the labour market. What needs to be explained is why certain groups of women challenged the dominant view of women's paid work as a stop-gap before marriage and instead argued for women to have the choice of pursuing an interesting career with good prospects. A wide range of influences would have shaped a woman's view of her work, but the most important common influences can be pinpointed. A woman's attitudes towards her work were shaped by private relationships, in particular whether she married or not, and by a more public relationship with her work. Four key aspects of this relationship were especially important and depended on the nature of the profession: its hierarchy, discipline, unity and extent of male domination. The more hierarchical, disciplined and fragmented the profession, the more difficult women found it to assert themselves within it. For this reason women's views frequently divided along occupational lines.

Debates over the impact of the depression in the 1930s have also been affected by gender history.[34] The debate over the impact of the depression on people's health circles around the role of working-class mothers. While a family's health was largely the responsibility of the women of the family, especially the mothers, 'official' condemnation for poor health was directed at working-class mothers. Mothers were culpable if they did not ensure cleanliness, along with healthy diets and lifestyles for their children. Celia Petty has discussed the allegations that 'inefficient' mothers aggravated the effects of poverty. She has challenged the methods and the alleged scientific basis of the Medical

Research Council's (MRC) studies. Reworking the data contained in two MRC reports, Petty has shown that moderate and severe protein energy malnutrition existed. She has also challenged the MRC's methodology which led it to the conclusion that ill-health was due to the mothers' slovenly standards, carelessness and unwise shopping. According to Petty, the data actually show how well working-class women coped with their inadequate resources.[35]

In contrast to the two world wars, and the labour market and the family in the first half of the twentieth century, the post-Second World War period has been relatively under-researched by gender historians. Instead, the field has been left almost entirely to sociologists and social policy experts, who have linked women's role in the labour market with welfare, whether provided by the state, voluntary organisations or informally. They have unpicked assumptions about women's role in the family which informed so many post-war welfare policies. Gender historians are now beginning to break into the post-war years, although lagging well behind traditional political historians. Jane Lewis's work is illustrative of a feminist approach in the way she organised her study of women in post-war Britain around the family, the labour market and the welfare state. She discusses major trends such as the growth of married women in the labour force, the huge leap in divorce rates since the 1970s, and the growth in the number of single mothers.[36]

There is also a growing interest in the relationship between gender and empire, although most of the work so far has tended to focus on the nineteenth century. Some work has been undertaken which links ordinary women's lives with grand imperial concerns. Twentieth-century interest in gender and empire was first aroused by an article by Anna Davin, who linked the empire with working-class women's role in the family. In the early years of the twentieth century, lowering the infant death rate in order to maintain a population to defend the British Empire and to work efficiently meant that what working-class mothers did with their children was a matter of imperial importance.[37] The link between notions of the family and its relationship to the empire can be further illustrated by the difficulties encountered by women who tried to get the nationality law altered so that a woman who married a foreigner would not lose her nationality: every interwar government refused to budge, partly because they argued it would undermine the unity of the family, partly – and more importantly – because it would undermine the unity of the empire if some but not all countries of the empire made changes to their nationality laws.

Only relatively recently have historians attempted to integrate gender and ethnicity, although this has been effectively pursued by Lara Marks who has argued that in the early years of the twentieth century ethnicity was as important as social and economic factors in influencing patterns of morbidity and mortality, and in social and health service provision in the East End of London.[38]

Other areas of traditional history have been worked on by gender historians, but so far their work has had little impact on those approaching the subject from a traditional standpoint. This is especially true of the history of political parties where recent work on women is ripe for integration into the traditional studies.

It is important that this great variety of gender history is continued and that it should become a part of mainstream history. In order to ensure that this happens it must be written in a language which is accessible; it should not be couched in academic jargon which hides insights from the uninitiated and obscures people's past experiences as effectively as did traditional history by its indifference. It should not be necesssary to have studied psychology in order to read and enjoy history. If this history is to be more than a purely academic pursuit, it must be written in language which is accessible to a wide readership and non-élitist; only then can it be employed as part of a contemporary feminist project. In order that women are not again discarded by history, moreover, it is important that current warnings are heeded and that women remain at the centre of a gendered historical methodology: keep women as the subject and gender analysis as the methodology.

Unless gender history is genuinely pursued, as opposed to the history of women, it will be kept in a side-current and regarded as an optional extra 'topic'. Gender history, rather than the history of women, has automatic implications for the whole methodology of historians. Gender history involves analysing processes and relationships between men and women, and between public and private worlds. Only when this is done can the claim be justified that gender history should affect the way we look at all areas of history.

At the same time as we are beginning to see the way in which gender history is leading to a re-reading of the great themes of history, it is important that it continues to contribute to the opening up of new areas of research, and to the breaking down of various categories of analysis, such as gender, class and ethnicity in order to show the variety of experiences. Post-structuralism has had an important influence on gender history so that historians are now interested in the personal and the particular of people's lives; no longer will it do to fit people into one of three boxes: class, gender or race. Gender historians can no longer agree over the validity of the category 'woman'; instead a number of historians are keen to emphasise the differing experiences of women according to their class, race, age, marital status, whether they were mothers or not, and their relationship to the labour market. How far this deconstruction should go is a matter of debate, and will continue to be so, not least because many feminist, gender and women's historians are constantly engaged in methodological debates.

Further reading

June Purvis (ed.), *Women's History: Britain, 1850–1945: An Introduction* (London: UCL Press, 1995) has a number of interesting chapters on a range of social, economic and political themes. See also D. Riley, *'Am I that Name?' Feminism and the Category of 'Women' in History* (London: Macmillan, 1988). Karen Offen, Ruth Roach Pierson and Jane Rendall (eds), *Writing Women's History: International Perspectives* (London: Macmillan, 1991), has chapters covering a number of countries, including Jane Rendall, 'History, and gender history in Great Britain'. Two essential journals are *Gender History* and *Women's History Review*. Other useful theoretical perspectives are provided by Joan Scott, 'Women in history', *Past and Present* 101 (1983) and 'Women's history', in P. Burke (ed.), *New Perspectives in Historical Writing* (Cambridge: Polity Press, 1991). A broader approach to issues of gender history can be found in the same author's *Gender and the Politics of History* (New York: Columbia University Press, 1988).

CHAPTER 15

Economic history

Jim Tomlinson

Economic history emerged as a separate academic discipline in the late nineteenth century. The first full-time university teacher of the subject was appointed in Britain in 1904, but it remained a tiny subject area until the general expansion of British higher education in the 1960s. In the 1970s a peak was reached with about fifteen departments of economic history then in existence, some of them called departments of economic and social history.[1] In the financially austere 1980s and 1990s the subject came under pressure, with the number of university teaching posts in decline and separate departments closed at the Universities of Nottingham, Aberdeen, Sheffield, Durham and Kent. While some 'sub-disciplines', notably business history, fared better, the general picture at the end of the twentieth century is of a subject on the defensive and finding it difficult to maintain its role in a harsh higher education environment.

This story of rise and decline in the fortunes of economic history is partly to be explained in institutional terms. The subject established itself early on at the London School of Economics (LSE) and has shared in the success of that institution. In the expansion of higher education in the 1960s and 1970s, the LSE-trained economic historians were able to staff many of the new departments and ride on the flowing tide of popularity of the social sciences. In the subsequent lean years small departments in many subject areas came under pressure as financial stringency unleashed a search for economies of scale and amalgamations, and the falling staff and student numbers and departmental closures in economic history were by no means unique. However, this institutional context cannot explain more than a fraction of the story of the fortunes of economic history. To understand fully that waxing and waning it is necessary to analyse the nature of the subject, and the difficulties it has had throughout its existence in establishing a separate and powerful identity.

The emergence of economic history in the late nineteenth century has to be seen against the contemporary background of its two neighbouring disciplines, history and economics. University history in this period was overwhelmingly dominated by political, especially diplomatic and constitutional history. Economic history was first taught in history faculties, but was very much on the margins of concern in such faculties.[2] On the other hand, late nineteenth-century economics was undergoing the 'marginal revolution', in which the subject increasingly worked on a deductive basis, developing models of economic behaviour from a small number of basic postulates about individual behaviour. While key figures in this revolution, such as Alfred Marshall, retained a keen interest in historical development, marginalism drove economics away from the broad mixture of inductive and deductive methods characteristic of classical political economy from Adam Smith to John Stuart Mill, towards a more strident emphasis on 'scientificity', defined in terms of deductive methods.[3]

The emergence of economic history can best be broadly understood as arising from criticism of both of these neighbouring disciplines. On the side of history, the neglect of economic forces in the shaping of both Britain's national development and its role as a world power appeared increasingly odd as economic weaknesses seemed, from the 1880s onwards, to be arousing both new political forces at home and new rivalries overseas. Equally, the tendency of economics to take on the guise of a universal method seemed to disable it from interest in or understanding of the shifting grounds of relative economic performance, as new countries challenged Britain's economic supremacy.

Economic history's emergence was in part the result of the intellectual 'space' created by the developments in history and economics at the end of the nineteenth century. 'History and Political Economy were divorced. In their separate states they were equally convinced, complacent and triumphant.'[4] Economic history challenged this complacency and triumphalism. In doing so it most obviously asserted the importance of understanding the economic past, which for their different reasons both history and economics neglected. But beyond that basic assertion of the importance of its subject matter, early economic history offered a broader challenge. While institutionally trying to free itself from history, early economic history was engaged in a methodological and ideological struggle with economics, and indeed much of the subsequent development of the subject has revolved around a never-resolved debate about the relationship between the two subjects.[5]

As already noted, economics was undergoing a methodological

revolution from the 1870s. The emphasis was on deriving universal patterns of behaviour from abstract postulates. By contrast, economic historians offered a more inductive framework, asserting the importance of institutions, with the implication that universal patterns of behaviour were unlikely to be found in a world of very different institutional arrangements.[6] This methodological dispute was at the same time ideological and political. Marginalist or neo-classical economics has, despite all its claims to scientific status, an in-built bias towards favouring market forces because of its assumption that the aim of economic activity is to satisfy individual consumer wants (rather than being concerned with either, for example, the welfare of producers as producers, or the interests of a nation state as a political entity), that those wants are best judged by the individuals concerned, and that, given a range of standard assumptions, markets will maximize the satisfaction of those wants. Such an assumptive world led most neo-classical economists to be natural supporters of *laissez-faire* in the late nineteenth century, though the strength of such support was obviously affected by forces other than just intellectual leanings. By contrast, most of the early economic historians were self-consciously 'reformers', in revolt against the limited state of late Victorian Britain. This, it should be emphasised, did not make them socialists. On the contrary, most of them saw the task as being the reforming of the state and the employing of it to strengthen British capitalism, both against the socialist enemy within and foreign rivals without. In sum, they tended towards support for the 'social imperialist' revolt against *laissez-faire* and 'cosmopolitanism' which gathered strength from the 1880s, but became notably stronger in the early years of the new century.[7]

The ideological and political differences between orthodox economics and economic history are most evident in the great debate about protection in the early years of the twentieth century. Advocacy of free trade had, of course, been a central plank of political economy from the end of the eighteenth century and this stance was strengthened rather than weakened by the rise of marginalism. On the other hand, the economic historians saw advocacy of free trade as based on precisely the kind of universalistic, deductive reasoning they abhorred. For them trade policy should be a route to national economic goals, and if protectionism would strengthen the British economy then it should be supported.[8]

The early economic historians tried to reform economics from within rather than create a new subject. But that endeavour failed. As one of the early economic historians, William Ashley, remarked in retrospect, 'The theoretical economists are ready to keep us quiet by giving us a little garden plot of our own; and we humble historians are so grateful for a little undisputed territory that we are inclined to leave the economists to their own devices.'[9]

That garden plot remained a very small one for several decades after it was first cultivated. Despite the founding of the *Economic History Review* as the flagship journal of the discipline in Britain in 1927, the subject remained institutionally weak throughout the interwar years.[10] Practitioners in this period divided into two broad camps. On the one hand there were the 'reformers', such as the Hammonds and Tawney. Unlike the pre-war reformers, their revolt against the economic and political orthodoxies of Victorian Britain led them not towards social imperialism but towards socialism. The focus of concern of the Hammonds was the social conditions of the working class during the industrial revolution period, and this work began a stream of broadly Leftist 'labour history' which was to continue long into the post-Second World War years. Tawney's work was much more diverse and less easily categorised, but shared the disdain of other reformers for the 'trivialities' of orthodox economics.[11] On the other side – and increasingly academically powerful within the small world of economic history – were those such as Clapham and Ashton who, while focusing their work on detailed empirical research, broadly shared the assumptions of orthodox economics. Clapham, however, combined a scepticism about the usefulness of some of the more abstract concepts of economics with a strong commitment to basic quantification as a primary feature of economic history.[12] Ashton was more explicitly hostile to the socialistic tendencies of labour history, and became an ideologue of a right-wing version of the history and social consequences of British capitalism.[13]

In the early post-war years it was those in the Clapham/Ashton school of economic history who predominated and, particularly because of their power base at Cambridge and especially the LSE, were able to dominate the subject in the years of expansion that followed. This domination was facilitated by the emergence of an increasingly separate discipline of social history which built on but went beyond the old 'labour history'. This new discipline was based in part on the growth of sociology in the post-Robbins expansion of the social sciences in higher education. Sociology seemed to provide social history with a theoretical framework which escaped the constraints of orthodox economics. Also important was the growth of a British Marxism, something which in an intellectual sense had been almost entirely absent in the 1920s and 1930s. Two features of this Marxism stand out. First, it was concentrated in history rather than, for example, in political theory or philosophy.[14] Second, this Marxist history showed little interest in economics. Apart from Dobb, the British Marxist historians such as Thompson, Hill and Hobsbawm showed little concern with or know-

ledge of economics in their work, and in that respect their approach
reinforced the existing division between the interwar 'social reformers'
and the economically informed economic historians.[15] While some of
the new departments established in the 1960s and 1970s were styled
economic *and* social history, separate departments (and journals) of
social history also grew up in these years, and this reflected a strength-
ening of the intellectual (and to a significant extent ideological) divide
between the two aspects of the subject.

The dispute over the methods appropriate to economic history which
characterised the years of birth of the subject returned in a different
but related form in the 1960s and 1970s. The origin point of this debate
was work in the United States, where, from the 1950s, what was later
to be christened 'cliometrics' emerged. This approach to economic
history reflected the fact that the institutional separation of economics
and economic history had never occurred in the United States, and
economic history was pursued mainly in economics departments. Cliometrics involved applying contemporary economic theory and statistical
techniques to economic history. One of its major practitioners has
argued that the most appropriate name for this approach is 'historical
economics', rightly in this way reversing the adjective and noun in
economic history to reflect the fact that the new approach was a branch
of applied economics.[16] While in principle the new approach emphasised
the importance of economics *per se* to historical problems, especially in
its early years, historical economics was in large part an application of
neo-classical economics to historical material. Temin, in his introduction
to one of the first collections of articles from the new field wrote: 'This
anthology of the new economic history has been assembled to introduce
the reader to economic history as a form of applied neo-classical
economics.'[17] The triumphalism of neo-classical economics is clearly
evident here, with the acceptance of the 'scientific' claims of that
economics and with history seen as a rich field in which the efficacy of
these methods could be demonstrated, while also suggesting that
economics could learn from history.[18] In practice the intellectual
movement has been mainly one way, with cliometrics representing a
further example of the tendency of economics to try and colonise other
social science disciplines, while there is little evidence of mainstream
economics being much affected by historical work.

If, methodologically, historical economics reflected the imperialist
claims of neo-classical economics, its popularity in the USA and to a
lesser extent elsewhere also reflected its central concern with economic
growth. Before 1939 the subject of economic growth had largely disappeared from the economists' agenda, but there was a re-birth of
concern with this topic after the war. This was driven partly by a

perception of the political importance of the huge gap that had grown up between the countries which had experienced industrialisation and rapid growth, and the great majority of the world's population who had not.[19] In addition, in the 1950s and 1960s, when the old interwar enemy of mass unemployment appeared to have been banished, governments in the advanced countries looked to more rapid economic growth as the way to increase the welfare of their populations and gain popular support.

Much of the early work of historical economics was concerned with the growth of the US economy, exploring both the dimensions and sources of that growth.[20] This focus on growth provided a bridge to other, including British, economic historians, even if they were not enthusiasts for the techniques of historical economics. On the other hand, this focus on economic growth served to narrow the agenda of economic history,[21] and reflected a lack of self-confidence in the discipline by its reliance on external forces to generate the problems to work on. (This point is returned to below in the discussion of the British debate on economic decline.)

The new American historical economics stirred deep emotions, especially when the question of the desirability of its spread to Britain was at issue. Partly this reflected some of the early topics addressed by this method. A pioneer example was the work of Conrad and Meyer on slavery, which purported to demonstrate that in economic terms slavery was buoyant and profitable in the American South before the civil war.[22] Such a position raised a host of entangled ideological and political as well as methodological and substantive problems. Less dramatic but almost as controversial in economic history circles was the use of the 'counterfactual' approach, where the importance of a cause (for example, the building of railroads) to an outcome (the rate of American economic growth) was assessed by attempting to estimate what would have happened in the complete absence of this cause. Some opponents of the new approach regarded this as the absurd apotheosis of history by the deductive method, while its supporters regarded it as a logical way to attempt rigorously to assess the significance of an alleged cause.[23]

The attempt to export historical economics from the USA to Britain ran up against a number of barriers. First was the divergence in the intellectual background and training of economic historians in the two countries. American economic history was largely done by economists who happened to specialise in history. The American system of graduate education gave them the skills to work with economic theory and modern statistical methods. By contrast, British economic historians typically learnt little formal economics or statistics, and most graduate education in the subject involved little 'system' at all – rather it was characterised by a very individualised research effort, often archivally-centred and with little concern for formal skills and techniques of any sort.

This difference in training was obviously linked to differences in perception about the nature of economic history. Many in Britain saw the American techniques as at odds with their view of the subject as close, not to economics, but to other historical disciplines in its attachment to close evaluation and deployment of source material as the primary method of working, with little explicit theorising, and strong attachment to 'commonsensical' frameworks to understand patterns of cause and effect. In part the clash between old and new economic history was a genuine difference of view about the nature of the intellectual enterprise. But there was, undoubtedly, in Britain a 'know nothing' attitude which turned ignorance of economics and statistics into a positive virtue rather than a weakness.

Barriers to entry of the new approach also reflected the perception of the imperialistic and arrogant claims of neo-classical economics. These claims were commonly driven by a prescriptive account of the nature of 'science', which economics asserted it had become because of its methodology. These claims about the status of economic knowledge would now be regarded with much more scepticism by both many economists and advocates of the new economic history than was the case in the 1960s and 1970s, when this idea that there is something called 'the' scientific method which every discipline ought to seek to follow had a much greater hold than today.[24] One of the most interesting postscripts to this whole debate has been the work of McCloskey, very much a pioneer of the new historical economics, but someone who has written extensively in criticism of this kind of 'scientistic' attitude to assessing the value of arguments in economics and economic history.[25]

Because so much of the new historical economics was driven by the assumptions of neo-classical economics, the normative aspect of that theory is clearly evident in many of the conclusions of the new work. Above all, those conclusions usually suggested that, by and large, market forces have generated desirable outcomes. McCloskey, somewhat reluctantly, accepts the existence of this tendency: 'The economist is no Dr. Pangloss, believing that all is for the best in the best of all possible worlds. Yet it must be admitted that he has Panglossian tendencies, to which he will occasionally surrender,' and, as he notes elsewhere in the same book, in disputes in historical economics 'usually what is at stake is optimism or pessimism about the working of the market'.[26] Such implications of the new historical economics reinforced the ideological hostility to its deployment in Britain, where faith in the market mechanism among social scientists at this time was generally in short supply.

While a great deal of the early work in the new historical economics was on American economic growth, another popular topic was British economic history, especially from the 1870s onwards. Pioneered by such writers as Burn in the 1940s, by the 1960s it was emerging as a commonplace among British economic historians that for nearly a century the British economy had been on a path of relative decline. This perception drew on the general political debate on economic decline which emerged in Britain at the end of the 1950s, but pushed back the beginnings of the problem to well before the First World War. Central to this argument was the idea that the decline was a consequence of an entrepreneurial failure, a failure of businessmen to invest and innovate at the 'desirable' rate to sustain Britain's economic momentum. Such an argument was a red rag to the bull of the new economic history, because it suggested irrational behaviour on the part of businessmen, and a failure of the market economy to maximise possible growth. Thus much of the early new work in historical economics set out to show that Britain did not suffer from entrepreneurial failure, but that the slowing rate of growth simply reflected shifting costs and market opportunities, in which businessmen responded rationally to changing market signals.[27] These arguments well illustrate the combination of iconoclasm and Panglossian tendencies which the new work so often embodied.

Given the institutional separation of British economic history from economics, the intellectual training (and prejudices) of most British economic historians, and the ramifications of the neo-classical basis of most of the new historical economics, it is unsurprising that this approach did not become dominant in Britain. But the new American product did throw British economic history on to the intellectual defensive, and put it in a weak position to defend its claims as an autonomous and worthy activity when the financial pressures of the 1980s and 1990s made themselves felt.

Cipolla has written of the problems of economic history in terms of the 'two cultures', leading to the subject's 'schizoid status half-way between history and economics'.[28] On the one hand economic history, like any history, must be concerned with reconstructing the diverse rationalities[29] of individual and collective actors in the context of their time, and must therefore resist the imposition of a trans-historical rationality that neo-classical economics embodies.[30] On the other hand its explanatory frameworks have to engage with (though not uncritically accept) those developed in economics. This is difficult to do when, in Britain, so many historians seem to be doggedly resistant to economics, an attitude which stems in no small part from the over-inflated 'scientific' claims of much economics (and new economic history) and the arrogance which so often flows from these claims. Historians' common

'know nothing' attitudes to economics are in part the perverse consequence of the peculiar development of that discipline, the severe
limitations of which are now being recognised by some of its most
distinguished practitioners.[31]

Anguished debates about method are not the staple of economic
history, though, as argued above, the methodological issue is very important in understanding the failure of economic history to establish a clear
identity. This failure also has its positive side, for it has allowed an
eclecticism of both subject matter and approach which at its best has
been highly productive. There is much less sense in economic history
than in orthodox economics that 'good work' in the discipline has to
conform to some preordained methodological norms, and this is entirely
healthy given the weak foundations for the 'scientific' claims for such
norms.[32] Alongside such eclecticism of methods, British economic
history has also exhibited great diversity of subject matter, and this again
has been a notable strength. But the economic history of *modern* Britain
has shown a strong tendency to focus on the issue of economic 'decline',
and the last part of this essay will outline some of the issues arising from
this characteristic of so much recent economic history research.

The idea that we can best understand the recent economic history of
Britain in terms of an overarching (relative) decline seems to have
originated in the late 1950s at the same time as perceptions of decline
were coming to dominate contemporary economic policy and political
debate.[33] Indeed, the impetus of this historical analysis seems to come
in part from the desire to seek for the roots of a contemporary malaise.
Of course, 'decline' in the British economy in more restricted senses
had long been diagnosed in Britain: for example, a pioneering article in
a new journal devoted to economic history had, in 1931, analysed the
weaknesses of Britain in responding to the growing competition from
American engineering goods as far back as the 1850–70 period.[34] But
the new 'declinism' of the 1950s was much broader in its implications.
The 'failure' of Britain was seen as continuous (since at least the 1870s)
rather than episodic, general rather than specific, deep-seated rather
than contingent. Over the next decades this idea of the recent British
economic past came to be almost universally accepted, and debate
focused not on the existence of the phenomenon but its causes.[35]

The debate about decline linked to the rising concern with economic
growth among both economists and economic historians in the 1950s
and 1960s, noted above. But the early British literature drew little on
growth theory, or indeed any other part of economic theory, and often
became little more than a list of the failings of British industry against
a standard of performance which remained ill-defined. There was little
attempt to specify in detail the rationalities of key actors in the economy

in the periods analysed, and this left an open door for the new historical economists who wanted to demonstrate that in Britain in the nineteenth century – like everywhere else at all other times – neo-classical rationality had prevailed, and things had, by and large, been for the best in the best of all possible worlds.[36] Here the weakness of much British economic history, in its inability critically to engage with economics, was rather cruelly exposed.

Another feature of declinism, and one which has perhaps been both the most persistent and the most unfortunate, has been the explanation of that decline in terms of 'culture'. In much of the declinist literature this term has been thrown around with abandon, though in effect it usually seems to be a concept which substitutes for rather than aids understanding. The obvious general problem with cultural explanations is the failure to demonstrate that successful capitalist economies require any particular cultural components, and in the absence of such specification the whole exercise appears ill-considered. Just how ill-considered was shown in two popular declinist works of the 1980s, by Wiener and by Barnett,[37] both in their different ways ascribing British decline to an 'anti-industrial culture', both gaining large readerships for their message, and both being profoundly unpersuasive.[38]

The success of such works, despite their evident weakness as historical understandings, reflected the ideological function that declinism has assumed. Both books in different ways offered a version of a 'New Right' history of Britain to match the contemporary political mood. Yet the striking feature of declinism has been how it has been taken up across the political spectrum, rather than being confined to Left or Right. There is a well-established Marxist account of British decline which in some respects mirrors Rightist accounts, though usually with somewhat more historical sense than the latter display.[39]

The dominance of declinism in writing about recent British economic history has had a number of unfortunate effects. First, as the previous paragraphs have suggested, declinism has created an audience for very poor history. Second, the idea of 'a hundred year decline' has given a much greater homogeneity to British economic performance over this period than the evidence would seem to justify. As conventionally measured by the growth of GDP relative to major competing nations, only in the period 1951–73 can British relative decline be said to have been large and sustained, and in this period a substantial part of the divergence can plausibly be ascribed to a 'catching-up' by the West European economies on Britain's substantial lead.[40] The failure to take this point on board in most discussions has led to over-generalised notions of decline becoming widespread, and allowing all kinds of flaccid generalisations to gain some credibility.

More specifically, the predominance of declinism has tended seriously to narrow the kinds of questions asked by economic historians about the recent economic past. Almost every feature of British society is put through the mill of 'what went wrong; how did this feature contribute to decline?'. An example of this is the discussion of the decline of sterling as the world's major currency, and the associated evolution of the 'sterling area' as a regional currency bloc in the 1930s through to the 1960s. Most accounts of this development examine (and usually condemn) this area for its supposed detrimental effects on British growth. The particular arguments used in these assessments have been powerfully criticised by Schenk,[41] but the point of importance here is how, by linking the analysis so often to 'decline', other interesting issues are sidelined. In this case, the sterling area could be looked at in the situation of British attempts to manage the national economy in a context of peculiarly complex international connections – economic, financial and political. Similarly, the emphasis on decline in terms of growth has led economic historians to give much less attention to distributional issues than was the norm for earlier generations of writers in the subject.

The above argument is not intended to suggest that any discussion of Britain in terms of decline is to be condemned. Clearly there have been failures of economic performance, and these should not be dismissed in the Panglossian fashion of neo-classical economics. But the generality with which the notion of decline has been used has militated against the close specification of problems that good economic history requires, with close study of particular episodes of 'decline' crowded out by the overarching and often fatuous generalisations about the 'hundred years decline'.[42] Such economic history would also require a critical engagement with notions of economic performance derived from economics. Most obviously, the whole emphasis on the growth of GDP as the measure of such performance requires much more critical attention. From within economics there is a long-standing and growing strain of criticism about the use of GDP to measure welfare which economic historians should take seriously, and it is to be hoped they can add their own contribution, for example by emphasising the conditions and efforts of producers in the production process as a proper component of a sensible overall measure of welfare. In this kind of work the 'two cultures' might perhaps fruitfully interact rather than growl at each other in mutual misunderstanding.

Further reading

The history of economic history as a discipline is most comprehensively covered in Donald Coleman, *History of the Economic Past: an Account of the Rise and Decline of Economic History in Britain* (Oxford: Oxford University Press, 1987). The early years of the subject, and the important debate within economics, have been covered by a number of authors including George Koot, *The English Historical Economists* (Cambridge: Cambridge University Press, 1987). For an idiosyncratic but interestingly different perspective on the discipline's development see Ronald Hartwell, 'Good old economic history', *Journal of Economic History* 33 (1973): 28–40. For a broader, European, view see Carlo Cipolla, *Between Two Cultures: an Introduction to Economic History* (New York, W. W. Norton, 1991). The new economic history is accessibly dealt with by Donald McCloskey, *Econometric History* (London: Macmillan, 1987), while his arguments about the need to reject the 'scientific' pretensions of economics, which suggest a more equal and positive relationship with other social sciences, including economic history, are best displayed in his *Knowledge and Persuasion in Economics* (Cambridge: Cambridge University Press, 1994).

CHAPTER 16

Business history

John Armstrong

If history as a discipline has been under attack and has seen a decline in numbers of faculty and prestige within academia, then business history is a counter-cyclical good. Over the last twenty or thirty years business history has come of age and grown in terms of research, publications and teaching and has become an accepted, professional field of study within history, with all the normal scholarly appurtenances. This chapter will endeavour to expound and support this argument, and also indicate the exceptions to this generally positive trend; explain how and why this has occurred; and finally suggest how the subject might develop in the future. It commences with a consideration of the nature of the area, goes on to a brief explanation of the origins of the subject, and then outlines the history of the development of interest in the area as a suitable subject for academic research.

An obvious starting point for a chapter such as this might seem to be to define the topic about which it is going to expound. However, an eminent business historian and past President of the Business Archives Council warned against this: 'it is fatal to ask "what is business history?".'[1] He felt that such an exercise was likely to lead not to objective statements of what it was but normative assertions 'of what it ought to be'.[2] Despite this injunction an attempt will be made to undertake both tasks, to look at what business history has been and what it may become.

We might do worse than start with the definition given by one of the early sages of the discipline, G. N. Clark, who was the initial incumbent of the Chichele Chair in Economic History at Oxford in 1932. He said what differentiated business history from other branches of the discipline was the sources that were employed; it was 'history based on the records of business itself as distinguished from the information about

business collected by governments or tabulated by economists and statis-
ticians'.[3] This would be seen as far too restrictive for the 1990s but still
contains some validity. Indeed Mathias's warning about definitions was
because he feared they would be too narrow and he advocated a broad
church approach – to be inclusive rather than exclusive. An attempt
must be made to arrive at a working definition.

As we shall see below, business history in Britain derived from
economic history and within economic history there had been a strand
dealing with industries, entrepreneurship and studies of individual
firms. It was these aspects on which early business history concentrated.
Thus one facet of business history is to examine the foundation, growth,
problems and demise of individual firms and from this endeavour to
derive some general rules. At the other extreme it might take theories
propounded by business and management specialists and try to see what
validity these have when tested against historical experience. For
example, did firms adopt the multidivisional form when they moved
from producing a single range of products into a diversified product
market? Although most business historians would endorse Clarke's ex-
hortation to use internally generated company records, these alone are
not adequate or defining sources. In addition, the records of government
can shed light on company law, contracts and contacts between business
and the state; legal disputes often resulted in large tranches of documentation. Further, newspapers, the financial press, and trade papers
are a potentially huge source of information on firms and industries.
These sources are external to the firm, but used by business historians.
The subject matter of business history is vast: ranging from accounting
history, through company law to multinationals, as well as the most
visible product – the scholarly monograph on an individual company's
history. Mathias's stricture is well taken and indeed endorsed: business
history is not a narrow subject. Any study which looks at continuity and
change over time, in any area of business or industry, or at any aspect
of how firms are founded, organised, grow and decline – or indeed
attempts to survey or explain the roots, motivation and characteristics
of entrepreneurship – is legitimately part of the discipline. Much of
the theory of business history has been imported from economics,
management, accounting, marketing or human relations and at its best
business history feeds back into these disciplines by indicating the
strengths and weaknesses of these theories when an attempt is made to
apply them to a specific historical context or situation. Clark's point is
important; any business history is likely to be enhanced by drawing
upon those records generated by business itself, but good business
history can draw entirely on externally created documentation.

The origins of business history as a discipline are subject to some dispute and one senior member of the profession has described as 'a trap', the question 'what is its origin, when did it begin', though later in the same address he then went on to outline an answer to just these questions.[4] So even if it is a trap, it is one which cannot be avoided – though care will be taken to tread gently.

The Germans seem to be the candidates who have the greatest claim for writing the first business histories. As early as 1952, when British business history was barely out of its teens, Fritz Redlich wrote an article tracing the earliest such German works to the 1820s and suggesting they had become extensive by the 1860s.[5] He also suggested that by 1900 the French had a substantial number of such publications. Thus primacy seems to lie on the Continent. However, as in many things the Americans, though later on the scene, went into the operation wholeheartedly. In the 1920s what has been described as 'a flurry of major activity' took place in the USA based in Harvard University.[6]

It was born out of three cognate areas: economics, economic history and business studies. It was partly a function of the establishment of business schools in the USA and the desire to seek the causes of America's rapid rise to economic prosperity. Part of this project was an attempt to explore entrepreneurship, trying to discover the sources of entrepreneurial flair, the essentials of entrepreneurship, and the motivation to succeed – and hence how it could be encouraged and fostered. One method of establishing this, it was thought, was to research and write up case studies of successful entrepreneurs and firms as an inductive way of unearthing the characteristics and motivations of high achievers. These were also seen as fruitful forms of study for future top managers of American corporations studying at business schools.

The 1920s, when America seemed to have reached a new plateau of permanent prosperity, led to its business leaders being idolised so that hagiographies abounded, as well as serious attempts to analyse and understand the process. Thus two journals were established within a couple of years of each other: the *Bulletin of the Business Historical Society*, which later became the *Business History Review*, was published in 1926 by Harvard University and is still going strong today; the short-lived *Journal of Economic and Business History* appeared only from 1928 to 1932. The former journal was the offspring of the Business History Society, which had been founded in the previous year. The crash of 1929 and the ensuing depression created an inimical climate for new journals, especially one celebrating America's business successes.

The British came to the field a little later and, on this side of the Atlantic, the progenitor was almost entirely economic history. Mathias has seen the roots of the subject as lying in three separate traditions: the hagiographic work of the mid to late Victorians such as Samuel

Smiles and works like *Fortunes Made in Business* and *Men of Note in Finance and Commerce*;[7] banking histories which began to appear from around 1900, presumably to convince customers of the solidity and longevity of these financial institutions; and industrial or company histories, pioneered by Manchester University Press.[8] One of the earliest British business history monographs was written by George Unwin and published in 1924 dealing with the cotton producing firm of Samuel Oldknow.[9] This sprang out of the contemporary interest in the industrial revolution. A few years later T. S. Ashton wrote the history of a small file-making entrepreneur based in Warrington, operating initially on the domestic system.[10] However, these were the precursors to the discipline and at the time seen more as case studies of specific aspects of economic history than business history *per se*. The 1930s provided a double stimulus to research in business history. The depression of 1929 to 1932 meant a large number of firms went out of business and some of their records became available for study. Responding to this, the Business Archives Council was established in 1934 to rescue and preserve business records and encourage their use as research sources in writing business history.[11] In Britain the subject took on a new vigour in the 1950s, spurred on by the publication of the multi-volume history of Unilever written by a Cambridge scholar, Charles Wilson.[12] At the time this was a radical departure for Cambridge and inaugurated one strand of business history – that of the commissioned history – which continues to the present day, and to which we shall return. At about the same time, in the late 1950s, a number of sponsored and unsponsored studies emerged[13] and a journal devoted to the subject was founded.[14] This might be seen as the second stage in the take-off of the discipline. A body of monographs was beginning to be formed. The journal provided the opportunity for smaller-scale contributions, as well as reviews of business history books and, as important, reviews of books in related areas such as economic theory, especially applied economics, management and the related functional areas such as accounting, personnel and marketing. However, at this point it was still perceived as essentially a sub-discipline of economic history, though beginning to achieve some independence, and there was very little formal tuition in it, certainly at undergraduate level. The 1960s saw the existing trends develop and it was not until the 1970s that the subject achieved another stage in its ascent and also started the search for its 'holy grail', which to this day remains elusive. The 1970s were significant for perhaps the first national conference in the field, held at Cranfield and organised by Professor Shankleman.[15] It was also important because its aim was to allow the business historians to talk to management educators and perhaps persuade them of the relevance of their subject. This became a 'holy grail' for business historians for at least the next decade. If management schools could be convinced that business history should be a significant part of their curriculum, a huge potential for teaching and the research associated with it would be opened up, and hence for the subject and its advocates. However, as management education already embraced a wide range of disciplines, each convinced of its academic superiority and hence equally sure that they needed more slots on the timetable, there was bound to be significant entrenched institutional opposition to a brash newcomer trying to, apparently, acquire precious time and resources. Hence the goal of securing business history as a subject within management education was as elusive as the holy grail and never attained.

The 1970s saw a huge expansion in research activity, the number of courses offered, and the range of scholarly monographs on the history of individual firms. They also saw the establishment of a regular annual seminar on business history organised by Professor Derek Oddy, initially at Ealing Technical College, then moving to the Polytechnic of Central London in 1978. This provided a forum for trying out ideas and allowing debate and discussion on the subject. The series still continues, with financial support from the ESRC, and the seminars are now held at the LSE under the auspices of the Business History Unit. It was the 1980s that saw the satellite achieve a stationary orbit. In that decade, perhaps helped by the new prestige, emphasis and utility placed upon entrepreneurs and business activities in a Thatcher–Reagan economic climate, a whole host of activities took place to institutionalise the subject. Bibliographies appeared, a multi-volume biographical dictionary was published: and various guides to help researchers proliferated, such as a guide to the origins and interpretation of business records, to the records of particular industries and on the methodology of business history. Hence the 1980s saw the subject come of age.[16]

As has already been explained, the business history monograph, essentially relating the history of an individual firm, dates back to the earliest days of the subject. It continued to flourish throughout the decades and is still an important element of the field today. However, as Professor Coleman has pointed out, most of the earliest such monographs were based on dead firms whose records happened to survive,[17] whereas later ones, perhaps beginning with Charles Wilson's pioneering study of Unilever,[18] were of businesses which were still active and, usually, at least moderately successful. The range of industries commissioning such tomes is immense, from biscuits and beer to soda and soap via newsagents and railways.[19] The spur to such a work was often an anniversary, a merger or takeover which threatened the separate existence of a long-established family firm, or at the insistence of a particularly history-minded chairman. One advantage of this genre is that it builds up a series of highly detailed case studies of how and why particular firms were founded, grew and prospered. In theory, from this body of cases a set of generalisations could be drawn which would demonstrate the common elements which made for business success. One issue of *Business History* endeavoured to do this, drawing on a limited number – thirteen – of published cases studies.[20] Despite some drawbacks it felt this activity was successful: 'the essays do demonstrate that it is possible to abstract and use the large body of data available in existing company histories'.[21]

However major reservations have been voiced about this essential pillar of business history publishing. One is that the company will be so careful of its reputation as to allow no criticism of its policies, and hence the book will be unanalytical and anodyne. This is largely true of some of the earliest company histories, written usually by journalists rather than by scholars, and often produced as public relations exercises. However, from the early days of scholarly company history it was understood, and usually specified in the contract, that it would be history – warts and all. This was sometimes eased by the end date of the study being sufficiently early as to preclude the probability of libel writs, and by the feeling that mistakes made in the past, and overcome, demonstrated the resilience of the firm and its ability to learn. Thus this was never a real problem.

More important is the criticism that the sample of firms studied in this way is not representative of the economy as a whole and hence any generalisations made are equally flawed. This arises because enterprises which commission histories tend to have two characteristics: they are successful, otherwise they would not still be around to hire the business historian, and they are large scale. The former may be less of a problem, although still a limitation, in that these successful firms are often the result of mergers and takeovers of other competing firms within the same industry. These firms which have ceased to exist as separate entities might be deemed 'unsuccessful' and as such the study of the constituent parts of a large-scale corporation will necessarily consider some unsuccessful firms, and the reasons for their lack of success.[22] Nevertheless these case studies will explain much less about why or how businesses fail; however, they may be used to try to generalise about why and how businesses succeed and grow. It will be difficult to isolate success factors if it is not known whether they were absent from unsuccessful firms. Hence the generalisations will be tentative but not totally invalid. The bias towards large-scale firms is more worrying. It is a valid comment that most commissioned histories are of the largest companies, whereas at any time these giant firms are a small minority of the total number of businesses in the economy. Indeed the 'typical' firm would be a small-scale family business – precisely the least likely type of firm to have its history written. This criticism can be applied yet more widely to the business history field, for much of the theory applied to business history derives from the work of Alfred D. Chandler in the United States,[23] and his focus is entirely on the very largest businesses. This is a significant drawback to the commissioned history, and we shall return to the topic later. A partial answer is similar to that of the successful versus unsuccessful firm problem. Most modern large firms did not spring into existence 'fully grown' but were initially small firms which gradually grew, partially by ploughing back profits and internal growth. Often they absorbed parallel firms which also were small at first. So the study of the early growth of a large company will involve consideration of how small firms grew. However, it means that the limitations of the generalisations made need to be appreciated; they apply more to large firms, but not necessarily so much to small ones.

A criticism often aimed at the commissioned history is that it is like the dinosaurs: large, slow moving and obsolete. It is rarely read except by other business historians, and certainly not by business people, economists or management educators. It may impress customers and employees but is too big, heavily written and specialised to interest them.[24] As such, these tomes preach only to the converted and have been seen as a waste of resources. Paradoxically, they have also been criticised from the opposite flank. Because they were commissioned, the client's known preference for a narrative company history will influence the author and hence the study will be insufficiently analytical of the company's policy and instead will be the work of 'inveterate empiricists'.[25] This concern with narrative history is not so damning if the author can ride two horses, if not simultaneously, consecutively. A number of company histories have combined the narrative progress of the specific company with an analysis of aspects of policy in enough depth to make a contribution to the theory. In this sense size may be an advantage as it allows multiple goals to be pursued.

Another charge laid at the door of the company history is that studies of individual firms give too narrow a focus. It is impossible to say how well or badly one business did except by comparison with its peers, the other enterprises in that industry. Thus what is required, it is argued, is comparative works of all the firms in an industry. It may be true that some of the early company histories were narrowly based, but later examples, being aware of this limitation, have tried to contextualise 'their' firm by placing it within the performance of the industry – looking at market share, returns, and such indicators. In this way a mini-study of the whole industry has been attempted. In addition many of the large firms which commissioned company histories were the result of mergers and amalgamations, and hence in part answered the charge by looking at a number of firms which were initially independent in the same industry, even though they later became amalgamated. For instance, Unilever in the 1950s comprised more than three hundred different companies which had been taken over. Hence a full study of the component parts of a large firm will require consideration of a number of businesses. In this way some of the criticisms can be circumvented.

So what of the future for the company history? There is no doubt it will continue to be produced. A number are currently in progress and imitation and inertia will ensure they continue. While companies continue to want in-depth studies and are prepared to pay for them, historians will be happy to produce them. And they are of value to the academic community, not just as case studies from which inductive generalisations can be made but also as in-depth studies of particular issues in business policy. They have their weaknesses but these can be overcome.

It was suggested previously that the 1980s saw the full acceptance of business history as a valid field of academic study. We shall now examine the various features that made this possible and which indicated the maturity of the subject.

In part this progress can be marked by publications. If a discipline is mature, presumably it will have a large number of relevant books and articles; and then, to aid scholars, a specialist bibliography will be needed. This occurred in 1987 for business history, when two separate bibliographies were published. They were not the first, for there had been Joyce Bellamy's bibliography of Yorkshire business histories produced back in 1970,[26] Horrocks's of Lancashire a year later,[27] and Rowe's of 'Northern' business histories at the end of that decade.[28] For many years *Business Archives*, the journal of the Business Archives Council, had carried an annual bibliography of works on business archives and history. However, Goodall and Zarach produced the first book-length bibliographies claiming national coverage.[29] It was ironic that after being without any general bibliographies, two should appear in the same year. Zarach's volume suffered from the limitation that it only covered books, whereas Goodall's was much more comprehensive, including articles as well, and, although slightly idiosyncratic in its layout, was much the more useful of the two. It contained over 3,700 separate items, which gives some idea of the growth in the subject to that date, whereas Zarach included about 2,200 entries. That the discipline continued to expand was evident both from the bibliography pages of *Business Archives* and from Zarach's issuing of a second edition – much enlarged, in 1994.[30] Although on very similar lines to the first edition, in that it continued to include only books, excluded some previously well-covered industries such as railways, tramways, cooperative societies and the press, and did not count books of less than fifty pages – it contained about 2,500 entries, demonstrating the growth in the subject in much less than a decade. In 1996 an *International Bibliography of Business History* was added to the shelves. It contained brief annotations on the best business histories in the world, essentially books only, and covered over three thousand entries.[31] This too was a sign of the subject reaching maturity on an international scale, as well as at a national level. Another service which might be offered to scholars when a subject reaches a degree of maturity is some guidance in methodology. This had occurred spasmodically from the founding of the subject, via occasional editorials and articles in the journals,[32] and some remarks in the opening sections of articles or books. Perhaps most seriously this topic was tackled in a booklet issued by the Historical Association in 1960[33] which was one of the opening shots in the campaign for acceptance of the subject. However, in 1987 two volumes were published, both being devoted to easing the work of the business historian. One volume by Armstrong and Jones was a guide to about fifteen of the most common types of business document, endeavouring to show how and why they originated and hence what sort of biases were inbuilt and the types of question that they might be used to answer.[34] The intention was that this book would encourage greater use of business records and smooth the path of potential business historians by charting some of the pitfalls and values of these sources. The second book, by Orbell, had a similar general aim but was directed particularly towards helping the researcher to find information on a particular company.[35] It was excellent in systematically explaining the various locations and sources which should be tried if a researcher was seeking evidence about a specific firm or group of businesses. Armed with these two volumes the business historian was more likely to be successful in seeking relevant records and using them carefully. This might have been well-trodden ground for the hardened business historian but for the tyro researcher, especially postgraduates embarking on a piece of research or amateurs doing local history or seeking family antecedents, the two volumes were a great help. Both books were written by individuals who were stalwarts of the Business Archives Council (BAC), one having edited its journal, the second its newsletter and the third having been the research adviser for the Council. The British business historian was particularly favoured in having the BAC for, as we shall see, it was particularly active in the 1980s and 1990s and perceived part of its role to be to publicise the whereabouts of historical business records and to encourage their use to write business histories. In this role it sponsored the publication of a number of helpful guides for business historians.

The guidance in methodology did not cease in the 1980s but was reinforced later. *Business History* in 1991 carried an article that claimed to be a 'good archive guide' dealing with a number of national, mostly London-based archives and explaining what types of documents they held, how they were accessed, the uses to which these documents might be put and the limitations of the sources.[36] Again it was mostly of value to the relatively inexperienced researcher, but contained some tips and shortcuts which even the experts might find useful. In the same year, an issue of *Business Archives* was devoted to the theme of the problems involved in writing business history, and how they were overcome in a number of cases. By explaining the difficulties encountered in writing the history of a nationalised transport industry,[37] a Scottish bank,[38] and a business biography of an individual generally known more for his socialism and artistry than his business acumen,[39] and showing how they had solved these problems, the authors were exposing their methodologies and providing examples of good practice which aspiring business historians could draw upon.

A third sign of maturity in the subject, and a great help to doing research in it, were the printed guides to sources in business history which were published in the 1980s. Again this was not new. As early as 1971 a guide had been issued to the historical records of the shipping industry.[40] Its aim was to list the location of all the records that had survived for each shipping company, explaining the type of documents that were extant for each firm and for what period they remained, and giving a brief history of each business in order to highlight the main corporate changes, takeovers, mergers and alterations in status which effected document creation and preservation. In this way a researcher seeking records on a particular firm could use this guide rather than writing round to dozens of county and city record offices, as well as the shipping companies themselves and the large number of specialist repositories. This guide set the standard for the guides that were to follow. In themselves they were fascinating works, showing the often huge number of firms that were ever known to have been in the industry (for example it was estimated there were over seven hundred firms in the shipping industry), the extent of mergers and acquisitions, and the range of types of documents generated.

The approach pioneered in this volume was continued with books on the records of insurance companies,[41] shipbuilding businesses,[42] and banking corporations.[43] Each of these guides aimed to catalogue the extant historical records in its industry and so save the researcher time and effort. They were usually the result of a survey to locate the surviving records and many were promoted by the BAC. In addition, the volumes on insurance and banking businesses contained introductory essays which outlined the historical development of the industry, so providing a context for the potted histories of the individual firms which followed. The guide to banking records also included a methodological section, explaining the types of specialist documents created by the industry and how they might be used by historians.

Thus a series of volumes on the historical records of particular industries began to be formed. In addition, the 1980s saw the result of a large-scale survey into what records survived of the earliest registered limited liability companies.[44] Limited liability was only made easily and cheaply available in 1856 and the survey approached firms which were still on the register in 1979 and 1980 and then listed those documents which still remained: their type, location and the periods covered. In addition, following the precedent set by the industry guides, a brief history was given of each individual firm. Thus the format was familiar but the subject matter was not. This was a broad survey providing details on the records of more than six hundred and seventy firms, ranging through a wide variety of industries and indeed including charities, societies and institutions as well as businesses. It was a large tome and, with its indexes, provided the researcher with an easy way of checking if any records survived of a particular firm, industry or location. Thus research into business history was being greatly facilitated. This was furthered when the BAC surveyed its own membership and published the results in a *Directory of Corporate Archives* in 1985, giving details of the type of records available, access policy, and whether a company history had already been written.[45] Again this was a great boon to researchers – so much so that copies soon ran out and a second edition was published only two years later, and a third edition a few years after that.[46]

Thus the subject in the 1980s was well served by guides to available source material, easing the researcher's task and encouraging the use of primary sources in business history. The guides continued to be produced, with the BAC launching a new series of industry guides in 1990, which by 1995 contained volumes on the brewing, shipbuilding and accounting industries,[47] with more promised on banking and pharmaceuticals. In addition, the Royal Commission on Historical Manuscripts, which had been building up for many years a companies index as part of its National Registry of Archives, issued the first two volumes in what promised to be a series of industry guides. The inaugural volume was on the textiles and leather industry and was soon joined by one on metal working.[48] These further contributed to the easing of the burden of research, so that the modern business historian has a wide range of printed guides to facilitate access to archival primary materials.

Another great step forward in the 1980s was the publication of the results of a large co-operative project based and organised at the Business History Unit (BHU) at the London School of Economics (LSE). This was the five-volume *Dictionary of Business Biography*, edited by David Jeremy.[49] It was a vast enterprise, containing biographies of nearly fourteen hundred businessmen, running to over four thousand four hundred pages, and drawing on more than four hundred different contributors. Since it covered only business people active from 1860 and avoided those still alive, it gave some indication of the huge number of business individuals that might be worth recording. As well as being a most useful tool for business historians as a first resort to ascertain basic ideas about individuals, it demonstrated the strength and solidarity of the profession in being able to undertake and see through such a huge undertaking. It was not alone. It deliberately excluded entrepreneurs active in Scotland because a companion project was under way north of the border. The results duly appeared in two volumes in 1986 and 1989, comprising nearly a thousand pages and covering about four hundred business people.[50] As a result of these two projects a significant database of business biographies was established. In addition, these dictionaries offered the possibility of large-scale comparative work on the origins, education, religion, and values of entrepreneurs, as well as their methods of working. This collective biography – prosopography – was not to prove easy to achieve as the data in the dictionaries was not compiled in like manner for all entries; so the practice was not as good as the promise, but a number of avenues were open. Also a new interest in business biography was sparked off. Subsequently a number of volumes appeared loosely on this theme.[51] Further, the glaring omissions revealed in the apparently 'authoritative' *Dictionary of National Biography* – and the bias in the few entries of business people that were included towards all aspects of their life *other than* the business side – may have been one factor in convincing of the need for a complete revamp of that austere institution.[52]

However, it was not merely a plethora of publications which marked the maturity of the subject. There were also a number of institutional moves which were important, such as the establishment of business history centres or units and the inauguration of chairs in business history at some universities. The first formal centre for business history was established as the Business History Unit (BHU) at the London School of Economics in 1979.[53] We have already encountered the BHU when discussing the *Dictionary of Business Biography*, which was one of its more prestigious products. The finance for the unit came largely from industry and it recruited a leading economic historian, Leslie Hannah, as its first director. Its focus was international and it hoped to attract commissioned histories of the many large London-based businesses on its doorstep. Although the BHU was the first formal example of such a unit, there were other groups which had preceded it. For example, in the mid-1970s Lanchester Polytechnic (which later became Coventry Polytechnic and then Coventry University) employed an SSRC grant to survey local business records and subsequently published the result.[54] A few years later it followed this success with a more specific survey of the industries for which Coventry is most famous, namely the motor and the cycle industries.[55] These were sterling efforts and, although not the result of a particular designated unit, they indicated the direction in which individual local centres could and did move: to survey extant local business records, publish the results as a guide, and then research and write up some of these local firms' histories. A good example of this pattern was Bristol Polytechnic (later the University of the West of England at Bristol), where a centre for business history was established in 1985 and within a few years a handsomely produced volume on several local businesses was published.[56] Strangely, although all of the essays were written by local historians from Bristol Polytechnic and Bath College, no mention was made of any institutional affiliation in the book. Also rather oddly, the volume on sources available for business historians in the Bristol region came out *after* the book of business histories.[57] This seems rather a widdershins way of doing it, but may indicate the thoroughness of the survey of local businesses to identify record collections.

Business history centres or units also became established at Glasgow and Reading. Glasgow was really the pioneer of institutionalised business history in the UK, for in the late 1950s the university established the Colquhoun Lectureship in Business History – the first British university post in business history.[58] The initial incumbent was Peter Payne, who went on to write many distinguished business histories on rubber, steel and electric firms as well as on more general business history topics.[59] As a result of the creation of this post, a number of important volumes appeared and the study of business history, the preservation of business records and their collection for study were an important part of the university's role, with the establishment of the Adam Smith archive of business records. Glasgow's pre-eminence in the business history field was further asserted in 1979 when Tony Slaven, another incumbent of the Colquhoun lectureship, was appointed to the first chair of business history in the UK, and in 1987 when an anonymous donation allowed the establishment of a formal Centre for Business History in Scotland.[60] The other main centre for business history that emerged in the 1980s was Reading University. A lectureship in business history was created in 1988 and because of the work already being carried out in the Department of Economics, and the research interests of the initial incumbent, Geoffrey Jones, a strong focus soon developed on multinational enterprise – both foreign firms coming into the UK and British companies investing abroad. The quality of this work was recognised in 1991 when Jones was awarded a chair in business history, still only the fourth in the UK. Reading became an important centre for conferences, seminars and workshops in business history. Other centres emerged in the 1990s such as Leeds, which published a useful volume of local business histories,[61] and Portsmouth, where a centre was established under the energetic direction of Peter Scott – an expert on the property market and the development of industrial estates. Thus by the early 1990s there were a number of centres of excellence in the subject and a handful of chairs. The subject had come of institutional age. It might be argued that for a subject to be successful as an undergraduate subject there needs to be more than high-quality research and a number of solid monographs. One essential is some scholarly journals which will make cutting-edge research easily and quickly available, provide a forum for debates and discussions, and contain book reviews and bibliographic essays. This will allow the student access to examples of the academic dialectic in practice and a source of evaluation of the latest works in the subject. Business history has been fortunate in this regard for many decades in that a number of journals in closely related areas often contained articles of relevance. For example, *The Economic History Review* and *The Journal of Economic History*, both of which commenced publication before the Second World War, could not but contain some articles on industry, entrepreneurship, multinationals and such topics which are central to both business and economic history. In addition, as we have seen, as early as 1926 the American *Business History Review* began publication and from its earliest days it contained articles on British topics and by British academics, as well as items on theoretical issues of interest to all business historians.[62] Thus there were a number of outlets available for research findings from an early date and students of the discipline could consult these journals. However, British business history took a large step forward in the 1950s when both *The Journal of Transport History* (founded in 1953)[63] and, more importantly, *Business History* began publication, the latter in 1958. The former journal was of importance because it often contained articles on the business aspects of transport history, such as the reasons for air transport companies being unprofitable in the 1920s,[64] the rivalry between two railway companies,[65] and the extent and causes of depression in British shipping firms just before the First World War.[66] In addition it contained review articles of major themes or topics in business history from the transport industry angle, such as Channon's piece on Chandler.[67]

Of much more significance, however, was the inauguration of *Business History*, published on a biannual basis by Liverpool University Press and edited by Francis Hyde, professor of economics at that institution, with an editorial team largely drawn from Liverpool.[68] It provided a British outlet for business history research to be showcased, for although it contained articles by foreign scholars and on non-British topics, the vast majority of articles were on British concerns and British scholars dominated the contents pages. It undoubtedly filled a gap in the scholarly literature and was an important step in establishing the credibility of the subject. The early volumes contained about nine or ten articles, reviewed between fifteen and twenty books, and ran to between 130 and 150 pages. The journal began a marked expansion in size in the 1970s after its publication was transferred from Liverpool to Frank Cass in 1972, though oddly there was neither editorial mention of the reasons for this change of publisher nor even a gracious vote of thanks to Liverpool for being midwife and nurse to the new arrival until it reached its teens.[69] Even more significant as a measure of health of the journal and the discipline was the decision to increase the frequency of publication, from twice to three times a year, in 1981. This represented a 50 per cent increase in size so that the 1982 volume, for instance, contained over three hundred and thirty pages and fifteen articles, reviewed fifty-three books, as well as having a conference report.[70] Only a few years later, in 1986, the journal became a quarterly – another significant increase in size and credibility. As a result, Volume 28 contained over five hundred and seventy pages, twenty-three articles and reviews of seventy-eight books.[71] It might be said, with justification, that the journal had truly come of age. Its size and frequency of publication matched those of the American *Business History Review* and most other prestigious social science journals. The scholar and the undergraduate student could stay informed about recent research, ongoing debates, the latest books, and their strengths and weaknesses.

In the 1990s two further significant developments occurred in regard to journals relevant to business history. In 1990 a brand-new journal was launched: *Accounting, Business and Financial History*, published by Routledge three times a year initially, falling to twice a year in 1991.[72] It aimed to encourage articles 'on the interface between the three named areas',[73] wishing to produce comparative and interdisciplinary research as well as the more straightforward pieces on aspects of financial and accounting history. In this respect it aimed to carve out for itself a rather different niche to that occupied by *Business History* and reflected the particular interests of the editorial team, who were based at Cardiff Business School and researched and taught in the area where accounting and business history met – looking not merely at the evolution of accounting history but also at the impact of financial considerations on business history. This successful launch was another sign of the high level of interest in the broad subject area. To reinforce the flow of articles to the journal, Cardiff held an annual autumnal conference which soon became an institution well attended by the faithful.

A further addition to the periodical literature of business history took place in 1994 when *Financial History Review* was started. Published by Cambridge University Press twice a year and with two of the leading financial historians as editors, it too aimed at a niche market with a high profile of publishing.[74] Banks were among the most supportive of in-house business archives policy, produced the most lavish histories, and were among the staunchest supporters of the business history field. With the 'de-communisation' of Eastern Europe, new interest in the circumstances surrounding the establishment and growth of financial institutions in the West became apparent. The extent to which Western financial history could be used as a guide for the newly privatised Eastern Europe provided an added incentive for the foundation of this journal.

Thus by the mid-1990s business history could boast of three journals published in Britain with eight issues per annum, as well as the American publications. This increase in output was a gratifying sign of the subject's health. In addition, the 1990s saw the publication of proper textbooks for the subject. Just like the bibliographies, whereas there had been none, two were published within a year of each other. For undergraduate teaching this was crucial since textbooks acted as a guide to the broad field, indicating where there was consensus and where debate, summarising and evaluating a large body of literature, and pointing students towards further reading. This is not to suggest no undergraduate teaching occurred or that no substitutes for textbooks were available earlier. One of the earliest books which did service in this regard was written by Sidney Pollard in 1965.[75] Although it argued a thesis about management techniques and policies in the industrial revolution, it was also a stimulating summary of policies on labour recruitment, accounting techniques and management methods, and as such could be profitably used by students. Its weaknesses, as a textbook for business history, were its time scale – stopping in the middle of the nineteenth century – and that it did not cover all of the aspects of business history that most courses saw as important, such as marketing the product and raising capital. Also, as no revised edition was forthcoming despite a Pelican paperback version coming out in 1968, it became increasingly dated. Another book that provided a useful introduction to the subject was Peter Payne's slim volume on nineteenth-century entrepreneurship.[76] Again it was never intended as a business history text, being one of the 'Studies in Economic History' series launched by the Economic History Society to bring current debates easily and cheaply to students. However, it had excellent coverage of the idea of entrepreneurship, the debate over the apparent decline in its quality in Britain in the nineteenth century, and the structure of the firm, as well as a bibliography of several hundred relevant items. Because it was intended primarily for students, it was clearly written and took little for granted. However, like Pollard's book, its time span was limited and it made no pretence of being a business history text, covering only some important aspects of the subject.

The appearance of Leslie Hannah's seminal work in 1976,[77] therefore, augured well as possibly the first real textbook for the topic. It was to that date the best. Its focus was essentially on the twentieth century with an introductory chapter on the late nineteenth century. Although its prime aim was to argue the case for the growth of a corporate economy and explain why and how that came about, in so doing it covered a number of topics central to business history, such as the role of government, the rationalisation movement, the growth of large-scale firms, the role of capital, and the stock exchange, among other things. Thus it filled a long-felt gap in the market and by combining it with the books by Payne and Pollard a reasonable coverage of the topic since the industrial revolution could be achieved. This was made even easier in 1977 when Supple produced a collection of essays providing some excellent case studies of aspects of business history,[78] such as the role of the government in the establishment of the national grid,[79] the introduction of a new product (machine-made cigarettes),[80] and an example of turnaround strategy.[81] Although the introduction was disappointing, the title promising a theoretical framework but failing to deliver, the essays made available to students in a reasonably priced paperback a range of case studies which added flesh to the skeleton of theory and generalisation. Thus equipped, a number of undergraduate courses in business history were able to be taught, but there was still felt to be a need for a real textbook on the subject, a need which was not fulfilled by the appearance of second editions of both Hannah's and Payne's books.[82]

As a result of this long-felt need, the first volume claiming to be a business history text appeared in 1994,[83] closely followed by another the next year.[84] The earlier book was a co-operative venture edited by Maurice Kirby and Mary Rose – who had separately written some important works on business history – bringing together eight other eminent economic historians to allow each to write on their particular area of expertise. It also claimed to cover the whole period since industrialisation, unlike Pollard, Payne or Hannah, and so appeared to make cheaply available (it was in paperback form) in one volume a comprehensive text on business history. It was undoubtedly a great step forward but its coverage was rather patchy, with some topics dealt with only in the earlier period (the volume was in two parts, the first covered from the industrial revolution until 1900, and the second from 1900 to an unclear end date). In some cases this made good sense, for there was little point in devoting space to multinational enterprises much before 1850, but some topics should have been dealt with in both sections – for example, the excellent chapter on family firms up to 1914 was not matched by a similar one on the period after 1914, yet the family firm in no way disappeared and one of the much-debated issues in British economic performance after 1920 is the extent and influence of familial managers rather than professionals. Similarly, there was a good chapter on how firms financed themselves up to 1850 but no complementary chapter on the later period, although again it is a crucial issue. Topics like marketing and the role of bookkeeping also needed more attention. Obviously it is too easy to criticise a book for what it does not do and there must be a limit on contents if it is to remain a reasonable size and price, and it was an excellent attempt. Perhaps greater editorial direction should have been imposed as to contents of individual chapters as well as to the topics covered; the volume might then have been a little more coherent.

The second text, mentioned above, was by John Wilson of Manchester University, claimed to cover the whole period from 1720 to 1994, and was rather different in its approach to that of Kirby and Rose. It placed more emphasis on testing the Chandlerian hypothesis that Britain adhered much more than America to personal or familial capitalism and that this peculiarity explains why British growth rates were poor. Wilson argues that at least until the 1940s the environment in which British firms operated was so different to that of the USA in terms of markets, the law, technology and other sociocultural factors, that it would have been quite inappropriate for British companies to have adopted American structures and strategies. To do this he needs to provide detailed comparisons between what was happening in Britain and in other developed countries – especially America, Germany and Japan – and hence several sections of his book are explicitly devoted to the policies and practices of foreign firms to act as a contrast to British business. Being single-authored, the book was more coherent than Kirby and Rose and more consistent in arguing a case throughout, but suffered from scant coverage of some topics such as marketing the product before 1870, and bookkeeping and the role of accounting techniques. However, despite any shortcomings, by the mid-1990s business historians had available a choice of textbook, significantly easing the teaching of undergraduate courses.

Perhaps the placing of the keystone in the arch of business history took place in about 1990, for it was then that the Association of Business Historians (ABH) was formed. Despite some caricatures of the British as being natural clubmen, they were late in establishing a national professional grouping compared to the Americans, Germans or Japanese. It had been talked about informally when groups of business historians met, for example at the Derek Oddy seminars or at Economic History Society annual conferences, but never pursued to a completion. A combination of circumstances conspired to make this the right time and a small council was established, a newsletter issued – the first appearing in April 1991[85] – and the inaugural conference was held at Glasgow, appropriately enough, in September 1991.[86] Business history had become 'professionalised' or, at least, an academic interest group had been established.

The group kept subscription levels low, to encourage wide membership, published a biannual newsletter entitled *Business History News* and organised a biennial peregrinatory conference at remarkably low rates, the second being at Leeds, with Warwick and Glasgow following on. Arising partly out of the success of this initiative, it was decided that a directory of business historians should be drawn up, not of British practitioners alone, but rather on an international basis. This project was masterminded by one of the inaugural council members of the ABH, David Jeremy, and published in 1994.[87] It provided a self-selected 'who's who' of the business history world covering about seven hundred and fifty individuals, facilitated networking, and acted as a register of research interests. As a result of comprehensive indexing – by period, industry, country and functional area within business – anyone wishing to hire a business historian could access one with relevant experience easily. The profession had become formalised, and catalogued. Thus by the early 1990s business history had all the trappings of an accepted field of scholarly study: it had truly come of age.

Although a decidedly hazardous task, some attempt needs to be made to indicate where business history is likely to go in the near future. It is difficult to disentangle prediction from normative judgements and thus there is an element of where it ought to go as well as where it will go. As previously suggested, the large company-sponsored monograph is likely to endure. Businesses like the prestige they bring and they are a vital building block of the discipline, providing in-depth study of business areas in particular companies. Since many authorities have called for more comparative work,[88] this too seems to be an area into which the discipline ought to and will move. Comparisons between firms in the same industry, comparisons of how firms in different industries react to a similar threat or opportunity, and comparisons between firms and industries in different countries[89] are all likely to be illuminating. Another frequently bemoaned gap in current business history is on coverage of the small firm sector – at least of those firms that not merely start small but stay small. One approach to this has been adopted by Lloyd-Jones and Lewis in their study of small firms in Sheffield,[90] another may be to look at a particular industrial estate or factory area,[91] a third might be to test some of the theories about flexible specialisation, industrial districts and the extent to which small firms can co-operate to provide externalities which large firms tend to internalise. These ideas have been pioneered by Piore, Sabel and Zeitlin but they are not easy to apply with any degree of rigour because definitions of what comprises an 'industrial district' are so loose and because the degree of co-operation required to fulfil the conditions has never been specified, and would be a difficult task.[92]

Undoubtedly networks and network theory are fashionable concepts in academia at the moment. These ideas have been applied to business history. One application is to apply network theory to those industries, like transport, and utilities such as gas, water and electricity, which are networks,[93] to see what new insights this will provide and how this has affected the relationship with the state. Another angle is to see business people as being linked into networks created by family, religion, schools, clubs, etc., and then to trace the importance of these links and how they explain connections and flows of, for instance, capital, information or partners.

The compilation of very large databases may be another road which business history will travel along. The decreasing cost of computing power and the ease of using database packages make this a more attractive route and it overcomes the problem of how far individual firms are representative and avoids the problem of small samples being biased. It assumes that the same sort of data can be collected from each firm in the population, which is frequently not the case, but in theory it should allow generalisations to be made with greater confidence. Jones and Bostock have tried this approach with foreign multinationals locating in Britain and come up with some convincing conclusions.[94]

Whatever routes may be predicted here, the most exciting new developments will be those it is impossible to predict. To date, business history has shown itself to be resilient, able to evolve to tackle new problems, eclectic in its use of theory from a wide range of disciplines, and has a wealth of sources on which to draw. It is likely to continue to develop and expand, evolving new methods and areas of interest.

Further reading

The best place for the totally uninitiated to start their reading is with one of the two recent textbooks: Maurice W. Kirby and Mary B. Rose (eds), *Business Enterprise in Modern Britain from the Eighteenth to the Twentieth Century* (London: Routledge, 1994) and John F. Wilson, *British Business History, 1720–1994* (Manchester: Manchester University Press, 1995). For succinct case studies, the volume of essays edited by Barry Supple is a good introduction. Both Les Hannah's work on *The Rise of the Corporate Economy* (London: Methuen, 1982) and Sidney Pollard's *The Genesis of Modern Management. A Study of the Industrial Revolution in Great Britain* (London: Edward Arnold, 1965 and Pelican, 1968) are currently out of print, but as both were produced in large numbers as paperbacks, they may still be found in second-hand bookshops and are excellent samples of the genre. Readers might also like to try dipping into one or two of the monographs mentioned in the main body of the text and listed in the notes. Choose a company in an industry that interests you. If uncertain as to whether a history exists, consult Goodall's or Zarach's bibliography, both listed in the notes to the chapter. A browse through some recent numbers of *Business History* will give an idea of current issues and debates as well as the breadth of temporal, geographic and thematic coverage that now comprises business history. A similar perusal of the *Business History Review* will demonstrate current American concerns and the difference of approach and methodology on that side of the Atlantic.

Notes

1. Historical writing

1. R. W. Chapman (ed.), *Boswell's Life of Johnson* (Oxford: Oxford University Press, 1953), p. 304.
2. J. Tosh, *The Pursuit of History*, 2nd edn (London: Longman, 1991), p. 113.
3. See for example, C. V. Wedgwood, *The King's Peace 1637–41* (London: Collins, 1955) or Winston Churchill, *A History of the English-Speaking Peoples*, 4 vols (London: Cassell, 1956–8).
4. J. Barzun and H. F. Graff, *The Modern Researcher*, 2nd edn (Fort Worth: Harcourt Brace Jovanovich, 1962), pp. 229–30.
5. D. Judd, *Empire: the British Imperial Experience from 1765 to the Present* (London: HarperCollins, 1996), pp. 94–7.
6. A. J. P. Taylor, *War by Time-Table: How the First World War Began* (London: MacDonald & Co., 1969), p. 45.
7. E. Gibbon, *Decline and Fall of the Roman Empire*, 1776–88, 1st edn (London: Everyman's Library, 1993), Chapter 3.
8. A. Marwick, *The Nature of History* (London: Macmillan, 1970), p. 152.
9. J. W. Burgon, *Lives of Twelve Good Men* (London: Murray, 1888), vol. 1, p. 73.
10. A. J. P. Taylor, *English History, 1914–45* (Oxford: Clarendon Press, 1965), p. 1.
11. R. Robinson and J. Gallagher, *Africa and the Victorians: the Official Mind of Imperialism* (London: Macmillan, 1961), p. 472.

2. History: theory and practice

1. P. Burke (ed.), *New Perspectives on Historical Writing* (Cambridge: Polity Press, 1991), pp. 3, 6.
2. Ibid., p. 4.
3. P. Burke, *History and Social Theory* (Cambridge: Polity Press, 1992), p. 14.
4. E. A. Freeman, *Methods of Historical Study* (1886), p. 44.
5. Burke (1992), p. 5.
6. Burke (1991), p. 4.
7. P. Burke, *The French Historical Revolution. The Annales School 1929–89* (Cambridge: Polity Press, 1990a), p. 7; P. Burke, 'Introduction', in Jacob Burckhardt, *The Civilization of the Renaissance in Italy*, trans. S. G. C. Middlemore (London: Penguin, 1990b).
8. J. Tosh, *The Pursuit of History. Aims, Methods and New Directions in the Study of Modern History*, 2nd edn (London: Longman, 1991), pp. 176–7.

9. B. Southgate, *History: What and Why? Ancient, Modern, and Postmodern Perspectives* (London: Routledge, 1996), p. 74.

10. Tosh (1991), p. 158.

11. Ibid., p. 135.

12. G. Elton, *The Practice of History* (London: Fontana, 1969), p. 70.

13. K. Jenkins, *On 'What is History?' From Carr and Elton to Rorty and White* (London: Routledge, 1995), p. 66.

14. K. Jenkins, *Re-thinking History* (London: Routledge, 1991), pp. 37–8.

15. Southgate (1996), p. 3.

16. Elton (1969), p. 31.

17. Jenkins (1995), pp. 68–9.

18. Ibid., pp. 8, 23.

19. Tosh (1991), p. 182.

20. Burke (1992), p. 7.

21. Quoted in Burke (1992), p. 9.

22. Tosh (1991), p. 161.

23. Ibid., p. 158.

24. Burke (1992), p. 3.

25. Ibid., p. 2.

26. Jenkins (1995), p. 8; Southgate (1996), p. 88.

27. Southgate (1996), p. 89.

28. Tosh (1991), p. 164.

29. Southgate (1996), pp. 90–1.

30. Tosh (1991), pp. 167–8, 172.

31. Ibid., p. 165.

32. Southgate (1996), p. 90.

33. Tosh (1991), pp. 163–4.

34. Ibid., p. 168.

35. Southgate (1996), p. 96.

36. Tosh (1991), p. 169.

37. Ibid., p. 174.

38. Ibid., p. 175.

39. Burke (1992), p. 16; Burke (1990a), p. 1.

40. Burke (1990a), pp. 6–7.

41. Burke (1992), p. 16.

42. Burke (1991), p. 6.

43. Burke (1990a), p. 2.

44. Burke (1992), p. 16.

45. Ibid., p. viii.

46. Burke (1991), p. 4.

47. H. White, *The Content of the Form* (Baltimore: Johns Hopkins University Press, 1987), p. 31.

48. Tosh (1991), pp. 51–2, 119.

49. Burke (1990a), pp. 94, 96–7.

50. Ibid., pp. 2, 4.

51. Tosh (1991), p. 108.

52. Ibid., pp. 171–2.

53. Burke (1991), p. 19. For a useful discussion of the ideas of Michel Foucault, see Patricia O'Brien, 'Michel Foucault's history of culture', in Lynn Hunt (ed.), *The New Cultural History* (Berkeley: University of California Press, 1989).

54. Burke (1990a), pp. 85–9.
55. Southgate (1996), p. 94.
56. Ibid., pp. 96–7.
57. M. Kinnear, *Daughters of Time. Women in the Western Tradition* (Ann Arbor: University of Michigan Press, 1982), p. 6.
58. Southgate (1996), p. 97.
59. Ibid., p. 97.
60. Ibid., p. 98.
61. Ibid., pp. 98–9.
62. Tosh (1991), p. 181.
63. Ibid., p. 179. The development of gender history is also discussed below in Chapters 13 and 14.
64. Southgate (1996), p. 99.
65. Jenkins (1995), p. 6.
66. Jenkins (1991), pp. 59–60.
67. R. Samuel, 'Grand Narratives', *History Workshop Journal* 29 (1990).
68. M. Bloch, *The Historian's Craft* (Manchester: Manchester University Press, 1992), p. 53.
69. Jenkins (1991), p. 38.
70. Southgate (1996), p. 75.
71. Ibid., p. 7.
72. Burke (1991), p. 6.
73. Southgate (1996), p. 9.
74. Burke (1991), pp. 3–4.
75. Ibid., pp. 17–18.
76. Southgate (1996), p. 70, citing J. E. Toews, 'Intellectual history after the linguistic turn: the autonomy of meaning and the irreducibility of experience', *American History Review* 92 (1987): 882. As Southgate indicates, Toews does not necessarily subscribe to this view.
77. Southgate (1996), pp. 72–3.
78. Ibid., p. 74.
79. P. Burke, 'History of events and the revival of narrative', in P. Burke (1991), pp. 233–48.
80. Southgate (1996), p. 124.
81. See, for example, Paul Thompson, *The Voice of the Past: Oral History*, 2nd edn (Oxford: Oxford University Press, 1988), and Jan Vansina, *Oral Tradition as History* (London: James Currey, 1985).
82. Burke (1991), pp. 12–13.
83. Jenkins (1995), p. 20.
84. Ibid., p. 88.
85. Burke (1991), pp. 4–6, 11, 16.
86. Ibid., pp. 10–11.
87. Burke (1990a), p. 89.
88. Southgate (1996), p. 54.
89. Ibid., pp. 8–9.
90. G. R. Elton, *Return to Essentials. Some Reflections on the Present State of Historical Study* (Cambridge: Cambridge University Press, 1991), pp. 28–9.
91. Tosh (1991), p. 182.

3. Public records

1. Public Record Office, Ruskin Avenue, Kew, Richmond, Surrey, TW9 4DU (Tel. 0181 392 5200). Opening hours: 9.30 a.m. to 5.00 p.m. Mon., Wed., Fri., Sat.; 10.00 a.m. to 7.00 p.m. Tues.; 9.30 a.m. to 7.00 p.m. Thurs. Closed on public holidays and for two weeks each year for stocktaking (these dates should be checked in advance). A reader's ticket is issued on production of proof of identity, such as a passport or driving licence.

2. On the change to agency status, see J. Cantwell, 'The new style Public Record Office: the transition from the old order', *Journal of the Society of Archivists* 14, 1 (1993).

3. G. H. Martin, 'The public records in 1988', in G. H. Martin and P. Spufford (eds), *The Records of the Nation. The Public Record Office 1838–1988, The British Record Society 1888–1988* (London: The Boydell Press/The British Record Society, 1990), p. 22. In the year 1993–94 alone, over half a million documents were produced to readers at Kew (Lord Chancellor's Office, *Thirty-fifth Annual Report of the Keeper of Public Records on the Work of the Public Record Office and the Thirty-fifth Report of the Advisory Council on Public Records 1993–94* (London: HMSO, 1994), Appendix 1).

4. An important exception is the records of the India Office, which are the responsibility of the British Library India Office Library and Records, 197 Blackfriars Road, London SE1 8NG (Tel. 0181 928 9531). See S. C. Sutton, *A Guide to the India Office Library, with a Note on the India Office Records*, 2nd edn (London: HMSO, 1971), and A. J. Farrington and G. W. Shaw, *Guide to Oriental and India Office Collections* (London: British Library, 1993). Nevertheless, an enormous quantity of records relating to British policy towards India can be found in the PRO.

5. Scottish Record Office, HM General Register House, Edinburgh EH1 3YY (Tel. 0131 556 6585); Public Record Office of Northern Ireland, 66 Balmoral Avenue, Belfast BT9 6NY (Tel. 01232 661621/663286).

6. Royal Commission on Historical Manuscripts, Quality House, Quality Court, Chancery Lane, London WC2A 1HP (Tel. 0171 242 1198). For guidance on the use of Parliamentary records, see D. Englefield, 'Parliamentary sources', in A. Seldon (ed.), *Contemporary History Practice and Method* (Oxford: Basil Blackwell, 1988).

7. See PRO Records Information leaflet 124, *Public Records outside the Public Record Office*.

8. During the year 1993–94, for example, records occupying nearly five thousand feet of shelving were transferred to the PRO (Lord Chancellor's Office, *Thirty-fifth Annual Report of the Keeper of Public Records*, p. 25).

9. See K. J. Smith, 'Sampling and selection: current policies', in Martin and Spufford (1990), p. 59.

10. Edward Higgs, 'The Public Record Office, the historian, and information technology', in Martin and Spufford (1990), p. 108.

11. M. Clay, 'Putting the records straight', in *FCO Historical Branch Occasional Papers No. 1* (London: FCO, November 1987), p. 9.

12. Cmnd. 8204, *Modern Public Records: Selection and Access* (London: HMSO, March 1981), para. 10.

13. Cmd. 9163, *Committee on Departmental Records: Report* (London: HMSO, July 1954), para. 241.

14. Sir H. Jenkinson, *Manual of Archive Administration*, 2nd edn (London: Lund, Humphries and Co., 1965), p. 149.

15. Smith (1990), p. 50.

16. Cmnd. 8204, paras 120–42 .

17. Smith (1990), p. 52.

18. Higgs (1990), p. 103.

19. See Smith (1990), p. 57; Edward Higgs, '"Particular instance papers": the historical and archival dimensions', *Social History* 10, 1 (1985): 89–94.

20. Cmd. 9163, para. 62.

21. N. Cox, 'The thirty-year rule and freedom of information: access to government records', in Martin and Spufford (1990), p. 75.

22. Parliamentary Debates (Commons), 9 March 1966, cols 561–3.

23. The thirty-year rule can be slightly misleading. Many files cover more than one year, and only become available thirty years after the date of the last item added to the file. In this respect, practice has varied between departments: the Foreign Office, for example, generally allowed files to 'run' for only one year; other departments, especially during the Second World War, allowed files to remain current for two or three years, or even longer.

24. This, arguably, distorted the 'natural' trend of historiography, encouraging a rash of studies of war-related topics, at the expense of serious research into the 1930s, an imbalance still being corrected.

25. Cox (1990), pp. 83–5.

26. Cm. 2290, White Paper, *Open Government*, July 1993; Lord Chancellor's Office, *Thirty-fifth Annual Report of the Keeper of Public Records*, p. 26.

27. An extremely lucid introduction to the archival principles which underpin PRO practice is provided by M. Roper, 'Modern departmental records and the Record Office', *Journal of the Society of Archivists* 4, 5 (April 1972): 400–2.

28. Roper (1972): 403.

29. N. Cox, 'Public Records', in A. Seldon (ed.), *Contemporary History, Practice and Method* (Oxford: Basil Blackwell, 1988), p. 85.

30. Detailed advice on how to cite PRO documents correctly is provided in the General Information leaflet 25 *Citation of Documents in the Public Record Office*.

31. Very useful introductions to this subject include D. N. Chester and F. M. G. Wilson, *The Organization of British Central Government 1914–1964* (London: Allen & Unwin, 1968), W. J. M. Mackenzie and J. W. Grove, *Central Administration in Britain* (London: Longman, 1957), and P. Hennessy, *Whitehall* (London: Secker & Warburg, 1989).

32. Lord Strang, *The Foreign Office* (London: Allen & Unwin, 1955); Sir Frank Newsam, *The Home Office* (London: Allen & Unwin, 1954); Sir Charles Jeffries, *The Colonial Office* (London: Allen & Unwin, 1956).

33. P. Hennessy, *Cabinet* (Oxford: Basil Blackwell, 1986); H. Roseveare, *The Treasury: The Evolution of a British Institution* (London: Allen Lane, 1969).

34. Examples include General Information leaflet 15, *Copyright* and Records Infomation leaflets 73 *The Records of the Cabinet Office* and 22 *The Records of the Foreign Office from 1782*.

35. Other important examples include B. W. E. Alford, R. Lowe and Neil Rollings, *Economic Planning 1943–1951. A Guide to Documents in the Public Record Office* (London: HMSO, 1992), and A. Thurston, *Sources for Colonial Studies in the Public Record Office Volume 1. Records of the Colonial Office, Dominions Office, Commonwealth Relations Office and Commonwealth Office* (London: HMSO, 1995). See General Information leaflet 11 *Publications* for further details.

36. Public Record Office, *Current Guide* (Kew: PRO Publications, 1996).

37. For some classes of record, the published *Guide to the Records of the Public Record Office* (3 volumes, London: HMSO, 1963–68) remains authoritative, and for a few older classes, the earlier *Guide to the Manuscripts Preserved in the Public Record Office* (2 volumes, London: HMSO, 1923–24) by M. S. Giuseppi should be consulted.

38. Public Record Office, *Kew Lists. The Microfiche Edition* (London: HMSO, 1988).

39. Information about volumes produced and membership can be obtained from the Secretary, List and Index Society, Public Record Office, Kew, Richmond, Surrey TW9 4DU.

40. See Records Information leaflet 90, *Photographs Held by the Public Record Office*.

41. Detailed advice on locating maps is provided in Records Information leaflet 91, *Maps in the Public Record Office*.

42. See Louise Atherton, *'Never Complain, Never Explain'. Records of the Foreign Office and State Paper Office 1500–c.1960* (London: PRO Publications, 1994), pp. 146–54.

43. Cox (1988), p. 75.

44. J. E. Hoare, 'Present-day records: the prospects for future historians', in *FCO Historical Branch Occasional Papers No. 1* (November 1987).

45. Remember to use a pencil – pens are not allowed because of the risk of damage to the documents. The Office can, however, accommodate readers who wish to use portable typewriters, lap-top computers or tape recorders.

46. M. Bloch, *The Historian's Craft* (Manchester: Manchester University Press, 1992), p. 53.

47. A very convenient guide to ministerial office-holders, which gives precise dates for terms of office, is D. Butler and G. Butler, *British Political Facts 1900–1985*, 6th edn (Basingstoke: Macmillan, 1986).

48. *Dictionary of National Biography to 1900*, 22 vols (Oxford: Oxford University Press, 1885–1900), with eight subsequent volumes, each covering a decade, for the period 1901–1980; *Who's Who* (published annually by A. & C. Black, London); *Who Was Who* (eight volumes to date, covering the period 1897–1990, with a *Cumulated Index 1897–1990*, London: A. & C. Black, 1991).

49. The precise dates of publication can be checked in the *Times Index*, published since 1906. Convenient collections have been published in *Obituaries from the Times*, in three volumes covering the period 1951–75 (Reading: Research Publications, 1975–79).

50. Rodney Lowe, *Adjusting to Democracy. The Role of the Ministry of Labour in British Politics 1916–1939* (Oxford: Clarendon Press, 1986).

51. See General Information leaflet 19, *Reprographic Copies of Records in the Public Record Office*, for details of processes and prices.

4. Archives

1. J. Foster and J. Sheppard, *British Archives. A Guide to Archive Resources in the United Kingdom*, 3rd edn (London: Macmillan, 1995), p. vii.

2. Dick Sargent, *The National Register of Archives: An International Perspective* (London: University of London Institute of Historical Research, 1995), p. 18.

3. R. J. Olney, *Manuscript Sources for British History: Their Nature, Location and Use* (London: University of London, Institute of Historical Research, 1995), p. 2.

4. For example: the Royal Commission on Historical Manuscripts, *A Standard for Record Repositories on the Constitution and Finance, Staff, Acquisition and Access* (London: HMSO, 1990); International Council on Archives, *ISAD(G): General International Standard Archival Description* (Ottawa: International Council on Archives, 1994) and *Draft ISAAR(CPF): International Standard Archival Authority Record for Corporate Bodies, Persons and Families* (Ottawa: International Council on Archives, 1995); M. Cook and M. Proctor, *Manual of Archival Description*, 2nd edn (Aldershot: Gower, 1989).

5. Much of this section is based on A. A. H. Knightbridge, *Archival Legislation in the United Kingdom* (London: Society of Archivists, Information Leaflet 3, 1985). This leaflet is due to be revised and republished.

6. Public Records Act 1958 s. 5(1) as amended by the Public Records Act 1967 s. 1.

7. There are many statutes which require companies to keep records for current business purposes, but few which relate to keeping archives for research purposes.

8. The most comprehensive and up-to-date guide is J. Foster and J. Sheppard's *British Archives. A Guide to Archive Resources in the United Kingdom*, 3rd edn (London: Macmillan, 1995). It has useful indexes including a subject index. Briefer details are given in Royal Commission on Historical Manuscripts, *Record Repositories in Great Britain: A Geographical Directory*, 9th edn (London: HMSO, 1992).

9. For details, see Public Record Office, *Beyond the PRO: Public Records in Places of Deposit* (London: HMSO, 1995).

10. A. Turton (ed.), *Business Archives* (London: Business Archives Council, 1991) is a useful introduction to business archives.

11. A useful, though out-of-date, summary of the remits of the organisations mentioned below is given in C. M. Short, *Advisory Bodies and Voluntary Organisations Concerned with Archives* (London: Society of Archivists Information Leaflet 6, 1989). Up-to-date information is given in Foster and Sheppard (1995), pp. xlviii–liv.

12. Foster and Sheppard (1995), p. ix.

13. For example E. L. C. Mullins (ed.), *Texts and Calendars: An Analytical Guide to Serial Publications*, 2 vols (London: Royal Historical Society, 1958, 1983) and *Guide to the Historical and Archaeological Publications of Societies 1901–1933* (London: Athlone Press, 1968).

14. These are described in detail in Sargent (1995), pp. 24–34.

15. Royal Commission on Historical Manuscripts, *List of Accessions to Repositories* (London: Royal Commission on Historical Manuscripts, 1957–1972) and *Accessions to Repositories and Reports Added to the National Register of Archives* (London: Royal Commission on Historical Manuscripts, 1973–1992 but now discontinued; digests now appear in specialist historical journals); also the HMC series, *Guides to Sources for British History*. Many published source guides are listed in Foster and Sheppard (1995), pp. lv–lxiv.

16. Chadwyck-Healey, *National Inventory of Documentary Sources in the United Kingdom and Ireland* (London: Chadwyck-Healey, 1985) is useful.

17. J. B. Post and M. R. Foster, *Copyright: A Handbook for Archivists* (London: Society of Archivists, 1992) is a useful guide. An updated edition is due to be published.

5. Libraries

1. There is an excellent, extensive but under-used literature of guidance for library researchers in history. Perhaps because the bulk of it is American and weighted towards American reference sources, it is relatively little known in Britain. This chapter frequently sketches and summarises points more fully expounded and demonstrated in a number of works. Especially recommended are Charles A. D'Aniello (ed.), *Teaching Bibliographic Skills in History: a Sourcebook for Historians and Librarians* (Westport and London: Greenwood Publishing, 1993) in which the chapters by Jane A. Rosenberg and Robert P. Swierenga, and David Y. Allen and John Attig are particularly suggestive; and the helpful if now slightly dated Thomas Mann, *A Guide to Library Research Methods* (New York: Oxford University Press, 1987). Both of these clearly explain the different characteristics of indexing in the range of reference sources. An older text, Jacques Barzun and Henry F. Graff, *The Modern Researcher*, rev. edn (San Diego, Calif: Harcourt Brace Jovanovich, 1987), is still a fruitful read for any budding researcher.

2. There is a full discussion of this point in Jane A. Rosenberg, and Robert P. Swierenga, 'Finding and using historical materials', in D'Aniello (1993).

3. For the most recent general account see Alan Day, *The British Library: a Guide to its Structure, Publications, Collections, and Services* (London: Library Association, 1988). This will require revision as the move into the new British Library building at St Pancras proceeds.

4. This was the case until recently. Discussions are being held with the other national and some university libraries with a view to distributing and co-ordinating responsibility for the national collection of British imprints.

5. SRIS has recently issued a useful pamphlet: Anne Summers, *How to Find Source Materials: British Library Collections on the History and Culture of Science, Technology and Medicine* (London: British Library, 1996).

6. There are occasional exceptions especially in special libraries where the contents of selected journals may be catalogued. Technology is beginning to make possible the viewing of article holdings by linking library catalogues to periodical index databases, but relatively few British libraries have this in place yet.

7. David Y. Allen and John Attig, 'Using catalogues and indexes', in D'Aniello (1993).

8. Mann (1987), pp. 26, 28.

9. *Walford's Guide to Reference Material*, vol. 2, *Social and Historical Sciences, Philosophy and Religion*, Alan Day and Joan M. Harvey (eds), 6th edn (London: Library Association, 1994) is particularly helpful in indicating the main reference works for a user tackling a new subject area. Volume 1 covers science and technology; volume 3, generalia, language and literature, the arts. Besides the advice on catalogues, there are useful discussions of the structures of the various types of reference sources in works already mentioned in note 1. See also Ronald J. Fritze, *Reference Sources in History: an Introductory Guide* (Santa Barbara: ABC-CLIO, 1990).

10. There are exceptions, for example Peter Catterall, *British History 1945–1987: an Annotated Bibliography* (Oxford: Basil Blackwell, 1990); Heather M. Creaton (ed.), *Bibliography of Printed Works on London History to 1939* (London: Library Association, 1993); and Richard W. Cox, *Sport in Britain: a Bibliography of Historical Publications, 1800–1988* (Manchester: Manchester University Press, 1991).

11. The standard historical listing of general directories is Gareth Shaw and

Allison Tipper (comps), *British Directories: a Bibliography and Guide to Directories Published in England and Wales (1850–1950) and Scotland (1773–1950)*, 2nd edn (London: Mansell, 1996).

12. For a short bibliography of these lists see D. J. Munro, *Microforms for Historians* (London: Institute of Historical Research, 1994), pp. vi–vii.

13. The most recent edition is available from the compilers at the University of London Library. This is a useful list, but it is worth drawing attention to its indexes as a straightforward example of the minimally edited 'easily-compiled' computer-generated indexes which need to be used with care.

14. Mann (1987), p. 154.

6. Computing techniques for historical research

1. I am most grateful to Silvia Sovic and Matthew Woollard, who read drafts of this chapter, for their helpful comments and suggestions.

2. The resources offered to historians by the Internet and their use of it is the subject of Chapter 8.

3. Peter Denley with Debra Birch and Raivo Ruusalepp (eds), *International Historical Computing Bibliography*.

4. See, for example, Michael Anderson, 'Households, families and individuals: some preliminary results from the national sample from the 1851 Census of Great Britain', *Continuity and Change* 3 (1988); 421–38; A. Armstrong, *Stability and Change in an English Country Town. A Social Study of York, 1801–1851* (Cambridge: Cambridge University Press, 1974); more broadly, E. A. Wrigley and Roger S. Schofield, *The Population History of England, 1541–1871* (Cambridge: Cambridge University Press, 1989 edn); and E. A. Wrigley, R. S. Davies, J. E. Oeppen and R. S. Schofield, *English Population History from Family Reconstitution* (Cambridge: Cambridge University Press, 1997). For other examples of computer-assisted research, see Frank O'Gorman, *Voters, Patrons and Parties: the Unreformed Electoral System in Hanoverian England, 1734–1832* (Oxford, 1989); R. J. Morris, *Class, Sect and Party: the Making of the British Middle Class: Leeds, 1820–50* (Manchester: Manchester University Press, 1990); R. Floud, K. Wachter and A. Gregory, *Height, Health and History: Nutritional Status in the United Kingdom, 1750–1980* (Cambridge: Cambridge University Press, 1990).

5. G. E. C[ockayne], *The Complete Peerage* (Gloucester: Sutton, 1982 edn).

6. This example is taken from Julie Flavell, *New York, New Immigrants 1900*. Teaching Frameworks for Historical Datasets, I (Glasgow: CTI Centre for History, Archaeology and Art History, 1996). This is a dataset developed for teaching purposes, with a full introduction and tutorial. It is obtainable from the CTI Centre (note 32 below for details).

7. See below, pp. 116–18.

8. A combination of fields can also be used for the link. However, for simplicity's sake the illustration which follows assumes the use of a single field.

9. Charles Harvey and Jon Press, *Databases in Historical Research* (London: Macmillan, 1996), Chapter 5; early versions in Charles Harvey and Jon Press, 'The business elite of Bristol: a case study in database design', *History and Computing* 3, 1 (1991): 1–11, and Charles Harvey and Jon Press, 'Relational data analysis: value, concepts and methods', *History and Computing* 4, 2 (1992): 98–109.

10. It is interesting that many of these characteristics of historical data are being noticed in other areas as well. This is having an impact on database theory, which is now gradually moving away from the relational database towards 'object-oriented' databases.

11. The History Data Service (see below, note 33) is in the process of drawing up a code of good practice for the documentation of databases.

12. For brief illustrations of the application of project management principles to historical computing, see Leen Breure, 'The management of historical computer projects', in Virginia Davis, Peter Denley, Donald Spaeth and Richard Trainor (eds), *The Teaching of Historical Computing: An International Framework*. A Workshop of the International Association for History and Computing, University of London, 26–28 February 1993, Halbgraue Reihe zur historischen Fachinformatik, A17 (St Katharinen: Scripta Mercaturae Verlag, 1993), pp. 49–54. See also Matthew Woollard, 'Small-scale project management', loc. cit., pp. 55–6.

13. General introductions are Konrad J. Jarausch and Kenneth A. Hardy, *Quantitative Methods for Historians. A Guide to Research, Data, and Statistics* (Chapel Hill and London: University of North Carolina Press, 1991); Catherine Marsh, *Exploring Data. An Introduction to Data Analysis for Social Scientists* (Cambridge: Polity Press, 1988); Roderick Floud, *An Introduction to Quantitative Methods for Historians* (London: Methuen, 1st edn 1973, 2nd edn 1979); William O. Aydelotte, *Quantification in History* (Reading, MA: Addison-Wesley, 1971). For illustrations of such historical research, William O. Aydelotte, A. G. Bogue and R. W. Fogel (eds), *The Dimensions of Quantitative Research in History* (London: Oxford University Press, 1972); E. A. Wrigley (ed.), *Nineteenth Century Society: Essays in the Use of Quantitative Methods for the Study of Social Data* (Cambridge: Cambridge University Press: 1972).

14. The records are from the Port of London Project, directed by Sarah Palmer. I am grateful to Dr Palmer for permission to use this data.

15. The word 'ideometry' has been coined to reflect this. Although it wins no prizes for attractiveness, it is accurate. Luciano Floridi, *L'estensione dell'intelligenza. Guida all'informatica per filosofi* (Rome: Armando Editore, 1996), pp. 161–7.

16. See M. Olsen and L.-G. Harvey, 'Computers in intellectual history: lexical statistics and the analysis of political discourse', *Journal of Interdisciplinary History* 18 (1988): 449–64; Alan Brier and Andrea Reiter, 'HAMLET. Methoden zur Ermittlung von Ähnlichkeitswerten von Kontextwörtern und ihre Anwendung in einer ideologiekritischen Zeitschriftenanalyse', in Manfred Thaller and Albert Müller (eds) *Computer in den Geisteswissenschaften* (Frankfurt: Campus Verlag, 1989), pp. 87–137. The best overall introduction to stylometry is Anthony Kenny, *The Computation of Style* (Oxford: Oxford University Press 1982), especially early chapters. An excellent historical case study is David I. Holmes, 'A multivariate technique for authorship attribution and its application to the analysis of Mormon scripture and related texts', *History and Computing*, 3, 1 (1991): 12–22. For an example of a substantial text retrieval project involving historical sources, Michael Leslie, 'The Hartlib Papers project: text retrieval in large datasets', *Literary and Linguistic Computing*, 5 (1990): 58–69; and http://www.shef.ac.uk/uni/projects/hpp/hartlib.html.

17. Best known is the Oxford Concordance Program (OCP), published in its most recent form as Micro-OCP (Oxford: Oxford University Press, 1989). There are no plans for a revised version. Textual Analysis Computing Tools (TACT), a public domain system produced by the University of Toronto, is under continuing development; the UK distributor is CTICH (see note 32 below), and details are

available on http://www.gla.ac.uk/Inter/Computerpast/ctich/WebFTP/tact.html. Longman's Mini-Concordancer is a more friendly but also a more limited system.

18. See the examples cited in Andrew Prescott, 'History and computing', in Christine Mullings, Marilyn Deegan, Seamus Ross and Stephanie Kenna (eds), *New Technologies for the Humanities* (London: Bowker Saur, 1996), pp. 231–62 (especially pp. 242–51).

19. Manfred Thaller (ed.), *Images and Manuscripts in Historical Computing*, Halbgraue Reihe zur historischen Fachinformatik, A14 (St Katharinen: Scripta Mercaturae Verlag, 1992); Jurij Fikfak and Gerhard Jaritz (eds), *Image Processing in History: Towards Open Systems*. Halbgraue Reihe, A16 (St Katharinen: Scripta Mercaturae Verlag, 1993); Peter Robinson, 'Image Capture and Analysis', in Mullings, Deegan, Ross and Kenna (eds) (1996) pp. 47–65 (see note 18); Peter Robinson, *The Digitization of Primary Sources*. Office for Humanities Communication Publications, 4 (Oxford: 1993).

20. For more information on the programme, see http://www.qmw.ac.uk/~gbhgis/.

21. As part of the Nineteenth Century Censuses Project (see note 30 below).

22. A simple introduction is Humphrey R. Southall and Ed Oliver, 'Drawing maps with a computer or without?', *History and Computing* 2, 2 (1990): 146–54. Some recent case studies are collected in Michael Goerke (ed.), *Coordinates for Historical Maps*, Halbgraue Reihe zur historischen Fachinformatik, A25 (St Katharinen: Scripta Mercaturae Verlag, 1994). For the more professional angle, David Wheatley, 'Geographic information systems in humanities research', in Mullings, Deegan, Ross and Kenna (eds) (1996), pp. 92–114 (see note 18); P. Mather, *Computer Applications in Geography* (Chichester: 1991).

23. Wolfgang Levermann, Thomas Grotum and Jan Parcer, 'Preservation and improved accessibility of the archives in the memorial Oświęcim/Brzezinka (Auschwitz/Birkenau)' in Gerhard Jaritz, Ingo H. Kropac and Peter Teibenbacher (eds), *The Art of Communication*, Proceedings of the Eighth International Conference of the Association for History and Computing, Graz, Austria, 24–27 August 1993, eds. (Graz: 1995), pp. 141–9.

24. Κλειω is currently available directly from the Max-Planck-Institut für Geschichte, Göttingen, through http://gwdu19.gwdg.de/kleio/. A general description of the underlying philosophy is Manfred Thaller, 'The historical workstation project', in Josef Smets (ed.), *Histoire et Informatique*, Vᵉ Congrès 'History and Computing' 4–7 Septembre 1990 à Montpellier (Perols: Josef Smets, 1992), pp. 251–60. A revised version appears in Josef Smets, 'The historical workstation project', *Computers and the Humanities* 25 (1991): 149–62. A fuller illustration can be found in Matthew Woollard and Peter Denley, *Source-Oriented Data Processing for Historians: a Tutorial for* κλειω, Halbgraue Reihe zur historischen Fachinformatik, A23 (St Katharinen: Scripta Mercaturae Verlag, 1993). On the image-processing features, see Gerhard Jaritz, *Images. A Primer of Computer-Supported Analysis with* κλειω *IAS*, Halbgraue Reihe zur historischen Fachinformatik, A22 (St Katharinen: Scripta Mercaturae Verlag, 1993). On the debate over the relative merits of κλειω and relational systems, and of 'source-oriented' and 'model-oriented' approaches, see Peter Denley, 'Models, sources and users: historical database design in the 1990s', *History and Computing* 6, 1 (1994): 33–43.

25. For orientation, see Steven Ruggles, 'Family demography and family history: problems and prospects', *Historical Methods* 23, 1 (1990): 22–30; J. Dennis Willigan and Katherine A. Lynch, *Sources and Methods of Historical Demography* (New York:

Academic Press, 1982); Kevin Schürer, Jim Oeppen and Roger Schofield, 'Theory and methodology: an example from historical demography', in Peter Denley, Stefan Fogelvik and Charles Harvey (eds), *History and Computing II* (Manchester: Manchester University Press, 1989), pp. 130–42; David S. Reher and Roger Schofield (eds), *Old and New Methods in Historical Demography* (Oxford: Clarendon Press, 1993); L. L. Cornell, 'Analyzing the consequences of family structure with event-history methods', *Historical Methods* 23, 2 (1990): 53–62; Nancy Tuma, 'Event history analysis', in Angela Dale and Richard B. Davies (eds), *Analyzing Social and Political Change. A Casebook of Methods* (London: Sage Publications, 1994), pp. 136–66; Paul D. Allison, *Event History Analysis. Regression for Longitudinal Data* (London: Sage Publications, 1984).

26. John A. Phillips, *Electoral Behaviour in Unreformed England* (Princeton, NJ: Princeton University Press, 1982); John A. Phillips, 'The many faces of reform: the reform bill and the electorate', *Parliamentary History Yearbook* 1 (1982); W. A. Speck and W. A. Gray, 'The computer analysis of poll-books: an initial report', *Bulletin of the Institute of Historical Research* 43 (1970), and 'The computer analysis of poll-books: a further report', ibid. 48 (1975); Derek Hirst and Shaun Bowler, 'Voting in Hereford 1679–1721', *History and Computing I* (1989): 14–19; Stephen W. Baskerville, '"Preferred Linkage" and the analysis of voter behaviour in eighteenth century England', *History and Computing* 1 (1989): 112–20; Frank O'Gorman, 'Electoral behaviour in England 1700–1872', in Peter Denley, Stefan Fogelvik and Charles Harvey (eds), *History and Computing II* (Manchester: Manchester University Press, 1989), pp. 220–38; John A. Phillips (ed.), *Computing Parliamentary History. George III to Victoria* (Edinburgh: Edinburgh University Press, 1994).

27. Neithard Bulst, 'Prosopography and the computer: problems and possibilities' in Denley, Fogelvik and Harvey (1989) (see note 26); Koen Goudrian, Kees Mandemakers, Jogchum Reitsma and Peter Stabel (eds), *Prosopography and Computer. Contributions of Medievalists and Modernists on the Use of Computer in Historical Research* (Leuven: 1995); Josef Smets, 'South French society and the French Revolution: the creation of a large database with CLIO', in Peter Denley and Deian Hopkin (eds), *History and Computing* (Manchester: Manchester University Press 1987), pp. 49–58.

28. Gerhard Botz, 'Oral history and computing', in Virginia Davis, Peter Denley, Donald Spaeth and Richard Trainor (eds), *The Teaching of Historical Computing: An International Framework*. A Workshop of the International Association for History and Computing, University of London, 26–28 February 1993, Halbgraue Reihe zur historischen Fachinformatik, A17 (St Katharinen: Scripta Mercaturae Verlag, 1993), pp. 63–8; Peter Teibenbacher, 'The computer, oral history and regional studies', in Denley, Fogelvik and Harvey (1989), pp. 286–90 (see note 25); Leonora Ritter, 'Oral history and the use of data base: a case history', *History and Computing* 2, 1 (1990): 12–16.

29. W. A. Armstrong, 'The use of information about occupation', in E. A. Wrigley (ed.) (1972), pp. 191–310 (see note 13); Gérard Bouchard, 'The Saguenay Population Register and the processing of occupational data: an overview of the methodology', *Historical Social Research* 32 (1984): 37–58; P. J. Corfield, 'Class by name and number in eighteenth-century Britain', *History* 72 (1987): 38–61; R. J. Morris, 'Occupational coding: principles and examples', *Historical Social Research* 15, 1 (1990): 3–29; Daniel I. Greenstein, 'Standard, meta-standard: a framework for coding occupational data', *Historical Social Research/Historische Sozialforschung* 16

(1991): 3–22; Edward Higgs, 'Structuring the past: the occupational and household classification of nineteenth-century census data', in Evan Mawdsley, Nicholas Morgan, Lesley Richmond and Richard Trainor (eds), *History and Computing III. Historians, Computers and Data. Applications in Research and Teaching* (Manchester: Manchester University Press, 1990), pp. 67–73; Kevin Schürer and Herman Diederiks (eds), *The Use of Occupations in Historical Analysis*, Halbgraue Reihe zur historischen Fachinfarmatik, A19 (St Katharinen: Scripta Mercaturae Verlag, 1993); Herman Diederiks and Marjan Balkestein (eds), *Occupational Titles and their Classification*, Halbgraue Reihe zur historischen Fachinfarmatic A27 (St Katharinen: Max-Planck-Institut für Geschichte in kommission bei Scripta Mercaturae Verlag, 1995).

30. The Leverhulme-funded Nineteenth Century Censuses Project, jointly administered by the History Data Service and the History Department of the University of Essex, is preparing codebooks for the machine-readable version of the 1881 Census of Great Britain. Contact Dr Kevin Schürer, Department of History, University of Essex, Colchester CO4 3SQ.

31. See *History and Computing* 4, 1 (1992) and 6, 3 (1994), special issues on record linkage; Baskerville (1989) (see note 26); Arno Kitts, David Doulton and Elizabeth Reis, *The Reconstitution of Viana do Castelo*, Research Studies in History and Computing 1 (Egham: Royal Holloway College, 1990); Ian Winchester, 'What every historian needs to know about record linkage in the microcomputer era', *Historical Methods* 25 (1992): 149–165; E. A. Wrigley, *Identifying People in the Past* (London: Arnold, 1973).

32. http://www.gla.ac.uk/www/ctich/homepage.html; email: ctich@dish.gla.ac.uk, or write to: CTI Centre for History, Archaeology and Art History, 1 University Gardens, University of Glasgow, Glasgow G12 8QQ.

33. The list of its holdings was published as *A Guide to Historical Datafiles Held in Machine-Readable Form*, compiled by Kevin Schürer and Sheila J. Anderson (London: AHC, 1992). The list is now incorporated in an on-line searchable list through BIRON (http://dawww.essex.ac.uk/services/biron.html). For the AHDS, see http://ahds.ac.uk/; for the History Data Service, http://hds.essex.ac.uk.

34. For on-line details, http://ihr.sas.ac.uk/ihr/wp/int.html, or http://ihr.sas.ac.uk/cwis/train95.html.

35. It is published by Edinburgh University Press.

7. Managing and funding research

1. Quoted, Donald Macleod, 'Head hunters', *Guardian Education*, 26 September 1995; Rees Davies, 'The research assessment exercise 1996 – a personal view', *Royal Historical Society Newsletter*, October 1995, p. 1.

2. Higher Education Funding Council for England, *Report on Quality Assessment 1992–1995* (Bristol: HEFCE, 1995), pp. 33–4.

3. Peter Beck, 'The history panel', in *Research Assessment: The Way Ahead. Conference Report* (Bristol: Society for Research into Higher Education/University of West of England, 1993), p. 17.

4. Lee Elliott Major, 'Games universities play in the struggle for research funding', *Guardian Education*, 23 April 1996.

5. Beck (1993), p. 26.

6. Ibid., p. 26.

7. *Times Higher Education Supplement*, 23 December 1994.

8. Sir Keith Thomas, 'The role of the British Academy in British academic life', *Address to Plenary Meeting of History at Universities Defence Group (HUDG)*, London University Institute of Historical Research, 28 October 1995; Davies (1995), p. 2.

9. Maurice Kogan, 'Assessment and productive research', in *Research Assessment: the Way Ahead. Conference Report* (Bristol: Society for Research into Higher Education/University of West of England, 1993), pp. 43–52; Davies (1995), p. 2.

10. Thomas (1995).

11. Michael Bush, 'Grading and degrading the dons', *The Independent*, 7 March 1996.

12. Lincoln Allison, 'A mountain of wasted words', *Daily Telegraph*, 18 May 1995.

13. Davies (1995), p. 2.

14. Beck (1993) pp. 21, 28; Bush (1996).

15. Davies (1995), p. 2.

16. Bush (1996).

17. *The Times Higher Educational Supplement*, 25 December 1992; Peter Beck, 'Subtle ways to avoid clowning by numbers', *The Times Higher Education Supplement*, 26 February 1993.

18. John Laver and Michael Jubb, *The Humanities Research Board of the British Academy: Structures and Strategies* (London: Humanities Research Board, 1994), pp. 1–5.

19. *ESRC Advanced Course Studentships 1996: Guidance Notes for Applicants* (Swindon: ESRC, 1996), p. 1.

20. *Guide to Postgraduate Studentships in the Humanities 1996* (London: Humanities Research Board, 1996), p. 1.

21. Ibid., p. 3.

22. Ibid, p. 9.

23. *ESRC Research Studentships 1996: Guidance Notes for Applicants* (Swindon: ESRC, 1996), pp. 6–9.

24. *ESRC* (1996), p. 19.

25. *ESRC Studentship Handbook 1995: A Guide for Postgraduate Award Holders* (Swindon: ESRC, 1995), pp. 61–9.

26. Ibid., p. 63.

27. *ESRC Recognition of Research Training Courses and Programme: Postgraduate Training Guidelines*, 2nd edn (Swindon: ESRC, 1996), pp. 22–4.

28. *ESRC* (1996), p. 19.

29. *ESRC* (1996), pp. 22–4.

30. *ESRC* (1996), p. 19.

31. *ESRC* (1996), pp. 25, 27.

32. Quoted in Graham Wade, 'On the money trail', *Guardian Education*, 7 May 1996.

33. *ESRC* (1995), p. 76.

34. Jean Wright, 'Left to their own devices', and David Plowright, 'My Ph.D. nightmare', *Times Higher Education Supplement*, 6 December 1991; James Meikle, 'Painful research', *Guardian Education*, 24 November 1992.

35. Brian Brivati, 'Stormy sixties love affair', *Times Higher Education Supplement*, 6 December 1991.

36. Martin Harris (chair), *Review of Postgraduate Education* (Bristol: HEFCE, 1996), pp. 15–17, 25, 27, 61.

37. Ibid., pp. 45, 57.

38. Ibid., pp. 8–9, 25, 56–7; Lee Elliott Major, 'Ivy League threat sets sabres rattling', *Guardian Education*, 21 May 1996.

39. Wade (1996) (see note 32).

8. The Internet for historians

1. Accurate figures on Internet connections and usage are notoriously difficult to come by and, in any case, are subject to rapid change: these figures represent best estimates derived from a web site which monitors Internet usage on a regular basis: the URL for this site is <http://www.admedia.aust.com/>. All World Wide Web Uniform Resource Locators (URLs) and addresses are current and accurate as of the end of April 1997.

2. This article was researched and written in 1996–7: the research was initially conducted on a 486 DX2-66 MHz networked workstation at the University of Westminster with 8 Mb of RAM using Netscape Navigator v.2 as the Web browser: this configuration was later upgraded to a Pentium P-133 with 16 Mb RAM using Netscape Navigator v.3.0. The final research was conducted using a pre-release version of Netscape Communicator.

3. See for example the Institute for Historical Review at URL <http://www.kaiwan.com/~ihrgreg/>.

4. 'Porn on the Net: Filth or Freedom of Speech', *The Daily Telegraph*, 27 March 1997.

5. The best place for the researcher to start looking into discussion lists is H-NET at Michigan State University (URL <http://h-net.msu.edu>) which has over 60 lists and by its own estimates in October 1996 was reaching 'over 30% of all history professors in the US, Canada and Australia'. These discussion lists cover a wide range of topics and time periods and include lists devoted to British and Irish History, Demographic History, Diplomatic History, Labor [*sic*] History, Women's History, Urban History, Business History and Military History. Some lists have over 1,000 subscribers. No charge is incurred for academic subscribers; all that is needed is an e-mail account.

6. When subscribing to a discussion list the new user should establish the subject matter, ground rules and etiquette of the list, usually available as posted 'Frequently Asked Questions' (FAQ) messages, before launching tactlessly into an open-ended and naive question or statement that has been exhaustively covered in the forum in the past.

7. The WWW URL for the M25 consortium is <http://www.M25lib.ac.uk/M25/>. For the COPACS system, the URL is <http://copac.ac.uk/copac/>.

8. The BIDS URL is <http://www.bids.ac.uk/>. Not currently available on-line but available on CD-ROM is CRIB (Current Research in Britain), which lists all UK academic staff and their research interests.

9. The URL for the Institute of Historical Research is <http://ihr.sas.ac.uk/>.

10. The URL for the *Canadian Journal of History* is <http://www.usask.ca/history/cjh/>.

11. The URL is <http://www.lib.byu.edu/-~rdh/wwi/>.

12. The URL for the Public Record Office website is <http://www.open.gov.uk/

pro/prohome.htm>. The Royal Commission on Historical Manuscripts URL is <http://www.hmc.gov. uk/>.

13. The URL is <http://www.kcl.ac.uk/lhcma/top.htm>.

14. This debate can be followed at the help section of the University of Alberta library site at URL <http://www.library.ualberta.ca/library_html/>.

15. The URL is <http://www.halcyon.com/jim/ussliberty/>.

16. The United States Naval Historical Center home page is at <http://www. history.naval.mil/index.htm>.

17. The URL is <http://webcorp.com/mccarthy/>.

18. The URL is <http://www.seattletimes.com/trinity/>.

19. The BUBL Information Service home page is at URL <http://bubl.ac. uk/>.

20. Before diving into the Internet users should take a deep breath and pause. They should choose their time for searching the Internet very carefully: there are peak periods – usually associated with when the United States is on-line – when the information 'superhighway' slows to a crawl as the bandwidth clogs up. At the time of writing the early to mid-morning is the optimum in terms of response times. Users should also configure their software to get the best possible speed, for example unless specifically searching for visual material, it is a prudent move to take advantage of the facility in most web browsers not to download images: there is often an inverse ratio between the presentation and the substantive content of a site.

21. The URL is <http://www.yahoo.co.uk> or <http://www.yahoo.com/>.

22. Two examples will suffice to illustrate the pitfalls that await the unwary. Entering the search term Suez in Yahoo produced some material relating to the history of the Suez Canal, including a picture of Benjamin Disraeli and a potted history of the Suez Canal, but also generated a large list of links that included hotels located near the Suez Canal and a doctor's practice whose name happened to be Suez. A search for the term Gaitskell produced a personal home page listing the interests of its creator, a Mr Gaitskell, which included a discography of the 1970s popular beat combo Mott the Hoople.

23. The 'History and Philosophy of Project Gutenberg' can be found at URL <http://www.sunsite.doc.ic.ac.uk/packages/Project Gutenberg/pg/history.html>.

9. Political history

1. G. R. Elton, *Political History: Principles and Practice* (London: Allen Lane, 1970), p. 3.

2. Juliet Gardiner (ed.), *What is History Today?* (London: Macmillan, 1988), pp. 22, 20.

3. Maurice Cowling, *Disraeli, Gladstone and Revolution* (Cambridge: Cambridge University Press, 1967), *The Impact of Labour* (Cambridge: Cambridge University Press, 1971), and *The Impact of Hitler* (Cambridge: Cambridge University Press, 1975).

4. See, for instance, Kenneth O. Morgan, *Labour in Power 1945–1951* (Oxford: Clarendon Press, 1984); and Peter Hennessy, *Never Again: Britain 1945–51* (London: Cape, 1992).

5. Steve Fielding, '"Don't know and don't care": popular political attitudes in Britain, 1945–51', pp. 106–25, in Nick Tiratsoo (ed.), *The Attlee Years* (London: Pinter, 1991).

6. See Robert Pearce, 'Truth and falsehood: George Orwell's prep school woes', *Review of English Studies* 43, 171 (1992): 367–86, and 'Revisiting Orwell's Wigan Pier' (forthcoming in 1997 in *History*).

7. A. J. P. Taylor, *English History 1914–1965* (Oxford: Clarendon Press, 1965), p. 602.

8. Lytton Strachey, *Eminent Victorians* (London: Chatto & Windus, 1918), introduction.

9. There is no shortage of material on Edwardian England or on Britain during the First World War. Three books, which themselves give bibliographical advice, can be reliably recommended: Donald Read (ed.), *Edwardian England* (London: Croom Helm, 1982); Cameron Hazlehurst, *Politicians at War* (London: Cape, 1971); and J. M. Bourne, *Britain and the Great War 1914–1918* (London: Edward Arnold, 1989).

10. C. L. Mowat, *Britain Between the Wars* (London: Methuen, 1955), p. 142.

11. Robert Skidelsky, *Politicians and the Slump: the Labour Government of 1929–1931* (London: Macmillan, 1967), p. 424.

12. See R. A. C. Parker, *Chamberlain and Appeasement* (London: Macmillan, 1993); and D. Dilks (ed.), *Retreat from Power: Studies in British Foreign Policy, vol. 1, 1906–39* (London: Macmillan, 1981).

13. See Stuart Ball, *Baldwin and the Conservative Party: the Crisis of 1929–31* (New Haven: Yale University Press, 1988). Ball's *The Conservative Party and British Politics 1902–1951* (London: Longman, 1995) has an excellent bibliography.

14. On the general strike, see Jeffrey Skelley (ed.), *The General Strike of 1926* (London: Lawrence and Wishart, 1976), which contains nine regional studies. On general elections, see Andrew Thorpe, *The British General Election of 1931* (Oxford: Oxford University Press, 1991) and Tom Stannage, *Baldwin Thwarts the Opposition: The British General Election of 1931* (London: Croom Helm, 1980).

15. See Philip Williamson, *National Crisis and National Government: British Politics, the Economy and Empire 1926–32* (Cambridge: Cambridge University Press, 1992); G. R. Searle, *Country Before Party* (London: Longman, 1995); John D. Fair, 'The Conservative basis for the formation of the National Government of 1931', *Journal of British Studies* 19 (1980): 142–64; David J. Wrench, '"Cashing in": The parties and the National Government', *Journal of British Studies* 23 (1984): 135–53; Stuart Ball, 'The Conservative Party and the formation of the National Government: August 1931', *Historical Journal* 29, 1 (1986): 159–82; Vernon Bogdanor, '1931 revisited: the constitutional aspects', *Twentieth Century British History* 2, 1 (1991): 1–25; Philip Williamson, '1931 revisited: the political realities', *Twentieth Century British History* 2, 3 (1991): 328–38.

16. See E. L. Ellis, *TJ: A Life of Dr Thomas Jones* (Cardiff: University of Wales Press, 1992); S. W. Roskill, *Hankey, Man of Secrets*, 3 vols (London: Collins, 1970–74); Peter Hennessy, *Whitehall* (London: Secker & Warburg, 1990).

17. For the variety of approaches taken to the study of British fascism, see Robert Skidelsky, *Oswald Mosley* (London: Macmillan, 1975); Richard Thurlow, *British Fascism* (Oxford: Blackwell, 1987); Kenneth Lunn, Kenneth Thurlow and Richard Thurlow (eds), *Fascism in Britain* (London: Croom Helm, 1980); Robert Benewick, *The Fascist Movement in Britain* (London: Allen Lane, 1972); D. S. Lewis, *Illusions of Grandeur* (Manchester: Manchester University Press, 1987); Melvyn D. Higginbottom, *Intellectuals and British Fascism: A Study of Henry Williamson* (London: Janus, 1992); Richard Griffiths, *Fellow Travellers of the Right* (London:

Constable, 1980); G. C. Webber, *The Ideology of the British Right* (London: Croom Helm, 1986); John D. Brewer, *Mosley's Men: The British Union of Fascists in the West Midlands* (Aldershot: Gower, 1984); and David Baker, *Ideology of Obsession: A. K. Chesterton and British Fascism* (London: I.B.Tauris, 1996). For a remarkably stimulating account by a non-historian, see John Carey, *The Intellectuals and the Masses: Pride and Prejudice Among the Literary Intelligentsia, 1880–1939* (London: Faber, 1992)

18. Martin Blinkhorn (ed.), *Fascists and Conservatives* (London: Unwin Hyman, 1990); W. J. Mommsen, and L. Kettenacher (eds), *The Fascist Challenge and the Policy of Appeasement* (London: Macmillan, 1983).

19. See Frank McDonough, 'The role of the individual in history', *History Review* 24 (March 1996): 40–42.

20. John Grigg, *Lloyd George* (London: Methuen, 1978 and 1985); David Marquand, *Ramsay MacDonald* (London: Cape, 1977); Keith Middlemas and John Barnes, *Baldwin* (London: Weidenfeld & Nicolson, 1969); David Dilks, *Neville Chamberlain*, vol. 1 (Cambridge: Cambridge University Press, 1984); Alan Bullock, *The Life and Times of Ernest Bevin: Minister of Labour 1940–1945* (London: Heinemann, 1967); Ben Pimlott, *Hugh Dalton* (London: Cape, 1985); Martin Gilbert, *Finest Hour: Winston S. Churchill 1939–1941* (London: Heinemann, 1983) and *Road to Victory: Winston S. Churchill 1941–1945* (London: Heinemann, 1986).

21. See, for instance, Clive Ponting, *Churchill* (London: Sinclair-Stevenson, 1994); Norman Rose, *Churchill: An Unruly Life* (London: Simon & Schuster, 1994); and Peter Neville, *Churchill: Statesman or Opportunist?* (London: Hodder & Stoughton, 1996).

22. Paul Addison, *The Road to 1945* (London: Cape, 1975); Kevin Jefferys, *The Churchill Coalition and Wartime Politics 1940–1945* (Manchester: Manchester University Press, 1991); Stephen Brooke, *Labour's War* (Oxford: Oxford University Press, 1992).

23. There is an excellent bibliography in Kevin Jefferys, *The Attlee Governments 1945–51* (London: Longman, 1992). See also Correlli Barnett, *The Lost Victory: British Dreams, British Realities, 1945–1950* (London: Macmillan, 1995). All the major figures from this period have been covered in recent biographies, apart from Cripps, who is the subject of a forthcoming study by S. G. Burgess.

24. Ben Pimlott (ed.), *The Political Diary of Hugh Dalton, 1918–40, 1945–60* (London: Cape, 1986), p. xviii.

25. David Cannadine, 'British history: past, present – and future?', *Past and Present* 116 (August 1987): 187.

10. Diplomatic history

1. In keeping with the title of this chapter the term 'diplomatic history' has been used throughout, but over the past thirty-five years the subject has evolved into a broader field which is frequently referred to as 'international history'. The reader should assume these terms to be interchangeable in this context.

2. W. N. Medlicott, 'The scope and study of international history', *International Affairs* 31 (1955).

3. D. C. Watt, *Personalities and Policies: Studies in the Formulation of British Foreign Policy in the Twentieth Century* (London: Longmans, Green & Co, 1965), p. ix.

4. D. C. Watt, *Succeeding John Bull* (Cambridge: Cambridge University Press, 1984), p. 3.

5. D. Reynolds, *Brittania Overruled: British policy and world power in the 20th century* (London: Longman, 1991); P. Kennedy, *The Realities Behind Diplomacy* (London: Fontana, 1981), p. 21. A similar argument is advanced by B. Porter, *The Lion's Share: a Short History of British Imperialism*, 3rd edn (London: Longman, 1993).

6. H. Butterfield, 'Delays and paradoxes in the development of historiography', in K. Bourne and D. C. Watt (eds), *Studies in International History* (London: Longmans, Green & Co, 1967), pp. 1–15; E. Robertson (ed.), *The Origins of the Second World War* (London: Macmillan, 1971), p. 9.

7. A shorter exposition by Fischer of his views can be found in 'World policy, world power and German war aims', in H. W. Koch (ed.), *The Origins of the First World War. Great Power Rivalry and German War Aims*, 2nd edn (London: Macmillan, 1984), pp. 128–88. Fischer drew some inspiration from the work of another German scholar, Eckart Kehr, an example of which can be found in H. U. Wehler (ed.), *Das Primat der Aussenpolitik* (Berlin: Walter de Gruyter, 1965).

8. Such 'revisionist' scholarship proliferated in the 1960s, but among the most representative examples are W. Appleby Williams, *The Tragedy of American Diplomacy*, 2nd edn (New York: Dell, Publishing Co., 1962) and G. Kolko, *The Politics of War* (London: Wiedenfeld & Nicolson, 1969). For a summary see N. Graebner, 'Cold war origins and the continuing debate: a review of recent literature', *Journal of Conflict Resolution* 13 (March 1969): 123–32.

9. Z. Steiner, *Britain and the Origins of the First World War* (London: Macmillan, 1977), p. 3.

10. Quoted in J. Barnes, 'Books and journals', in A. Seldon (ed.), *Contemporary History: Practice and Method* (Oxford: Blackwell, 1988).

11. A. J. P. Taylor's *Origins of the Second World War* (London: Hamish Hamilton, 1961) was reprinted in 1963 with a new introduction, 'Second thoughts'.

12. D. C. Watt, 'Appeasement: the rise of the revisionist school', *Political Quarterly* (1965). See also W. N. Medlicott, *The Coming of War in 1939* (London: Historical Association Pamphlet 36, 1963).

13. A. Marwick, *The Nature of History*, 3rd edn (London: Macmillan, 1989), pp. 101–3; T. Mason, 'Some origins of the Second World War', *Past and Present* 29 (December 1964), reprinted in E. Robertson (ed.) (1971), pp. 105–35.

14. F. H. Hinsley, *Power and the Pursuit of Peace: Theory and Practice in the History of Relations between States* (Cambridge: Cambridge University Press, 1963), pp. 5–7.

15. See for example, P. M. H. Bell, *The Origins of the Second World War in Europe* (London: Longman, 1986); and A. Iriye, *The Origins of the War in Asia and the Pacific* (London: Longman, 1987).

16. For a perspective spanning the first two hundred years of the Foreign Office, see Roger Bullen (ed.), *The Foreign Office and Foreign Policy 1898–1914* (London: 1982) which arose from a conference sponsored by the London School of Economics on the occasion of the Foreign Office's two hundredth anniversary in 1982.

17. A. Adamthwaite, *The Making of the Second World War* (London: George Allen & Unwin, 1977), p. 22.

18. J. Lepsius (ed.), *Die Grosse Politik der europaischen Kabinette, 1871–1914* (Berlin: DVPG, 1922–27); G. P. Gooch and H. V. Temperley, *British Documents on the Origins of the War, 1898–1914* (London: HMSO, 1926–38).

19. T. Desmond Williams, 'The historiography of World War II', in E. Robertson (ed.) (1971), p. 39; *Documents on German Foreign Policy 1918–1945* (London: HMSO, 1954–).

20. L. Woodward, *British Foreign Policy During the Second World War*, 5 vols. (London: HMSO, 1970–76).

21. R. Butler amd M. Pelly (eds), *Documents on British Policy Overseas* (London: HMSO, 1984).

22. A. L. De Porte, *Europe Between the Superpowers: the Enduring Balance* (New Haven: Yale University Press, 1979); D. Reynolds, 'The origins of the cold war: the European dimension 1944–45', *The Historical Journal* 28, 2 (1985): 497–515.

23. For a helpful summary of the state of the Cold War debate at the end of the 1980s, see G. Warner, 'The study of cold war origins', in D. Armstrong and E. Goldstein (eds), *The End of the Cold War* (London: Cass, 1990).

24. Warner, ibid.

25. J. Kent, 'The British Empire and the origins of the cold war, 1944–49', in A. Deighton (ed.), *Britain and the First Cold War* (London: Macmillan, 1990).

26. D. Reynolds, 'Roosevelt, Churchill and the wartime Anglo-American alliance, 1939–1945: towards a new synthesis', in W. Roger Louis and H. Bull (eds), *The Special Relationship:Anglo-American Relations Since 1945* (Oxford: Oxford University Press, 1986).

27. There is a clutch of articles which provides an insight into this question: P. G. Boyle, 'The British Foreign Office and American foreign policy, 1947–48', *Journal of American Studies* 16, 3 (1982): 378–89; R. Ovendale, 'Britain, the USA and the European cold war 1945–48', *History* 67 (1982): 217–36; R. Frazier, 'Did Britain start the cold war: Bevin and the Truman doctrine', *Historical Journal* 27 (1984).

28. D. C. Watt, *Succeeding John Bull* (1984) (see note 4).

29. On the question of defence see J. Kent and J. W. Young, 'The Western Union concept and British defence policy, 1947–48', in R. Aldrich (ed.), *British Intelligence, Strategy and the Cold War* (London: Routledge, 1992), pp. 166–92.

30. J. W. Young, *Britain and European Unity 1945–92* (London: Longman, 1993); but see also S. Greenwood, *Britain and European Co-operation since 1945* (Oxford: Historical Association, 1992).

31. Reynolds (1991), p. 238; S. George, *An Awkward Partner* (Oxford: Oxford University Press, 1990), p. 40.

32. G. Wint and P. Calvocoressi, *The Middle East Crisis* (Harmondsworth: Penguin, 1957), pp. 88–9, is an example of contemporary studies which set out the case for collusion. D. Reynolds, review article in *English Historical Review*, April 1992: 417–20; G. Warner, 'Aspects of the Suez Crisis', in E. Di Nolfo (ed.), *Power in Europe? Great Britain, France, Germany and Italy and the Origins of the EEC 1952–1957* (New York: Walter de Gruyter, 1992).

33. D. Cameron Watt, 'Between Great Britain and Little England', *Times Literary Supplement*, 11 February 1994, pp. 10–11.

34. G. Craig, 'On the pleasure of reading diplomatic correspondence', *Journal of Contemporary History* 26 (1991): 369–84.

35. The theme of 'Memory and counter-memory' is the subject of an issue of *Representations* 26 (Spring 1989). The background of this subject is explored by P. H. Hutton, *History as an Art of Memory* (Hanover, Vt.: University Press of New England, 1993).

36. G. Himmelfarb, 'Telling it as you like it. Post-modernist history and the flight from fact', *Times Literary Supplement*, 16 October 1992, pp. 12–15.

37. B. Cummings, 'Revising "Postrevisionism", or the poverty of theory in diplomatic history', in *Diplomatic History* 17, 4 (Fall 1993).

38. C. Thorne, *Border Crossings: Studies in International History* (Oxford: Basil Blackwell, 1987). See also M. Kaldor, *The Imaginary War* (Oxford: Basil Blackwell, 1990), pp. 55–148.

11. Military history

1. John Keegan, *The Face of Battle* (London: Cape, 1976), pp. 41–2; David Skaggs, 'Michael Howard and the dimensions of military history', *Military Affairs* 49, 4 (1985): 181–2; Tim Travers, 'The development of British military historical writing and thought from the eighteenth century to the present', in David Charters, Marc Milner and J. Brent Wilson (eds), *Military History and the Military Profession* (Westport, Conn.: Praeger, 1992), pp. 23–44.

2. Travers (1992), pp. 23–44; Ian Beckett, 'The pen and the sword: reflections on military thought in the British Army, 1854–1914', *Soldiers of the Queen* 68 (1992): 3–7; Chief of the General Staff, *Design for Military Operations: The British Military Doctrine* (London: Chief of the General Staff, 1989).

3. John Keegan, 'The historian and battle', *International Security* 3 (1978–9): 140–42.

4. Brian Bond, 'Introduction', in Brian Bond (ed.), *The First World War and British Military History* (Oxford: Oxford University Press, 1991), p. 9; Ian Beckett, 'Frocks and brasshats', in Bond (ed.) (1991), pp. 89–112.

5. Ian Beckett, 'Total war', in Gary Sheffield and Colin McInnes (eds), *Warfare in the Twentieth Century* (London: Unwin Hyman, 1988), pp. 1–23; also reproduced in Clive Emsley, Arthur Marwick and Wendy Simpson (eds), *War, Peace and Social Change in Twentieth Century Europe* (Buckingham: Open University Press, 1989), pp. 26–44.

6. Travers (1992), p. 39.

7. Beckett (1988), pp. 1–23; Geoffrey Holmes (ed.), *Britain After the Glorious Revolution* (London: Macmillan, 1969); John Brewer, *The Sinews of Power: War, Money and the English State, 1688–1783* (London: Unwin Hyman, 1990); Clive Emsley, *British Society and the French Wars, 1793–1815* (London: Macmillan, 1979); John Childs, *Armies and Warfare in Europe, 1648–1789* (Manchester: Manchester University Press, 1982).

8. David Chandler and Ian Beckett (eds), 'Introduction', in D. Chandler and I. Beckett (eds), *The Oxford Illustrated History of the British Army* (Oxford: Oxford University Press, 1994), pp. xv–xvii; Edward Spiers, *The Late Victorian Army, 1868–1902* (Manchester: Manchester University Press, 1991); John Fuller, *Troop Morale and Popular Culture in the British and Dominion Armies, 1914–18* (Oxford: Oxford University Press, 1990).

9. J. Brent Wilson, 'The morale and discipline of the BEF, 1914–18', unpublished MA thesis, University of New Brunswick, 1978; David Englander and J. J. Osborne, 'Jack, Tommy and Henry Dubb: the armed forces and the working class', *Historical Journal* 21, 3 (1978): 593–621; Gary Sheffield, 'Officer/man relations, morale and discipline in the British Army, 1902–22', unpublished PhD thesis, University of London, 1994.

10. Jeremy Gibson and Mervyn Medlycott, *Militia Lists and Musters, 1757–1876* (Birmingham: Federation of Family History Societies, 1989).

11. Peter Simkins, 'Everyman at war: recent interpretations of the front line experience', in Bond (1991), pp. 289–314; Maurice Shadbolt, *Voices of Gallipoli* (Auckland, 1988), p. 11; Ian Beckett, 'Revisiting the old front line', *Stand To* 43 (1995), pp. 10–14.

12. Simkins (1991), pp. 291–3; Alistair Thomson, *Anzac Memories: Living a Legend* (Oxford: Oxford University Press, 1994); Ian Beckett, 'The British Army, 1914–18: the illusion of change', in John Turner (ed.), *Britain and the First World War* (London: Unwin Hyman, 1988), pp. 99–116. For an indication of the current work on the visual representation of war, see the annual issue of the *Imperial War Museum Review*.

13. Ian Beckett, *The Amateur Military Tradition, 1558–1945* (Manchester: Manchester University Press, 1991) has a full bibliography of such publications by record societies.

14. 'What is military history?', *History Today* 32, 12 (1984): 5–13; Ian Beckett and Keith Simpson (eds), *A Nation in Arms: A Social Study of the British Army in the First World War* (Manchester, Manchester University Press, 1985); review by John Terraine, *Daily Telegraph*, 21 June 1985; review by Gwynn Harries-Jenkins, *British Book News*, September 1985, p. 536.

15. J. Terraine, *Daily Telegraph*, 21 June 1985; Simkins (1991), pp. 312–13.

16. Tim Travers, *The Killing Ground: The British Army, the Western Front and the Emergence of Modern Warfare, 1900–1918* (London: Unwin Hyman, 1987); Tim Travers, *How the War Was Won: Command and Technology in the British Army on the Western Front, 1917–18* (London: Routledge, 1992); Trevor Wilson and Robin Prior, *Command on the Western Front* (Oxford: Blackwell, 1992); John Bourne, 'British divisional commanders during the Great War', *Gunfire* 29 (1994): 22–30.

17. Ian Beckett, 'Low-intensity conflict: its place in the study of war', in Charters, Milner and Wilson (eds) (1992), pp. 121–30.

18. David Charters, *The British Army and Jewish Insurgency in Palestine, 1945–47* (London: Macmillan, 1989); Tom Mockaitis, *British Counter-insurgency, 1919–60* (London: Macmillan, 1990); Charles Townshend, *Britain's Civil Wars: Counter-insurgency in the Twentieth Century* (London: Faber and Faber, 1986); Ian Beckett, 'The study of counter-insurgency: a British perspective', *Small Wars and Insurgencies* 1, 1 (1990): 47–53.

19. Joyce M. Horn (ed.), *Historical Research for Higher Degrees in the United Kingdom* (London: University of London Institute of Historical Research, 1995): *List 56 Parts I and II, Theses Completed 1994 and Theses in Progress 1995.*

20. John Childs, *The Army of Charles II* (London: Routledge, 1976); John Childs *The Army, James II and the Glorious Revolution* (Manchester: Manchester University Press, 1980), John Childs, *The British Army of William III, 1689–1702* (Manchester: Manchester University Press, 1987); Alan Guy, *Economy and Discipline: Officership and Administration in the British Army, 1714–63* (Manchester: Manchester University Press, 1984); John Houlding, *Fit for Service: The Training of the British Army, 1715– 95* (Oxford: Oxford University Press, 1981); Tony Hayter, *The Army and the Crowd in Mid-Georgian England* (London: Macmillan, 1978). A good introduction to the state of research on the British army is to be found in Chandler and Beckett (eds) (1994), especially the bibliography, pp. 467–76.

21. Brian Robson (ed.), *Roberts in India: The Military Correspondence of Field Marshal Lord Roberts, 1876–93* (Stroud: Alan Sutton for Army Records Society, 1993); John Laband (ed.), *Lord Chelmsford's Zululand Campaign, 1878–79* (Stroud: Alan Sutton for Army Records Society, 1994).

12. Imperial and Commonwealth history

1. Sir John Seeley, *The Expansion of England* (London: Macmillan, 1884), p. 1.

2. Mary Kingsley to John Holt, 5 August 1898, quoted in Robert Pearce, *Mary Kingsley: Light at the Heart of Darkness* (Oxford: Kensal Press, 1990), p. 115.

3. David Fieldhouse, 'Can Humpty Dumpty be put together again?', *Journal of Imperial and Commonwealth History* 12, 2 (1984): 9–23.

4. Juliet Gardiner (ed.), *The History Debate* (London: Collins, 1990), pp. 88–9.

5. Mary H. Kingsley, *Travels in West Africa* (London: Virago, 1982), p. 129.

6. J. A. Mangan, *Athleticism in the Victorian and Edwardian Public School* (Cambridge: Cambridge University Press, 1981); J. A. Mangan (ed.), *Making Imperial Mentalities* (Manchester: Manchester University Press, 1990); Donald Leinster-Mackay, 'The nineteenth-century preparatory school', in Mangan (ed.), *Benefits Bestowed?* (Manchester: Manchester University Press, 1988); see also Robert Pearce 'The prep school and imperialism', *Journal of Educational Administration and History* (January 1991): 43–53; R. Roberts, *The Classic Slum* (Manchester: Manchester University Press, 1971).

7. Shula Marks, 'History, the nation and empire', *History Workshop* 29 (1990): 117.

8. An excellent starting point for study in this field is D. W. Dean, 'Conservative governments and the restriction of Commonwealth immigration in the 1950s: the problems of constraint', *Historical Journal* 35, 1 (1992): 171–94.

9. Peter Griffiths, *A Question of Colour* (London: Leslie Frewin, 1966); D. E. Butler and Anthony King, *The British General Election of 1964* (London: Macmillan, 1965). See also Robert Pearce, *Patrick Gordon Walker: Political Diaries 1932–1971* (London: The Historians' Press, 1991).

10. John Gallagher and Ronald Robinson, 'The imperialism of free trade', *Economic History Review* 6, 1 (1953): 1–15. For another wide-ranging article which rings the changes since the 1950s, see Wm Roger Louis and Ronald Robinson, 'The imperialism of decolonization', *Journal of Imperial and Commonwealth History* 22, 3 (1995): 462–511. This article argues that formal empire ended, as it had begun, 'as a variable function of integrating countries into the international capitalist economy'. It lacks the assured simplicity of the 1953 article but is particularly rich in bibliographical references.

11. D. A. Low, 'The Asian mirror to tropical Africa's independence', in Prosser Gifford and Wm Roger Louis (eds), *The Transfer of Power in Africa* (New Haven: Yale University Press, 1982).

13. Social history

1. G. M. Trevelyan, *English Social History* (London: Longman, 1944).

2. The *Bulletin of the Society for the Study of Labour History* changed its name to the *Labour History Review* in 1990.

3. See the General Editor's introduction on 'People's history', in R. Samuel (ed.), *Village Life and Labour* (London: Routledge and Kegan Paul, 1975), pp. xiii–xxi.

4. See P. Thomson, *The Voice of the Past* (Oxford: Oxford University Press, 1988).

5. See C. Roberts, *The Logic of Historical Explanation* (University Park: Pennsylvania University Press, 1996), pp. 134–45, for a recent discussion.

6. H. Trevor-Roper, 'Fernand Braudel, the *Annales*, and the Mediterranean', *Journal of Modern History* 44 (1972): 475.

7. See M. Vale, 'The return of the event', *Times Literary Supplement*, 16 August 1996, pp. 34 et seq.

8. 'The revival of the narrative: reflections on a new old history', in L. Stone, *The Past and the Present* (London: Routledge and Kegan Paul, 1981).

9. Roberts (1996), p. 145.

10. M. Vale, *Saint Louis* (Paris: Gallimard, 1996).

11. Hélène Cixous, quoted by C. Weedon, *Feminist Practice and Post-Structuralist Theory* (Oxford: Blackwell, 1987), p. 67, cited in B. Southgate, *History: What and Why: Ancient, Modern and Postmodern Perspectives* (London: Routledge, 1996). Gender history is also discussed in Chapters 2 and 14 of this volume.

12. R. J. Morris and G. Morton, 'Where was nineteenth century Scotland?', *The Scottish Historical Review* 73 (April 1994): 97.

13. B. Southgate (1996), p. 122.

14. See B. Reay, *The Last Rising of the Agricultural Labourers* (Oxford: Clarendon, 1990).

14. Gender history

1. The implications of gender history are also discussed in Chapters 2 and 13.

2. S. Rowbotham, *Hidden from History: 300 Years of Women's Oppression and the Fight Against It* (London: Pluto, 1973).

3. June Purvis, 'From "women worthies" to poststructuralism? Debate and controversy in women's history in Britain', June Purvis (ed.), *Women's History: Britain, 1850–1945: An Introduction* (London: UCL Press, 1995), pp. 12–14 and passim.

4. It is no accident that the women's history seminar at the Institute of Historical Research, London, sweeps the centuries.

5. Sally Alexander, *Becoming a Woman and Other Essays in 19th and 20th Century Feminist History* (London: Virago, 1994), p. xii.

6. Catherine Hall, *White, Male and Middle Class: Explorations in Feminism and History* (Cambridge: Polity Press, 1992), p. 4.

7. Carolyn Steedman, *Landscape for a Good Woman* (London: Virago, 1986).

8. Andrew Davies, *Leisure, Gender and Poverty: Working-Class Culture in Salford and Manchester, 1900–1939* (Buckingham: Open University Press, 1992).

9. Joan Sangster, 'Telling our stories: feminist debates and the use of oral history', *Women's History Review* 3, 1 (1994): 5–28.

10. Elizabeth Roberts, *Women and Families: An Oral History, 1940–1970* (Oxford: Blackwell, 1995). See also Elizabeth Roberts, *A Woman's Place: An Oral History of Working-Class Women, 1890–1940* (Oxford: Blackwell, 1984).

11. Judy Giles, *Women, Identity, and Private Life in Britain, 1900–50* (London: Macmillan, 1995).

12. Liz Stanley, 'Women have servants and men never eat: issues in reading gender, using the case study of Mass Observation's 1937 day-diaries', *Women's History Review*, 4, 1 (1995): 98.

13. Ellen Ross, 'Survival networks: women's neighbourhood sharing in London

before World War 1', *History Workshop Journal* 15 (Spring 1983): 4–27.

14. Ellen Ross, *Love and Toil: Motherhood in Outcast London, 1870–1918* (Oxford: Oxford University Press, Oxford, 1993), p. 9 and passim.

15. Elizabeth Roberts (1984), p. 163 and passim.

16. Carolyn Steedman, *Childhood, Culture and Class in Britain: Margaret McMillan, 1860–1931* (London: Virago, 1990).

17. Seth Koven, 'Henrietta Barnett 1851–1936', in Susan Pedersen and Peter Mandler (eds), *After the Victorians: Private Conscience and Public Duty in Modern Britain* (London: Routledge, 1994), pp. 30–53.

18. Barbara Cain, 'Feminist biography and feminist history', *Women's History Review* 3, 2 (1994): 252–54; Jane Lewis, *Women and Social Action in Victorian and Edwardian England* (Aldershot: Edward Elgar, 1991).

19. Olive Banks, *Becoming a Feminist: The Social Origins of 'First Wave' Feminism* (Brighton: Wheatsheaf, 1986).

20. Johanna Alberti, *Beyond Suffrage: Feminists in War and Peace, 1914–28* (London: Macmillan, 1989).

21. Liz Stanley, 'Moments of writing: is there a feminist auto/biography?' *Gender and History* 2, 1 (Spring 1990): 62.

22. Claudia Koonz, *Mothers in the Fatherland: Women, the Family and Nazi Politics* (London: Jonathan Cape, 1987).

23. Helen Jones, *Duty and Citizenship: The Correspondence and Papers of Violet Markham, 1896–1953* (London: The Historians' Press, 1994).

24. Dea Birkett, and Julie Wheelwright, '"How could she?" Unpalatable facts and feminist "heroines"' *Gender and History* 2, 1 (Spring 1990): 49–67.

25. Anna Davin and Alun Howkins, 'Editorial', *History Workshop Journal* 19 (Spring 1985): 1.

26. Michael Roper and John Tosh (eds), *Manful Assertions: Masculinities in Britain Since 1800* (London: Routledge, 1991), p. 8 and passim.

27. Joanna Bourke, *Dismembering the Male: Men's Bodies, Britain and the Great War* (London: Reaktion Books, 1996).

28. John Macnicol, *The Movement for Family Allowances 1918–45: A Study in Social Policy Development* (London: Heinemann, 1980).

29. Penny Tinkler, 'Sexuality and citizenship: the state and girls' leisure provision in England, 1939–45', *Women's History Review* 4, 2 (1995): 193–217.

30. Denise Riley, '"The free mothers": pronatalism and working women in industry at the end of the last war in Britain', *History Workshop Journal* (Spring 1981): 59–118.

31. Penny Summerfield, *Women Workers in the Second World War* (London, Croom Helm, 1984).

32. Sheila Blackburn, 'How useful are feminist theories of the welfare state?', *Women's History Review* 4, 3 (1995): 369–94; Jane Lewis, *The Politics of Motherhood: Child and Maternal Welfare in England, 1900–1939* (London, Croom Helm, 1980); Susan Pedersen, 'Gender, welfare and citizenship in Britain during the Great War', *American Historical Review* 95 (October 1990); Susan Pedersen, *Family, Dependence and the Origins of the Welfare State: Britain and France, 1914–1945* (Cambridge: Cambridge University Press, 1993); Seth Koven and Sonya Michel (eds), *Mothers of a New World: Maternalist Politics and the Origins of the Welfare States* (London: Routledge, 1993).

33. Helen Jones, *Health and Society in Twentieth-Century Britain* (London: Longman, 1994).

34. Margaret Mitchell, 'The effects of unemployment on the social condition of women and children in the 1930s', *History Workshop* 19 (1985): 105–27.

35. Celia Petty, 'The Medical Research Council's inter-war dietary surveys', *Society for the Social History of Medicine Bulletin* 37 (1985): 76–8.

36. Jane Lewis, *Women in Britain since 1945: Women, Family, Work and the State in the Post-War Years* (Oxford: Blackwell, 1992).

37. Anna Davin, 'Imperialism and motherhood', *History Workshop Journal* 5 (Spring 1978): 9–65.

38. Lara Marks, *Model Mothers: Jewish Mothers and Maternity Provision in East London, 1870-1939* (Oxford: Clarendon, 1994). Henry Srebrnik has looked at differences in the 1930s between two white ethnic groups of women, Jews and Irish, in the East End of London. He points to their differing political allegiances: the Jewish women tended to support the Communists, the Irish women the Fascists and Mosley. According to Srebrnik, ethnic differences were more important cultural markers and indicators of personal identity than class or gender. Henry Srebrnik, 'Class, ethnicity and gender intertwined: Jewish women and the east London rent strikes, 1935–40', *Women's History Review* 4, 3 (1995): 283–99.

15. Economic history

1. Data on different aspects of the rise and decline are given in Negley Harte, 'Trends in the publications on the economic and social history of Great Britain and Ireland', *Economic History Review* 30 (1977): 20–41; Donald Coleman, *History of the Economic Past: an Account of the Rise and Decline of Economic History in Britain* (Oxford: Oxford University Press, 1987), Chapter 1.

2. Negley Harte (ed.), *The Study of Economic History* (London: Cass, 1971), pp. xviii–xix.

3. George Koot, *The English Historical Economists* (Cambridge: Cambridge University Press, 1987).

4. Coleman (1987), p. 33.

5. For example, Nicholas Crafts: 'Economic history', in John Eatwell, Murray Milgate and Peter Newman (eds), *The New Palgrave Dictionary of Economics* (London: Macmillan, 1987), pp. 37–42.

6. The study of institutions, especially those that embody property rights, has become popular among some economists and economic historians in recent years, but usually interpreted from within an orthodox economics framework. To some extent this has been a revival of late nineteenth-century arguments. See Richard Hartwell, 'Good old economic history', *Journal of Economic History* 33 (1973): 28–40.

7. Koot (1987).

8. Alan Friedberg, *The Weary Titan: Britain and the Experience of Relative Decline* (Princeton, NJ: Princeton University Press, 1987).

9. Quoted in Koot (1987), p. 187.

10. Theo Barker, 'The beginnings of the Economic History Society', *Economic History Review* 30 (1977): 1–19.

11. On Tawney see Jay Winter (ed.), *History and Society: Essays by R. H. Tawney* (London: Routledege and Kegan Paul, 1978).

12. John Clapham, 'Empty economic boxes', *Economic Journal* 32 (1922): 305–14.

13. Thomas Ashton, 'The treatment of capitalism by historians' in Friedrich Hayek (ed.), *Capitalism and the Historians* (London: Routledge and Kegan Paul, 1954), pp. 33–63.

14. Howard Kaye, *The British Marxist Historians* (Cambridge: Polity Press, 1984).

15. Maurice Dobb, *Studies in the Development of Capitalism* (London: Routledge and Kegan Paul, 1946).

16. Donald McCloskey, *Econometric History* (London: Macmillan, 1987), p. 14.

17. Peter Temin, *New Economic History* (Harmondsworth: Penguin, 1973), p. 8.

18. Donald McCloskey, 'Does the past have useful economics?' *Journal of Economic Literature* 21 (1983): 434–61.

19. Hans Arndt, *The Rise and Fall of Economic Growth* (Melbourne: Longman Cheshire, 1978).

20. Temin (1973), pp. 9–10, 17.

21. Barry Supple, 'Economic history and economic growth', *Journal of Economic History* 20 (1960): 548–56.

22. Alfred Conrad and John Meyer, 'The economics of slavery in the Ante-Bellum South', in Conrad and Meyer (eds), *Studies in Econometric History* (London: Chapman and Hall, 1965).

23. Richard Fogel, *Railroads and American Economic Growth* (Baltimore: Johns Hopkins Press, 1964).

24. William Parker (ed.), *Economic History and the Modern Economist* (Oxford: Blackwell, 1986).

25. Donald McCloskey, *The Rhetoric of Economics* (Brighton: Wheatsheaf, 1986).

26. McCloskey (1987), pp. 24, 74.

27. Donald McCloskey, *Economic Maturity and Entrepreneurial Decline: British Iron and Steel 1870–1913* (Cambridge, MA: Harvard Unversity Press, 1973). It is important to this argument that the entrepreneur is defined 'in the general sense of a businessman or manager rather than in the restricted sense of a *good* businessman or manager, that is, an innovating Schumpeterian entrepreneur' (p. xiii, emphasis in original).

28. Carlo Cipolla, *Between Two Cultures: an Introduction to Economic History* (New York: W. W. Norton, 1991), p. 74.

29. On the importance of thinking in terms of diverse rationalities rather than the dichotomy of rational/irrational, see Barry Hindess, *Choice, Rationality and Social Theory* (London: Unwin Hyman, 1988).

30. In this regard, neo-classical economics is like a certain kind of Marxism that seeks to expose the workings of class behind the scenes; in a similar way, this kind of economics seeks to expose the workings of individual maximising behaviour.

31. Robert Solow, 'Economics: is something missing?', in Parker (1986), pp. 21–9.

32. McCloskey (1986).

33. Jim Tomlinson: 'Inventing "decline": the falling behind of the British economy in the post-war years', *Economic History Review* 49 (1996).

34. Duncan Burn, 'The origins of American engineering competition, 1850–70', *Economic History* 2 (1931): 225–45.

35. There are, as always, exceptions to this generalisation. See especially Barry Supple, 'Fear of failing: economic history and the decline of Britain', *Economic History Review* 48 (1994): 441–58; David Edgerton, *England and the Aeroplane* (London: Macmillan, 1991).

36. Donald McCloskey (ed.), *Essays on a Mature Economy: Britain after 1840* (Princeton, NJ: Princeton University Press, 1971), introduction.

37. Martin Wiener, *English Culture and the Decline of the Industrial Spirit, 1850–1980* (Cambridge: Cambridge University Press, 1981); Correlli Barnett, *The Audit of War* (London: Macmillan, 1986). Apart from anything else, both these authors display the disabling effects of a lack of economics.

38. Bruce Collins and Keith Robbins (eds), *British Culture and Economic Decline* (London: Weidenfeld & Nicolson, 1990).

39. A very early example of this approach is P. Anderson, 'Origins of the present crisis', *New Left Review* 23 (1964): 1–32.

40. Robin Matthews, Charles Feinstein and John Odling-Smee, *British Economic Growth, 1856–1973* (Oxford: Clarendon Press, 1982), p. 31.

41. Catherine Schenk, *Britain and the Sterling Area: from Devaluation to Convertibility in the 1950s* (London: Routledge, 1994).

42. Friedberg (1987).

16. Business history

1. Peter Mathias, The Association of Business Historians, Inaugural Lecture, Glasgow, September 1991, p. 2.

2. Ibid.

3. Negley B. Harte (ed.), *The Study of Economic History* (London: Cass, 1977), p. 77.

4. Mathias, ABH inaugural lecture, p. 2.

5. Fritz Redlich, 'The beginnings and development of German business history', *Bulletin of the Business Historical Society* (September 1952).

6. Mathias, ABH inaugural lecture, p. 10.

7. *Fortunes Made in Business: Series of Original Sketches. Biographical and anecdotic from the recent history of industry and commerce*, vols I and II (London: 1884), vol. III (London: 1887); *Fortunes Made in Business: Life Struggles of Successful People* (London, 1901–2); H. H. Bassett, *Men of Note in Finance and Commerce* (London: 1900–1).

8. Mathias, ABH inaugural lecture, pp. 7–9.

9. George Unwin, *Samuel Oldknow and the Arkwrights. The Industrial Revolution in Marple and Stockport* (Manchester: Manchester University Press, 1924).

10. Thomas S. Ashton, *An Eighteenth-Century Industrialist: Peter Stubs of Warrington, 1756–1806* (Manchester: Manchester University Press, 1939).

11. Peter Mathias, 'The first half century: business history, business archives and the Business Archives Council', *Business Archives* 50 (1984): 1–16.

12. Charles Wilson, *The History of Unilever* (London: Cassell, 1954).

13. For example: R. S. Sayers, *Lloyds Bank in the History of English Banking* (Oxford: Oxford University Press, 1958); Eric M. Sigsworth, *Black Dyke Mills* (Liverpool: Liverpool University Press, 1958); Francis E. Hyde, *Blue Funnel: A History of Alfred Holt and Company of Liverpool from 1865 to 1914* (Liverpool: Liverpool University Press, 1956).

14. *Business History*.

15. See A. M. Bourn, 'Business history and management education', *Business History* 17 (1975): 17–25.

16. For example: Bernard W. E. Alford, *W D & H O Wills and the Development*

of the UK Tobacco Industry (London: Methuen, 1973); William J. Reader, *Metal Box: A History* (London: Heinemann, 1976); Harold Nockolds, *Lucas: The First 100 Years* (Newton Abbott: David & Charles, 1976 and 1978).

17. Donald Coleman, 'The uses and abuses of business history', *Business History* 29, 2 (1987): 142.

18. Wilson (1954).

19. T. A. B. Corley, *Quaker Enterprise in Biscuits: Huntley & Palmer of Reading 1822–1972* (London: Hutchinson, 1972); Terry R. Gourvish and Richard G. Wilson, *The British Brewing Industry 1830–1980* (Cambridge: Cambridge University Press, 1994); W. J. Reader, *ICI: A History, Vol. I. The Forerunners 1870–1926* (Oxford: Oxford University Press, 1970); A. E. Musson, *Enterprise in Soap and Chemicals: Joseph Crosfield & Sons Limited, 1815–1965* (Manchester: Manchester University Press, 1965); Charles Wilson, *First with the News. The History of W H Smith, 1792–1972* (London: Jonathan Cape, 1985); Terry R. Gourvish, *British Railways 1948–73: A Business History* (Cambridge: Cambridge University Press, 1986).

20. *Business History* 29, 4 (1987).

21. A point well made by Peter Mathias in his lecture to the inaugural meeting of the Association of Business Historians, in September 1991.

22. Ibid., p. vii.

23. Alfred D. Chandler Jnr, *Strategy and Structure: Chapters in the History of the American Industrial Enterprise* (Cambridge, Mass.: MIT, 1962), *The Visible Hand: The Managerial Revolution in American Business* (Cambridge, Mass.: Harvard University Press, 1977); *Scale and Scope: The Dynamics of Industrial Capitalism* (Cambridge, Mass.: Harvard University Press, 1990).

24. Coleman (1987), p. 144.

25. Les Hannah, *Entrepreneurs and the Social Sciences. An Inaugural Lecture* (London: LSE, 1983), p. 4.

26. Joyce M. Bellamy (ed.), *Yorkshire Business Histories. A Bibliography* (Bradford: Bradford University Press, 1970).

27. Sally Horrocks, *Lancashire Business Histories: A Contribution towards a Lancashire Bibliography* (Manchester: Manchester University Press, 1971).

28. D. J. Rowe, *Northern Business Histories: A Bibliography* (London: Library Association, 1979).

29. Francis Goodall, *A Bibliography of British Business Histories* (London: Gower, 1987); Stephanie Zarach, *Debrett's Bibliography of Business History* (London: Macmillan, 1987).

30. Stephanie Zarach, *British Business History. A Bibliography* (London: Macmillan, 1994).

31. Francis Goodall, Terry Gourvish and Steve Tolliday (eds), *International Bibliography of Business History* (London: Routledge, 1996).

32. T. S. Ashton, 'Business history', *Business History* 1, 1 (1958): 1–2; B. E. Supple, 'The uses of business history', *Business History* 4, 2 (1962): 81–90; F. E. Hyde, 'Economic theory and business history', *Business History* 5, 1 (1962): 1–21; K. A. Tucker, 'Business history: some proposals for aims and methodology', *Business History* 14, 1 (1972): 1–16.

33. Theo C. Barker, Roy H. Campbell, Peter Mathias and Basil S. Yamey, *Business History* (London: Historical Association, 1960).

34. John Armstrong and Stephanie K. Jones, *Business Documents, Their Origins, Sources and Uses in Historical Research* (London: Mansell, 1987).

35. John Orbell, *A Guide to Tracing the History of a Business* (London: Gower, 1987).

36. John Armstrong, 'An introduction to archival research in business history', *Business History* 33, 1 (1991): 7–34.

37. Terry Gourvish, 'Writing British Rail's history', *Business Archives* 62 (1991): 1–9.

38. Charles W. Munn, 'Writing a business history: The Clydesdale Bank', ibid., pp. 10–16.

39. Charles Harvey and Jon Press, 'Researching a business biography: the career of William Morris', ibid., pp. 17–27.

40. Peter Mathias and Alan W. H. Pearsall, *Shipping: A Survey of Historical Records* (Newton Abbott: David & Charles, 1971).

41. H. A. L. Cockerell and Edwin Green, *The British Insurance Business 1547–1970* (London: Heinemann, 1976).

42. L. A. Ritchie, *Modern British Shipbuilding. A Guide to Historical Records* (London: National Maritime Museum, 1980).

43. Leslie S. Pressnell and John Orbell, *A Guide to the Historical Records of British Banking* (London: Gower, 1985).

44. Lesley Richmond and Bridget Stockford, *Company Archives. The Survey of the Records of 1000 of the First Registered Companies in England and Wales* (London: Gower, 1986).

45. John Armstrong (comp.), *Directory of Corporate Archives* (London: Business Archive Council, 1985).

46. Lesley Richmond and Alison Turton (comps), *Directory of Corporate Archives* (London: BAC, 1987 and 1992).

47. Lesley Richmond and Alison Turton (eds), *The Brewing Industry: A Guide to Historical Records* (Manchester: Manchester University Press, 1990); L. A. Ritchie (ed.), *The Shipbuilding Industry. A Guide to Historical Records* (Manchester: Manchester University Press, 1992); Wendy Habgood (ed.), *Chartered Accountants in England and Wales: A Guide to Historical Records* (Manchester: Manchester University Press, 1994).

48. Royal Commission on Historical Manuscripts, *Records of Business and Industry 1760–1914: Textiles and Leather* (London: HMSO, 1990); R. H. Campbell, *Records of British Business and Industry 1760–1914: Metal Processing and Engineering* (London: HMSO, 1994).

49. David J. Jeremy (ed.), *Dictionary of Business Biography*, 5 vols (London: Butterworth, 1984–6).

50. Anthony Slaven and Sidney G. Checkland (eds), *Dictionary of Scottish Business Biography, 1860–1960*. Vol. I, *The Staple Industries* (Aberdeen: Aberdeen University Press, 1986); Vol. II, *Processing, Distribution, Services* (Aberdeen: Aberdeen University Press, 1989).

51. For example, Richard P. T. Davenport-Hines (ed.), *Speculators and Patriots. Essays in Business Biography* (London: Frank Cass, 1986).

52. Martin Daunton, '*The New Dictionary of National Biography* and business history', *Business Archives Sources and History* 68 (1994): 1–4.

53. John Armstrong, 'Business history and management education', *Proceedings of the Annual Conference 1988* (London: BAC, 1988), p. 64.

54. Joan Lane (comp.), *Register of Business Records of Coventry and Related Areas* (Coventry: Lanchester Polytechnic, 1977).

55. Jane Lowe, *A Guide to Sources in the History of the Cycle and Motor Industries in Coventry, 1880–1939* (Coventry: Coventry Polytechnic, 1983).

56. Charles Harvey and Jon Press (eds), *Studies in the Business History of Bristol* (Bristol: Bristol Academic Press, 1988).

57. Jennifer Green, Philip Ollerenshaw and Peter Wardley, *Business in Avon and Somerset. A Survey of Archives* (Bristol: Bristol Polytechnic, 1991).

58. Peter L. Payne, 'Reflections on the Company Acts, business archives and the nature and growth of the firm', *Proceedings of the Annual Conference 1994* (London: BAC, 1994), pp. 3 and 77.

59. Peter L. Payne, *Rubber and Railways in the Nineteenth Century* (Liverpool: Liverpool University Press, 1961), *Colvilles and the Scottish Steel Industry* (Oxford: Clarendon Press, 1979), *The Hydro: A Study of the Development of the Major Hydro-Electric Schemes Undertaken by the North of Scotland Hydro-Electric Board* (Aberdeen: Aberdeen University Press, 1988), *The Early Scottish Limited Companies 1856–1895* (Edinburgh: Scottish Academic Press, 1980).

60. Armstrong (1988), p. 64.

61. John Chartres and Katrina Honeyman (eds), *Leeds City Business, 1893–1993: Essays Marking the Centenary of the Incorporation* (Leeds: Leeds University Press, 1993).

62. For example, 'The Wedgwood Papers', *Business History Review* 1, 8 (1927): 12–16; 'Three books that made furniture history', *Business History Review* 1, 9 (1927): 1–9; 'The first Thames tunnel', *Business History Review* 5, 3 (1931): 8–12.

63. *The Journal of Transport History*, 3rd series, 14, 2 (1993): iv–ix.

64. E. Birkhead, 'The financial failure of British air transport companies, 1919–1924', *The Journal of Transport History* 4, 3 (1960): 133–45.

65. Philip S. Bagwell, 'The rivalry and working union of the South Eastern and London Chatham and Dover railways', *The Journal of Transport History* 2, 2 (1955): 65–79.

66. Derek H. Aldcroft, 'The depression in British shipping, 1901–1911', *The Journal of Transport History* 7, 1 (1965): 14–23.

67. Geoffrey Channon, 'A. D. Chandler's "visible hand" in transport history: a review article', *The Journal of Transport History* 2, 1 (1981): 53–64.

68. *Business History* 1, 1 (1958).

69. See *Business History* 13 and 14 (1971 and 1972).

70. *Business History* 24 (1982).

71. *Business History* 28 (1986).

72. *Accounting, Business and Financial History* 1, 1 (1990).

73. Ibid.: 2.

74. *Financial History Review* 1, 1 (1994).

75. Sidney Pollard, *The Genesis of Modern Management. A Study of the Industrial Revolution in Great Britain* (London: Edward Arnold, 1965; Pelican, 1968).

76. Peter L. Payne, *British Entrepreneurship in the Nineteenth Century* (London: Macmillan, 1974).

77. Leslie Hannah, *The Rise of the Corporate Economy* (London: Methuen, 1976).

78. Barry E. Supple, *Essays in British Business History* (Oxford: Oxford University Press, 1977).

79. Leslie Hannah, 'A pioneer of public enterprise', in Supple (1977), Chapter 11, pp. 207–26.

80. Bernard W. E. Alford, 'Penny cigarettes, oligopoly and entrepreneurship', in Supple (1977), Chapter 3, pp. 49–68.

81. Charles Wilson, 'Management and policy in large-scale enterprise', in Supple (1977), Chapter 7, pp. 124–40.

82. In 1983 and 1988 respectively.

83. Maurice W. Kirby and Mary B. Rose (eds), *Business Enterprise in Modern Britain. From the Eighteenth to the Twentieth Century* (London: Routledge, 1984).

84. John F. Wilson, *British Business History, 1720–1994* (Manchester: Manchester University Press, 1995).

85. *Business History News* 1 (1991).

86. Ibid: 5, and 2 (1991): 1.

87. David J. Jeremy (ed.), *An International Directory of Business Historians* (Cheltenham: Edward Elgar, 1994).

88. For example, Gourvish (1991): 1; Coleman (1987): 149; Mathias, ABH inaugural lecture (1991), pp. 5–6.

89. As pioneered by Chandler (1990). Two recent works on comparative railway history deserve a mention: F. Dobbin, *Forging Industrial Policy: The US, Britain and France in the Railway Age* (Cambridge: Cambridge University Press, 1994); and C. A. Dunlavy, *Politics and Industrialisation: Early Railroads in the United States and Prussia* (Princeton, NJ: Princeton University Press, 1994).

90. Roger Lloyd-Jones and M. J. Lewis, 'Personal capitalism and British industrial decline: the personally managed firm and business strategy in Sheffield 1880–1920', *Business History Review* 68 (1994): 364–411.

91. John Armstrong, 'The development of the Park Royal industrial estate in the interwar period: a re-examination of the Aldcroft/Richardson thesis', *The London Journal* 21 (1996): 64–79.

92. Charles Sabel and Jonathan Zeitlin, 'Historical alternatives to mass production: policies, markets and technology in nineteenth century industrialization', *Past and Present* 108 (1985): 133–76; M. J. Piore and Charles Sabel, *The Second Industrial Divide: Possibilities for Prosperity* (New York: Basic Books, 1984).

93. James S. Foreman-Peck, 'Network industries and the nineteenth and twentieth century British economy', *ReFRESH* 19 (1994): 1–4.

94. Frances Bostock and Geoffrey Jones, 'Foreign multinationals in British manufacturing, 1850–1962', *Business History* 36 (1994): 89–126.

Index